The Literary Art and Activism of Rick Bass

The Literary Art and Activism of Rick Bass

Edited by

O. Alan Weltzien

The University of Utah Press

Salt Lake City

Printed on acid-free paper

06 05 04 03 02 01 00
5 4 3 2 1

Library of Congress Cataloging-in-Publication Data

The literary art and activism of Rick Bass / edited by O. Alan Weltzien.
p. cm.
Includes bibliographical references and index.
ISBN 0-87480-697-6 (pbk. : alk. paper)
1. Bass, Rick, 1958—Criticism and interpretation. 2. Environmental literature—History and criticism. 3. Environmental protection in literature. 4. Ecology in literature. 5. Nature in literature.
I. Weltzien, O. Alan (Oliver Alan)
PS3552.A8213 Z76 2001
813'.54—dc21 2001003165

Contents

Acknowledgments

IN OBVIOUS AND less obvious ways, a critical anthology represents a set of collaborative acts. The present volume was inspired by the common interests of certain Western Literature Association (WLA) scholars who kept discovering themselves on similar panels devoted to the burgeoning career of Rick Bass. I want to thank these individuals, most of whom have contributed to this anthology, for their example and interest. I particularly acknowledge the suggestions of my friend, Terrell Dixon, for conceiving this project, which first occurred to me at a small round bar table in Banff, Alberta, during the 1998 WLA Conference.

After writing the Western Writers Series booklet (1998) on Rick Bass, it seemed a logical step for me to tackle this bigger project. I have learned more about Bass from every contributor and thank them for their work and their patience with me. I also want to thank three individuals. My wife, Lynn Myer Weltzien, provided encouragement and interest. My editor and friend, Dawn Marano, has provided steady instruction and support and proven herself a model editor. Most of all, I want to honor the work and example of Rick Bass himself, who so loves a corner of my adopted state and who provides us all with new ways to assess the relationship between art and environmental activism. His books keep resonating in my heart.

Introduction

> *Art or activism? Why not both? Why worry about burning out in activism, or failing in art? What else are our lives but diminishing tapers of wax, sputtering already in long flame? Rot or burn, it's all the same to the eye of time . . .*
>
> *Art, or activism? They shadow one another; they destroy one another: but they share the same inescapable, irreducible bedrock fuel—passion. Love, or fury. They will always be near one another, in an artist's heart—or the temptation of both of them will always be present, in an artist's heart; and for me, there just came a point one day where I was spending too much energy trying to keep the two apart. It seemed artificial, unnatural, brittle, to have two similar passions, sharing the same root-stock . . . to exclude or excise one of them from my life, for the sake of another, did not feel true or healthy. I would rather fail at both than be disloyal to one, even if succeeding at the other.*
>
> Rick Bass, *Brown Dog of the Yaak* (114, 118–19)

I. "The Writer, the Fighter"

American nature writing has always been a writing about place, and often a celebration of particular places. Such writers have always known that a concerted study of their particular chosen landscape contributes, through synecdoche, to the goals, particularly preservationist goals, of naturalist writing everywhere. By the 1990s, a generation after the landmark Wilderness Act (1964) and the first Earth Day (1970), both environmentalism and nature writing had matured in a number of ways. Their continuing maturation is marked, in part, by increasing patterns of convergence. In his conclusion to *Voices in the Wilderness*, however, Daniel G. Payne argues that nature writers at the century's end are "less likely to be the immediate force" for green reform than were the Aldo Leopolds and Rachel Carsons, for example. Instead, he characterizes them as political gadflies who must insistently strive to reach, through their work, "the mainstream of American culture" (168–69, 175). Though he sees himself as a moderate, Rick Bass plays the part of a gadfly whose diversity of writing seeks to preserve wilderness and to influence mainstream American culture to think and act more ecologically.

If the twentieth century saw increasing rates of environmental degradation and preservation, increasing grounds for both despair and hope, as well as the arrival of environmentalism as a major moral and political movement, Rick Bass emerges as an epitome of contemporary nature writing. By the 1990s he had become a bellwether writer because of his defiant blending of roles: he appears equally dedicated to the writer's life and to political activism in defense of his chosen place, the extremely rural northwestern corner of Montana called the Yaak. "Yaak" is a Kootenai word meaning "arrow," and one can easily construe much of Bass's polemical journalism as a series of arrows shot into the thick, complacent hide of attitudes that sanction, for example, the continued squandering of the country's remaining old growth forests not already set aside in parks or wilderness areas. Writers like Bass want to prick our content and arouse our reformist energies. Certainly nature writing was receiving more scholarly and pedagogical attention than ever before by the twentieth century's end, as evidenced by the rapid growth of such organizations as ASLE (Association for the Study of Literature and Environment), on the Advisory Board of which Bass has served, incidentally, since its inception. The country may also have more environmental activists and first-rate nature writers than ever before. Yet Bass seems to me a bellwether figure due to his conspicuous marriage of these identities.

It's a perilous marriage, as published interviews attest and, occasionally, Bass's writing thematizes. A long profile appearing in the *Seattle Times* (21 December 1997) titled "The Writer, the Fighter" captures Bass's dual career as well as some of its problems and costs. Another article printed in the *Great Falls (Montana) Tribune* ten months later (8 October 1998), titled "Fervant [*sic*] Outdoorsman Lives and Writes for the Wilderness," describes Bass's *raison d'être* and quotes senior Western writer William Kittredge's pronouncement—and nudge: "'His real genius is in fiction. He's a stunningly imaginative guy and his great books will be fiction—if he writes them.'" Bass's courageous example suggests a path of influence that does lead to political action for many of his readers, who admire his fiction and have written letters or e-mails to preserve the remaining roadless areas in his Yaak Valley, for instance. As one measure of Bass's own commitment to cause—a familiar grassroots credo—he has been active in the Orion Society, the Montana Wilderness Association (MWA), and, closer to home, the Yaak Valley Forest Council (whose website is listed in *Brown Dog of the Yaak,* 79) for many years. Like Wallace Stegner and Wendell Berry and Edward Abbey, he crosses genres and publishes prolifically. He has repeatedly described the different roles that fiction and nonfiction occupy in his life; unsurprisingly, some readers prefer the fictionist to the essayist and vice versa. Bass crosses other, less common borders, since he came to writing from a background in petroleum geology and since he's both a Texan and a Montanan. In his setting and his naturalist discipline, it's hard not to see Bass as a direct descendent of Henry David Thoreau who also combines the rapture of John Muir and the obstinacy, orneriness, and eloquence of Abbey.

I first heard of Rick Bass from an Oregon man in the early 1990s, when I was teaching at an elderhostel on some Montana writers. He asked me if I'd read *Winter: Notes from Montana* (1991), and as always I hurried to fill another gap. Then I read backward and forward in Bass, trying to keep up with his rate of production. In the summer of 1997 my wife, younger son, and I drove up the Yaak River Valley from Troy and camped at the Pete Creek (Kootenai National Forest) campground, a few miles west of "downtown" Yaak, for a few days so that I could acquaint myself with Bass country. About three-quarters of Lincoln County, Montana, is within Kootenai National Forest and includes Montana's lowest elevations.

During that visit I hiked up Northwest Peak and Mt. Henry, both boasting fine old Forest Service lookouts and the latter featuring "the best little look outhouse in Montana"; one evening, dodging mosquito swarms, we walked into Hoskins Lake, off the Vinal Creek Road and not far from Bass's place. I drank a beer in the Dirty Shame, unofficial community center and one of three buildings comprising Yaak, and talked with the barman, a friend of Rick's. I also studied larch trees. In spite of clearcuts, stretches of the land's skin rubbed raw, the valley looks green and feels far away: almost heaven, as John Denver once sang and as Bass repeatedly writes. Here, in 1987, Bass and Elizabeth Hughes, who later became his wife, chose to make their stand—what Bass later describes in *The Book of Yaak* (1996) as "the notion that settling-in and stand-making is the way to achieve or rediscover these [blood-rhythms of wilderness]" (13).

Again, Bass's own example of this credo explains, in part, his rapidly rising reputation and influence. The volume of published work alone, for a writer barely in mid-career, forces us to sit up and take notice. From 1985 to 2002, for example, he published seventeen books (including *Fiber,* 1998) and dozens of uncollected essays and stories: three collections of short stories and two of novellas, ten nonfiction books, and a big novel he spent a decade writing. Bass published two books a year in 1989 and 1995, and in 1998 he published three. A survey of the career reveals his steadily deepening environmentalism, as studies such as Terrell Dixon's essay "Rick Bass" document. Certainly Bass introduces, however faintly, some ecological themes in his first book, *The Deer Pasture* (1985), which is set in his first geography, the Texas Hill Country. By the time Bass returns to the Hill Country as the setting for his title novella "The Sky, the Stars, the Wilderness" (1997), his thinking about ecology—about self and place, and self in place—has matured a great deal. Setting often becomes the main character, infusing every element of the ostensible protagonists. Bass has Anne, inheritor and guardian of the Prade Ranch, brag: "We have eight times the diversity of other places in the West because we are at the edge of all four of those [named geographic-vegetation] zones. Unlike any other place on earth, perhaps, this is where it all comes together" (132).

For some, though, the urgency and the occasional stridency of his polemical journalism deflect attention from his often magical fiction and detract from his overall reputation; for others, they only enhance it. The Yaak River, flowing southwest, originates just over the Medicine Line (except for the South fork); and in many respects his more recent career issues from a pressured sense of being up against the line. For Bass, the international boundary means much more than that; the Yaak constitutes a regional, climatic, botanical, zoological, and personal border country and, by the time of *Fiber,* a synecdoche for the American West. As a multivalent border country, it provides a source of energizing tensions that fuel his career. Those perceived tensions between nonfiction and fiction, for example, explain his appeal and centrality as a contemporary nature writer.

In his essay "Getting Along with Nature" (1982), Wendell Berry defines the notion of edge, or ecotone, in a way that illuminates Bass's border countries: "the phenomenon of edge or margin . . . we know to be one of the powerful attractions of a diversified landscape, both to wildlife and to humans" (*Home Economics,* 13). In his life and fiction (e.g., Anne in "The Sky, the Stars, the Wilderness" and Mel Estes in *Where the Sea Used to Be*), he proposes an ethical border country wherein the individual practices stewardship in a sustained close proximity to the wild. And Bass uses the Medicine Line as a magical border, whimsically yet seriously proposing Canada as a nearly limitless site and source of greater wildness, potentiality, and freedom. Yet more often than not, from stories such as "Choteau" (1989) or "The Valley" (1995) to novellas such as "Platte River" (1994) or "The Myths of Bears" (1997) to the more recent "The Hermit's Story" (1998), characters cross the Line (usually northbound) in order to recross, and this border country presumes return or recursion, without which identity remains incomplete. In standard map representations, bigger Canada sprawls just above the United States, and characters move up, sometimes aiming for the top, some transcendence, from which they must come down. In terms of natural resources endowment and rates of logging (primarily west of the Continental Divide), Canada represents a magnified mirror image and often baleful reference point for Bass's activism (e.g., "The Heart of a Forest," 1997).

The setting of *Where the Sea Used to Be* (1998), the culmination of Bass's fiction to date, exemplifies Berry's endorsement of the edge or liminal space, source of that diversity essential to Bass's worldview. "The second, hidden" Swan Valley, the novel's primary presence, appears a remote Shangri-La accessible only through Canada, so with Wallis and his predecessors we cross the Line in the novel's beginning to hook back south. Bass parodies his place and its reputation among some Montanans by having a (first) Swan Valley—a real Montana valley, long and narrow, drained by the Swan River and about 125 miles southeast of the Yaak—storekeeper sardonically comment to Wallis, "'It's mostly dope addicts and hippies. . . . Criminals. It's right on the Canadian line. Part of it goes over into Canada. They say there are about twenty or so people living up there. Dark, wet—way back in the woods. A ghost town. They get a lot of wolves up there'" (*Where the Sea Used to Be,* 13). Only winter puts on hold the predaceous forces of development symbolized by Old Dudley Estes. It's a place of and for outsiders, self-sufficient individualists often protesting late-twentieth-century corporate America and actively seeking simpler or at least more biocentric modes of life. A place to slough off the ephemeral and pursue the durable. A valley with an extraordinarily articulate voice, which, even before *The Book of Yaak,* gained some bardic authority. That voice, whether producing nonfiction or fiction, has dedicated itself to a defense of place, whether the Yaak or other landscapes through which he walks as visitor.

The 24 June–1 July 1996 issue of the *New Yorker* included an "Easel" by Bruce McCall titled "The Montana Salon Convenes" (105). The scene realistically summarizes any valley in western or central Montana where miles of rolling benchland—more miles than one imagines—gradually rise (often along alluvial fans) to meet a local mountain range. McCall includes a couple of small canyons, one stand of timber in the left distance, and one irrigated pasture. In the foreground, one cowboy, with six-shooter raised, sits in an easy chair, glancing over his left shoulder at us. In the easel's middle, a hundred or more yards beyond the first dude, two more dudes sit on couches, not quite facing one another and a space apart. In the middle distance on the right, another male stands next to the driver's door of his old pickup; farther away (and presumably farther away from one another) are three other figures, the first seated next to a campfire. The roll-call caption below the "Easel" reads: "Richard Ford, Annick Smith, Jim Harrison, Beverly Lowry, William Kittredge, and Tom McGuane. Absent: Rick Bass."

Even as it rehashes sundry Old Western cliches and includes writers who are certainly not year-round Montanans, the *New Yorker* picture recognizes the Montanan scale of space and, more importantly, the Intermountain literary renaissance in which Montana writers play a prominent part. The *New Yorker* has its little joke on the semireclusive Bass, youngest writer on this list, highly visible in his self-consciously chosen, well-known Yaak obscurity. Like Thoreau, Bass has gone "way back in the woods" to live deliberately, often coming out but always eagerly returning; unlike Thoreau, Bass seems permanently wedded to his Walden. Bass lives a lifelong epistemological quest in the Yaak, resembling Thoreau the naturalist-chronicler of the *Journals*. In published interviews he repeatedly stresses the endless lessons to be learned in the woods, and his writing reflects the excitement of his ongoing, infinitely nuanced adjustment to place: often, but not always, the Yaak. This seems to me the primary theme of "The Sky, the Stars, the Wilderness" and *Where the Sea Used to Be*.

Though a private individual, Bass has told portions of his own story occasionally in interviews or journalism. I believe his most revealing autobiographical writing, however, remains "Crossing Over" (1992), the essay he wrote for *Petroglyph*, "A Journal of Creative Natural History Writing" published by his alma mater, Utah State University. Among other things, "Crossing Over" evokes the beginnings of this native Texan's love affair with the Rockies and his conversion to a new physical and metaphysical West, one defined by wilderness advocacy. If any single book changed his path, it was Abbey's best-known novel, *The Monkey Wrench Gang* (1975), which Bass read over Thanksgiving in 1976, midway through his first semester at Utah State. In fact, Bass has, for many, inherited Abbey's mantle through his career to date. Reading Abbey and taking courses from longtime Utah State University professor (and *Western American Literature* editor) Thomas Lyon probably shaped the future writer as much as anyone during his undergraduate years. He teases his essay title, stating both that he "crossed over" to wilderness advocacy then and that he "*refuse[s]* to cross over: that wildness, and love of wildness, is still natural within us, a thing we're born with, and can only lose, rather than gain—and that the trick is to *keep* from crossing over, and to stay in the shrinking wild habitat of the soul of which we've been made guardians" (23). Again, Bass centers his paradox on the concept of liminal space—the soul as border country—but here he conceives the space as one to be crossed *and* to resist crossing. No credo defines Bass more than the relationship of wildness to wilderness and the interior and exterior status of wildness (e.g., the title of his second book, borrowed from a Robert Frost poem: *Wild to the Heart,* 1987). His oeuvre, particularly since *Winter,* his first "Montana" book, plays variations, sometimes stark or strident variations, on this theme.

I have already suggested Abbey as a primary stream of influence; Bass is a literary son who sometimes writes out of anger and who takes risks through the infusion of self in his work, including the risk of contradiction and inconsistency. He often lays it on the line, and his candor and earnestness, let alone his prophetic voice, disconcert or anger some readers. Bass risks remaining, in Daniel G. Payne's terms quoted earlier, a "political gadfly" rather than an "immediate force" for environmental reform. Perhaps his circle will continue expanding more through his (eco)-fiction, as William Kittredge implies, than through his nonfiction. Though shy and modest and quiet in his personal manner, Bass is nothing if not intense, and that intensity, leaking in diverse ways through his writing and often expressing the wildness theme mentioned above, describes his attraction. New and veteran Bass readers respond intensely to his intensity, and for legions of environmentalists he has become a key spokesman. Consider, for example, his well-known public reading of *Fiber* on the morning of 19 July 1997, the final day of ASLE's second biannual conference, in Missoula, Montana. By the time Bass reached the final, notorious part IV, he broke down and was barely able to complete his reading. His naked anguish moved many and embarrassed others, and a vigorous e-mail debate ensued in the following weeks questioning and evaluating his sincerity. How best do we respond to the visible, public weight of emotion in defense of one's place? Why do some construe such emotion as indecorous and unseemly? Both that story and its public debut push our buttons and force us to take a stand—not always Bass's stand.

Stephen J. Lyons's short, unflattering review of *Fiber* serves as one measure of the controversy a writer like Bass arouses. Those writing about Bass praise him far more than disparage him. Indeed, on the same *Northern Lights* page with Lyons's condemnation, one reads two laudatory short reviews, by Michael Branch and Mary Sojourner. But Lyons's criticisms of Bass might serve as a lightning rod for his detractors or those increasingly frustrated or dismissive of his marriage of art and activism. Lyons reads *Fiber* as a contemporary political tract wherein the Bassian narrator scolds like the righteous (and rightist) William Bennett. He mocks Bass's shift to prophetic anger in *Fiber*'s Part IV: "When Bass turns on us in the last chapter we plunge into one of those magical, millennial confluences when the left sounds exactly like the right. Bass has arrived. He is now native. . . ." In my judgment, Lyons ignores the postmodern energies and varieties of tone in *Fiber* as well as its ostensible status as fiction. Yet this kind of response represents a perhaps unsurprising discomfort with Bass's contemporary expression of that rhetorical tradition of anger traced, in the present volume, by Michael Branch. Sometimes literary anger, however autobiographical, makes us angry, even contemptuous. Lyons certainly suggests a sour view of nativism. Bass, however, revels in his cheekiness.

Though he has published so much already, Bass, not yet in his midforties, writes with a young writer's voice and temperament. Certainly his sometimes breezy, adolescent language enlarges his appeal. "Goofy" is an honorific title in Bass's world, and from the first paragraph of *The Watch* (1989) he reveals a wide range of goofiness and flashes of the bizarre. He takes on a variety of rhetorical postures in his efforts to awaken and arouse and is not afraid to talk cool or act the buffoon. In *Brown Dog of the Yaak*, for example, Bass recounts his meeting with friend and mentor Barry Lopez at a Montana social occasion as if he were a bumbling sidekick positioned near an oracle. Immediately following Lopez's speech, Bass reports that he compliments him, repeating "a little louder," "'*you're a smart mu'h-fu'h*'" (117). Bass not only writes youthfully and occasionally outrageously (e.g., the infamous, antirhetorical "fuck you" near *Fiber*'s end), like his friend Doug Peacock; also like Peacock and others, Bass takes risks of lessening rather than enlarging his audience through his disdain, and occasional contempt, for what he deems the inadequacies of professional field science. Certainly his anger about wolf biology, for instance, manifests itself by the time of *The Ninemile Wolves* (1992) and develops further through Anne and Mel, key authorial alter egos in "The Sky, the Stars, the Wilderness" and *Where the Sea Used to Be*, respectively. Bass's voice, mixing goofiness and weirdness and outrage and lament with a stunning lyricism, has become one of the most representative voices, particularly environmental voices, of our time.

Bass's *Brown Dog* initiated Milkweed Press's Credo Series, yet another marker of his status as a writer. Its subtitle, *Essays on Art and Activism*, again underlines Bass's dual career, and it represents, to date, his most recent statement about a duality that he refuses to accept as such. Series editor Scott Slovic begins his profile "Rick Bass: A Portrait" by echoing Bass's opening, intoning, "I know a writer with a bomb in his heart," and the metaphor fits, since "this artist is a beast, the possessor of a furiously intense imagination and the storytelling voice of a born-and-bred raconteur" (124). But the metaphor points out Bass's dilemma and his irritating quality for the unsympathetic. What will prevent the bomb from exploding, or imploding? Or, if it ticks indefinitely, how does it remain a bomb? Will it defuse, slacken, lose its explosive potential? How will Bass sustain his intensity, that ferocity, as a writer? How does it stay fresh and not wear thin with repetition for writer or readers? This writer has become famous for modulating into propaganda at the end of an essay (or *The Book of Yaak* or *Fiber*) or presentation, asking the readers or audience to write letters or send contributions on behalf of preserving the Yaak's remaining roadless areas. But he doesn't want visitors, let alone new residents, in the valley, as I was in July 1997. Please help, but don't come (e.g., "the handful of residents here would frankly be unhappy to see you," *Brown Dog*, 11–12). The defense of one's place, like the unpredictable oscillation between nonfiction and fiction, comes at a cost.

Reversing the imaginative direction of fable, one can, without great effort, assess Bass through the megafauna about whom he's written. Years ago for *Audubon* he wrote about woodland caribou, an ungulate rare and perhaps vanished below the Medicine Line. He also idealistically imagines himself not unlike the timber and gray wolves, intensely familial but forever threatened and on the move within their chosen territory (if not dislocated beyond it), that we follow in *Ninemile Wolves* and *The New Wolves* (1998). And though he writes in comically ursine terms about his friend Doug Peacock in *The Lost Grizzlies* (1995), the elusive mystery and majesty of possible San Juan Mountains grizzlies becomes again not only wish fulfillment but a rich source of projection. In *Lost Grizzlies* Bass evaluates and shifts between the contrary angles of vision of predator and prey (116–17). By *Fiber* he speaks both as a "snarling wolverine" and, like his valley, the mythical "hunch-shouldered griffin high in a snag looking down on the rest of the American West" (47). He sees far and is prepared to breathe fire. Above all, Bass resembles Colter, his beloved Brown Dog of the Yaak "with a bomb in his heart," whose disappearance, in the fall of 1997, occasions Bass's sustained eulogy that becomes two of his most recent books. Colter, quintessence of the Yaak and subject of *Brown Dog*'s first essay, constitutes the ideal benchmark and context from which to define place ("The Yaak"), activism, and art, the respective subjects of the next three essays; he shines brilliantly, providing a luminosity that writers themselves may lack but that their materials and habits of composition reflect (11). Such a superior hunting dog "carries a brilliance in his blood," and though his modesty would recoil from such a comparison, Bass strives for the same power and illumination. He deepens the self-portraiture in *Colter* (2000), his newest nonfiction book, which extends the commemorative act of *Brown Dog*.

If in fact environmentalism and nature writing manifest increasingly rich patterns of convergence, then Rick Bass represents one of the best unfolding examples of the risks and rewards of that convergence. We read him not only to experience the joys, infinitely varied, of being in place in the natural world. We also read him as a test case: as one eager to close the gap, however yawning or imperfectly closeable, between art and activism, or being in place and taking political action to defend that place. In "Politics in American Nature Writing," Scott Slovic proposes "a spectrum with epistemological rhapsody at one extreme and political jeremiad at the other" for the genre (108). He cites Bass's *Ninemile Wolves* as a text voicing "rather shrill political messages" (104) and, noting the familiar limitations of the jeremiad—an essential mode of discourse for writers like Bass—echoes Daniel Payne in affirming that "the more significant, long-term transformation of values is the work of writers who emphasize fundamental epistemological discoveries and whose political concerns, if any, are blurred with or deeply embedded in the epistemological" (105). Yet Slovic's "preliminary taxonomy" reveals a consistent "movement from epistemological nature writing to political nature writing" (101). Further, his interpretation of a John Nichols text, wherein he construes Nichols using jeremiad and rhapsody "in tandem," perfectly describes Bass's overall effect: "Our repeated exposure to this conjunction of the dire and the beautiful leaves us more intensely aware of both the problems in the world today and our own attachment to the world" (106).

A startling "conjunction of the dire and the beautiful" summarizes Bass's achievement in his nonfiction but also, indirectly, in his fiction. A writer like Bass, who typically presents rhapsody and jeremiad "in tandem," and invokes anger and elegy and lyrical affirmation, for example, on the same page, resists if not defies Slovic's reductionist "spectrum." His supple shifts in rhetorical posture and his sometimes virtuosic style elude such a scheme just as Montana's Ninemile Valley wolf pack, years ago, dodged the "net" and "weave"—the primary metaphors for government science and bureaucratic entrapment in *The Ninemile Wolves.* Bass's career to date shows us some of the potential ways in which nature writing and environmental activism stimulate and shape one another. He charts one possible course. We celebrate Bass, however, not just for his courageous art-activism fusion, but for that fresh and strange territory he disclosed in the early stories (e.g., in *The Watch*) and has been exploring ever since. Consider the opening of "The Hermit's Story," first published in the *Paris Review* (Summer 1998) and the title story of his newest collection (2002):

> An ice storm, following seven days of snow; the vast fields and drifts of snow turning to sheets of glazed ice that shine and shimmer blue in the moonlight as if the color is being fabricated not by the bending and absorption of light but by some chemical reaction within the glossy ice; as if the source of all blueness lies somewhere up here in the north—the core of it beneath one of those frozen fields; as if blue is a thing that emerges, in some parts of the world, from the soil itself, after the sun goes down.
>
> Blue creeping up fissures and cracks from depths of several hundred feet; blue working its way up through the gleaming ribs of Ann's buried dogs; blue trailing like smoke from the dogs' empty eye sockets

> and nostrils—blue rising like smoke from chimneys until it reaches the surface and spreads laterally and becomes entombed, or trapped—but still alive, and smoky—within those moonstruck fields of ice.
>
> Blue like a scent trapped in the ice, waiting for some soft release, some thawing, so that it can continue spreading. (16)

This rhapsody in blue dazzles our eye and imagination as we follow the narrator through the story's frame and accompany Ann, her client, Grey Owl, and his "half . . . dozen speckled German shorthaired pointers" on a late autumn journey to Saskatchewan, to the flashing, iridescent bottom of a frozen lake. A pulsating blue light show, it suggests the subterranean power of Rick Bass, a writer whose earnestness and personal commitment sometimes cause discomfort. It will be of more than passing interest to witness the ways in which his bomb continues ticking.

II. The Landscape of Art and Activism

Rick Bass was born in Fort Worth, Texas, in 1958 but grew up in Houston suburbs—a setting he later uses in the story "Swamp Boy" (1995). He first discovered his attraction to the outdoors and traditions of storytelling at the family deer lease in the Texas Hill Country, which I've called his first geography. As an adolescent he made the momentous decision to go to college in the Rockies, at Utah State University, where he played football and majored in petroleum geology. But, as already noted, he read Abbey and studied under Thomas Lyon, both of whom marked his future. After college Bass went to work, primarily in Mississippi, as a petroleum geologist but gradually discovered his preference for exploring wilderness areas and writing. As he found his own voice in his first two essay collections, *The Deer Pasture* and *Wild to the Heart*, he read Eudora Welty, Barry Hannah, and Jim Harrison, who all influenced it. His third book, *Oil Notes* (1989), bids farewell to his earlier occupation and serves as a transition to his new life as writer. Two years before its publication, Bass and Elizabeth Hughes made a second momentous decision by moving from Mississippi to the Yaak Valley, in Montana's northwest corner. Neither writer nor place has been the same since.

The usual lag between a living writer's work and sustained scholarly attention to it grows wider in Bass's case because of his pace and volume of production. He has always been widely reviewed, and by the time he published *The Watch* and *Winter,* his fourth and fifth books, respectively, he was commanding considerable attention. The former announces Bass's arrival as a fictionist and original voice; the latter commemorates their first six or seven months in Montana. Bass and Hughes married in 1991; their first daughter, Mary Katherine, was born the following year and their second, Lowry Elizabeth, in 1995—the year Bass published both *In the Loyal Mountains,* his second short story collection, and *The Lost Grizzlies,* his book about the possible survival of grizzlies in Colorado's San Juan Mountains. The following year he published *The Book of Yaak,* which as much as any work confirms his twinned identities of psalmist and prophet. Bass's first wolf book, *The Ninemile Wolves,* tracks part of the wolf reintroduction effort in northwest Montana in 1989–91; his second, *The New Wolves,* published six years later, chronicles the effort to reintroduce the Mexican wolf, or lobo, in Arizona's Blue Mountains. In 1998 Bass also published both his big novel, *Where the Sea Used to Be,* which he'd been working on over a decade, and *Fiber,* his most unusual short fiction to date. In 1994 he published his first collection of novellas, *Platte River;* three years later he published his second, also a triptych, *The Sky, the Stars, the Wilderness.* Since his novel and *Fiber,* Bass has published two more nonfiction books, *Brown Dog* and *Colter;* his third short story collection, *The Hermit's Story,* came out in 2002. Bass shows no signs of slowing his breathlessly swift production.

By the early 1990s anthologies devoted to nature writing (e.g., *On Nature's Terms: Contemporary Voices,* eds. Thomas J. Lyon and Peter Stine) often included a Bass selection or two. The bibliography submitted by Bass for *Brown Dog of the Yaak* lists, in addition to 14 books, 139 journal, magazine, and newspaper publications, 63 anthology appearances, and 11 published interviews, all since 1987 (141–54). Scholarly collections such as *Green Culture: Environmental Rhetoric in Contemporary America* (ed. Carl G. Herndl and Stuart C. Brown), which features Scott Slovic's essay quoted earlier, occasionally glance at his work. In spite of Bass's prodigious output, however, apart from reviews or the infrequent essay such as Slovic's, he has received little scholarly attention. As mentioned earlier, in 1996 Terrell Dixon surveyed Bass's career for a generic survey, *American Nature Writers;* Dixon was the first to invoke the concept of border country in Bass, in his *Western American Literature* essay-review of *In the Loyal Mountains* (1995). More recently, I provided an overview of Bass's career in a Western Writers Series booklet (1998), though by the time of publication, it was out of date by two books including the novel and many shorter pieces.

The present volume recognizes Bass's growing stature and provides his work with the steady scholarly attention overdue it. As will be seen, many of the essays directly address the energizing tensions marking Bass's double landscape—those myriad borders or ecotones he continues to cross. I earnestly hope that this volume enlarges and clarifies the conversation about Bass and sends more readers in search of Bass titles they do not yet know. Given his width and breadth, an anthology such as this inevitably shows holes: there are facets or topics in his work that contributors have not addressed or have insufficiently addressed. It is nothing new to realize that the writer and his work remain larger than our commentary about them. While this book studies Bass less comprehensively than might be wished, it nonetheless takes a long and steady view at many parts of his career. Many of the ideas and issues analyzed in these essays will also carry over into Bass's future work and provide an interpretive framework for evaluating it.

The opening essay provides us with a close-up view of Bass's personality and style. Thomas J. Lyon's profile portrays Bass as a gifted student at Utah State University who inevitably grows into the writer he has become. Bass's intensity—his enormous appetite and hectic pace—radiates from his pages. Scott Slovic's interview, "A Paint Brush in One Hand and a Bucket of Water in the Other," originally published in *Weber Studies* in 1994, provides us Bass's own voice in mid-career, by which time his commitment to art and activism, reflected in Slovic's title, had emerged in full force. In his introduction, Slovic describes a Rick Bass in 2001 who differs in rhetoric and perspective from the Bass of this interview or *The Book of Yaak* and *Fiber,* for that matter. After these personal snapshots, subsequent essays range across Bass's career, with a slight majority focusing upon the nonfiction. The book observes a rough chronological order: the final essays tend to focus upon the more recent fiction and nonfiction. Jim Dwyer's focus is wide, as he surveys Bass's fiction in terms of comparative traditions of magic realism. Dwyer endeavors to define Bass's use of magic realism by isolating and tracing three themes, comparing earlier treatments with later elaborations, and emphasizing Bass's contributions to a subgenre more often associated with Native American and South American writers.

I have placed essays primarily treating the same topic or texts next to one another, presuming that the logic of juxtaposition maximizes our understanding and appreciation of diverse treatments. Thus, Jonathan Johnson analyzes Bass's Transcendentalist inheritance by contrasting several foundational themes in Thoreau's *Walden* with Bass's articulations of them in *Winter.* Thomas Bailey's essay, by contrast, stays closer to *Winter,* assessing its transitional place in Bass's oeuvre by highlighting two of his main personae: the psalmist and the prophet. I regard *Winter* as probably the crucial transition in Bass's writing, without which the subsequent career is inconceivable. Other pairings emerge, I hope, self-evidently. An essential—perhaps the essential—theme in Bass elaborates Thoreau's famed dictum from "Walking": "In wildness is the preservation of the world." Richard Hunt's essay studies this theme in the context of another facet of Bass's Transcendentalist inheritance, the capacity for wonder, particularly as both appear in his three books devoted to wolves and grizzly bears. That capacity, in Hunt's view, becomes the vehicle for Bass's conspicuous literary advocacy.

The next half-dozen essays tackle, in various ways, Bass's duality as writer and activist, fictionist and essayist. Diana Ashe assesses the personal dimensions—for example, the self-consciousness and subjective intrusiveness—of Bass's journalism by contrasting it with the markedly different style and assumptions characteristic of John McPhee, an older writer who frequently turns to environmental topics. Gregory Morris approaches some of the same territory in defining Bass as a significant ecojournalist—a term that made its appearance only near the end of the twentieth century. Henry Harrington traces the development of *The Ninemile Wolves,* Bass's first megafauna book, by contrasting Bass's attitudes toward and treatment of the Ninemile Valley (Montana) wolf pack with the more traditional journalist treatment seen in Sherry Devlin's series of articles appearing slightly earlier in the *Missoulian* (the Missoula, Montana, newspaper). Using Bass's three megafauna books as his primary texts, Richard Kerridge studies Bass's inheritance of a Romantic epistemology epitomized in the poet William Wordsworth. Kerridge traces Bass's dependency on "the sacredness and remoteness of thresholds" in validating mystical knowledge and expresses reservations about Bass's traditionalist conception of these thresholds. Kerridge, like several other contributors, assesses Bass's expressions of liminal space or border countries.

Karla Armbruster's and Michael Branch's essays evaluate what I earlier called the energizing tensions, implicit and explicit, in Bass's duality. Armbruster locates Bass in a long American tradition of "literary environmental advocacy" and probes various dilemmas inherent in his style of advocacy, in the process clarifying Bass's shifting art-activism dialectic. Employing a forgivable, perhaps inevitable pun, Branch concentrates on what he calls Bass's three "Yaak-tivist" books (*The Book of Yaak, Fiber,* and *Brown Dog of the Yaak*), summarizing reviewers' and readers' positive and negative reactions as a springboard for locating Bass in some broader rhetorical traditions. Specifically, he reads the more recent Bass, marked by disconcerting juxtapositions of tone and style, through American traditions of the jeremiad and the elegy, claiming that Bass works in venerable subgenres but that his clashing combinations of jeremiad and elegy mark off something more original.

The final four essays focus more on Bass's fiction than on his nonfiction. Terry Gifford looks steadily at Bass's most unusual recent short story (published as a separate volume by the University of Georgia Press), *Fiber,* arguing that it is a stellar example of a new direction in nature writing, which he defines as a "post-pastoral georgic." My essay, "Sounding the Depths of Rick Bass's Ancient Seas," highlights Bass's background in petroleum geology and considers *Oil Notes* as a primer for the subsequent career. I argue that the ancient seas represent Bass's most essential trope and that plotting its appearances, particularly in (and between) the novella (his first published short story) and novel of the same name, *Where the Sea Used to Be,* enables us to assess his steadily maturing environmentalism. I believe Bass uses geology as metaphor, particularly John McPhee's notion of deep time, to evoke an idealistic, biocentric credo. Terrell Dixon arrives at nearly the same place in his essay, where he judges the novel as a superior enactment of what he calls imaginative restoration and "the novel of ecological education." My conclusion, "Self-Portrait with Dogs," reads Bass's newest nonfiction book as an exemplum of living in place and gaining those "blood-rhythms of wilderness" advocated in *The Book of Yaak.*

If Bass is only in mid-stride, these essays allow us to understand his past and present in more depth than ever before. With them we honor the length and exuberance of the unfolding career; from them we may speculate with more care and insight about the territory he has staked out for himself and where he might go from here. *Brown Dog* shows Bass conceding the perilous marriage of art and activism, recognizing that, for him at least, they cannot exist apart from one another. There is no reason to believe that Bass will burn himself out; rather, he will keep that bomb ticking, whether the remaining roadless cores in the Yaak stay that way or not. I wonder what poststructuralist, post-pastoral directions Bass's fiction might take. I wonder if William Kittredge's judgment, quoted earlier, will be realized: whether Bass will write more novellas or novels of ecological education. I wonder how he will extend his ecojournalism and advocacy so that he becomes even more a defender of place, not just his place. I wonder how he will avoid repeating or parodying himself. Will shrillness bury his grace, as reviewers such as Stephen Lyons presume? I also wonder how he will extend the lessons of wildness and deep time to a readership and general population that, contrary to himself, lives in cities or suburbs. How do the lessons of the woods apply to urban ecology and nature writing?

I will put down my crystal ball, as it is unnecessary. For now, it is sufficient to honor the big career to date and salute the unflinching integrity of the writer. I have learned deeply from Rick Bass, as have most of his readers; his passion and intensity move us and arouse our own.

Works Cited

Abbey, Edward. *The Monkey Wrench Gang*. New York: Avon, 1975.

Bass, Rick. *The Book of Yaak*. Boston: Houghton Mifflin, 1996.

———. *Brown Dog of the Yaak: Essays on Art and Activism*. Credo Series. St. Paul: Milkweed Press, 1999.

———. *Colter: The True Story of the Best Dog I Ever Had*. Boston: Houghton Mifflin, 2000.

———. "Counting Caribou." *Audubon* (May/June 1995): 72–84, 114–15.

———. "Crossing Over." *Petroglyph* 4 (1992): 17–23.

———. *The Deer Pasture*. College Station: Texas A & M University Press, 1985.

———. *Fiber*. Athens: University of Georgia Press, 1998.

———. "The Heart of a Forest." *Audubon* (January/February 1997): 39–49, 96–98.

———. *The Hermit's Story*. 2002.

———. *In the Loyal Mountains*. Boston: Houghton Mifflin, 1995.

———. *The Lost Grizzlies: A Search for Survivors in the Colorado Wilderness*. Boston: Houghton Mifflin, 1995.

———. *The New Wolves: The Return of the Mexican Wolf to the American Southwest*. Toronto: Burford & Lyon, 1998.

———. *The Ninemile Wolves*. Livingston, Mont.: Clark City Press, 1992.

———. *Oil Notes*. Boston: Houghton Mifflin/Seymour Lawrence, 1989.

———. *Platte River.* New York: Houghton Mifflin, 1994.
———. *The Sky, the Stars, the Wilderness.* Boston: Houghton Mifflin, 1997.
———. *The Watch.* New York: Norton, 1989.
———. *Where the Sea Used to Be.* Boston: Houghton Mifflin, 1998.
———. *Wild to the Heart.* New York: W. W. Norton, 1987.
———. *Winter: Notes from Montana.* Boston: Houghton Mifflin/Seymour Lawrence, 1991.

Berry, Wendell. *Home Economics.* San Francisco: North Point Press, 1987.

Dixon, Terrell. Essay Review of *In the Loyal Mountains. Western American Literature* 30 (1995): 97–103.

———. "Rick Bass." In *American Nature Writers,* ed. John Elder, vol. 1, 75–88. 2 vols. New York: Scribner's, 1996.

Lyon, Thomas J., and Peter Stine. *On Nature's Terms: Contemporary Voices.* College Station: Texas A&M University Press, 1992.

Lyons, Stephen J. Review of *Fiber. Northern Lights* 14:2 (Winter 1999): 32.

Murray, John. "Of Winter and Wilderness: A Conversation with Rick Bass." *Bloomsbury Review* (April/May 1991): 9–10, 14.

New Yorker, 24 June–1 July 1996, 105.

Payne, Daniel G. *Voices in the Wilderness: American Nature Writing and Environmental Politics.* Hanover, N.H.: University Press of New England, 1996.

Slovic, Scott. "A Paint Brush in One Hand and a Bucket of Water in the Other: Nature Writing and the Politics of Wilderness: An Interview with Rick Bass." *Weber Studies* 11 (Fall 1994): 11–20, 22–28.

———. "Politics in American Nature Writing." In *Green Culture: Environmental Rhetoric in Contemporary America,* ed. Carl G. Herndl and Stuart C. Brown, 82–110. Madison: University of Wisconsin Press, 1996.

———. "Rick Bass: A Portrait." In *Brown Dog of the Yaak.* Credo Series. St. Paul: Milkweed Press, 1999.

Stobb, Bill. "The Wild into the Word: An Interview with Rick Bass." *Interdisciplinary Studies in Literature and Environment* 5:2 (Summer 1998): 97–104.

Weltzien, O. Alan. *Rick Bass.* Western Writers Series 134. Boise: Boise State University Press, 1998.

———. "Rick Bass's Art-Activism Dialectic and Postmodern Ecofiction; Or, a 'Fiber' Tougher Than 'Anything Made of Wood.'" *Interdisciplinary Studies in Literature and Environment* 7:2 (Summer 2000): 81–93.

Teaching and Learning

An Appreciation of Rick Bass and His Writing

THOMAS J. LYON

WHEN I HAD Rick Bass in class at Utah State University ("Advanced Expository Writing," I think it was), I knew next to nothing about the subject—nothing really to the purpose, as Thoreau would say. I was an English professor and as such could criticize and analyze fairly plausibly, perhaps, but as for actually doing any good writing and being able to help students from the inside, well, that was another matter. Having little intimate knowledge of it, I probably even doubted that real writing could be taught at all. The only sharable thing I had going, as a teacher, was that I delighted in certain writers, certain pieces of writing. A passage of Ernest Hemingway—for example, where Jake and Bill are being driven up into the Spanish mountains, while Cohn sleeps, and the country is there so sharply you can smell it—would make me feel that all my cells were lined up and breathing clearly. I couldn't help voicing the exhilaration, and some students, inevitably, joined in the fun.

Rick was one of the ones who grinned back. He was a geology major and sometimes wore a T-shirt that said "Subduction Leads to Orogeny," a line showing high etymological consciousness, I thought, and his writing, as I remember (it has been a quarter of a century or so), had both image-detail and playfulness, wit. You dream of seeing those qualities in student writing. You dream of them in your own writing. In class discussion, Rick responded vibrantly to Edward Hoagland's unpredictable metaphors. Describing what it would be like if an African leopard dropped onto you out of a tree, Hoagland said it would feel "like a chunk of iron wrapped in a flag." We loved that—it opened up the world of what writers do.

In after years, I continued teaching, which is to say, not-writing, but Rick had somehow in or out of class or who knows how contracted the virus. He followed geology to Mississippi, looking for oil, but his own cells had been altered by the West, the mountains, and he was writing now, and he kept coming back. He says in *Wild to the Heart* that he could leave Jackson, Mississippi, at noon on a Thursday, drive across Arkansas and Texas and half of New Mexico, have fifty-seven hours in the Pecos Wilderness, and be back at work in Jackson Monday morning!

The well for all that energy is what he found instead of oil. He discovered that way under the surface of what passes for normal life, that which the rest of us have settled for, there is a beating heart. The mountains and writing and the wildness of things all came together for Rick in those first years after college, and at some point he did what Willa Cather said writers had to do: gave himself, gave the gift of sympathy, to his subject. The secret of writing is to love. You probably don't hear that in a classroom—it's something nonconceptual. It's something you do. The more you do it, the fuller the well stays.

When far northwestern Montana became the lodestar for Rick, but there were still good reasons to be in Texas part of the time, he would make more of those long road trips, almost shruggingly, as if it was just part of what life was about. Logan, Utah, was on the way or close enough, and he would stop. There'd be a knock on the door, and I'd open it to see him shyly but confidently vibrating on the front steps, radiating energy, on his way to the mountains and the new home, just taking a bit of a break, letting the dogs out of the truck for a while. Homer and Ann, the russet and black hounds, would course over the yard with their noses to the ground, under the trees, around the house a few times, while we talked. The mud-splattered four-wheel-drive Nissan looked as if it had entirely eschewed paved roads between Texas and Utah. I don't know if I fully appreciated what Utah looked like to Rick at those times—the mountains rising up at the edge of town, the little white Great Basin clouds blowing by overhead. His heart was open and awake. Talking, bouncing on the steps a little like a boxer or a runner at a traffic light, he seemed to hear something I didn't, some kind of high keening, a subtle, constant invigoration. The dogs poured together over the landscape, sniffing it. In minutes they were persuaded back into the cab and Rick was backing down the gravel driveway and wheeling quickly around toward the north.

Where he was headed was the new home of his heart, the Yaak. If what you want is big-scale wilderness, with the original animals and the original trees, moss and deep duff and clean wet air fecundating everything, you go northwest. It's as close as we can come, anymore, to a land commensurate with our capacity for wonder and our ability, if we still have it, to reach out in actual emotion to the world, feel the life, see and absorb the variety, get our feet wet in it. Rick had placed himself somewhere big enough and wild enough to take full loving, and his well was overflowing. The books began to pour out.

And now there was a measure for everything else. If you really see the wild, feel it, then the tame is suddenly and sadly apparent for what it is. Rick did time at Austin and Beloit, among other teaching stints. His essay entitled "Beloit" is as felt a description of the college/English Department/faculty/guest writer scene, the whole hopeful, conflicted, ironic situation, as I've ever read, including Bernard Malamud's funny deconstruction of Oregon State. This essay shows that the wild reference had been absorbed and incorporated. I'm not talking about satire: that's too easy. "Beloit" has fellow-feeling. We are all in this thing together—that's what wildness wakes up in us. Tame life is separate, each one getting one or two or ten up on the others.

The beauty of enlarged life is shown so clearly in the novella "The Sky, the Stars, the Wilderness" that it makes me want to stand in front of a class again—be some kind of teacher of literature or writing. Probably all I would do, though, is say "*Read this.*" Read it with every ounce of heart you've got, wrap your arms around it, have it by you at breakfast, take it to work. Memorize it! Then we'll talk. No, we won't talk, we'll just walk together up Logan Canyon, up Mill Hollow, walk the home ground, hear the yearning birds of spring, know we have this story in common in our lives. We'll know that this feeling of reaching out to the rocky cliffs and the aspens and the fir trees is our first allegiance. Everything good comes from love.

Unfortunately, neither the Yaak nor anyplace wild is safe. Rick came back down to Utah when the highway people wanted to channel Logan Canyon for some reason—something about "Level of Service" and "driver perceptions"—and he raised a lot of money for the friends of Logan Canyon and Logan River. He did it simply by declaring his sense of the sacred—what you put yourself on the line for. That night a lot of people saw how feeling for the land can be described and communicated and brought forth as action.

Meanwhile, the Yaak was (and remains) under threat. The wild is priceless, above money completely, but that doesn't mean somebody can't make money off it. If you can make money off something, you magically find that politicians and bureaucrats support you. They will do the trench work, find ways to justify logging the Yaak, for example, making it seem normal and natural. If you, on the other hand, are just trying to *protect* something, a valley, say, and you don't have money but you do have some knowledge of biological diversity, and also the energy coming from allegiance, then if you work day and night and send mailings to everyone you know and try to reason with politicians and throw everything into your writing about the place, baring your life and soul, you may get a hearing. At least you'll show your readers what commitment really means, really demands, and what love of the land, the world, really is. In our time these are not small contributions. That is *Fiber.*

Two summers ago, among a large gathering of academics, mostly English professors, who had formed an organization on the maverick ideas that nature has being and standing and that writing about nature is a respectable human activity, I heard Rick speak about the Yaak. ("Speak" isn't really the word.) In this conference, before Rick arrived, there had been intense discussion about just how activist the organization should be. Should it take positions on environmental matters? If it did so, would it lose standing with the academic establishment? But why then was the organization created, anyway? There was a lot of figurative hand-wringing. But at least this discussion took place, some of us said. You'd never hear it at the Modern Language Association.

Rick's talk took the audience down below the political surface. ("And there is getting down to the deepest self!" said D. H. Lawrence. "It takes some diving.") We went down into where the feeling of primal connection is, and simultaneously out to the mind-body's living partners and peers, the trees, the trout, the running river, the hills. Rick took his audience to where nature writing starts and to why it exists. And we saw that the source-touching consciousness doesn't, can't, exist in a vacuum. We are in a serious situation. We are dismantling the integrity and beauty of the world, just by living without caring enough. Could there be a stranger pathology? In the face of this, failure to take a stand isn't just cowardly; it could be the mistake of all time.

Without saying it in so many words, Rick told us that unless feeling is total, it's nothing. He *taught,* and the English professors listened in flawless silence. They may never have seen a writer so truly claimed by his subject, so in love. When he left, hurrying up the auditorium aisle with his head down, going home to the well, they stood and cheered. As I rose with the rest, I suddenly began to believe that real writing could be taught, after all. Maybe it could even be learned.

Works Cited

Hoagland, Edward. "Hailing the Elusory Mountain Lion." In Thomas J. Lyon, *This Incomperable Lande.* Boston: Houghton Mifflin, 1989.

Lawrence, D. H. "The Spirit of Place." In *Studies in American Literature.* New York: Viking, 1964.

A Paint Brush in One Hand and a Bucket of Water in the Other

Nature Writing and the Politics of Wilderness

SCOTT SLOVIC

"SUPPOSE YOU ARE GIVEN a bucket of water," Rick Bass once wrote in the *American Nature Writing Newsletter* ("20515 House/20510 Senate," Spring 1993). "You're standing there holding it. Your home's on fire. Will you pour the cool water over the flames or will you sit there and write a poem about it?" (4). Thus he posed what was for him, at the time, the nature writer's chief dilemma: "literature versus politics."

For the past decade and a half, Bass—storyteller, rhapsodist, polemicist—has been working at a torrid pace, producing more than a book per year and, at the same time, traveling across the country to read from his work and participate in lobbying efforts on behalf of wilderness preservation in America, particularly in the Yaak Valley. On 23 March 1993, when the following interview was taped in San Marcos, Texas, Rick was back in his home state to work on the article that would eventually be published as "On Willow Creek," first in the *Los Angeles Times* and later in the Nature Conservancy's anthology *Heart of the Land: Essays on Last Great Places* (1994). The most memorable lines from this essay—"When we run out of country, we will run out of stories. When we run out of stories, we will run out of sanity" (12)—suggest a sense of urgency, even desperation. The preservation of beautiful and meaningful places is connected with the author's—and perhaps society's—very sanity. When it was published a few years later, *Fiber*, especially with its plaintive conclusion—"Somebody help. Please help the Yaak. . . . Somebody please do this. Somebody please help"—extended the feeling of urgency to an almost unbearable level. At the time, Bass fretted that all the time and energy devoted to telling artful stories was preventing him from acting to save the world's threatened places, while anything spent on activism was undermining his art. Six and a half years after doing the interview, as he worked on *Brown Dog of the Yaak* during the grief-filled weeks following his dog Colter's mysterious disappearance, Bass wrote: "Art, or activism? Why not both? Why worry about burning out in activism, or failing in art? What else are our lives but diminishing tapers of wax, sputtering already in long flame? Rot or burn, it's all the same to the eye of time" (114).

More recently, some strange new rhetorical shifts have occurred in Bass's work. His two presentations at the Orion Society's June 1999 millennial extravaganza, Fire & Grit, mark the emergence of a newly detached and philosophical Rick Bass and the return of the charmingly antic storyteller whose comedic sensibility, evident early on in *The Watch,* had become increasingly submerged in activist angst and frustration by the mid-1990s. The essay "The Community of Glaciers" recounts Bass's efforts on behalf of a small "pro-roadless group" in the Yaak, which resulted in the author's shocking dismissal from the volunteer steering committee by a vote of 39 to 3 (15–16). "Wearier, if not smarter," he writes, "I have retreated to the far perimeters of the community, for now. The place where everyone wants me, the place where perhaps even the landscape wants me, and hell, perhaps even the place where, when all is said and done, I myself want to be—though it does not feel that way to me" (17). The essay proceeds to contemplate the processes by which social change and glacial erosion occur, especially the concept of glacial slowness and imperceptibility. "I do not mean to dismiss our little fires, nor our fiery hearts," he concludes. "I mean only to remind us all that our lives, our values, are a constant struggle that will never end, and in which there can never be a clear 'victory,' only daily challenge. . . ." (22). This sounds like the world-weary statement of a wilderness warrior now retired from the trenches rather than the desperately fierce whoops of *The Book of Yaak* and *Fiber.* And yet, taken in context, "The Community of Glaciers" can be seen as an effort to retrench and gain perspective, a gathering up of wisdom and resolve for the next phase of the artist-activist's life. The day before he presented "The Community of Glaciers" at Fire & Grit, Bass read a hilarious, self-mocking essay called "Bear Spray Stories," subtly setting up his audience for the more sober critique of activist hubris. "Every time I get sprayed, I have to laugh. It's like, how dumb can I get? But each time it happens, I tell myself it won't happen again: that there's no way I'll make that mistake twice," he writes (1).

Beneath the guise of a series of slapstick stories, Bass seems to be stating a powerful message for artists and activists and everyone else: life is funny, painful, uncontrollable, and sometimes all too predictable. Things don't always work out as we want or expect, but it's important to keep striving, loving, and believing.

This 1993 interview with Bass elicits some of the author's core literary strategies and beliefs about language and the social function of art. Although we can see in 2001 that Rick Bass has clearly evolved into a different kind of writer and activist than he was a decade ago, or even three or four years ago, it is instructive to read his earlier remarks in order to appreciate the context of his major early books and to see how far he has come in recent years.

Slovic: Edward Abbey has written, in *Desert Solitude,* that we need wild places even if we never go there, even if we never leave the confines of asphalt and right-angled spaces. Somehow I get the sense, though, that you could never actually be content without the opportunity to spend time in the actual, physical wilderness—is that true?

Bass: Yes, and I think it was true for Abbey. And when he said, "we," I think he was speaking about mankind, and pretty much excluding himself.

Slovic: What if, for some hypothetical reason, you found yourself obligated to be in a city like Houston or any city—

Bass: Forever?

Slovic: Not forever, but for several months or half a year or a year. What kind of solace or vicarious satisfaction could you get by reading your books or someone else's books about wild places?

Bass: That's an interesting question. Basically, that's what I did the first twenty-five or twenty-seven years of my life. But, again, I was determined to take control and go to a place that I desired, or to a way of life that I desired.

Slovic: Is this what you were doing in your early years as a writer while working in Jackson? Were you reading? I know that you were taking brief excursions, the ones you recorded in *Wild to the Heart,* but were you also reading things and deriving some sort of alternative wilderness experience from those?

Bass: Well, I was, and that's a real nice question because a lot of the books I read to derive that alternative wilderness experience I wasn't living and yet was striving for were not so-called "nature writing." I mean, there were the works by Flannery O'Connor, which have plenty of wilderness experience in them, or wildness. And Eudora Welty and Barry Hannah and a lot of the southern writers. Just a lot of great books. Saul Bellow.

Slovic: So there's something that seems to transcend the subject matter on the surface—a kind of wilderness even in Saul Bellow's writing.

Bass: Sure. *Herzog,* where the goofy guy is running around on the airstrip. Yeah, definitely. I was not getting it in my life physically, in my walking across the land, and so I was yearning for it, and so yeah—it's kind of like i.v. or something in the hospital. You're not well, but you could be a hell of a lot sicker if you didn't have the tube in you.

Slovic: So wilderness literature serves as a kind of saline solution that helps you survive until you can get to the real thing.

Bass: It helps slow down your atrophying, and if you get your act together, you can get out. Or if you stay on the tubes, you're eventually going to atrophy.

Slovic: Much of your writing, it seems to me, explores the idea of what it means to be happy. At one point, in *Oil Notes,* you say, "I'm learning that you can't map happiness." Can you explain what you mean by that? Aren't you, as a writer, seeking paradoxically to "map" your happiness, to define it and account for it?

Bass: Yeah. Or I can try.

Slovic: Is it right that your writing, to a great extent, is an effort to explore what it means to be happy?

Bass: I can't answer that. If it is, I'm not aware of it and don't really want to be aware of it. It might be more about the ability to control or the inability to control, and then you make your peace with the relative inability to control the specifics of your life. You know, if you can give that up and learn to look at the smaller things and things other than yourself, I think some growth and happiness will come out of that. And I think you'll treat things better, treat the land better, treat each other better—

Slovic: Is this one of the nebulous feelings that you have said you often start a story with—

Bass: I'm sure so. It's not something I'd set out to prove or disprove. That's one reason I'm awkward and hesitant to even talk about it.

Slovic: Is there something dubious about the very enterprise of interviewing a writer or being interviewed as a writer? Are there certain shadowed spaces that you'd prefer not to shed light on because that's where the creativity comes from?

Bass: There are for me. Yeah, that's it in a sentence. For me, anyway.

Slovic: Do you think it might be different for writers who are critics, too? What do you find in your own conversations with writers? Do writers who are also critics shy away from analyzing their own work?

Bass: Good question. I don't ever ask anybody else about their work because I assume it would be painful for them to go down and come up with something meaningful or relevant—I just wouldn't ever dream of asking them. I just read their work, but I'm sure there are writers out there—I don't know, there are all different kinds of writers. It's just that for me it can be real deadening, and I have to have basically pretty vast reserves of well-being and peace in order to talk about it. I don't even like to drink a lot anymore before an interview, which used to help a lot because it got me through the interview, but then I had double reserves to make up—I had to make up artistically or creatively for that which I had spent, but then I also had to get over the hangover, so it just set me two days back instead of maybe one day back. It does leave an echo rattling around in my skull if I talk about it.

Slovic: I wonder if there are ways in which an interview, rather than being a kind of intrusion, could actually generate new ideas or chart new directions for you to explore—things that would certainly not be exhausted through the conversation.

Bass: It happens occasionally, very rarely. But it happens enough to make it worth doing. And I feel like there's an obligation—if somebody is interested enough to read your interview or interested enough in your work to want to hear something about it. I guess it feels like an obligation to me—it's part of the work. But I would be coy to say that it doesn't cost. It does—it does cost me, it always has, and I suspect it always will. But, like you say, I've gotten some good things out of interviews—or not always interviews, but sometimes out of book reviews or something. I had one posted on the board in my office for a long time—and it was very helpful for several years. It had to do with vitality, vitality in the human experience. That notion still stays with me, and it was nothing I had been conscious of, but I realized it was a part of my work and it was an important part. But again, that can be the very danger to a writer—knowing too well the direction you're going.

Slovic: Uh-huh.

Bass: Shit, it's not as hard as digging a ditch. I mean, I'm whining about interviewing!

Slovic: Just talking.

Bass: Yeah, just telling the truth. For better or worse.

Slovic: At one point in *Oil Notes* you say, "There are people I know who dabble, who want to write—no, who want to be writers. But they're married, or have children, or have a job, or watch the news. There's no time." Now that you're married and have a baby daughter, does it complicate the effort to find a balance between work and family? Barry Lopez also commented once in an interview that he writes about these trips to distant parts of the world, wild parts of the world, that other people who have busy jobs and families can't get to. What do you think about the complexity of trying to balance a family and your work as a writer?

Bass: I think finding a solution is complex, but the application is very easy. You get into a rhythm that fits your life and at that point it's easy—getting there may be hard.

Slovic: So at this point, with your daughter, Mary Katherine, a year old, are you still trying to find that balance?

Bass: Well, I've had little trouble adapting to it. I've been real lucky. You know, writing is real important to me, the stories that I'm telling—but no more important than my family or than myself, my time alone. Every bit as important to me as writing is being able to walk, especially in the summer and fall. I just walk all afternoon until dark. Yeah, it's important. Now the equation's changed with her, but I've found balance, a schedule, a routine that works and that still allows me to devote as much energy to the family and to the woods as I do writing.

Slovic: Do you walk more than you write?

Bass: Oh, goodness yes. Goodness yes.

Slovic: So you walk maybe six or more hours a day.

Bass: Yeah, in the summer, usually eight and sometimes ten. And in the fall, usually more than six. At the short ends of the year, between four and six.

Slovic: What do you do in the winter? Do you ski? How do you get out?

Bass: I ski. I don't ski for as long as I walk, but I get a lot of work done in the winter.

Slovic: You said earlier this afternoon that you write for three, maybe three and a half, hours a day. During the winter, when you're kind of snowed in, do you spend more hours actually writing?

Bass: No, not really. Maybe thirty minutes more—maybe three and a half hours instead of three.

Slovic: Is that to make sure that you're always writing at a peak of freshness and attentiveness?

Bass: Yeah. Sure. Better for me to quit early than to go on too long, because I undo anything good that I've accomplished, I'll just unravel it. There's this point where, when I'm tired, I back off—I'm not focusing as hard and it's just like pulling a thread out and unraveling everything that came before. It's very destructive.

Slovic: Back to the idea of wildness and wilderness—but we'll try not to make it too abstract. One of your short stories that I like very much—partly because of its loving depiction of the Texas Hill Country near where we are right now—is the piece called "In the Loyal Mountains" [*Southwest Review* (Summer 1990)]. Would you describe this place, the "Loyal Mountains" [located in the real-life Loyal Valley, north of Fredericksburg and about eighty miles northwest of Austin], as a "wilderness"? Or is it too close—does remoteness from urban civilization have anything to do with how wild a place is? Can wildness happen even in a city park or in an area like the Hill Country, not too far from cities like Austin and San Antonio?

Bass: It depends not just on the individual, but on the time in that person's life. It depends on so many variables that—it sounds like a copout—I truly can't answer that other than yes and no.

Slovic: You seem to be saying that the sense of what wilderness is depends on the individual's state of mind.

Bass: On the individual's state of mind at the moment. I mean, one day I can be on the back northeast corner of the Deer Pasture, and that place is wild just because it's the back corner and it's farthest away from camp, it's farthest away from anything, it's its own place. The boundaries and borders are set by the contours and geology, the outcrops, the vegetation, the whole ecotype—not by human prescription—so it's a wild place. At dusk it's a wild place. And when I've been hunting all day and come there to sit down and just rest and be quiet, it's a wild place. If I hit it at ten o'clock in the morning and I drive a jeep in to within a quarter-mile or something of it rather than having to hunt it all day, it is not a wild place—on that day. If I've been at home in Yaak for three or four months and have been out hiking every day, going back and forth, crossing into Canada, it's not a wild place—a place is not wild for me during that phase or moment unless there's something in there that—like Doug Peacock says—"something that can kill and eat you." And it just differs from day to day and moment to moment.

Slovic: I once heard Donald Hall, the writer who lives on a farm in New Hampshire, contrast his own lifestyle with that of Wendell Berry, in fact he was introducing Wendell Berry at the time—and he said something like, "I'm a writer who lives on a farm, and Berry is a writer who lives on a farm and not only writes, but works the land and has some kind of material engagement with the land beyond merely living there." What degree of contact or engagement with the land do you think is necessary for a rural writer? Would your relationship with the Yaak wilderness change if you began farming or ranching there? Or can you not even imagining doing something like that?

Bass: I can imagine it. Only if it were something I wanted to do, and it's not. It's not that I don't want to do it—it's just that what I want to do is walk in the woods, and so that's what I do and that's the way I engage with the landscape. If farming or ranching were what I wanted to do, then it would be best for me as a writer to do that. There is a certain value to be gotten from repression—that is, from not doing the thing that you want to do with regard to your art, but I assume that we're talking on the scale of a life and not a year, and in the long run it's going to be better for both my life and my work if I engage myself with my subject—

Slovic: Engage by way of walking. Is walking a similar sort of discipline—

Bass: No, it's not discipline—it's just an engagement, it's a form of touching the subject. For me, that has the sound of an old wives' tale or a myth—that one writes best about one's subject when only imagining it rather than being engaged in it. It just has that feel of bullshit to it. There's no rule or law I know of or that I've experienced in my life that says engagement with my subject is going to compromise my ability to imagine. If anything, it stimulates my imagination—it stimulates it wildly to get out and engage myself with the landscape and with the subject. That's the trouble with so much student art, student writing—it's too detached, it is not engaged.

Slovic: A few years ago, Don Mitchell published a short essay called "Dancing with Nature" [*The Bread Loaf Anthology of Contemporary American Essays* (Hanover and London: Middlebury College Press/University Press of New England, 1989)], in which he criticizes nature writers who do not also work, by way of agriculture or something else, in order to subsist from the very land they're writing about. I sense that you're suggesting that that isn't necessarily a valid argument. Maybe even a writer's work is a means of subsistence, maybe even when the writer walks, or even sits and observes—

Bass: Yeah, that movie—*Barton Fink*—both makes fun of and praises "the life of the mind." I mean, the life of the mind can be made fun of, but it still exists—it's not as strenuous or physically rigorous an existence as the life of the lower back, but it is still a life if you allow it to be, if you engage in your subject . . . in whatever form you want to. If that's what you want to do, if that's the limit of the engagement you want to achieve—just sitting at the desk and dreaming moony-eyed about a vase—then what's fair is fair. It's just important to be honest about it—if you want to be scrambling up over the farthest ridge you can see, then if you're not doing that, you're shorting and cheating your subject.

Slovic: Annie Dillard has said with regard to her book *Pilgrim at Tinker Creek* that of course she spent time wandering around in rural Virginia while she was working on it, but while actually writing, she would enclose herself in a study at the Hollins College library and shut the window blinds, locking herself into this artificial, viewless place—so that, as she puts it, "imagination can meet memory in the dark," in a creative space that's somehow disengaged from the subject. Does this make sense to you?

Bass: Well, it does. I think the important thing is that she did the groundwork with her subject, and now she's talking more about the physical process of writing. She's in touch with the flows and rhythms of her body and her mind simultaneously, she's not excluding one from the other, she's sharing the two, the mind and the body. She took the body out across the land, and then brought it back and engaged the mind with it. I think that's a masterful—

Slovic: So what would be the problem if she happened to pull up the blinds and actually see the landscape she's trying to write about? Why should that cause an interference?

Bass: Her style of work. And her rhythms of body and mind at that moment call for her to be in the dark—so she's doing what she wants to do and she's being where she wants to be, and that's why her writing is so great. The trouble with abstractions is they are very easily broadcast over the entire population, and what works for one person is then thought to be the correct way for everybody else, and that's just not so.

Slovic: So that each writer, each thinker, has a different way of processing ideas.

Bass: I think that the good ones do, and that they're just in touch with the logic of their system, their natural system.

Slovic: Let me read a quotation to you—the statement from Robert Frost that serves as the epigraph from *Wild to the Heart:* "I lead a life estranged from myself . . . I am very wild at heart sometimes. Not confused. Just wild—wild. . . ." What does it mean to be "wild at heart"? And why the subtle difference between Frost's phrase "wild at heart" and your own title?

Bass: Well, my title, *Wild to the Heart,* was dealing with the subject, which was the land and the people in those essays, and those things were, to me, wild. And, I'm speaking for Frost, which I don't have the authority to do, but it's my guess, my interpretation, that that beautiful statement of his refers to a kind of flutteriness, something within, not an external subject such as land or another person, but an internal subject of himself.

Slovic: So to be "wild at heart" is to have a kind of internal wildness that isn't connected to one's relationship to an external experience.

Bass: Right. It's not necessarily connected to the external. I just think of it as a fluttering within.

Slovic: So your own essays emphasize experience, doing things, activities.

Bass: Just engaging with things that are perceived to be wild. Other than one's interior.

Slovic: One of the things your writing does so well—I've noticed this with all of your writing, but especially your books like *Wild to the Heart*—is to convey your intense love of wild places, your pleasure at being outdoors and experiencing the natural world. I could imagine this feeling striking a chord even with your readers who aren't predisposed toward rustic living—city readers. How do you feel about the possibility that your books, in the process of teaching people to value the wilderness, might be contributing to the threat of overuse, to what Edward Abbey used to call "industrial tourism"?

Bass: Yeah. Well, I understand the question, the pragmatism of it, but it seems secondary rather than primary. I'm thinking of somebody saying, "Aren't you worried about too many people coming to church? They're going to wear out the pews." I mean, that's what the church is for.

Slovic: Is that what the wilderness is for?

Bass: Yeah, the wilderness is for wild things. And I think that the people that are drawn to it, to the wilderness, are going to be—

Slovic: They'll be wild things?

Bass: I think more or less they'll fit, and if they don't fit, I don't think they'll stick around. I think they'll get out pretty quick.

Slovic: What if, in the process of accommodating the people who decide they want to come to the wilderness, roads are built, hotels are built, Yosemite is turned into a huge circus rather than a place where wild activities can occur freely?

Bass: Again, I think that's secondary. To stay within the analogy, it would be like saying, "Well, what if someone comes to church with a machine-gun and begins shooting people?" That may happen, but you have to go for the salvation, not for the protection. It could happen, but hopefully in my writing and in people's hearts, they will be touched by the land and behave in such a way that will not bring it harm and in fact will be inspired to fight their hearts out for it. That would be the kind of person I would want to encourage in my writing, and so maybe it's too naïve but I don't worry about, I don't picture, drivers of Winnebagos clamoring for a road up onto some grueling place I've reached and written about. I see more wild people trying to go out and find similar places for themselves, finding them, becoming engaged in them, falling in love with them, and fighting the rest of their lives to protect those things from being wiped off the face of the earth.

Slovic: So in your celebratory writing about the Yaak Valley, the idea is that the Yaak represents a *kind* of place, not a homing beacon—

Bass: Oh goodness, yeah. It's ugly. I mean, it's a homing beacon for me because it's home, but it's ugly, it's not a place people want to go visit. It's got clearcuts and it rains a lot and you can't see anything, there are no vistas. It's an ugly place to visit—it's an okay place to live. It's the perfect place for me to live because it's just what fits my warped mind, the twisted contours of brain—what are those things called?—the loops and coils. . . . Anyways, it fits, it's a good fit for me, but it probably wouldn't be for anyone else in the world.

Slovic: So it doesn't have the things we would call picturesque, it's not a Yosemite?

Bass: Goodness, no. Goodness, no.

Slovic: Stephen Harrigan, the contemporary Texas nature writer, has said that his main goal in writing about the natural world is to make the world accessible to the reader's imagination. To achieve this, he sometimes commits the so-called grievous sin of anthropomorphism in depicting animals, attributing humanlike consciousness to whales and other creatures. How do you feel about anthropomorphism as a literary technique? What are your own goals in writing about wildlife—for instance, in your recent book, *The Ninemile Wolves*?

Bass: I don't much care for rabid anthropomorphization, and certainly, as in his book *Water and Light,* Harrigan doesn't do that—I think he just speaks his heart's truth with regard to the notion that there are things we don't understand and things we can't control about animals' inner beings. And I think the best nature writers and the most compassionate people acknowledge this—it takes a kind of bravery and it's something our culture has not thought about in a long time, the fact that animals are beings, to state the obvious. So if I were going to make a mistake, I think it's time that we do make a mistake in the direction of anthropomorphizing rather than disallowing character and soul and sentiment and feeling in a species. Of course, as it's been pointed out, it makes it much more convenient for us to abuse that species—or that man, woman, or child—if that individual is not considered a sentient being. It's a form of manipulation, domination, control—all of the things that are bad for art, as well as life.

Slovic: When you wrote the original article on wolves for *Outside* magazine, were you working on assignment? Did they ask you to do it or did you suggest—

Bass: Yeah, I suggested a 2,500- to 3,000-word article about the state of the union of wolves in the Lower Forty-eight, and I fell in love with the story of *The Ninemile Wolves.* I thought it was a much stronger metaphor than all the other stories and decided to be specific rather than abstract.

Slovic: Does your writing process change at all when you're doing something on assignment, when you have a deadline? You tend to write so quickly that—

Bass: No.

Slovic:—that it may not affect you anyway.

Bass: I've been real fortunate to work with great editors who humor me. After I have gone on assignment and come back, I write everything I want to say in the manner I want to say it. I write for myself first. Then I send it to them and say, "Look I had to do this because I knew if I did it the way we discussed earlier it would take energy out of me so that when I came back to do it again I wouldn't be able to apply that pureness of form to it. This is the way I want to tell the story. I know full well the minute I pick up the pen that this probably isn't going to work for you, but I have to do it first to keep from injuring it. I'll get this out of my system—then, whatever I've got left, I'm going to give you seconds." And they put up with it. I guess they figure anybody goofy enough to write twice about the same thing when you could write once about it and get paid for doing it once deserves what he gets.

Slovic: So did you write a version of the article that was very much different than what actually appeared in the magazine? Or did they not tamper with it too much?

Bass: No. There was some work with it, but it wasn't too much different. It was a lot of cutting and rephrasing. But no, I turned in the whole 140-some-odd pages to them. I just did a piece for *Traveler* magazine on the rain forests in Hawaii, and turned in 140-some-odd pages to them, and they loved it. You know, I've been lucky to work with good editors who just say, "Well, write what needs to be written and we'll deal with the words later." They've just been interested in good writing, and it's a nice luxury.

Slovic: In *The Ninemile Wolves,* the book that emerged from the *Outside* article, you repeatedly associate the reintroduction of wolves in Montana with the idea of "hope," with a vague yearning. What is it exactly that the wolves represent for you? Why is their return so important?

Bass: I guess the dangerous word for me in that question is "exactly." They represent a chance to heal, a chance for forgiveness or mercy or grace with regard to our culture. You know, we made mistakes. It's a second chance. And it's a generous thing for wolves' spirits to engage in, to even suffer for our presence. They could avoid us—or I think they could. I know I'm speaking for them, but . . . it feels to me like they can sense that there are people in the West now who would honor them were they to return, and so they will give us a second chance, which is a very generous thing, and return, and that's what's happening.

Slovic: This is a very controversial topic in Montana and elsewhere. I've read some articles that suggest that animals like wolves are no longer appropriate in ranching territory or near suburban communities where there might be children playing outside. Do you give any credence at all to such arguments?

Bass: No. If anything is inappropriate it's people living in those places where the wolves were first and should be, rather than the other way around. No, I think we're being given a second chance for engagement with the world rather than a setting up of boundaries and borders and fences. "Wolves on this side, cows on this side, people on this side, and trees on that side"—that's where we turned wrong the first time. Hopefully we'll get it right this go-around.

Slovic: Toward the end of the book you discuss the wolf's "spirit." In the appendix called "Wise Blood," for instance, you mention wolves' "spirituality and mystique," their "disproportionately large souls." I find this an interesting approach to the heated political battle over wolf reintroduction, and I wonder if you could explain why you decided to end your book in this rather mystical way. How is this strategy likely to soften opponents' resistance, to enlarge their views? Or is this not really your goal? Is the book written to summon readers who might already be sympathetic?

Bass: It would be neither of those things. The reason I wrote the book was to honor loss. These wolves have fought valiantly for survival in this day and age, and they've come up short several times, but they always did what it took at the last instant to at least keep one of their members alive and to stay in the world. And I wanted to make sure that was not forgotten, I wanted to put it down for the record and get all the facts right and all the dates. I wanted to have everything right so that . . . it just seemed almost obscene to let it escape into something less than a memory or something less than honor. What they did was a thing of amazing integrity, amazing force, amazing power, amazing passion, and I did it for the wolves, but I also realize now that they gave quite a gift to our own culture, if we would just listen to that story.

Slovic: In our conversation you've repeatedly suggested the importance of writing as a way of paying respect to an idea or a phenomenon of one kind or another—for instance, the wolves. The importance of a deep devotion to the subject matter. Do you think much about your readers when you're writing? Do you think about what kinds of people this might be for?

Bass: No, I don't. I just think about the subject and try not to do anything that the subject would not want me to do. I try to stay within the logic of the system and not manipulate it or control it. I just try to engage with it rather than control it.

Slovic: What about the connections, though, between telling a story in writing and telling a story out loud when you actually have a group of listeners sitting there—for instance, when Mary Katherine is older and maybe she's with you and a group of her friends on a hike, and you sit down to tell them a story, which you think in the back of your mind might teach them something. How would the idea of telling a story out loud for a didactic reason, for an effect on an audience, differ from writing a story that might have such an effect, except that the audience is less visible?

Bass: I guess it depends, of course, on the writer. Again, I tend to look at the subject and speak in a manner—by speak, I mean with the pen—in a manner that will not cause the subject to take offense and walk away. It's a way of engaging with the subject and relating to it, with it. I just want to keep from messing up that brief moment of recognition between me and the subject, that brief—or not brief—engagement. I've always been struck by the notion that with children or any other audience—if you speak in that manner, the audience is going to listen. If you maintain that integrity and honesty between the writer and the subject, then it's going to have a feel, an attraction, to it. I just think too many mistakes can be made if you turn your eyes from the subject toward the audience. Because then when you look at the audience you look back at yourself, and then back at the audience and back at yourself, and the subject, like some shy deer, could drift away back into the woods. And then when it's time to turn around and look back at the subject, it's gone, and you're messed up.

Slovic: In *The Deer Pasture,* you write that deer hunting is "not a hunt for the deer, an outside factor, but rather a hunt for the hunter inside—a tracking of his own self." When hunters realize this, you suggest, they "begin photographing deer or just watching them instead of shooting them all the time." This reminds me of the ideas that Aldo Leopold presents toward the end of *A Sand County Almanac,* the argument that young men hunt to kill animals and gather trophies, but eventually they learn to appreciate the aesthetic and spiritual and perhaps the ecological dimensions of the world, and the idea of killing wild things loses its appeal. Have your own feelings about hunting changed at all since your move to Montana? Do people in the Yaak Valley view hunting in the same way that Texans do?

Bass: With the notion by Leopold, I wouldn't follow the premise too far that aesthetics or spirituality or any of those other byproducts are compromised by the act of hunting. What I'm saying is that I think certain people can hunt all their lives and gain increasing engagement and understanding of both themselves and their subject, and passion for hunting, all the way through their lives. That is not the trend historically or biologically in our species these days. The tendency seems to be as one gets older, like Leopold says, that one loses the desire to kill and almost the desire to hunt. I'm certain a lot of that is controlled biologically—and so to try and control it outside of your body and mind just based on something society is trying to tell you you should or shouldn't do, I think that's dreadfully wicked, wretched, wrong-headed, fatal. That kind of thinking and mentality is fatal to survival as a species, it's fatal to the imagination, fatal to being honest and true to yourself, which is the only way any individual is going to survive, and the individual has to survive for the population to survive, etc., etc.

And yeah, with age it changes drastically every year. I know a lot of people my age—and even younger, and quite a few older—who don't shoot anymore at all. They still go out, but they don't shoot.

Slovic: But do they carry guns?

Bass: Yeah, but of course I also know people who even give up their guns. I haven't given up my guns because [my wife] Elizabeth and I both love wild game, and it's very much a tradition and very much one of the fabrics of our lives, the shooting and cleaning and preparing and cooking and sharing of—I know it sounds like a corny word—but that bounty. Sadly something dies in our doing it, but something is nourished.

Slovic: Have you read Richard Nelson's book—

Bass: No, I haven't—I sure aim to, I hear a lot about it, and I like his work that I've seen.

Slovic: He writes quite reverently about deer hunting in particular and the whole process you were just describing, the cleaning and preparation—

Bass: It's not something that just I do. It's something that my family and I do together and have always done together. Nonetheless for the last couple of years I've found myself not shooting deer that, in years past, I would have shot in an instant, and I'm troubled by it—not really troubled, it's just something else to contend with in a life. I mean, you change throughout your life, and that's just the way it goes. I'm somewhat frightened to think that there will be a day when

I will not be able to shoot a deer, when I just absolutely will not be able to shoot one all season long, but I'm not going to fight it. When I get to that point, if I get to that point, I hope I'll be honest enough to not keep—

Slovic: Why would you reach such a point?

Bass: I don't know.

Slovic: You mean psychologically—

Bass: Yeah. Or who knows? Psychological, biological. Who knows? I do know for the past couple years I've passed up big deer that before I would have shot instantly, and I just sat there and looked at them and they looked at me, and they went on. And then I felt confused about it afterward, but I'm proud that I at least had the honesty to not shoot if I didn't want to. Nonetheless, before the season was over, I realized we didn't have meat and we needed it, and I was able to get over my mooniness. But it's interesting—that's what's nice about life, it's not static.

Slovic: We all change.

Bass: Yeah.

Slovic: We're circling back to issues that we've discussed before, but in *Oil Notes* there is a really interesting scene where you write about a kid named Jimbo, an illiterate bully, who nonetheless used language with a kind of genius when he taught you how to pitch a baseball. Is this what you're up to as a writer, an elaborate, extended effort to teach your readers to "listen to the earth," as you put it in that same passage? For instance, when you write letters to people in Congress—in your more political writing nowadays.

Bass: Without question. What Jimbo was trying to teach me that time when he was trying to teach me to throw a baseball—it was not teaching, it was trying to share, and that was where beauty and the genius and the inspiration and the purity and the force came from. He was trying to share everything he had about it in as few words as possible, and trying to transcend the difference between us in order to share the subject—and it was a gift. And yeah, I think the best writing shares that same passion, that almost desperate passion.

Slovic: In your letters to politicians are you trying to teach or just to share the value of the things you're writing about—

Bass: It's like I said in that little essay I sent you ["A20515 House/20510 Senate"]. I'm just trying to put out brush fires. You know, I'm standing there with a paint brush in one hand and a bucket of water in the other hand. And if there's no fire around, I'll paint a pretty picture; but if a fire's burning, I've got to dump water on it. So I do separate in my mind, totally, the didactic or political writings from the art. It's hard to do, but I try.

Slovic: Do you think there is the possibility of merging the two, the political and the aesthetic?

Bass: It's like merging gas and flame. I don't have that possibility and I think it's an incredible danger—it can lure you really close to the edge, and I'm in no way tempted to pursue it any further. I already have pushed it about as far as I care to.

Slovic: So is there a distinction, in your mind, between environmentalist writing and environmental writing, writing that is cognizant of nature or the environment?

Bass: Yeah. In one form, you're asking for something, and in the other form, you're looking for something. There are going to be shades of gray everywhere between, but the two are incredibly different and I think they should stay different—in your mind anyway, in *my* mind. And I think it corrupts either to merge them, with regard to my writing—to pretend that a piece that's trying to get letters for wilderness protection is something other than that again goes back to artifice and lack of honesty, which is ultimately bad for the work, I think.

Slovic: Has your attitude toward development—for instance, toward the petroleum industry—changed at all? Petroleum exploration, of course, is something that has the potential to cause a great deal of change in wilderness areas. There has, at various times, been a desire to explore areas like the Arctic National Wildlife Refuge to see if there are oil reserves there. Has your attitude toward petroleum exploration changed since you got out of the business?

Bass: No. I've always been horrified by the idea of oil and gas exploration going into wild places. It doesn't belong there. It never has and it never will. Similarly, I have never been against and never will be against drilling for oil and gas, as long as there's a need for it, on private lands and in landscapes that will not be harmed by it. It's not drilling for it that harms the world. It's burning it. You drill an eight-and-seven-eighths-inch hole into the ground—and on some farmer's land in north Alabama, which is where I worked, it never harmed anything more than basically eight and seven-eighths inches. I may sound like a spokesman for the petroleum industry, but I have to say that—it didn't hurt anything in that country. On the other hand, I've spent months and months and months of my life testifying in court and writing articles about trying to keep the oil and gas industry out of the North Fork of the Flathead and the Badger Two-Medicine Area in northwest Montana and other places.

When I was looking for oil, I had the time of my life. It was a beautiful and wild thing to be looking down 350 or 400 million years into the past for something that may or may not be there. It was very much a predator-prey relationship—it was thrilling. It was what I wanted to do. Now I want to write, so I don't have time for it. My concern with the oil and gas industry is not with the industry itself, beyond the tankers with the flimsy-assed single hulls and the cavalier notion that they won't be held accountable for environmental damage, but my gripe is with ourselves as consumers and the way we waste it—waste energy of all forms, not just hydrocarbons and not just the oil and gas, which are so much cleaner than coal or nuclear waste. And by clean I mean on all levels, not just the air, but the accumulated effects, such as health. I wish that as consumers we would push harder for at least natural gas in automobiles rather than liquid petroleum, but again it's the consumers—we're responsible. It's not the oil and gas companies that are responsible—that's childish, that's chickenshit to blame them. If we're going to start blaming, we need to blame ourselves and work from there. They're not going to change just because we're unhappy, because we ask them to. You're not going to change because I ask you to do something, and I'm not going to change because you ask me to do something. You have to do it yourself.

Slovic: What is it that's going to stimulate that new responsibility on the part of the consumer?

Bass: Hopefully, artists and culture—

Slovic: So artists have the potential to effect that kind of change.

Bass: If they look at in the proper scale, which is over generations—yes. Again, as a culture we've become so attuned to the fifteen-second change, such a short-term electronic pace. We say, "Aww, artists can't make a difference," because that book was published last year and it's remaindered this year. You've got to try harder and just keep trying harder—you can't give up. But the oil and gas industry is not going to change, and they have no obligation to change.

Slovic: They respond to their market.

Bass: Right.

Slovic: What about the timber industry, which is directly threatening the part of the world that you're particularly trying to preserve?

Bass: It's out-and-out theft. They're stealing timber from federal lands. We're paying them to steal the timber. We might as well just give them money and let them distribute money to the workers rather than ruining the landscape and distributing the money to the workers—from the taxpayers. It is a civil war in the West, and it's a scandal, I think, that exceeds any in our nation's history since slavery. It encourages brutality, it encourages greed, it encourages domination, it encourages in the short term everything that is destructive to the thing that matters most to us, which is the future. People outside of the West probably are not able to imagine the magnitude of the destruction and the passions and polarizations on that issue. It's a scandal.

Slovic: As you speak right now, you are explicitly and directly defending these places that are being ruined by the timber industry. But in your work often, in a much less direct, much subtler and more deeply affecting way, you're interested in the same idea of protection. That's one of the motifs that emerge in "Platte River" [*Paris Review* (Winter 1992)]. Your main character there, Harley, is a lineman, whose job it was to protect the runner in football, which serves as a metaphor for all the other things that he learns to protect, he wants to protect. I wonder if, on a larger scale, wilderness writing is an act of protection.

Bass: Without question. And that's why I'm convinced that, for me, love of something is going to be stronger than hate of something. And I think any cause I have to further, I'm better able to further it by helping people fall in love with those values or that subject that I'm trying to preserve rather than trying to make them hate the side that's trying to take it away. And I think every nature writer operates under that logic. It's very easy for critics to look at people like Abbey and Peacock, the angry writers—and Joy Williams—and say, "Oh, these people are writing diatribes and that's why they're so strong. And then you've got somebody passionate like Terry [Tempest Williams] or Barry Lopez, and they're writing for something." I disagree. I think that *all* of those writers are writing for something, that they're celebrating the beauty and spirit of something primarily and addressing their outrage secondly. Certainly when you think of outrage, you think of Abbey and Peacock, but if you're familiar with all their work and with their lives, when you think about their writing or their lives, you think about first the love they had for the subject, and the outrage is only a measurement of that love—it's not a form of hatred, it's a form of love. It's just a different voice.

Slovic: At the risk of being redundant, but as a way of wrapping up this discussion of writing and wilderness, maybe you could read the last paragraph from the essay "River People" [*Wild to the Heart*] aloud and comment on it, which would merely be an extension of what you've been saying.

Bass: [Reading] "If it's wild to your own heart, protect it. Preserve it. Love it. And fight for it, and dedicate yourself to it, whether it's a mountain range, your wife, your husband, or even (heaven forbid) your job. It doesn't matter if it's wild to anyone else: if it's what makes your heart sing, if it's what makes your days soar like a hawk in the summertime, then focus on it. Because for sure, it's wild, and if it's wild, it'll mean you're still free. No matter where you are."

Yeah, like you say, it does run some redundancy. To me, it's a question of integrity versus artifice—

Slovic: There must be something that is wild to everyone's heart, even to people in the timber industry perhaps—

Bass: Exactly. Oh, God, yes. I mean, a chainsaw, if you're up there running it and you're engaged with it, it's a lovely process. There's not anybody on our side asking them to stop cutting trees, because we use as many of them as anybody. We're just asking them to step back and look at a larger picture—

Slovic: Where they're cutting from—

Bass: And the way they're cutting them—

Slovic: Clearcutting being the problem.

Bass: Right. There's nothing wilder than a chainsaw.

Works Cited

Bass, Rick. "Bear Spray Stories." Presented at Fire & Grit: Working for Nature in Community. An Orion Society Millennium Conference. Shepherdstown, West Virginia, 22 June 1999.

———. *Brown Dog of the Yaak: Essays on Art and Activism*. Minneapolis: Milkweed Editions, 1999.

———. "The Community of Glaciers." Presented at Fire & Grit: Working for Nature in Community. An Orion Society Millennium Conference. Shepherdstown, West Virginia, 22 June 1999.

———. *Fiber.* Athens: University of Georgia Press, 1998.
———. "On Willow Creek." In *Heart of the Land: Essays on Last Great Places,* ed. Joseph Barbato and Lisa Weinerman. New York: Pantheon, 1994.
———. "20515 House/20510 Senate." *American Nature Writing Newsletter* 5:1 (Spring 1993): 3–5.

"The Unbelievable Thing Usually Goes to the Heart of the Story"

Magic Realism in the Fiction of Rick Bass

JIM DWYER

IMAGINE THAT EACH member of a group of people unfamiliar with Rick Bass reads just one essay or story. Readers of the early essays might describe a geologist with a strong sense of place. Those who read his later essays might applaud the passionate defender of the Yaak, noting that his work reflects extensive knowledge of geology, natural history, and conservation. Those who read only his fiction might wonder if they were talking about the same person. Isn't this the author whose characters perform superhuman feats of strength and endurance, one whose work is laden with myth and magic? As in the tale of the blind men describing the elephant, each could describe some elements, but none could provide an accurate overall assessment. Bass is a multifaceted individual who seems equally at home walking in the woods, gutting an elk, rallying support for a cause, or writing powerful, emotionally engaging fiction. His work is similarly multifaceted and difficult to categorize.

First, consider what it *isn't*. According to M. H. Abrams, "The romance is said to represent life as we would have it be—more picturesque, fantastic, adventurous, or heroic in actuality; realism, on the other hand, is said to represent life as it really is" (*A Glossary*, 174). Clearly, there are both romantic and realistic elements in Bass's work. He may incorporate natural history, but he could hardly be considered a literary naturalist, since naturalism eschews the spirituality that pervades his fiction. Instead, he employs vivid, detailed descriptions of nature to create "super-realism" that reveals both physical and spiritual aspects of life. While he employs fable, he could hardly be labeled a fabulist. He may be writing in the postmodern era, but his work is generally free of such devices as dislocations of time and space or textual self-commentary. Exceptions include the excerpts from Old Dudley's notebooks in *Where the Sea Used to Be* (1998) and the genre-busting *Fiber* (1998).

Alan Weltzien notes that the novellas comprising *Platte River* (1994) contain "flashes of the bizarre" (*Rick Bass*, 39). He further asserts: "The title of William O'Rourke's *Chicago Tribune* review, 'Rick Bass' Near Mythic Tales of Big Country and Big People,' understates, if anything, the novel combination of fairy tale and realism Bass essays" (39). According to reviewer Sam Walker, "The three novellas . . . are full of events that push the envelope of the plausible, and his mythical narrative style harks back to a time when most men sat in hunting lodges telling tall tales" ("Author's Tall-Tale Novellas," 13).

Bass's tales are embedded in strikingly realistic prose. He "sets you up" by creating characters or landscapes you identify with and "knocks you down" with unexpected events. A good example can be found in *Where the Sea Used to Be*. Bass establishes young Colter as a sympathetic character who loves nature, works hard to support his widowed mother, mourns the loss of his father, and becomes friends with newcomer Wallis. He teaches Wallis about the lives of the animals and the people of the Swan, establishing himself as a down-to-earth young man. Our empathy increases when he nearly freezes to death visiting his father's corpse at night and is condemned as a "pure-God, nasty little savage" by the despicable Dudley (*Where the Sea Used to Be*, 124).

When Colter tells Wallis, "Come on, I'll show you something" (183), one assumes that he is about to transmit some wood-lore. Instead he takes Wallis to Joshua, a folksy Orpheus who may be the most fantastic figure in all of Bass's fiction. In a poverty-stricken valley populated by a few dozen people who hunt, fish, trap, scavenge, forage, and garden to eke out a meager existence dwells a brilliant artist whose only work is building coffins: "There were fantastic, brightly painted, animal shaped coffins stacked on sawhorses throughout the barn" (184). Some are buried, others are hung in trees or placed in caves, and others, "[s]wans, usually" (185), are floated downriver, rather like a Viking funeral. By having no-nonsense Colter introduce us to Joshua, Bass lends him credibility.

Reestablishing bonds between humanity and nature is a common thread in Bass's fiction and essays. He creates emotional ties between the reader and the characters, creatures, and landscapes of his stories through a combination of super-realism and fantastic but plausible events and imagery. Does he succeed? Robert Wilson attests: "These novellas strike me in this way, as attempting to convince me of things that I wouldn't ordinarily believe, and succeeding at it more often than not. *The unbelievable thing usually goes to the heart of the story,* to the mystery of human personality and motivation" ("*Platte River*," D, 51; emphasis added). The "unbelievability" is precisely what causes us to question our beliefs: "What was *that* about?"

Bass's best fiction succeeds because it depicts the world realistically and then challenges our assumptions through fantastic characters or phenomena. His less successful pieces fail to do so. Consider the contrast between the characters and settings in *Where the Sea Used to Be* and those in "Field Events," "Cats and Students, Bubbles and Abysses," and some of the Houston stories. Mel, Wallis, and Matthew are complex characters, unusual in certain ways, but always credible. A. C. and Piss Ant aren't remotely real. Since it is difficult to identify with them, their stories aren't compelling. A. C. seems to be larger-than-life, but the same might be said of Old Dudley. One difference in our acceptance of the two is that Dudley's limitations are presented simultaneously with the more mythic elements, whereas A. C.'s only "human" aspects are his initial shyness and his ability to fall in love. The other difference is contextual: with the exception of Lori, the characters in "Field Events" seem one-dimensional, while those in *Where the Sea Used to Be* are more complex.

Magic Realism

How might we characterize Bass's strange brew of vivid natural history writing, quirky characters, bizarre events, mysticism, myth, and calls to action? Given the many "fresh and strange" (Lowell, "Country Love," 11) elements in his work and his subversive intent in deploying them, it appears to be magic realism. Magic realism as a genre was created in Latin America by Alejo Carpentier, Jorge Luis Borges, Jorge Amado, Gabriel García Márquez, and others. African writers such as Chinua Achebe and Wole Soyinka have employed it, as have some gay writers, many Native American novelists, and two direct influences on Bass: Eudora Welty and William Faulkner.

García Márquez observed that the writer "can bring light to this very chamber [of destruction and oppression] with words . . . [to create] a minor utopia" ("Solitude," 208). The agenda of magic realism is to expose and resist oppressive and destructive forces. Bass feels as much an "outsider" as most magic realists. He uses art in a subversive fashion, resisting the industrial destruction of the natural world, the mythical world, and the human psyche. His work is a withering critique of an overly materialistic consumer-based society, the other side of the same coin that spawns the political oppression that Third World magic realists rebel against. It seems only natural that he would adopt the literary strategy of magic realism, considering its opposition to forces of oppression and industrial destruction.

Bass utilizes magic realist techniques such as inserting fantastic elements into otherwise realistic accounts, but should he be considered a magic realist? Michael Berryhill makes the case that "Bass has almost single-handedly created North American magical realism, part Paul Bunyan, part Herman Melville, and all of it solidly, believably his" ("Bass Hunts Black Gold," 21). John Skow demurs, asserting that "categories kill, and so to say 'Oh, yeah, magic realism' is to veer several degrees from true north. These narrations are what they are, which is true of only the strongest kind of imagining" ("Wilderness Within," 97).

I agree that Bass is not a "traditional" magic realist in the South American style but contend that he has fundamentally expanded the genre. Whereas distortions, exaggerations, and fantasies are typically used to create magical elements, much of the magic in his writing arises from his almost super-realistic descriptions of nature itself. Bass displays the "hidden wisdom" *within* the everyday reality of the natural world. We just need to look more closely to see it. The celebrated American poet Rita Dove has "had people point out passages that they think of as having elements of magical realism, and all I can think is: isn't reality *magic?*" (Walsh, "Isn't Reality *Magic?*" 152). Bass champions the mystical aspects of nature. Mel Estes echoes Dove's and Bass's sentiments when she tells her class that "what other people call 'magic' was once a normal and everyday response to life everywhere else in the world" (*Where the Sea Used to Be,* 215).

Reading Bass, I am sometimes reminded of an exhibition of Japanese super-realistic painting I attended around 1970. I assumed that the work was photography, but with an unusual painterly quality that rendered it almost hallucinatory. Similarly, the paintings in an exhibit by Chuck Close "look so much like photographs that museum guards must be posted . . . to prevent visitors from running their hands over the canvases to make certain that they were not just photographs" (Gelderman, "Hyperrealism," 358). While only a few of the viewers were actually "tripping" at the time, virtually everyone seemed to be similarly enraptured. Many left the exhibit with different eyes, as it were, observing the world more closely and feeling more intrinsically part of it. The painters had achieved a super-realistic effect through incredible detail, and even the dark, rainy pieces had a subdued luminosity. William Howarth observes that writer John McPhee "buffs and polishes a fact until it becomes a greater reality," much as the painters' work seemed buffed and polished (*The John McPhee Reader*, xvi). So, too, with Bass (his use of painterly techniques is considered in greater detail below).

This paper considers Bass's use of magic realism by examining the weird, wild, and wonderful images and events in his fiction. They can be divided into a few basic themes, which are often interwoven and cannot be completely separated: (1) feats of great or even superhuman strength and endurance, quests, and other legendary elements; (2) the physical and spiritual links between human beings and other animals and the land; and (3) the magic inherent in the natural world, often expressed in terms of "glowing" and "luminosity." His writing evolves from an emphasis on the superhuman elements in his earliest work, to deeper considerations of the relation between humans and nature, to the inherent magic of nature in his later work.

Monstrosity, Macho, and Myth

Many of Bass's characters are fine physical specimens hardened by heavy work and harsh conditions. Others are misshapen, often reflecting a troubled psychological or spiritual state. As noted on the jacket of *In the Loyal Mountains* (1995), "While Bass' work is grounded in an uncompromising vision of the truth, he magnifies elements until they acquire fantastic proportions." Consider Old Dudley, who initially seems to be just another demanding oil tycoon. Through his journal entries, obsessive behavior, and weird occurrences such as his impregnation of Amy, Bass creates a bizarre character that the reader can accept with relatively little suspension of disbelief. He accomplishes this by depicting not just Dudley's "larger than life" elements, but his familiar flaws, prejudices, and peculiarities. On one hand he's just another unreasonable, cantankerous old curmudgeon, but on the other he's the very personification of "our aberrant hunger to devour everything on or below the earth's surface"

(Boyes, Review, 463). Our disgust and anger toward Dudley are also directed at what he so forcefully represents, as Bass's magic realism engages and enrages the reader.

In his earlier work, particularly *The Watch* (1989), Bass overrelied on fantastic characters, pulling them from his authorial bag of tricks like a clumsy apprentice magician. Big Ed of "Juggernaut" claims he once had a pet lion that stabbed a child with a claw hidden in its tail: "All female lions have a claw hidden in their tail . . . *No,* it's true," he adds, anticipating his students' skepticism (*Watch,* 107). Ed has a "scarecrow wife . . . seven feet tall" (109) and moonlights on a semipro hockey team. The narrator of one story (Bass?) can run down the beach with a couch on his back, looking like an ant scurrying with a leaf. Macho meets magic as he and Kirby imagine riding mythical horses into the Gulf: "Both of us on white horses, riding out into the waves, chest deep, neck-deep, then the magic lift and float of the horse as it began to swim, the light feeling of nothing, no resistance" (190).

In the title story, Jesse's abnormality is both emotional and metabolic. After working himself into world-class bicyclist shape he becomes so obese that he abandons his bike in favor of a go-cart. Peculiarities can sometimes be useful: when the narrator of "Mississippi" hangs his sheets in the summer sun, he can maintain an erection all night. "Cats and Students, Bubbles and Abysses" features two other physical anomalies. The narrator is 5 foot 6, weighs 195 pounds, and can "dead lift 700 pounds and run a marathon in under three hours six minutes" (93), an almost superhuman combination. His roommate Piss-Ant is 7 feet tall, weighs a skeletal 165, and can somehow fold himself into his MG sports car. Even their cat is strange: "He's a bad ass: he only eats raw pigeons. You know how cats can be finicky" (94). Unlike Bass's later stories, which blend realism and the surreal seamlessly, these characters seem contrived.

The characters who inhabit *Platte River* are almost superhuman. Harley is a former pro-football player, and his lover, Shaw, an ex-fashion model. Leena in "Mahatma Joe" possesses great stamina and is impervious to cold. She swims in the icy river daily, even when she must chop a hole in the ice to do so. "Field Events" takes this theme to an extreme: ". . . the big man came around the bend, swimming upstream, doing the butterfly stroke. He was pulling a canoe behind him, and it was loaded with darkened cast-iron statues . . . the big man leapt free of the water with each sweep of his arms, arching into the air like a fish and then crashing back down into the rapids" (*Platte River,* 45). The "big man," A. C., performs ballet with a cow on his shoulder. These characters seem cartoon-like, larger than life but not significant enough to be the stuff of legend. They compare poorly to Glenda, the much more credible world-class runner in "Fires." Glenda requires discipline, a regular training regimen, support, and protection to accomplish her athletic goals. Like Leena's, though, Glenda's passion for frigid water seems dubious: "... she'd sit down in the cold water like an animal chased there by hounds" (*In the Loyal Mountains,* 42).

The quest is one of Bass's primary mythic themes. In "Field Events" it is for world records and then for love, while in "The Watch" Jesse seeks athletic greatness before joining Hollingsworth's quest for his father. Many stories feature quests for food or oil, wilderness survival, or a return to nature. A. C.'s love is strengthened when his lover uses a car to pull him out of rapids that not even he can conquer. "Closer and closer she'd pull him, reeling in the wet rope, dragging him up on shore, bending over and kissing his lips until his eyes fluttered, bringing him back to life every time" (*Platte River,* 95).

The narrator of *Fiber* sometimes becomes "the log fairy," surreptitiously loading logs onto other loggers' trucks. He pictures "houses and homes getting stronger... as they feed on my magical forest, and then I imagine those strong homes raising strong families... It's a fantasy to be sure, but you tell me which is more real: an idea, such as a stated passion or desire of one's... human emotions or a hundred inch, 250-pound green juicy fir on one's mortal shoulder" (20–21). The Paul Bunyan legend is thereby reversed. Bass simultaneously transforms a very different legend as the pixie-like tooth fairy becomes a burly logger—a case of "subversion by inversion." The novella form seems to bring out the fantasist in Bass, the obvious reason being that the additional length provides more room.

Bass's big novel, *Where the Sea Used to Be,* incorporates many legendary and mythic elements including Paul Bunyan, *Moby Dick,* and Native American cosmology. A variety of quests occur simultaneously: Dudley, Matthew, and Wallis seek oil; Mel quests after wolves; Colter prepares for a long journey deeper into nature and the past; various romantic and sexual quests arise; and Matthew and Wallis survive an epic hunting trip. It's not surprising to find figures of heroic proportions in the novel's "second Swan Valley" since one almost has to be superhuman to survive the bitterly cold winters. Wallis nearly freezes under his jeep before Mel revives him and skis ten miles carrying him on her back.

Along the way they encounter a rock wall that "seemed to Wallis to make the scenery not more bucolic, but wilder, as if they were going back in time, back to some time before true fences" (19). It was begun by Matthew but has become a community project, a rite of spring, the physical manifestation of a quest for community. Matthew's fence unites the community in a common task. Rather than dividing the land or facilitating its exploitation, its purpose is social and symbolic.

The theme of superhuman strength is personified in Matthew: building the wall, carrying propane refrigerators on his back as a boy, dousing himself with gasoline so he could light himself up like a human flame to startle the swans, etc. Even after impaling himself on a screwdriver in a disastrous fall from an oil rig, he leads a rugged two-week-long elk hunt that would kill most people. Phil Hanrahan calls this one of "the best quest episodes in our literature" ("Timeless Dreams," 12). Richard Bernstein, though, complains that "Mr. Bass's aim is undermined by his propensity for a self-conscious, epic-heroic mysticism that at times approaches self-parody... in a Paul Bunyanesque tall tale mode that requires a good deal of credulity" ("Searching for Oil," 9). It seems implausible that Matthew should even attempt such a hunt after a serious injury, but once the hunt begins, such misgivings are forgotten as the reader is swept away in a seductive narrative as powerful as a blizzard.

The Human Animal

One of Bass's implicit directives is that we must acknowledge the attributes we share with other animals to understand ourselves. This is no sugarcoated utopia: human relationships may be of the predator-prey variety, and death must occur for new life to flourish. His unsentimental view leads him to explore the boundary between wildness and domesticity, crossing back and forth like a wolf thinning a herd before escaping back into the forest. Terrell Dixon observes that Bass's "stories explore relationships between the city and nature, looking at the prospects for co-existence and at the ways in which urban dwellers can connect with place and with the wild" (Review, 99).

In "Mexico," Kirby raises a giant catfish in a front-yard swimming pool that is deep enough to contain stumps, gravel, old trees, and an old Volkswagen. Alan Weltzien observes: "On the first page of Bass's first short story collection, he wastes no time showing the reader something quite strange. The swimming pool, cliched symbol of suburban affluence, is rendered unfamiliar, bizarre" (*Rick Bass,* 22). The pool might be viewed as an attempt to reconnect with nature in the suburbs. "The Wait" includes a potent animal image: "'I dreamed you were in my garbage can last night,' Kirby tells Jack matter-of-factly. 'I dreamed you were a raccoon, banging around in the garbage, sorting through my trash.' 'Uh-huh,' says Jack, seemingly amused at the thought of being taken for a raccoon" (*Watch,* 116). The narrator's father in "In the Loyal Mountains" is a developer and golfer, a marked contrast to his "wild" brother, Zorey, whom he calls "Animal." The not entirely feral Zorey owns a small plane that seems much "like a tethered animal" (*In the Loyal Mountains,* 163). Zorey treats the narrator and his girlfriend to dinners in the finest restaurants in Houston, but his wild side emerges anew as he guts quail in the cab of his truck and cooks them over cans of Sterno.

"The Watch" introduces the motif of human predator-prey relationships. Seventy-seven-year-old Buzbee and his sixty-three-year-old son, Hollingsworth, operate a "ratty ass grocery" (*Watch,* 50) with virtually no customers. Driven to distraction by his son's ceaseless babbling, Buzbee escapes to the swamp, where he creates an odd little settlement for women who have escaped abusive situations. They disappear, ghostlike, into the swamp whenever danger approaches. Despite their blundering ineptitude, Jesse and Hollingsworth eventually capture Buzbee and chain him to a stake. When "Swamp Boy" collects specimens, a gang of schoolmates chases him: "We followed him like jackals, like soul scavengers . . . we'd shout and whoop and chase him down like lions on a gazelle, pull that sweet boy down and truss him up with rope and hoist him into a tree" (*In the Loyal Mountains,* 23). As in *Lord of the Flies,* the boys beat him and break his glasses. The nearby forest includes a "buffalo ring" where a herd of bison made a last stand against a pack of wolves. "You could feel magic in this spot, could feel it rise from centuries ago and brush against your face like the cool air from the bottom of a deep well" (26). The boys make wolf masks and chase Swamp Boy, who "sounds like the lost calf" (33). Whereas wolves kill only to survive, the boys engage in sheer cruelty. Mimicking elements of nature must take place in the context of a deeper understanding, which these boys lack.

Harley and Shaw of "Platte River" have a volatile relationship marked by passionate bursts of sex alternating with Shaw's frequent escapes. The story takes a strange twist when one of Harley's former teammates, Willis, invites him to lecture to his classes in northern Michigan. On the day before the lecture, when they go fishing, Harley hooks but loses a fish, an occurrence eerily similar to his relationship with Shaw. When he becomes inarticulate in class he breaks down and confesses that as a football player "I never learned to let anything go past me . . . I was too damn fucking good. It turned me into a fucking *crustacean*" (140). The only way Harley can understand his human foibles is to think in zoological terms.

Elaine Kendall claims that "'Fires' is a departure from the fantastic tone of the others: it's almost a romance" ("Two Lands," E4). This is somewhat true, but the themes of predator-prey relationships and fantastic strength are nevertheless present. "Whenever one [woman] does move in with me, it feels like I've tricked her, caught her in a trap" (*In the Loyal Mountains,* 38). Note the many variations in the predator-prey theme, from aggressive pursuit and harassment in "The Watch" and "Swamp Boy" to Harley's frustration in trying to "keep" Shaw and the more passive and subtle relationships in "Fires." Terrell Dixon is generally correct in observing that "[t]he first two stories [in *Platte River*] continue and expand the magical realism of 'The Watch' in narratives that incorporate elements of the tall tale, fable, and myth; the title story is a more traditional, Hemingway-like tale of men and women and steelhead fishing in Michigan" ("Rick Bass," 86). "Platte River" and "Fires" demonstrate that the themes of the quest, possession and loss, physical strength, and the human as animal are present even in Bass's most straightforward fiction.

These themes dominate "The Myth of Bears": "Trapper is so old and tired that every August he just sits in the sun in front of the cabin with his head bowed, trying to gather up the last of it" (*The Sky, the Stars, the Wilderness,* 5). Trapper is a thirty-five-year-old man worn down by the privations of a trapping life in the Yukon. He is canine, though, in his own way: "In Trapper's nighttime fits, he imagines that he is a wolf, and that the other wolves in his pack have suddenly turned against him and set upon him with their teeth . . ." (6). His lover, Judith, is more like a moose: "She's six feet tall (Trapper is five-nine), and her shoe size is thirteen . . . the inward curve of her feet makes it so she doesn't need snowshoes" (5). Disturbed by his worsening fits, Judith escapes into a raging blizzard: "It is not that he is a bad man, or that I am a bad woman, she thought. *It's just that he is a predator, and I am prey*" (9; emphasis added). Trapper feels "[b]etrayed, abandoned. He'd thought she was *tame.* He'd not understood she was the wildest, most fluttering thing in the woods" (12). He resolves to track her down and tie her to a stake in the yard, a fate similar to Buzbee's in "The Watch."

Trapper and Judith play a cat and mouse game in extreme conditions. Judith covers great distances with little more than the clothes on her back, kills deer with a knife, and burrows into the snow at night as the temperature drops to fifty-five below. Trapper is guided both by practical wood-lore (moving like a wolf) and by heavenly forces: he can hear the northern lights. In a flashback to Judith's Uncle Harm's childhood, Harm and a friend follow a Hansel and Gretel trail of corn that a grizzly bear dropped after raiding their fields. The trail leads to a penned-up cave where the bear has been fattening four or five pigs. The boys flee when they sense that the bear is considering adding them to his herd. "'Cave's still up there,' Harm had told Trapper. 'Pig skeletons, too. And dog skeletons. Never did find a bear skeleton on that mountain. Could have been that bear was God'" (32). By interpolating this earlier story into the text, Bass emphasizes its spiritual aspects, possibly even conferring Godhood upon a bear.

Bass then considers Trapper's spiritual state: "[Trapper] trembles but without feeling as he watches the ghosts of the animals return to the sky. There *is* no spirit world, he thinks. There is just her, whom he wants to capture, on the other side of the river. If he can capture her . . . all will be made new again. Spirit world, my butt, he thinks . . ." (37). He may *think* this, but his actions indicate that he believes in a spirit world and in interconnectedness with other animals. Plainly, though, he does not believe everything he hears: "A myth of bears, Trapper thinks: they'll bring others of their own kind, caught in a trap, food, to ease their hunger, to give comfort. Wolves, yes—he'd seen that often—but never bears" (42). Lauren Cobb observes: "By embedding this strange love story with the tall tales, myths, and realistic details of a trapper's life, Bass seems to suggest the human urge to romanticize the other—whether a lover or a grizzly bear—is both an attempt to fill in the blanks of our knowledge, and a heartfelt response to the mythic dimensions of existence" (Review, 388). Trapper may have trapped her, but the equation between them has changed. In the end she demands that he tell her he loves her, but now she is gripping *his* wrist. This story ends the predator-prey relationship in a statement of interconnectedness.

Several stories in *In the Loyal Mountains* explore what Alan Weltzien calls "the interstices between wilderness-wildness and domesticity-tameness" (*Rick Bass,* 44). They "provide us with a complex and moving look at how Rick Bass envisions the power(s) of place" (Dixon, Review, 98). Five stories in particular—"The History of Rodney," "The Valley," "Antlers," "Days of Heaven," and "Where the Sea Used to Be"—can be considered variations on this theme. Renewal out of ruin is portrayed in "The History of Rodney" when a new oxbow in the Mississippi River "strands" the town. Instead of humans returning to nature, it returns to them. A young couple shares a huge abandoned mansion with a tree growing through the floor, an owl in the attic, and pigs under the porch. The couple lights the house with jars of fireflies "and then we laugh as we love, with their blinking green bellies going on and off like soft, harmless firecrackers, as if they are applauding" (10). Even the graveyard provides an animal image: "the skeleton of a deer impaled high on the iron spikes of the fence.... The skull seems to be opening its mouth in a scream" (15).

The hardscrabble subsistence economy of the Yaak is introduced in "The Valley." Electricity, roads, and money are all in short supply. People hunt and forage, make home brew, and feed roadkill to their sled dogs. What little technology is available is put to unusual uses. The tavern owner announces community barbecues with an old emergency warning siren. At one such event old Mr. Terjaney's overheated accordion explodes when he spills beer on it, electrocuting himself: "We thought he'd done it on purpose—perhaps this was a special function of the instrument when he pressed a certain button.... We even cheered at first" (56–57). "Antlers" describes a wild Halloween party where everyone is adorned with antlers: "Mock battles occur when the men and women bang the antlers against each other" (66). They get towed home behind trucks, still wearing the antlers, which "feel natural after having them lashed to our heads for so long" (66). Much of the story explores attitudes about hunting, which range from cold-bloodedness to reverence for the hunted to horror. Suzie, whose own wildness takes the form of serial monogamy, expresses the last sentiment. The narrator decides that "[a]ll this time I'd been uncertain about whether it was right or wrong to hunt if you ate the meat and said those prayers. And I'm still not entirely convinced one way or the other. But I have a better picture of what it's like to be the elk or deer. And I understand Suzie a little better too" (73). Accepting your animal nature, connecting with your inner wildness, stimulates deeper self-realization.

Even the developers in "Days of Heaven" engage in animalistic ritual. While butchering a moose, "Zim reached over and smeared it [blood] on Quentin's cheeks, applying it like makeup, or medicine of some sort" (144). This mock ceremony fails to trigger any healing shift of consciousness: "They'd nailed the moose's head, with the antlers, to one of the walls, so that his blue-blind eyes stared down at his own corpse. There was a baseball cap perched on his antlers and a cigar stuck between his big lips" (145). Despairing, the narrator adopts a different totem: "I sat very still, like that owl, and thought about where I would go next, after this place was gone. Maybe, I thought, if I sit very still, they will just go away" (147). This clearly wishful thinking, though, implies the need for action.

Bass's zoological analogies are replaced with geological ones in the story "Where the Sea Used to Be." He reminds us that geology is intrinsically connected to zoology by describing the basin as "an ancient, mysterious, buried dry sea . . . [from] an Age of Sharks, thousands of varieties of sharks in the warm waters in those days—empty, beautiful, hundreds of miles of empty beaches, a few plants, windy days, warmth, no one to see anything, the most mysterious sea that ever was" (*The Sky, the Stars, the Wilderness*, 55). Weltzien observes: "The ancient sea chooses Wallis and tests his mettle. Also, it expresses in Bass's career a fundamental, even chthonic connection of self with earth; it figures as a legacy, a residual core of wildness—external and internal—waiting to be tapped" (*Rick Bass*, 21). Indeed, Wallis "felt as if he were oil, far below the ground, trapped in a thin layer of rock. He felt that when the drilling bit hit his formation, and pierced the very top of it, he would come out: blowing, all of it, a fire, a roar" (*The Sky, the Stars, the Wilderness*, 68).

Bass conjures up the consciousness of injured birds caught beneath the ice in "The Hermit's Story": "The austere times were the very thing, the very imbalance, which would summon the resurrection of that frozen richness in the soil—if indeed that richness, that magic, that hope did still exist beneath the ice and snow. Spring would come like its own green fire, if only the injured ones could hold on" (30). Resurrection, hope, and magic are not merely human constructs, but are inherent in nature. Emerging from the lake, Ann and Gray Owl find their way home, but only after the dogs choose the correct direction. Ann learns to see things from the dogs' perspective: "how the world must have appeared to them when they were in that trance, the blue zone, where the odors of things wrote their images across the dogs' hot brainpans. A zone where sight, and the appearance of things—*surfaces*—disappeared, and where instead their essence—the heat molecules of scent—was revealed, illuminated, circumscribed, possessed" (31). The familiar themes of boundaries, human-animal relationship, feats of survival, and luminosity are intertwined.

Bass fills *Where the Sea Used to Be* with animal imagery, where it works its way ever deeper into the reader's consciousness. Wallis encounters herds of deer and elk that "wore their antlers like kings" (12). Antlers are a common image in his earlier work: used as rakes in "Mahatma Joe," party hats in "Antlers," part of the dishonored moose corpse in "Days of Heaven," and the illusion of a rabbit with antlers in "The Sky, the Stars, the Wilderness." The novel *bristles* with antlers. They serve not just as weapons and snow shovels for ungulates, but as burial cairns, substitutes for flowers, get-well presents, trail markers left in the trees during the snowy winter, signals of the biggest game for hunters, wilderness drinking mugs, coffin decorations, a shrine in a tree, and even as images for "how a thing could be twisted or flexed only slightly to become totally different" (328). They "form a gleaming double tree" (385) above the ground when an elk is pit-roasted, gather falling snow "as if with outstretched mahogany hands" (416), "catch the stars" (417). They carve furrows in the snow, with their weight carving similar lines in Matthew's back, as he drags a dead elk. Young Colter supports himself and his mother by gathering antlers and selling them. Colter describes how rodents eat the antlers and hawks eat the rodents so the antlers are absorbed in the hawks. "Think of it . . . a flying antler" (104). Wallis imagines building "fences, walls, even houses from those white spars" (294). Matthew and Wallis see "a swarm of antlers moving to the forest" (430) and bag their elk when the biggest one in the herd is drawn to the antlers that Matthew is dragging.

We typically think of a mask as a disguise, and a masquerade as a ritualistic fantasy, but the denizens of the Yaak seem to use antlers as a sort of antimask. They simultaneously acknowledge their animal nature as intrinsic to their individual identities and strengthen the bonds of their human community.

The animal imagery comes alive in "the coyote game." Mel, Wallis, Dudley, Matthew, and Helen sprinkle deer urine on their ankles, burrow into the snow, cover themselves with hides, and wait. When they jump up, "the coyotes tucked their tails and galloped away, looking back over their shoulders, streaking back into the woods. It was cruel, Wallis supposed, but he had to laugh at what must have been going through their minds: wondering if that was where humans came from—if they came up through some vent in the earth" (156). According to the Hopi emergence myth, humans arose from the world of the dead to that of the living through a passage from the underworld. Supposing that the coyotes may have "wondered" along the lines of myth may be an example of what Bass himself calls "rabid anthropomorphism." "I don't much care for rabid anthropomorphism. . . . [But] I think it's time that we do make a mistake in the direction of anthropomorphizing rather than disallowing character and soul and sentiment and feeling in a species. Of course, as it's been pointed out, it makes it much more convenient for us to abuse that species—or that man, woman, or child—if that individual is not considered a sentient being. It's a form of manipulation, domination, control—all of the things that are bad for art, as well as life" (Slovic, "Interview," 21). The similarity between these sentiments and those of García Márquez is quite striking.

Bass's anthropomorphism is yet another application of magic realism. According to Kate Boyes, "What seems bizarre eventually makes sense. . . . Bass' breathtaking language takes readers beyond the familiar, comfortable urban mind (the mind that intellectualizes relationships with nature, the mind that *might be tempted to argue about anthropomorphism*) and shows us the natural world through the wild mind . . ." (Review, 463–64; emphasis added). When Bass attributes what we might consider human thoughts to animals, he does so in a seemingly accurate way, avoiding exaggerations or cliches. For example, wolves do bring food to other wolves caught in traps. Hence anthropomorphism becomes plausible, providing another way to shift the readers' consciousness to a more primal level.

Life, death, and extinction take a decidedly anthropomorphic spin in "The Sky, the Stars, the Wilderness," particularly in the passages about Chubb's death and cremation. "I watched the hawk to see if it was Chubb. Strange things happen in the animal world when a loved one dies, that's a fact. They honor our passage with more reverence than we do theirs" (*The Sky, the Stars, the Wilderness,* 160). Chubb insisted that nighthawks are goatsuckers, much to the consternation of Grandfather, who consigns Chubb to "previous generations of blind, inattentive, head-bobbing myth mongers" (116). A stickler for accuracy, Grandfather believes that "[t]he natural history of Texas is being sacrificed upon the altar of generalization! You must pay attention! You must know the names before they're lost!" (98). He goes on to argue that "the world was going to hell in a handbasket, and it was because of a loss of attention to detail, a lapse in our glorious God-given ability to *observe*" (116).

In a passage reminiscent of Robinson Jeffers's "Sky Entombment," Anne proclaims that "*There are no boundaries.* It is all wrapped up together, all hawk-and-boar tumble, and if God does not take us out by the hawk, we will be eaten by the vultures" (*The Sky, the Stars, the Wilderness,* 121). She believes that the "heart of it all is mystery, and science is at best only the peripheral trappings to that mystery" (123). In college she had scorned "so much hoop-jumping bullshit in the world of science and no more sacred awe" (181). One hears Bass speaking alternately through Grandfather and Anne. "At the end of our spectacularly destructive century, Anne steps forward as a descendent of all Bass's earlier voices, defining herself as a survivor, fundamentally connected with some measure of wilderness, as we all should be" (Weltzien, *Rick Bass,* 48).

Bass also employs reverse anthropomorphism. The players in the coyote game became deer, Harley a crustacean, Judith an ungulate, Trapper a wolf, Jack a raccoon, A. C. a porpoise or a giant fish. Grandfather seems to be metamorphosing into a bird as death approaches. The boys who preyed on "lost calf" Swamp Boy are called jackals, lions, and wolves. Bass likened himself to a skin-shedding insect or snake and to a snapping wolverine in *Fiber.* Such transformations encourage readers to acknowledge the primal aspects of the "human animal." This practice dates back at least to Ovid's *Metamorphoses* and is used in many fables. By depicting sympathetic humans as animals, Bass encourages us to be more childlike in accepting our own wild attributes: wear the antlers, be the elk, albeit a human sort of elk.

Wildness is more than exterior wilderness since it is also an aspect of human nature. In "Mahatma Joe" nobody wears any clothes on "Naked Days" during the warm Chinook winds. The story revolves around a strange alliance between an aging evangelist and a young woman named Leena. "Joe believed that vegetables could calm angry souls, that meat—flesh!—was a temptation of Satan's creation" (*Platte River,* 6). When Joe and his wife, Lily, laboriously plant huge gardens, using antlers as rakes and pitchforks, he talks to the fields and seeds: "'Beans! Tomatoes! Kumquats!' snapped the old man, swinging as if his life were riding on it" (25). This passage recalls Frank Zappa's song "Call Any Vegetable": "Call any vegetable! / Call it by name! / And the chances are good /

that the vegetable will respond to you." Joe and Zappa both use *specific* names, much like Grandfather of "The Sky, the Stars, the Wilderness." Although "Mahatma Joe" has both comic and surreal elements, Joe is deadly earnest. By virtually baptizing the vegetables, he gives them identities and evangelizes them to become part of his great mission in life, sanctifying both them and himself.

Canoeing over the spot where Lily died, "Joe and Leena looked down and saw her, perfectly preserved in the frigid waters, lying on the bottom, looking the same as she ever had, looking up at them through twelve feet of water as if nothing had happened, as if no days had ever gone by" (42). A similar image recurs in *Where the Sea Used to Be* when Wallis and Colter view Colter's father's corpse through the ice. "Everything's still the same on him as it was when the day he went in . . . and his hair is still waving in the current . . . only longer. It kept growing after he died" (81). In the first incident the illusion of stasis is created, whereas in the second change takes place and life continues after death.

"Isn't Reality *Magic*?"

Bass's greatest artistic strength may be his ability to portray the magical aspects of life in both subtle and spectacular ways. He uses detailed descriptions to create super-realistic settings, as if to say "look closely and you will see the wonder of life." Sympathetic characters are enraptured by nature, while unsympathetic ones either fail to appreciate natural wonder or want to "improve" it, irredeemably destroying the magic. Super-realism, or hyperrealism, is sometimes found in contemporary painting, fiction, and drama. Carol Gelderman observes:

> Before the advent of the "new" realism, the art of the realistic play, like all art for that matter, was a recreation of the world in man's image. Hence, the central ingredient was not the subject of the play, but man's relationship to it. . . . The hyperrealist, by contrast, insists on the irrefutable existence of reality outside of and distinct from that faculty: "the world *is* quite simply. That in any case is the most remarkable thing about it," as Robbe-Grillet wrote. The hyperrealistic dramatist . . . says that the only way to see the world as it is, is to render it with as little distortion and personal overlay as possible. ("Hyperrealism," 358)

Toby Silverman Zinman notes that in "[s]uper-realist plays . . . motion is away from the conceptual toward the perceptual, away from idea toward fact and event. . . . That sense of layers, of something underneath . . . is basic to the very technique of super-realism" ("Sam Shepard," 423, 425). Indeed, one of Bass's hallmarks is eschewing the reinterpretation of natural scenes and events, preferring to depict "something underneath": luminosity, mystery, the spirit world, magic. With the exception of *Fiber,* Bass generally does not provide authorial asides about the narrative. The message to stop and preserve the wild roses is usually implicit, but sometimes characters like Anne, Grandpa, and Mel state it explicitly.

Novelist Hugh Hood defines the common ground between super-realist writing and painting: "an art which exhibits the transcendental element dwelling in living things. I think of this as true super-realism" ("Sober Colouring," 30). He argues that "the spirit is totally *in* the flesh. If you pay close enough attention to things, stare at them, concentrate as hard as you can not just with your intelligence, but with your feelings and instincts . . . you will begin to apprehend the forms in them" (32). Although Bass's cosmology may be more complex than Hood's, they seem to agree that spirit is inherent in all living things and that the destruction of the physical world is also a desecration of the spiritual. Like a super-realist painter Bass "lights things up" by providing painstaking detail and by directing his authorial light to accentuate certain points. He frequently describes the effects of light in various natural settings, employing the words "luminous," "glowing," and even "magical." The luminosity comes from within rather than from any exterior lighting or intellectual overlay.

We initially encounter luminosity in one of Bass's earliest stories, "Choteau." Galena Jim Ontz steals a cement truck, mixes a load of cement with blue galena ore, and drives away, accidentally splashing some into the creek, "making a little dam, [which] sparkled with an eerie blue light that seemed almost to come from within, like some beautiful new form of life, maybe even life being created, inside the mixer" (*Watch,* 37). He then spills "a wide trail of galena, as if some beautiful animal had been wounded and was leaving a glowing blue spoor . . . and it's beautiful in the moonlight, shining in the light like an electric blue blaze" (37). Terrell F. Dixon notes the irony of this act: "For all its glitter . . . the paved road has made access to the wilderness easier and more permanent, and thus it has begun the process of transforming the wild" ("Rick Bass," 82).

In "The Sky, the Stars, the Wilderness" mystical elements take realistic forms. Bass invokes a powerful sense of wonder through realistic narrative full of natural history. One might argue that this is his finest melding of nature writing and fiction. Jennifer Greenstein notes that Bass's "luminous writing . . . makes every image seem as if it were illuminated by the sun's rays on a crisp winter day" ("Nature," L7). Lauren Cobb notes that "[o]ne of Bass's achievements . . . is his revelation of the magical, the fantastic, existing within the real" (Review, 388). These reviewers, as if through osmosis, have absorbed Bass's own use of "luminous" and "magical."

At the onset of the title novella we learn that Anne's mother is "planted" at the exact center of the ranch: "That was the word Mother used . . . I realize now the gift of that word—giving Father a way to think of her after she's left her body: as a memory, a force growing out of the soil, and rock" (91). Anne considers herself as much a part of the land as her mother is and is dedicated to preserving it. In death, after all, the only way the mother can have any continuing impact is through her daughter's actions.

Bass highlights nature's inherent glow. Moths are called "luminescent," while birds, fireflies, and scorpions are "luminous." Human intervention sometimes enhances the magic. Anne and her brother, Omar, catch turtles and armadillos, paint designs and names on them in phosphorus, and release them into the river. "They'd be glowing bright as the moon . . ." (110). One day Anne finds the corpse of a golden eagle so huge that "[a]t first I thought it was a man wearing feathers. . . . The closer I got, the more luminous the body seemed to get . . ." (147). She carries it into the woods, lashes it to a tree as if poised for flight, and then dreams "of the oak tree flying; that eagle had taken flight and carried the great tree away with him . . ." (149). "The summer's shimmering heat" makes Chubb and Grandfather appear to be "half-man and half-tree" (127). On a February trip to a Mexican beach, shimmering transforms the image of a rabbit into that of a deer: "We'd set about after the deer wondering why a deer would have antlers in winter . . . and it seemed for a moment not as if there had been a mistake on our part, but as if there had been a magic trick: as if the earth itself . . . had changed the deer into a rabbit in the blink of an eye" (143).

Bass speaks through Anne again when she says: "We must participate in the world that has birthed us. We must not sit around . . . while the waters trickle past. We must join the waters" (162). Being part and parcel of nature means active engagement with it, and a failure to be part of the flow of nature is a form of death. Environmental protection, seen in this context, is a form of self-preservation.

Chubb almost literally joins the waters when he is cremated and his ashes placed in a watering can in his car by the river. They can separate his ashes from those of the cedar used to cremate him because "Chubb's ashes would be more blue, would almost glow in the dark . . ." (163). Luminescence after death implies eternal life, an inextinguishable flame. Anne's eulogy takes the form of a screech owl cry, causing birds to sound their own alarms. As stroke-diminished Grandfather approaches death, he loses the ability to speak but learns to sing like a bird.

"The Sky, the Stars, the Wilderness" closes with a lyrical meditation on life, death, and the complexity of our relation to the land: "You can rot or you can burn but either way, if you're lucky, a place will shape and cut and bend you, will strengthen you and weaken you. You trade this life for the privilege of this experience—the joy of a place, the joy of blood family, the joy of knowledge gotten by listening and observing. . . . You find that you have always been in the middle of a metamorphosis, constantly living and dying. . . . And you feel for the first time a sweet absence . . ." (189). Anne's thoughts turn to memories of scorpion hunting with Omar: "And when we'd find one, we'd fill him with the light from our flashlights, then shut the lights out and follow him, glowing in the dark, across the caliche streambeds, across the slick rock, and across the hills, following him until the glimmer faded, and there was only silence" (190).

"The Hermit's Story" has a similar glow: "An ice storm, following seven days of snow; the vast fields and drifts of snow turning to sheets of glazed ice that shine and shimmer in the moonlight as if the color is being fabricated not by the blending and absorption of light but by some chemical reaction within the glossy ice . . . as if blue is a thing that emerges, in some parts of the world, from the soil itself, after the sun goes down" (16). Ann, a dog trainer, has delivered a new pack of dogs to Gray Owl in Canada. During a six-day training session they become lost, and Gray Owl falls through the ice of a frozen lake. Ann is surprised to find him unharmed in a giant ice cave formed when the water drained out of the lake after a freeze. What seemed to be an unforeseen danger becomes shelter from the cold. Cattails used as torches ignite gas pockets, "and all around these little pockets of gas would light up like when you toss gas on a fire—those little explosions of brilliance like flashbulbs—

marsh pockets igniting like falling dominoes or like children playing hopscotch . . . [until] the puff of flame would blow a chimney-hole through the ice . . . and they could feel gusts of warmth . . ." (27).

This "surface" is not just figurative: it is literally the frozen surface of the lake. The first appearance (that the ice was safe to walk on) and the second (that the area below the ice would be dangerous) are both false. This may seem incredible, but Bass's description of how the ice cavern was formed convinces us otherwise. He thus inverts both our expectations and the creation myths in which death is found below ground and life above. This is a good example of how "[t]he unbelievable thing . . . goes to the heart of the story." In his early work, Bass relied on bizarre characters or incidents to "make magic," with inconsistent results. Over time he seems to step back to let wildness itself tell its tale. His super-realistic writing gives voice to plants and animals, and the landscape itself emerges from the background. As Kate Boyes notes, "'the land' as an abstract concept is transformed; the land becomes a conscious living being that literally shapes human hungers and the actions taken to satisfy those hungers" (Review, 463). The mythic elements occur more naturally in the later fiction. Consider the contrast between Bass's evocations of the Paul Bunyan legend in "Field Events" and in *Where the Sea Used to Be*. Expressed in painterly terms, one might say that he has a larger palette of themes and techniques to work with.

Where the Sea Used to Be

Those readers more experienced with Bass's oeuvre can appreciate this novel as the product of all his previous work. It draws not just on the earlier story of the same name but on other stories and novellas. Bass emphasizes isolation by presenting a lower Swan and a higher "second, hidden one . . . the one nobody knew about, the one the century had not been able to reach. They said that the second Swan Valley was like a shadow of the first" (9). "Shadow" presages mystery in a place beyond the beyond: "You go to the end of the world. . . . Go til you begin to hear wolves, til you see their big pawprints in the snow along the road. Go until the road stops" (14). The valley, the story, and the conflict begin at the boundaries between civilization and nature, between myth and science. The Swan is just one of several versions of the Yaak in Bass's fiction and epitomizes all threatened landscapes. Science's failure to recognize the spirituality of nature is emphasized early on: "'Spruce and pine trees have a physical quality.... Cedar is a tree of spiritual qualities. This deer's not ready to die yet. He'll stay in the spruce and pines as long as he can. Only when he knows he's ready to die will he go down in the cedars'" (36). Mel, a wildlife biologist, has transcended academia's artificial boundaries: "Scientists will give you some mumbo-jumbo about physiological responses.... They'll talk about thermal regulation and reduced fucking phototropism. The truth is simpler. The deer are leaving this layer of earth and are going to the next kingdom, and the cedars are a bridge between these two worlds. Science has never been all the way right about anything" (36).

Bass lends credence to such sentiments by having Anne express them in "The Sky, the Stars, the Wilderness" and Mel elaborate them here. Both are professional biologists, and both feel so strongly about science's limitations that they describe science profanely: "bullshit" and "fucking phototropism." Bass makes this point symbolically by having Mel rearrange the bones of the dead deer into a running form. Later Matthew and Wallis find the body of an elk they have shot, "hung up in a jumble of blown-down timber that he'd tried to leap... the latticework of it supporting his huge body above the ground so that it looked as if he were still alive, and only in mid-leap" (424). Mel places a salmon carcass in a creek, a metaphysical attempt to attract live salmon up a river that has been dammed/damned. These incidents address the issues of wildness, boundaries, and death in slightly different ways.

Helen exhibits strong spiritual connections with animals. As death approaches, she dreams that "a man had been spying on her, lusting for her old body" (320). She awakens to find the nose and paw prints of a bear on her window and sets out meals for it, "as a child would make a tea party for an imaginary guest" (320). Though the bear dines nightly, she can't catch him; so she waits outside at night. The bear approaches: "moving so carefully, so stealthily, as to seem like a man in the costume of a bear.... [They eat.] When it had finished, it looked at her a moment longer—woman and bear illumined in blue starlight; the bear's damp eyes and nose gleaming and its claws shining at the table like silverware" (342–43).

A magical glow pervades the book. Salamanders are "fluorescent," ice and comets "luminous," and the woods feature the interplay of shadow and glowing light. Humans and animals share this magic, and humans must defend it. One of Mel's students angrily admonishes the road builders. "You don't need to be drilling here. . . . It's not right. It'll upset the way things are—the way the animals are—their lives. . . . Their cultures. . . . Their relationships to the land" (365). Just as Bass seems to be sliding into "rabid anthropocentrism" again, he redefines cultures as "relationships to the land."

Before playing the coyote game, Mel reads from John Niehardt's transcription of *Black Elk Speaks:* "Crazy Horse dreamed and went into the world where there is nothing but the spirits of all things. That is the real world which is behind this one and everything we see here is something like a shadow from that world. . . . 'Oh, God,' Dudley said, 'worse than poetry, *Indian* shit'" (153). Dudley represents the opposite consciousness, the one that has justified the rape of the land and the extermination of vast numbers of plant and animal species as well as most Indians. He takes whatever he wants, riding roughshod over anyone and anything. He is an expert on raptors, but only because he is a falconer, controlling them so they will kill at his command.

Dudley's sexuality and sense of myth are similarly exploitative. "I dream the dream of the crystalline-marble woman, twelve feet tall . . . I combine my seed with her and give birth to the future" (187). He actually had one sculpted, "anatomically correct . . . every orifice was present . . ." (222). Mel's shiver leaves no doubt about its use. During a visit to the valley he impregnates Amy. "Dudley had been standing a good six feet away from her when he had gone off. It was almost like a spray . . ." (312). The myth of the Immaculate Conception is thus utterly perverted. Dudley's cosmology is encapsulated in diary entries interspersed throughout the book. "We have already achieved our perfection. . . . The shackles are removed. Man is free to possess the earth" (350). "Man *is* God!" (361). His arrogance and single-minded pursuit of oil are reminiscent of Ahab's fixation with Moby Dick. The whale and the valley are both natural forces to be drained for their oil. Both will be destroyed if they are conquered, but despite relentless pursuit both eventually destroy their potential exploiters.

If life in the Swan is magical, death is even more so. Joshua knows Helen has died because he can hear wolves responding to the mourning howls of the villagers two ridges away. When Wallis fastens her Thunderbird casket in a tree, he feels as if "when finished, [it] would assume life and fly away" (382). "Many of them had had their watches stop, they noticed, around the time that they had been burying Helen, and this unnerved them . . ." (385). Dudley gets the royal treatment: burial in a malachite woman-shaped coffin floating downstream. If Dudley is Ahab, then Joshua is Queequeg; but instead of Ishmael (Wallis) being saved by a floating coffin, the valley is saved when the dead Ahab floats away.

Reviewing the novel, Phil Hanrahan noted that Bass "animates it with myth, tall tales, the sublime and ridiculous both, and he renders its environment . . . with such breathtaking clarity you swear you'd been there before, and were simply remembering as you read" ("Timeless Dreams," 11). That "clarity" is the fruit of super-realism. Eugene McAvoy declares that it is "[b]eautifully executed, at once majestic and minute . . . a glorious myth for a world devoid of, yet desperate for magic" ("The Land," J2). He misses what may be Bass's key point: magic is not absent from the world, but is everywhere. If this were simply a fable, the moral might be "open your eyes, heart, and soul to the wildness that you are part and parcel with and defend it."

Conclusion

Bass's career displays his increasing maturation and environmentalism, which in his case go hand in hand. The early stories lack the thematic unity of his later collections and tend to be overreliant on quirky characters. His later characters continue to be somewhat unusual but are more credible. Myth is better integrated into the stories as he develops the theme of the physical and spiritual unity of the natural world. Although depictions of the inherent magic of the natural world can be found early on, this does not emerge as a central theme until *The Sky, the Stars, the Wilderness.*

It is difficult to imagine any form better suited to his agenda than magic realism. Depicting the natural world in an extremely accurate manner provides a basis for dramatic conflict and a springboard for dives into myth. He is occasionally guilty of "gilding the lily," but does so to call attention to the lily's natural grandeur. If he depicted an unrecognizable world with green sky and purple water, why should we care about its preservation? Since his sky and water encompass a wide and subtle range of blues and grays, the message cannot be so easily rejected. Consider two possible meanings of the word "myth." In our fast-paced world "myth" is often used in a negative sense as an "old wives' tale," an anachronism, or even a lie. Traditionally, though, myths are used to convey timeless truths and to provide cultural cohesion and meaning. (Those "old wives" and old hunters, after all, passed on a great deal of wisdom over time.)

Magic realism allows the writer to combine the realistic and the mythic so we can comprehend life at a deeper level. Throughout its relatively brief history it has provided a voice that is inherently contrary to destructive political and social forces. Bass has expanded that critique to oppose industrialism and consumerism, the packaging, selling, and squandering of our natural and spiritual resources. Magic realism advances his environmentalism.

Given the critical and popular success of *Where the Sea Used to Be,* one might assume that Bass would continue to write fiction. Passages in *Fiber* call that into question. After describing the first three phases of his life as geologist, artist, and activist, Bass tells us that "now I am into my fourth life, one that is built around things more immediate than the fairy-wing days of art. Even this narrative, this story, is fiction, but each story feels like the last one I'll do—as if I've become like some insect or reptile trying to shed the husk of its old skin . . . neither you nor I can really be sure of how much of any story is fiction, or art, and how much of it is activism" (4).

Bass describes the unusual trajectory of his life: "most people start out being radical and then gravitate toward moderation . . . but for me it has been the opposite—as if the land up here is inverted, mysterious, even magical, turning humans, and all else, inside out, in constant turmoil, constant revolution" (40). Fully submitting oneself to nature's magic is transformative, liberating, and radicalizing. Bass finally confesses that there is "no story . . . no fairy logs. I am no fugitive, other than from myself" (45). He then attacks both the destruction of the environment and the ineffectiveness of many environmental organizations. "And I understand that I am a snarling wolverine, snapping illogically at everything in my pain, snapping at everyone—at fellow artists, and at fellow environmentalists" (49–50). He concludes with the very unwolverine-like act of pleading for help in saving the Yaak.

As Bass explained in an interview with Scott Slovic in 1994: "I'm standing there with a paint brush in one hand and a bucket of water in the other hand. And if there's no fire around, I'll paint a pretty picture; but if a fire's burning, I've got to dump water on it. So I do separate in my mind, totally, the didactic or political writings from the art. It's hard to do, but I try" ("Interview," 26). In *Fiber,* Bass refuses to make such a separation. While I share his great frustration with the rapid and rapacious destruction of wilderness and wildness, I would urge him not to abandon his own wild, often weird fiction. His paint brush seems to have a magical capacity to fling more water than most other writers' fire hoses.

Works Cited

Fiction by Rick Bass

Fiber. Athens: University of Georgia Press, 1998.
"The Hermit's Story." *Paris Review* 147 (Summer 1998): 16–32.
In the Loyal Mountains. New York: Houghton Mifflin, 1995.
Platte River. New York: Houghton Mifflin, 1994.
The Sky, the Stars, the Wilderness. New York: Houghton Mifflin, 1997.
The Watch. New York: Norton, 1989.
Where the Sea Used to Be. New York: Houghton Mifflin, 1998.

Critical Works

Note: For reviews from Internet sources, section (when available) and beginning pagination are indicated.

Abrams, M. H. *A Glossary of Literary Terms.* Fort Worth: Harcourt, 1993.

Bernstein, Richard. "Searching for Oil, and Maybe Love, in the Snow." *New York Times,* 1 July 1998, E, 91.

Berryhill, Michael. "Bass Hunts Black Gold." *Houston Chronicle,* 26 July 1998, 211.

Black Elk. *Black Elk Speaks.* Ed. John Neihardt. New York: Morrow, 1932.

Boyes, Kate. Review of *Where the Sea Used to Be. Western American Literature* 34 (2000): 463–64.

Cobb, Lauren. Review of *The Sky, the Stars, the Wilderness. Georgia Review* (Summer 1998): 388–89.

Dixon, Terrell F. Review of *In the Loyal Mountains. Western American Literature* 30 (1995): 97–103.

———. "Rick Bass." In *American Nature Writers,* ed. John Elder, 75–88. New York: Scribner's, 1996.

Durix, Jean-Pierre. *Mimesis, Genres and Post-Colonial Discourse: Deconstructing Magic Realism.* New York: St. Martin's, 1998.

Frost, Robert. *The Poetry of Robert Frost.* New York: Holt, 1969.

García Márquez, Gabriel. "The Solitude of Latin America: Nobel Address 1982." In *Gabriel García Márquez: New Readings,* ed. Bernard McGuirk and Richard Cardwell. Cambridge: Cambridge University Press, 1987.

Gelderman, Carol. "Hyperrealism in Contemporary Drama: Retrogressive or Avant-Garde?" *Modern Drama* 26:3 (September 1986): 357–67.

Golding, William. *Lord of the Flies.* New York: Coward-McCann, 1962.

Greenstein, Jennifer. "Nature a Driving Force in Bass' Novellas." *Grand Rapids Press*, 22 March 1998, L, 71.

Hanrahan, Phil. "Timeless Dreams, Fables Bring Valley to Life." *Milwaukee Journal Sentinel*, 19 July 1998, 111.

Hood, Hugh. "Sober Colouring: The Ontology of Super-Realism." *Canadian Literature* 49 (Summer 1971): 28–34.

Jeffers, Robinson. *Collected Poetry*. Stanford: Stanford University Press, 1988.

Kendall, Elaine. "Two Lands Linked by a Mystical Quality." *Los Angeles Times*, 27 June 1995: E, 41.

Lowell, S. "Country Love and Naked Laundresses." *New York Times Book Review*, 5 March 1989, 11.

McEvoy, Eugene. "The Land Is Sole Source of Myth and Mystery in Beautiful Novel." *Virginian Pilot*, 26 July 1998, J, 21.

McPhee, John. *The John McPhee Reader*. Ed. William Howarth. New York: Farrar, Straus, Giroux, 1976.

Mellen, Joan. "Trivialization and Laziness Trivialize Magic Realism." *Baltimore Sun*, 29 August 1999, F, 121.

Sciallaba, George. "Geology and Transcendence in Montana." *Boston Globe*, 28 June 1998, C, 21.

Skow, John. "The Wilderness Within." *Time* 150:24 (8 December 1997): 97.

Slovic, Scott. "An Interview with Rick Bass." *Weber Studies* 11:3 (Fall 1994): 11–29.

Walker, Sam. "Author's Tall-Tale Novellas Push the Envelope of the Plausible." *Christian Science Monitor*, 8 March 1994: Books, 131.

Walsh, William. "Isn't Reality *Magic?*: An Interview with Rita Dove." *Kenyon Review* 16:3 (Summer 1994): 142–55.

Weltzien, O. Alan. *Rick Bass*. Boise: Boise State University Press, 1998.

Wilson, Robert. "*Platte River* Flows from Rick Bass' Powerful Prose." *USA Today*, 25 February 1994: D, 51.

Zappa, Frank. "Call Any Vegetable." In *Absolutely Free*. New York: Verve, 1967.

Zinman, Toby Silverman. "Sam Shepard and Super-Realism." *Modern Drama* 29:3 (September 1986): 423–30.

Tracking the Animal Man from Walden to Yaak

Emersonian Notions of Self, Nature, and Writing in Thoreau's Walden *and Rick Bass's* Winter

Jonathan Johnson

To a late-twentieth-century passerby, Walden is a lost Eden. A small New England lake packed all summer with swimmers and perpetually threatened by condominium development, Walden—the wild, solitary, embracing Walden that Thoreau knew—has not made it. Walden survives only as a relic, a worn monument to wildness. Maybe, on Sunday afternoons in August, the lake momentarily stirs something, some animal self all but forgotten by a few of the quietly desperate who look back as they load up their empty coolers and beach chairs and drive the expressways back to the suburbs of Boston or Portsmouth. But Walden the *experiment* is alive and well and living in northwest Montana. *Winter,* Rick Bass's journal of the first winter he spent living in the remote Yaak River Valley, maintains and examines many of the same Emersonian principles that Thoreau took with him into the woods a century and a half ago.

Walden is arguably the most influential book of nineteenth-century American nature writing, and *Winter* is its contemporary descendent in terms of experience, vision, and even style. By comparing these two works, we can discover what has, at least for one man, become of those Emersonian principles—the celebration of the capable and independent individual, the active belief in a unified and encompassing nature that infuses and sustains the self, and the conviction that artistic creation is the exercise of the independent human will in concert with nature. The suitable habitat for a Thoreauvian experiment may have shrunken drastically.

But Bass is like a member of some endangered species that has relocated to what is left of the American wilderness, where he holes up and reminds us of what Ralph Waldo Emerson and Thoreau knew: that nature can transform us.

In his essay "Self-Reliance" Emerson writes: "There is a time in every man's education when he arrives at the conviction . . . that though the wide universe is full of good, no kernel of nourishing corn can come to him but through his toil bestowed on that plot of ground which is given him to till" (259). *Walden* is the record of just such a time in the education of Thoreau. Thoreau, cultivating the "ground which is given him" (or, more accurately, loaned him) by Emerson, would show in concrete, quantified terms exactly how self-reliant he becomes, how much his circumstances (his food, shelter, and warmth) are a function of his independent will. And the measure of that independence is poverty, a baseline of next to nothing (a borrowed ax and a few acres on which to squat) from which to act with complete autonomy and see his circumstances improve. Emerson writes that "a cultivated man becomes ashamed of his property, out of a new respect for his nature" (281).

By the same principle Thoreau expresses a kind of pride in frugality, on which he bases his first chapter, "Economy." He methodically charts six tables in the chapter to show the cost of the cabin, the income he obtained by his crop and by day laboring, the cost of his provisions, and his calculated "outgoes," from which he subtracts all his income to show how little he consumed beyond that with which he started. The specificity of these tables is outdone only by the detail with which Thoreau describes farming his bean-field, recounting precisely what he accomplishes by day and by season.

Rick Bass, a former petroleum geologist from Texas and Mississippi who has driven his battered orange Nissan pickup with 180,000 miles northwest through the Rockies looking with Elizabeth Hughes for a place to settle and write and live off the land, is as aware as Thoreau that poverty is a means to freedom, the foundation upon which to build a willful and self-reliant life. "We were so damn poor," he writes in the prologue to *Winter,* "defiantly poor, wondrously poor—but not owing anyone anything, and in the best of health" (2).

At the opening of *Winter,* Bass and Elizabeth have moved into a remote lodge in the Yaak (like Thoreau, they do not buy the place, but hire on as caretakers for the absent owner) and almost immediately begin to prepare for the harsh, bitter Montana winter that is rapidly approaching. Like Thoreau, Bass prepares with a fierce frugality, always mindful of exact expenses and requirements and with an eye toward reducing both, toward spending and consuming the least humanly possible. One morning he writes: "I'm waiting for the propane truck to drive up. I'm going to buy 900 gallons of propane for the stove and generator (69.9 cents per gallon). For the family that lived here before me—husband, wife, two babies—that would have been three or four months' worth. I am going to make it last five or six months" (12). While he does not use actual charts, as Thoreau does in "Economy," Bass does keep close tabs on what things are costing him throughout the fall and into early winter, frequently noting such details, as when he writes, "I bought 2,270 feet of buckskin larch from Breitenstein yesterday for $120" (111).

Bass takes no less account of how he spends his time than Thoreau does, outlining his daily schedules of getting firewood (the crucial work of survival, which becomes a central subject of the journal). "With my crooked saw," he writes, "yesterday afternoon I was able to muscle through twelve cuttings of it, plus twelve of a smaller, younger log. I think I still have about six or seven more cuts to make off the big guy, and then another one almost like him, plus two more smaller ones—about five cords in all" (112). He recognizes that "no kernel of nourishing corn can come to him but through his toil" and lives by this principle as if his and Elizabeth's lives depend on his own skill, his own competence, as they well might on such an isolated ranch, six miles from the nearest phone, without electricity in a country where the temperature can fall to eighty below with the wind chill.

Still, like Thoreau, Bass has come to the woods of his own volition and could leave just as easily. Neither crosses so far into the wilderness that he is beyond the physical boundaries of no return. But that is not the goal for either writer. What they court is not danger or exposure (though Bass seems to revel a little in grim possibilities) but an awareness of the direct correlation between one's actions and one's well-being. This awareness is apparent in Bass's seriousness as he reads and rereads the sixty-page instruction book for his chainsaw: "I'd rather be walking through the woods or sitting by the river reading poetry, but this is something I've got to learn. This is something that is going to keep us warm" (63).

However, Bass makes no premature claims about his own self-reliance. He knows that he is a newcomer to the Yaak landscape and that he must turn to others, mostly long-time residents, for examples of true independence and competence. Bass describes a bind in his saw bar that he has inadvertently allowed to develop, which makes him appear awkward in front of his neighbor:

> Breitenstein looked on incredulously as I went about my woodcutting again, straining against the bind, sawing and pulling and heaving and tugging like a man wrestling with a whale. When Don T. and Breitenstein cut, their big saws sink so easily through the wood; they merely guide the saw with one hand, showing off, holding the saw like the rudder of a gentle sailboat. (121)

As *Winter* progresses, a learned interdependence follows newfound independence as Bass seeks out and learns from his neighbors in the Yaak community; the people of Yaak, with their seemingly effortless and graceful wilderness living, become a measure of capabilities that Bass himself would develop.

While the social dimensions of Thoreau's life on Walden Pond are fewer than Bass's in Yaak and solitude permeates *Walden* more than it does *Winter*, Thoreau does turn to his fellow woods dwellers for examples of natural self-reliance. The Canadian woodcutter that Thoreau meets serves this function. In Thoreau's assessment, the woodcutter's innocence seems matched only by his capability and potency in the woods:

> In him the animal man chiefly was developed. In physical endurance and contentment he was cousin to the pine and the rock. I asked him once if he was not sometimes tired at night, after working all day; and he answered, with a sincere and serious look, "Gorrappit, I never was tired in my life." (102)

The woodcutter is the embodiment of the effortless, yet powerful, self-reliant man Emerson describes when he writes (again in "Self-Reliance"): "It is as easy for the strong man to be strong, as it is for the weak to be weak" (271). The self-reliant individual's will comes into happy accord with circumstances (by powers of both creation and perception), so that "a true man belongs to no other time or place, but is the centre of things. Where he is, there is nature" (267). The woodcutter's belonging is so complete, so total, that Thoreau not only sees what he calls "animal man" developed in him but also recognizes his unique satisfaction, a kind of innocent wisdom in his harmony: "Looking round upon the trees he would exclaim,—'By George! I can enjoy myself well enough here chopping; I want no better sport'" (102).

The naturally self-reliant character or "animal man" is important for Thoreau and for Bass because he represents a state of being against which to measure their own relationships to nature. The woodcutter is both stronger than Thoreau and less sophisticated. His capabilities as an "animal man" are counterbalanced by his innocence. Thoreau writes: "The intellectual and what is called spiritual man in him were slumbering as in an infant.... I did not know whether he was as wise as Shakespeare or as simply ignorant as a child" (102–3). The goal of Thoreau's transcendentalism is to become what Emerson so famously called "a transparent eyeball," a state in which, as Emerson described it in *Nature,* "I am nothing; I see all; the currents of the Universal Being circulate through me; I am part or particle of God" (10). The constant striving for concreteness, decisiveness, and physicality of image, behavior, and even writing style in *Walden* stems from Thoreau's project (following Emerson) to define and foster a more heightened, authentic, religious human experience that does not orbit slavishly around the analytical intellect and result in rote acts of rational will. And the reduction of the self to a physical entity is one step toward such a state for Thoreau—a step so problematic that it becomes, for all practical purposes, a noble end in itself.

Much of the tension in *Walden* is generated by the paradox inherent in this desire of Thoreau's: a sophisticated, relentlessly analytical spirit who reflects extensively on himself and his environment, he concludes that he can achieve a more profound connection with the Universal Being and therein be fulfilled by becoming less sophisticated, less analytical, less thoughtful and more instinctive. And he would then examine his transformation on the page! But because Thoreau comes to the woods as an artist and educated man, he is unable completely to abandon his intellect. The character sketch of the woodcutter affords him the opportunity to indulge and embody his idea of the innocent purely connected to nature while remaining authentic to his own sophistication. Thoreau is constantly mindful of his failures, however minor, when he eats more than animal man would require, affords himself more of a dwelling than the bare necessity, or puts his furniture back into the house after cleaning, when "so much more interesting most familiar objects look out of doors than in the house" (80).

Thoreau is constantly looking for examples of what he calls that "aboriginal" or "savage" character, the truly perfect match of self and natural circumstance that he is one step short of achieving on his path toward an ultimately self-reliant, religious awareness. In the woodcutter he finds a man so self-reliant that all he need employ to be square with the world is his will. Of course, Thoreau and Emerson would wed such primal, physical authenticity to instinctive poetic awareness, to self-reliant *insight.* (As Emerson writes in the "Prospectus" chapter of *Nature,* "The invariable mark of wisdom is to see the miraculous in the common" [47].) But it is the animal part of the self-reliance equation that Thoreau sees in the woodcutter, insofar as he lives in accord with his natural character.

The Yaak is full of woodcutters (like Breitenstein) to whom Bass looks for examples of physical self-reliance. And there are others as well. Bass describes helping a neighbor who is trying to halter another neighbor's horse, Fuel:

> Fuel spooked and ran right at Mike, but instead of dodging Fuel, Mike hit him head-on, high in the chest, tackling him. He reached up and grabbed Fuel around the neck, as if bulldogging him, and then got dragged around the corral for a while—never letting go, lifting his feet to keep from being trampled—until Fuel was finally calmed down, or maybe was worn down. (55)

In the face of such heroic behavior, Bass is reduced to an almost childlike spectator, "standing on the other side of the corral, the safe side," trotting out to hand Mike the halter. Meanwhile, Mike continues, unshaken, to display superhuman (almost absurd) courage and strength and even a little brutality: "He held on to Fuel's nose with one hand, pulled Fuel's ear down and bit it, and slipped the halter on with his free hand" (55). Here it is not only his inexperience that keeps Bass from becoming like his neighbors, but his very nature. While he invests considerably more energy in his social life in Yaak than Thoreau does at Walden, Bass is also a writer, reflective and self-aware, who remains partly detached. For both men the physical must perpetually compete with the imaginative. Like Thoreau, he considers building his own place with Elizabeth but decides against it, admitting "that sharpening a pencil is a great mechanical adventure for both of us; we're a little artsy, I'm sorry to say" (2). He knows he is "a writer in a valley of workers" (10). At the end of October, with snow a possibility at any time, he notes, "I didn't get the thirty cords I wanted to have by this date. Writers. Half-assed at everything, it seems, except, occasionally, their writing" (77).

Bass's self-deprecation grows out of an impatience with his inability to immerse himself wholeheartedly in the physical and get beyond his "artsy," abstracting disposition, though he is more successful than he gives himself credit for at managing that contradiction. He gets up "eighteen, maybe twenty cords," and on the heels of chastising himself for not having gotten up more, he writes, "I'll get another load today" (77)—all the while burning some of the same wood every morning while out writing in the greenhouse he uses for a studio.

As with Thoreau and the woodcutter, it is not the strength and courage Bass most admires in the people of Yaak, but their connection with their home, the way they fit. Like the woodcutter, Bass's neighbor, Tom, is not only capable, a former champion bronc rider able to shoot big bucks with "homemade bow and arrows made of cedar"; he is also serene, the picture of an ageless "animal man," who "belongs to no other time or place, but is the centre of things." While the people of Yaak are varied and complex (more varied and complex than Thoreau's innocent, content woodcutter), they "belong," in Bass's eyes, to the landscape. They are "part and particle" of their universe. "One day back in the fall I saw Tom," Bass writes, "walking down the road in his moccasins, which Nancy had made for him, smoking a pipe (one he'd carved), and holding a big red-tailed hawk on his arm while his dog, Nuthin', a german shorthair, ran along beside him, sniffing for grouse..." (133).

This is not to say that Bass does not discover *some* element of "animal man" in himself—quite the contrary. Noticing one day how far from everything he has moved, how far from all familiar people, his family and friends, he also notices that his old, familiar self seems distant. "I'm falling away from the human race," he writes. "I don't mean to sound churlish—but I'm liking it. It frightens me a little to realize how much I do like it. It's as if you'd looked down at your hand and seen the beginnings of fur. It's not as bad as you might think" (73). What he is sensing under his skin is the presence of nature, the same presence he perceives in the mountain landscape, the foundation of everything revealed, to one who looks long and hard enough, in everything (even in the less than completely worldly Bass himself).

Though both Thoreau and Bass seek (and ultimately find) solitude and a resulting connection to the spirit of their landscapes, nature has another effect on both writers: reconnecting them to other human beings. In the chapter "Solitude," Thoreau describes society as a state of affairs in which "we live thick and are in each other's way, and stumble over one another, and I think that we thus lose some respect for one another. Certainly less frequency would suffice for all important and hearty communications" (95). Masses dilute the will and stand between the individual and the moral landscape, through which one can discover one's own self-reliance and belonging. Society does not conform to the "ethical character" of nature, as Emerson calls it, and Bass, saturated by society, is perhaps even more disgusted and frightened than Thoreau was a hundred and fifty years before him. Where cities are the "ova of insects" (204) on the leaves of the tree of creation for Thoreau, cities are a cancer, an immediate, mortal threat to creation for Bass. "I'm hiding up here—no question about it," he admits. "The decay in our nation is frustrating. We truly are becoming senile. I feel as if we are very near the end; each time I go to a city I feel it more and more. All I want to do is get back to Yaak, back to snow, back up into the mountains" (92). Nature still retains the power to renew Bass and reveal to him that he is directly responsible for his own well-being and that he belongs to the world. On this, he actually cites Thoreau. "It's not that we're total hermits," Bass writes, describing the inhabitants of the isolated valley, "only that most of us want, as Thoreau said, to examine our lives, as well as the world we live in—a world that, up here, is not controlled by others as much as by, believe it or not, one's self" (115).

Self-imposed solitude is not, for either writer, a rejection of other people but a rejection of greater social constraint in favor of self-reliance and unmediated experience. Far from being merely isolating, nature actually restores human relationships by restoring human beings, returning them to themselves and, by extension, to one another. Through solitude in nature, Thoreau and Bass come to value connections to others and to view those connections as based not on physical proximity but on mutual participation in creation. In his essay "The Over-soul," Emerson describes creation as "that great nature in which we rest, as the earth lies in the soft arms of the atmosphere; that Unity, that Over-soul, within which every man's particular being is contained and made one with all other; that common heart" (385–86). As the individual in nature perceives the universal Over-soul in every particular, so he soon recognizes that people, as natural beings, express the same unity, the same "common heart." Bass writes, "It has everything to do with people, as well as the land, up here—even though there's only thirty or so of us. It's like we're a *herd*" (68). He cleverly claims the metaphor "herd" from its common, negative connotations of conformity and reinvents it as an expression of a community shaped and defined by the landscape on which it lives.

For both authors, the landscape grants grace. Nature not only allows Bass and Thoreau to see the same Over-soul in others; it actually restores and renews human beings, morally, spiritually, and physically, bringing them back to what they are not in society as a whole—their original, pure selves. Thoreau describes spring as an event of tremendous human grace:

> In a pleasant spring morning all men's sins are forgiven. Such a day is a truce to vice. While such a sun holds out to burn, the vilest sinner may return. Through our own recovered innocence we discern the innocence of our neighbors. You may have known your neighbor yesterday for a thief, a drunkard, or a sensualist, and merely pitied or despised him, and despaired of the world; but the sun shines bright and warm this first spring morning, re-creating the world, and you meet him at some serene work, and see how his exhausted and debauched veins expand with still joy and bless the new day, feel the spring influence with the innocence of infancy, and all his faults are forgotten. (209)

Nature reunites us with one another: nature shines in the other as in ourselves. But the central human relationship that nature restores and reinforces, which gives us our sympathy and insight for others, is the relationship of the individual to his own true nature. It is only "through our own recovered innocence" that we may begin to perceive the innocence and vitality in others. The relationship to nature is basic, the necessary condition for all other relationships.

In the renewal of our relationship to nature (and thereby others) and in the recovery of our innocence, youth—and a return to a youthful condition—is crucial because in youth we learned that we were alive by the embrace of nature. "The wind has always been there. Ever before you knew love, you knew the wind," writes Bass (79). Before moral complexity, before our sacrifices and adaptations to society, before our bodies betrayed us and began the long slide into walking decay, we knew ourselves as natural beings. The project of the adult who enters the woods is, for Thoreau and Bass, to achieve what Emerson describes in *Nature* when he writes that "in the woods too, a man casts off his years, as the snake his slough, and at what period soever of life, is always a child. In the woods is perpetual youth" (10). The woods instruct. Nature is constant, the model and source of all other love. The Yaak Valley awakens Bass to what is prior, what he has known since childhood, what is timeless in himself. "I am coming to life myself up here in this valley," he writes. "I've taken a broadax to my life. . . . I know I won't live forever. Why does it feel as if I will?" (85–86).

Thoreau, too, perceives the eternal in the individual, a timelessness in himself that is the timelessness of creation. Toward the beginning of the chapter "Spring" in *Walden* his attention focuses on little streams of water eroding the side of an embankment. These he describes in detail and at great length in this famous passage, remarking on the shapes of the "little streams" as they "overlap and interlace one another" and the transformation of the landscape into an apparently living entity as the streams, like branches or arteries, form "a sort of architectural foliage more ancient and typical than acanthus, chicory, ivy, vine, or any vegetable leaves" (203). For Thoreau, the landscape, in its details and entirety, *is* an expression of a "common heart" both "ancient and typical" that forms the core of all deep observations, and all of creation and Thoreau himself can be accounted for as one living entity unified by one Over-soul. "I am affected," Thoreau continues in the same passage, "as if in a peculiar sense I stood in the laboratory of the Artist who made the world and me,—had come to where he was still at work, sporting on this bank, and with excess of energy strewing his fresh designs about" (203).

Spring, in which for Thoreau "all men's sins are forgiven," holds the same power of instruction for Bass. In early December he refers to that still-far-off season of the coming year; "then I will come out of it in the spring, different, cleaner, not born again so much as built up. I'll laugh at more things, and not get so angry at decadence, at laziness, at deceit and the theft of time, the theft of truth, starting with the President and going all the way down to the grocery store" (103).

Though Bass does anticipate the restorative power of spring, he does so from the perspective of winter. Indeed, *Winter*, which begins in mid-September and ends in mid-March, is set fairly consistently in that long Montana season. In this regard, Bass's focus is narrower than Thoreau's, who treats the entire year in *Walden*. Yet Bass manages to accomplish much of what Thoreau does. While Thoreau uses the erosion of spring runoff as a metaphor for the power and unity of creation, Bass chooses winter itself as his metaphor for the force that connects all things.

For Bass, winter is nature at its most destructive, most fracturing, yet winter is also that "within which every man's particular being is contained and made one with all other." Winter's necessity, winter's common threat, sharpens Bass's perception, makes him sympathetic with the animals outside his cabin, the coyote as well as the mice who "surround the barn, hiding in the hay, getting ready for winter too." All nature (predator and prey, observer and observed) lives, as Bass himself does, under winter. The mouse in the field may be eaten, "but the coyotes and the owls, they are responsible to the force of winter, to the brunt of its coming powers. It exerts a competitive, rather than unifying force on the whole forest" (36). Like the stream of runoff water carving away at the bank beside Walden, winter "is dynamic rather than static," and ultimately, paradoxically, it connects. "They catch mice the way I gather wood," Bass writes. "We're all close, we're all tied together" (36).

"I sometimes believe," Bass reflects after describing an evening spent watching the northern lights, "that this valley—so high up in the mountains, and in such heavy woods—is a step up to heaven, the last place you go before the real thing" (61). The Yaak Valley, like Walden Pond, is a place in which nature seems closer to the source of creation, closer to the "Over-soul." Both settings seem more real, places of religious significance and common divinity, the near regions of paradise, where, as Emerson writes, "there is no screen or ceiling between our heads and the infinite heavens" (*Essays and Lectures,* 387).

In his sections on winter ("House Warming," "Former Inhabitants; and Winter Visitors," "Winter Animals," and "The Pond in Winter"), Thoreau, like Bass, celebrates the self-reliance of wood-gathering, the human fellowship fostered in a snug cabin by the cold and snow outside, and the myth-making power of the season, exclaiming, "The Great Snow! How cheerful it is to hear of! When the farmers could not get to the woods and swamps with their teams, and were obliged to cut down the shade trees before their houses, and when the crust was harder cut off the trees in the swamps ten feet from the ground, as it appeared the next spring" (178). Thoreau opens "Winter Visitors" by describing the power of winter isolation in the woods and the way that winter isolation makes him think of himself as animal: "When the snow lay deepest no wanderer ventured near my house for a week or a fortnight at a time, but there I lived as snug as a meadow mouse, or as cattle and poultry which are said to have survived for a long time buried in drifts, even without food" (177).

Both Thoreau and Bass keenly observe the animals around them in winter, and *Winter* and *Walden* contain similar, beautifully detailed descriptions of creatures moving across the snowscape. But Thoreau's writings on winter remain largely descriptive and narrative, whereas Bass articulates in meditative, poetic writing the full religious power of the season. The landscape of winter, heartbreaking and desolate as it remains, is still primarily where Bass finds the deepest expression of grace, of the Over-soul. He describes standing out in a snow flurry, reveling, as Thoreau does, in his solitude, while pushing the experience further into Emersonian territory:

> I watch individual flakes; I peer up through the snow and see the blank infinity from which it comes; I listen to the special silence it creates.
>
> Anything I'm guilty of is forgiven when the snow falls. I feel powerful. In cities I feel weak and wasted away, but out in the field, in snow, I am like an animal—not in control of my emotions, my happiness and furies, but in charge of loving the snow, standing with my arms spread out, as if calling it down, the way it shifts and sweeps past in slants and furies of its own, the way it erases things until it is neither day or night—that kind of light through the day—dusk, several hours early, lingering, lingering forever.
>
> I am never going to grow old. The more that comes down, the richer I am. (90)

The snow brings with it a kind of sameness, a wash that would blur the particulars, the mountains, the pines, the cabin, the sky, and himself into one shade. Winter empowers him, rejuvenates him, and forgives him because it contains him as it contains the valley. Both Thoreau, who envisions himself preserved "without food," and Bass, who feels he is "never going to grow old," find in winter the truth of Emerson's assertion: "In the woods is perpetual youth." But beyond empowerment, rejuvenation, and forgiveness, Bass finds in winter the Emersonian Over-soul. Everything specific in nature, each snowflake, disappears into "the blank infinity from which it comes," and the snow "erases things," even the distinguishing power of light, "until it is neither day or night." For Bass nothing could be more fortunate than this erasure, and he embraces the snow, "calling it down" to erase even himself so that he becomes an animal, instinctual, his will dissolved into the world. He can never grow old because he, like everything around him, is taken up by the erasing snow, sees himself in the dusky light comprised of no specific thing and everything, washed together.

Like the "special silence" of the encompassing snow around Bass, "the path of things is silent" for Emerson, who asks, in his essay "The Poet": "Will they suffer a speaker to go with them?" (459). The writer's role and privilege is to be that aspect of creation that gives voice to the whole. Indeed, the collapse of the self into nature is actually the genesis of some of the most powerful passages in Bass and Thoreau, exactly as Emerson forecast when he wrote: "Only itself can inspire whom it will, and behold! Their speech shall be lyrical, and sweet, and universal as the rising of the wind" (386). Nature acts as a partner in the act of creation, inspiring and allowing Bass and Thoreau to become spokesmen for the landscape, to speak in the voice of nature. They "participate [in] the invention of nature," as Emerson puts it. He describes the poet's recognition of the unity of nature and of the self as "the intellect being where and what it sees, by sharing the path, or circuit of things" (459). In solitary observation of nature, the self apprehends personality, indeed its own personality, in the world. Thoreau describes a rare mood of loneliness that settled on him during a rain soon after he moved into his cabin:

> I have never felt lonesome, or in the least oppressed by a sense of solitude, but once, and that was a few weeks after I came to the woods, when, for an hour, I doubted if the near neighborhood of man was not essential to a serene and healthy life. . . . In the midst of a gentle rain while these thoughts prevailed, I was suddenly sensible of such a sweet and beneficent society in nature, in the very pattering of the drops, and in every sound and sight around my house, an infinite and unaccountable friendliness all at once like an atmosphere sustaining me, as made the fancied advantages of human neighborhood insignificant, and I have never thought of them since. (92)

The embrace of nature is more than recompense for the separation from other people; indeed, the general absence of other people seems to be a necessary condition of the author's capacity to accept that embrace. Far from the "human neighborhood" (from which Thoreau occasionally hears trains and church bells and Bass hears chainsaws and gunfire) nature can be heard, and the conversation between artist and environment becomes reciprocal. Thoreau hears the bullfrog's trump and the whippoorwill's song and responds with a "[s]ympathy . . . [that] almost takes away my breath" (91). And the self's sympathy toward nature is returned with that "infinite and unaccountable friendliness" that sustains him. Emerson would call that friendliness the character of the Over-soul, and it responds to Thoreau's sympathy in kind. He writes: "Every little pine needle expanded and swelled with sympathy and befriended me. I was so distinctly made aware of the presence of something kindred to me . . . that I thought no place could ever be strange to me again" (93).

Bass reacts to the same "presence of something kindred" with just as strong a sense of belonging. The "infinite and unaccountable friendliness" of Yaak enters him, alters him in ways that seem to strip him bare of old associations and his whole former character. He writes: "The coyote's barks are accumulating, becoming part of my life, and I am turning away from my old life and walking into a new one" (68). The change in Bass that his dialogue with nature brings about is so thorough, so elemental, that he writes of it in the quasi-religious terms of rebirth. His new life is filled with meditative perceptions of the world, especially animals and landscape. At the same time as he is seeking out the world, the world is moving in, "accumulating," filling him, "becoming part of [his] life." A man who has been made new by this daily discourse with nature, Bass composes as if in concert with the Yaak Valley, with nature itself. His affectionate descriptions become sympathetic projections of himself. He assumes the landscape, speaks with and ultimately for it, fills with coyote howls and howls back, participating in what Thoreau calls that "sweet and beneficent society in nature."

One of the most exquisite passages in *Winter* begins with a simple detail: "Ravens call out as they fly through snow. They're surprised by it, I think, it starts up so quickly—one second a gunmetal sky, and the next all the snow emptying out of that gray color" (134). What starts as an observation of the ravens (with a spark of sympathetic speculation about what the ravens are thinking) quickly turns into an imaginative, participatory experience as the ravens become a singular raven:

> That touches new corners of my brain, things never before seen or even imagined: the sight of a raven flying low through a heavy snowstorm, his coal-black, ragged shape winging through the white, the world trying to turn him upside down, trying to bury him, but his force, his speed, cutting through all that snow, all that white, and headed for the dark woods, for safety. For a few beautiful moments there's nothing in my mind but black, raven, and white. My mind never clearer, never emptier. (134)

The raven becomes not merely an object but a partner with (or analogue for) Bass, who would, in Emerson's words, "participate in the invention of nature." With the initial perception comes the awareness of his own relationship to the event; the raven has shown something of Bass to himself. The "new corners" of Bass's brain fill with the raven—both imagistic perceptions of the raven's movement, "flying low through a heavy snowstorm," *and* understanding of the raven's experience, of his struggle and grace and escape from "the world trying to turn him upside down." The sentence itself presses forward with force, with speed, picking up momentum, heading, with the raven and Bass's imagination, toward safe cover of the dark woods, where, briefly, nothing exists but those "new corners" of his brain, the deep, animal part in which "there's nothing . . . but black, raven, and white."

But Bass is not only a spokesman for nature in the poetic sense that Emerson had in mind; he also speaks for the Yaak Valley and nature in general as an environmental advocate. Bass's relationship to the landscape becomes colored by threat and tension, which he recasts as much as he can into calls for change in social behavior. "It's time to stop cutting the old-growth forests," he demands. "We'll cut them all, and then the same cries of more jobs, more money, will go up, and where'll we be then?" His peace shattered and his tone disturbed, he continues, "I don't mean to rant. I'm trying to keep this polite, low-key, respectful. Quiet. Falling snow. But inside I rage" (39).

Here we come to the key difference between Bass and Thoreau, reflective of the difference between Thoreau's world and ours. Bass is a late-twentieth-century ecologist and (like most late-twentieth-century ecologists) a terrified one. It is a difference in degree and focus. "We need the tonic of wilderness," Thoreau writes in "Spring." "We need to witness our own limits transgressed, and some life pasturing freely where we never wander" (211). But Thoreau does not make the leap to a direct call for collective ecological stewardship. His cause is intellectual and spiritual authenticity, with the focus on awakening and saving the individual human spirit. The health of the wilderness on which this awakening and salvation depends is taken more or less for granted.

For Thoreau and Emerson, if we do not perceive perfection in nature, it is because we are not seeing clearly. In the "Prospectus" chapter of *Nature,* Emerson writes, "The ruin or the blank, that we see when we look at nature, is in our own eye" (*Essays and Lectures,* 47). There is an environmental crisis for Thoreau and Emerson, but it is primarily a psychological and spiritual problem, in which, as Emerson explains, "[t]he axis of vision is not coincident with the axis of things..." (47). The damage is in the observer, not the observed—at least mostly. In the *Walden* chapter "The Ponds," Thoreau poignantly foreshadows increasing destruction to the woods—a lament that has become common in contemporary nature writers such as Bass. Thoreau writes: "When I first paddled a boat on Walden, it was completely surrounded by thick and lofty pine and oak wood.... As you looked down from the west end, it had the appearance of an amphitheater for some kind of sylvan spectacle" (131). But in the intervening years logging has taken many of the lofty pines and oaks; "the woodchoppers have... laid them to waste" and robbed him of some of the forest's inspiration. "My Muse may be excused if she is silent henceforth. How can you expect the birds to sing when their groves are cut down?" he asks (132).

The destruction of nature, the writer's partner in the creative act, is a far greater threat to Bass, who lives at a time when wilderness has been horribly diminished. Thoreau is certainly troubled at the destruction in his time, but it is not an obsession for him. Now society has spread across the country and chased the writer far up into one of the last corners of wilderness, and even there he can hear the saws and the over-stacked logging trucks rumbling out of Yaak Valley with the last of the ancient larches. "Living up here in the woods—just a mile or two from Canada—I feel as if I've got my back up against a wall, and, like the caribou, there are increasingly fewer places where I'll fit in" (39). Ecological threat is a threat to Bass's ability even to *find* a moral landscape—a landscape in which he can escape society's influence, in which he can live as a self-reliant, natural man—a landscape comprised of coyotes and crows for whom he can speak.

Bass, like Thoreau, writes out of love, but that love is made urgent, perhaps even heightened, by fear and loss. Speaking about the caribou that have been run out of the valley by logging and overhunting, he writes that "there are names on the old map that break my heart, names like Caribou Creek and Caribou Mountain.... But I missed out. There aren't any caribou up on Caribou Mountain now. Just ghosts" (37). *Winter* is filled with promise that Bass can prove competent and belong among his neighbors, that he will be embraced and transformed by nature. But the promise of *Winter* is accompanied by the threat that the Yaak Valley, the partner of his own imagination, will be destroyed, and he will be left to speak for ghosts.

Emerson and Thoreau can be called environmental writers in that they describe and champion a saving relationship between ourselves and nature. Many of the seeds of the greater American ecological consciousness were sown by both men, but for them the project of natural engagement remains largely one of personal fulfillment. Under the threat of ruin, those seeds grow to fruition in Bass. The relationship that he comes to advocate and to which he aspires would bring about salvation of both self and environment.

Perhaps this loyalty to nature, bred from his need for and fear of losing it, is why Bass stays in the Yaak at the end of *Winter*, whereas Thoreau finds himself ready to leave his cabin at the end of *Walden*. In his "Conclusion" Thoreau calls on us not to cling to any particular circumstances or setting, but to make our native territory our own minds. "Be a Columbus to whole new continents and worlds within you, opening new channels, not of trade, but of thought," he writes. "Every man is the lord of a realm beside which the earthly empire of the Czar is but a petty state, a hummock left by the ice" (213). From this perspective, the cabin at Walden is not a destination, not a found home, but one anchorage in the journey. Having received the spiritual instruction and nourishment he sought there, he feels free to go: "I left the woods for as good a reason as I went there. Perhaps it seemed to me that I had several more lives to live and could not spare any more time for that one" (214). But Bass believes he has lost too much time already to the diseased world outside his valley and can spare no more. "You've changed," Bass's father tells him as the two fly-fish the south fork of the Yaak River.

> "No, I haven't," I said, just as comfortably, still casting to the little fish. We were catching them almost at will. I suppose I was pretending that I had always realized what I needed—deep, dark woods, and a quietness, a slowness—and that I hadn't been floundering for thirty years trying to figure this out, trying to get along in cities, trying to move fast. (161)

Having received a season's worth of his own spiritual instruction and nourishment in the woods, and having found there the tracks of his animal self, Bass is ready to claim (and defend) the Yaak as both "earthly empire and realm of thought":

> Winter covers some things and reveals others. I admire the weasels, the rabbits, and the other wild creatures that can change with the sea-

> sons, that can change almost overnight. It's taken me a long time to change completely—thirty years—but now that I've changed, I don't have an interest in turning back.
>
> I won't be leaving this valley. (162)

The relocated Bass has become Bass the native species. For inhabitants of this contemporary world, these are words of hope. Bass finds himself and his place in creation through loving, poetic attention and physical engagement just as Thoreau did. For all our abuse of nature in the years between *Walden* and *Winter,* nature, at least in a few places, retains the power to save the wilderness in us. And according to Bass, we must answer that good fortune by finding in us the power to save wilderness.

Works Cited

Bass, Rick. *Winter.* New York: Houghton Mifflin, 1991.

Emerson, Ralph Waldo. *Essays and Lectures.* Ed. Joel Porte. New York: Library of America, 1983.

Thoreau, Henry David. *Walden.* New York: Penguin Books, 1980.

Rick Bass's *Winter*

Self-Discovery in a Cold Place

Thomas Bailey

I can picture getting so addicted to this valley, so dependent on it for my peace, that I become hostage to it.

(*Winter,* 40)

If you go slowly enough, six or seven months is an eternity. . . . even a week can last forever.

(*Winter,* 162)

Rick Bass's *Winter,* written between his arrival in the Yaak in the late summer of 1987 and early 1991 (when it was published), details with some care his first season in the landscape that was to come to dominate his life and his fiction. Although there is never a doubt in Bass's (or the reader's) mind that his arrival in the Yaak has been personally momentous, no one, least of all Bass, would have predicted his passionate and deepening involvement with this place and the degree to which it would influence his subsequent personal, economic, and artistic choices. *The Ninemile Wolves, The Book of Yaak, The Sky, the Stars, the Wilderness, Fiber, Where the Sea Used to Be,* and *Brown Dog of the Yaak*—in short, all of Bass's major works since 1991—are rooted in and grow out of his political and artistic concerns as he discovers them living in Yaak. "[W]e have stumbled into the pie, Elizabeth and I, finding this valley," he writes. "We have fallen into heaven" (30).

It is perhaps not surprising, then, that Bass chose to structure *Winter* in journal form as a series of intermittent, interwoven narratives composed in the language and rhetoric of the Psalms (39). The tone of much of the book is one of intense and fairly constant praise, punctuated by what might be called prophetic fury.

Just as psalmists lift their eyes unto the hills and find help and sustenance there, nature writers such as Bass who employ the psalm as a narrative device look to the natural world as a refuge from human society and culture. Nature represents safety, serenity, escape: "Thou leadest me beside the still waters, thou makest me to lie down in green pastures, thou preparest a table before me in the presence of mine enemies." For both writer and psalmist, the soul's quest for God (or peace) is always couched in terms referencing nature: "as the hart longs for the water brook, so longs my heart for Thee." To find God in the natural world is "natural," completely appropriate, and especially intense since it means finding God in the present moment. Bass's language throughout *Winter* is as rhapsodic and spiritual as a psalmist's, especially in its descriptions of nature and natural phenomena.

It is worth noting that much of the book is about the quest for appropriate language through which to evoke nature, and the language of the psalm comes to seem more appropriate to Bass as he becomes comfortable in the Yaak, as his personal geography becomes congruent with his chosen worldly and quotidian place. When that place is won, his language can become more prophetic, dealing scornfully with human culture and its mechanistic economic exchange and with what the human-wrought future will bring. Prophecy, it is worth noting, is rarely optimistic; it expresses a passionate concern for place, for environment, for the world itself, through rhetoric intended to protect the psalmist's perfect place. Bass the psalmist must perforce become a prophet to protect the place he is coming to love. Contemporary nature writers like Bass must be both psalmists and prophets. Praise and blame arise from the same source, after all; the writer lives passionately in his place, and describes it to us; and he passionately defends his place against all that might bring it ruin. As Bass himself puts it: "I keep singing psalms in this journal. But the light isn't anything without the darkness out there to define it. And even in these dream-mountains there's darkness, on the perimeter of the valley, hemming it in: the knowledge that the valley can, like everything, change, and be lost" (39).

Composed almost entirely of daily entries over the course of the months from the middle of September until the middle of March, *Winter* records an uninhibited and perhaps unintentional (or not fully considered) revelation of self. Bass deals charmingly and apparently ingenuously with his fears, his doubts, his neurotic tendencies, his vulnerabilities. He shows himself, not surprisingly, to be a man of enormous personal charm and charisma, highly charged, intense, anxiety-ridden, at times unpleasant and naïve. But he is always questing, always pushing his mind and body to experience and imagine life on what George Eliot calls "the other side of silence" (*Middlemarch*, 159). Because of this, the formal choice of the journal (the book's subtitle is *Notes from Montana*) is particularly apt: this book moves with the suppleness, indirectness, and subconscious thematic coherence of a long poem, proceeding with ease from topic to topic, from image to image. Bass is consciously placing himself in the company of autobiographers such as William Wordsworth and Walt Whitman and powerful contemporary writers such as Josephine Johnson (*The Inland Island*) and Linda Hasselstrom (*Windbreak*), whose writing insists that in exploring the self's relation to the natural world something absolutely essential about that self is revealed.

Furthermore, in the literary tradition of Thoreau, Annie Dillard, Pattiann Rogers, and Amy Clampitt, Bass subordinates exact chronology or dominant plot and substitutes a narrative structure with several recurring themes: losing his greenhorn status, cutting wood to keep the house secure against the cold, and becoming aware of weather and adapting to a winter climate. Like these writers, Bass finds a sacred place, learns to live in and love it, and then defends it against despoilment. Each searches for what Dillard calls "the tree with the lights in it" (*Pilgrim at Tinker Creek*, 35–36), the spot on earth that contains and mysteriously reveals God, however mystically and outside the usual claims of language. Yet in his emphasis on the irrational, the lucky, the heavenly, Bass sets himself apart from his contemporaries and reveals himself as a modern practitioner of the ancient rhetorical art of the psalm:

> This valley shakes with mystery, with beauty, with secrets—and yet it gives up no answers. I sometimes believe this valley—so high up in the mountains, and in such heavy woods—is like a step up to heaven, the last place you go before the real thing. (61)

The first of the recurring themes is announced in the early pages of *Winter*, describing the opening months of his stay: Bass shows himself acutely aware of his status as a newcomer, as a greenhorn, a familiar and prevalent figure of Western American literature that can be traced back to the works of nineteenth-century authors such as Mark Twain, Bret

Harte, and Owen Wister. The outsider must prove himself to those who already successfully inhabit the place and, by doing so, demonstrate the right to take up residence there. Almost palpably eager to learn, Bass is treated with great respect by the old-timers of Yaak Valley and soon has a wide circle of acquaintances and friends. But Breitenstein, a resident grouch and conservative, threatens Bass—and it is his approval that Bass is most eager to win. Having been raised with the high standards of performance of his forceful father, Bass calls himself "mo-ron" when he feels he has done something particularly silly or stupid. He projects his fear of incompetence on Breitenstein, worrying that Breitenstein will find his stuck car and think him "a pilgrim" or an unhandy woodsman. These fears, insofar as they are autobiographical, are heightened by Bass's peculiar dual nature: he is poet and engineer, a man of obsessive physical energy as well as intense imaginative empathy, a frantic gatherer of firewood as well as a contemplative man. Insofar as these fears are metaphysical, they are heightened by the psalmist's need to be capable in and intimate with the natural world and the prophet's need to be capable of defending it.

Breitenstein does indeed catch the greenhorn out. He talks about "building a deck," a suggestion that Bass interprets literally, only to discover that it means making an orderly pile of logs in his forest for the lumber truck to pick up. When Breitenstein discovers Bass's mistakes, he says, "I guess you've never been in the woods before" (127). Avoiding a fight, an argument, or a defense, Bass simply replies, "Hell, I'm just learning how a chain saw works." And that, says Bass, "took some of the good red air out of his lungs."

Although he eventually earns Breitenstein's respect and makes his passage from greenhorn to an accepted member of the community, Bass reflects unsentimentally on the lesson of this early episode. He had misunderstood Breitenstein, but had known better than to ask for clarification: "[Y]ou don't ask for anything in this country. Not for the time of day, not for help building your house, not for a tow when you're stuck.... the basics of communication—words—have never evolved out here, not yet, with the distances so great and the people so few, and I hope they never will. Actions are the way to communicate, not words.... [a] country of mutes, but also of doers, not sayers" (128).

In more ways than one, it is a funny place for a writer, much less a psalmist, to be. The motivation to write *Winter,* Bass says, comes from within, the need to understand his place and create it imaginatively, while in the Yaak the call to action comes mainly from without, from the culture; so the book he is creating is for himself, not for his neighbors. It is age-old dilemma of the journal writer: why should I write this, and for whom? If, on some level, doing is more important than saying, can action that *is* language ever have true social and cultural relevance? Bass is clearly troubled by this conundrum and in some sense shows himself to be more sensitive and less sure (and, consequently, more accessible) than such narrators as Dillard, Thoreau, and Rogers, whose professed grasp of the world and its natural beauty is often intimidating in a way that Bass's never is.

In a way, though, the Yaak is exactly the right place for a writer of Bass's propensities. He subscribes, certainly, to the world of macho "doing" and silence, which offers him release for his physical intensity even as it seems to embody a moral clarity he longs for. But he also needs that silence in order to nurture and sustain his own interior world of language and its endlessly discretionary levels of meaning and feeling. Writers "act" in silence, imagining and committing language to paper. And however "wordless" the natural world, however taciturn the residents of the Yaak Valley, Bass's effort in *Winter* is to use the language of silence to explain silence—a job for a psalmist.

In the recurring narrative concerning woodcutting, however, it is interesting to note that the passion and exaltation of Bass the psalmist fall away. Determined to be self-sufficient when winter sets in without having to rely on propane, "the fuel of affluence" (114), Bass directs a seemingly inordinate amount of physical energy into cutting, gathering, and stacking wood. He tells of cutting and hauling in twenty tons of wood a day, of working late into the night, of splitting and stacking woods so vigorously and continuously that he wears out several pairs of gloves a day. He tells of the frustrations of having a truck with a shot transmission and his difficulty in getting it fixed. The urgency is not being without transportation; his old, beat-up Falcon seems to fill the bill heroically. Rather, not having a truck limits how much wood gets gathered and stacked.

"Can't get enough wood!" he announces for the first time on September 15. Later in that same entry: "I went and picked up a truckload of wood.... Here and there on the slash piles I'll find some larch, which is the driest of woods up here and burns hot; it's everyone's favorite." On October 6: "I went to cut wood today.... for over an hour: big logs, with the newly sharpened saw.... I cut and cut, until I was dripping sweat." Yet on October 10: "I need a lot more wood." And on October 14: "I'm thinking about how I love getting wood. I moan about it.... and yet I really, really enjoy that feeling: lifting the great logs,... splitting them, stacking them, the pile growing higher, the protection against the cold." But on October 31 Bass writes: "I did not get all the wood in.... I've got some wood, a lot of wood—eighteen, maybe twenty cords—but I'm burning some of it every day now out here in the greenhouse and in the kitchen stove. I didn't get the thirty cords I wanted to have by this date." Then on November 3, "I am surprisingly calm.... I have most of my wood in." Finally, on January 17, Bass reports: "Last night I finished cutting, splitting, and hauling out the last of the larch I'd bought from Breitenstein."

Bass's obsessions yield neither to physical exhaustion nor to psychic depletion. Still, in the energy expelled, the sheer intensity of the quest, Bass again shows a capacity for complete absorption into the quotidian requirements of the world, and his prose does for physical labor—daily, practical, unglorified—what rhapsody can do for prayer and praise: elevate and honor it.

The obsession with wood is underpinned by profound moral implications that are constantly on Bass's mind. He knows that if there were more than thirty families in the Yaak Valley the demand for wood as fuel would be unsustainable. He knows, moreover, that to burn larch, a noble tree, is somehow morally suspect. But the larches he is cutting up are called "buckskin" larches, dead forest giants killed by a fire decades before and standing all these years in the forest, waiting to fall and rot. "Almost atomic in the heat [they throw] out" (111), the long, huge logs are cut out of his woods by Breitenstein and sold to the locals who want to burn them as firewood. As to the living trees, Bass admits that "[t]he European larch is like the giant redwood; its own greatness is what's killing it. It's the tree everyone wants: it's heavy, dense, yet splits easily..." (112).

The question of burning larch, even though it is deadwood, nags Bass. "Am I a plunderer, a taker, for going into the woods on a snowy evening... for the soul and body of one of these trees.... dead but magnificent, and that will never be again? I don't know" (113). As with most questions in this perplexing book, this one remains unanswered, at least directly. Bass worries and comes back to it often before finding reconciliation. The question of burning larch does not yield to logic, but it does yield to art. Bass imagines himself a kind of "log fairy," saving remnants and parcels of the meaningful past and delivering them to Houston. Readers of *Fiber* will find the narrator of that title foreshadowed in this one:

> I'm going to save some larch for my children. . . . Perhaps this spring I'll drive to Houston pulling a sixty-foot larch tree behind me. . . . and leave it in their front yard for the children to grow up with. (114)

But Bass's guilt concerning the larch is never completely assuaged. And guilt leads us back, as he sees it, almost inexorably to questions of morality, worship, and faith. The loss of the trees is owing to the corruption of the natural world brought about by human greed. They are consumed because they are worth money, they save money, and they make life easy. Bass participates in this exchange, but he feels it as a prophet must, maintaining all the while his outspoken prophetic point of view toward capitalism and its evils.

A psalmist celebrates the "nowness," the "isness" of the natural world; the prophet, an expert in subtraction as well as logic, is ironically vexed by the same thing: the knowledge that things, unless heeded, decay, fall away—that the coming world will be worse than the present one. These larch trees and the world they represent are being destroyed, and there is no escaping the responsibility for their disappearance. Leaving his friends surprising evidence that the larch once existed is simply whim in the face of enormous loss: the fool singing to Lear on the heath, the comic's joke about dying. But Bass refuses to succumb to a sense of futility. He knows how beautiful the natural world is and how imperiled; in evoking its presence, he can speak convincingly on its behalf as both poet and prophet.

This is most clearly seen in Bass's passionate attention to climate, to the vagaries of wind and rain and snow; he is determined "to winter" in the Yaak in the fullest possible sense. One reason for this passionate attention is purely autobiographical: Bass is a southern boy who has never lived through a winter before, especially not one as snowy and cold as he hopes that this one will be. The second reason is tautological: nature writers are obsessed by weather, claiming for their art an extraordinary consciousness of the world and absorption into it. This absorption is not merely rehashed nineteenth-century Romanticism, but a much more hard-edged modern romanticism rooted in science and in accurate and obsessive observation. When Bass allows himself to be utterly taken in by the weather, which is after all the biggest, most powerful and random force determining our lives, he becomes an agent for understanding the interplay of self and world in a new ecological read of things. Obsessed as any sailor or farmer, Bass watches the weather and its changes, struggles to interpret it, to comprehend how wintering changes him and his neighbors, to understand what winter *is.* To this end, he uses all of his linguistic skills to create an imagined world that he can shape through language just as his surroundings are shaped by the weather, by the real world. His place, then, is at once in geography and in the imagination. He is going with Wallace Stevens ("The Snow Man") to where, having "been cold a long time," he "beholds / Nothing that is not there, and the nothing that is" (ll. 4, 14–15).

Beginning with his record of his first full day in the valley, September 13, Bass alerts the reader to his commitment to observation, acknowledging that he is "eager to see how rain falls here" (9). Nothing, not even rainfall, is prosaic to the nature writer, whose job it is to make distinctions others might miss. "When it starts to snow," he notes a paragraph later, "I'm going to write in the greenhouse.... while I look out at winter, when it gets here" (9). He quickly turns his attention from noun to verb, however, from season to concept, when he addresses wintering in the Yaak. He is already busy trying to imagine it and simultaneously foreshadowing the limitations of language here, the wordlessness of this place, which he will come to know: "That's what they talk about most when they talk about winter: the silence" (12).

Autumn, the season of preparation, dominates much of the first half of the book. But Bass focuses on what is to come, keeping track of the snow contest at the Dirty Shame, fantasizing as a greenhorn about winning it. He examines every cloud to see if it is a "snow cloud," hoping it is, "knowing.... that it, the great cold, lay out there in the future, a certainty" (64). At last, on November 16: "It started snowing today" (83). His excitement is palpable: "It's like guests showing up.... guests from out of town.... It's going to be strange falling asleep tonight, knowing that snow is landing on the roof. It's here. We're here. Nobody's leaving" (84). The austerity of the season is profoundly moving to him: "I don't mind the cold. The beauty is worth it." And as winter's beauty and silence fall, Bass explains why: "I am coming to life... up here in this valley" (85). The restraint of the season bites in, and he throws himself more and more completely into lyrical observation. "We've had two nights and days of solid snow, big flakes, falling feathers.... I'm following a river of snow leading all the way... home" (89).

This obsessive observation of weather, what it means and how it looks, begins to take on the aspects of a moral investigation, a deepening set of speculations on the relationships between self and society, self and natural world. On November 24, for instance, Bass writes: "I watch individual flakes; I peer up through the snow and see the blank infinity from which it comes; I listen to the special silence it creates. Anything I am guilty of is forgiven when the snow falls. . . . I am like an animal—not in control of my emotions . . . but in charge of loving the snow . . . the more that comes down, the richer I am" (90). This is at once a paradox and a profound spiritual insight. It is the negation and austerity of winter, equating richness with snowflakes and possessing them by looking at them. Sensing winter's purity and offer of complete self-possession, Bass knows that the depth of this experience is at least in part an escape from the culture that, viewed from the Yaak in winter and from a prophet's point of view, he has truly come to hate. He feels pure in his escape, because the world of money, exchange, culture—that inescapable world of the future—is so deeply flawed. "I'm hiding out up here—no question about it. The decay of our nation is frustrating. We are truly becoming senile . . . each time I go to a city I feel it more and more. All I want to do is get back to the Yaak, back to the snow" (92).

However much Bass might sound like a Jeremiah without portfolio in such a passage, the religious intensity of his liberation from the larger culture as he settles in to winter in the Yaak is real, and he is too sensitive and smart not to question his own thinking, his own motives. "I'm wondering if I've already fizzled out, died, and up here, in the snow and the mountains, I have already begun an afterlife. I think that is what it may be" (93)—a new twist certainly on his earlier notion of having "fallen into heaven." In its strong moral language and elements of moral quest, his narrative of surviving and understanding winter becomes central to Bass's gaining a fundamental identity and a recognition and sense of home in the Yaak.

The Yaak is literally and symbolically an unflawed present. In the moral metaphysical quest that shapes *Winter,* journal writing conjoins with the needs of the psalmist, who loves that place, and the prophet, who protects it. "It's not like we're total hermits, only that most of us want, as Thoreau said, to examine our lives, as well as the world we live in—a world that, up here, is not controlled by others as much as by, believe it or not, one's self" (115). In this complete act of understanding, Bass has come home, grown up, earned his spurs, become one with his place, become its defender: he has become that which he unknowingly or naïvely set out to be when he left Houston with Elizabeth, their two dogs, and the old Nissan pickup. He has won through.

Inevitably, however, the season changes; Bass finds the loss of his first winter hard. It means the passing of silence, of austerity, of safety. "I need to stay loyal to it," he says, "but I dream of grass" (159). On March 4 he runs a hoe through the soil in the greenhouse, and "[i]t felt as strong an act of infidelity as can be imagined" (158). As the snow melts, his hide-out is vanishing. Having not only survived winter but settled into the local ways of doing things, burning the wood that he cut himself, Bass finds his values clarified and resolved: "There are two worlds for me—and for anybody, I think—and I do better in one than in the other. I used to be able to exist in both, but as I pay more and more attention to the one world, the world of the woods and of this valley, I find myself, each day, less and less able to operate in the other world" (159); "I have changed. . . . My heart has changed too" (160); "I won't be leaving this valley" (162).

The supply of wood in the shed having lasted, with his deepest personal identity stripped and shined and honed, cleansed and reified by this experience of cold danger and clear beauty of the past season, Bass has prepared himself for a period of significant literary productivity to follow. Quotidian experience, observed by an intently tuned and focused moral imagination, has revealed the true nature of that world as well as the moral imperative to protect it; has shown him his place in the world as woodcutter and citizen, psalmist and prophet.

Works Cited

Bass, Rick. *Brown Dog of the Yaak: Essays on Art and Activism.* Minneapolis: Milkweed Editions, 1998.

———. *Fiber.* Athens: University of Georgia Press, 1998.

———. *The Ninemile Wolves.* Livingston, Mont.: Clark City Press, 1992.

———. *The Sky, the Stars, the Wilderness.* Boston: Houghton Mifflin, 1997.

———. *Where the Sea Used to Be.* Boston: Houghton Mifflin, 1998.

———. *Winter: Notes from Montana.* Boston: Houghton Mifflin/Seymour Lawrence, 1991.

Buell, Lawrence. *The Environmental Imagination.* Boston: Harvard University Press, 1995.

Clampitt, Amy. *Collected Poems.* New York: Alfred A. Knopf, 1998.

Davies, Donald, ed. *The Psalms in English.* London: Penguin Editions, 1996.
Dillard, Annie. *Pilgrim at Tinker Creek.* New York: HarperCollins/Perennial Classics, 1988.
Dixon, Terrell. "Rick Bass." In *American Nature Writers,* ed. John Elder, 75–88. New York: Scribner's, 1996.
Eliot, George. *Middlemarch.* London: Penguin, 1981.
Hasselstrom, Linda. *Windbreak: A Woman Rancher on the Northern Plains.* Berkeley: Barn Owl Books, 1987.
Johnson, Josephine W. *The Inland Island.* New York: Simon & Schuster, 1969.
Rogers, Pattiann. *Firekeeper: New and Selected Poems.* Minneapolis: Milkweed Editions, 1994.
Stevens, Wallace. *The Collected Poems.* New York: Alfred A. Knopf, 1954.
Thoreau, Henry David. *Walden.* New York: Norton, 1966.
Whitman, Walt. "Song of Myself." In *The Norton Anthology of Poetry,* 961–85. New York: Norton, 1970.
Wister, Owen. *The Virginian.* New York: Grosset & Dunlap, 1945.
Wordsworth, William. *The Prelude, 1850 Edition.* Oxford: Oxford University Press, 1962.

Witnessing to the Wild

Rick Bass and the Advocacy of Wonder

RICHARD HUNT

THOMAS MOORE WRITES THAT the process of ecology is "the mysterious work of finding a home for the soul" ("Ecology," 144). Throughout his nonfiction books, Rick Bass does that work, and in the process he has found a home for his own soul: the Yaak Valley in northwestern Montana. But his interest—and his work—transcends the inward focus suggested by Moore's epigram, asking readers to look outward, toward what he sees as the necessity of wildness. For Moore, it is the human soul that forms the "one necessity" that Annie Dillard describes in "Living Like Weasels" (34): one central focus around which to understand our lives and attentions. For Bass, that one necessity is wildness, essential not just for the human soul but for the "soul" of the entire biotic community. Indeed, his celebration of wildness in all its manifestations recalls Thoreau's injunction: "In wildness is the preservation of the world" ("Walking," 112).[1]

Bass emphasizes the need to protect "[t]he wildness that is life" (*Lost Grizzlies,* 167), which is crucial not just to wild places and wild species but also to humans, regardless of whether we partake of those places or see those wild animals; for "the blood-rhythms of wilderness which remain in us . . . are declaring, in response to the ever-increasing instability of the outside forces that are working against us, the need for reconnection to rhythms that are stable and natural" (*Book of Yaak,* 13). Nowhere are those "blood-rhythms" more important to Bass than in his efforts to preserve the Yaak Valley. In his earliest efforts to generate support for preserving the Yaak, his extensive catalogues of the valley's biological diversity rival—in number of species if not individuals—the reports of seventeenth-century European explorers of North America's Atlantic coast.

In a letter dated 17 December 1993, for instance, he lists over one hundred species of mammals, birds, and fishes—and over sixty species of plants—that live in the Yaak Valley. In a subsequent letter he writes of the logging interests that have been, in his words, "savaging the valley for three decades now" and notes that his letter-writing campaign is intended to bring this practice to public attention (Letter, 21 December 1994). In these and other letters,[2] Bass suggests that getting the word out to enough people ought to initiate a public movement to stop the logging companies and U.S. Forest Service from stripping the forests and carving logging roads through the Yaak's roadless areas, writing that "[t]he biology of Yaak Valley is the best argument for protecting it" (Letter, 10 April 1994). Sadly, his optimism has waned in recent years; he writes in his most recent book, *Brown Dog of the Yaak* (1999), that the increased public attention to the issue of wilderness preservation has not stopped the savaging he describes. "In ten years I've published about fifty magazine and newspaper articles arguing for wilderness protection for those last roadless cores in the Yaak, to a cumulative readership of over 50 million people. And still, not one stone, not one gram of soil, is protected" (87). But even so, he continues, "that's no reason to back away. We just have to hope others come along behind us who love the place as much as we do" (87). Where he once described the Yaak as genetic corridor between Canada and Mexico, he now describes it as resembling "some newly forming Malaysian archipelago drifting from the mainland, . . . not the land bridge I believe it should be—a source—but instead, an island" ("Raccoons of Yaak," 24). Yet the cause is not hopeless: "The fact that nothing's gone extinct in the Yaak—that its full diversity of individuals and relationships is still, even if tenuously, preserved—provides more avenues, more corridors, for life, and life's potential for 'magic,' to travel" (*Brown Dog of the Yaak,* 112–13). Though he has begun to despair over the valley's future, he moderates that despair by weaving through it his appreciation of the wonder he has always known in the Yaak.

Bass and Elizabeth Hughes (they married in 1991) first arrived in the Yaak Valley in September 1987. *Winter: Notes from Montana* (1991) describes his initial season in what would become the focus of both his literary efforts and his environmental activism. They moved to Montana for their art—he to write, she to paint—seeking "a place of ultimate wildness, with that first and last yardstick of privacy: a place you could walk around naked if you wanted to . . ." (3). They found just the place in the Yaak Valley; Bass reports that they "knew immediately that this was where we wanted to live. . . . We had never felt such magic" (5). But however magical the valley may have appeared, the place was not without problems that even as a relative stranger he could not overlook.

For one thing, he calls attention to the destructive effects of rapid growth on the nearby town of Libby, whose "seams are fixing to pop" (*Winter,* 28); he also notes in passing the presence of mining operations that threaten the valley's water quality. But in this early book Bass would still prefer to concentrate primarily on his home "back up in the woods," where he's "unable to see what's going on" in town (29). He and Elizabeth merely retreat, "trying to put it out of our minds." "We have stumbled into this pie," he continues, "finding this valley, this life. We have fallen into heaven" (29, 30). Yet soon after his arrival he realizes that the valley has become more than just a heavenly place where he can concentrate on his writing career; he can foresee becoming "so dependent on [Yaak] for my peace, that I become a hostage to it" (40). In many ways the valley itself is the real hostage, not to Bass but to both the logging interests that he describes as savaging its few remaining uncut hillsides and Congress, which continues to refuse his call for wilderness designation to protect what little remains of the valley's wild state.

Nor does Bass overlook the important role of human wildness in his argument that wildness must be preserved and protected, writing that "as human beings we still have at our core an essence, a yearning for and affiliation with wilderness, and that we can only be pushed and herded so far" (*Book of Yaak,* xiv). He wants to believe that "anyone who hears about the valley, and the complete disregard with which its wilderness has been treated in the past . . . will be moved to help" (*Book of Yaak,* 109). Yet his chronic publicizing has failed to impress the powers that be. Two things become clear from this failure. First, neither the description of the Yaak's biological importance nor the revelation of the devastation being inflicted upon it is adequate, in the view of policy-makers and the mass public, to warrant the sort of change in the economics of timber extraction necessary for the preservation of wildness in the Yaak. Even the presence of the most charismatic of megafauna—wolves or grizzlies—apparently counts as nothing in the face of the continued plunder.

To a wilderness activist, a second point necessarily follows the first: a new perspective must be found to preserve the sort of wildness Yaak represents before it is entirely despoiled. But as the Australian environmental philosopher Warwick Fox points out, "Logic . . . is no help to us either way in proceeding from the fact of our interconnectedness with the world to the practical question of how we should live" (*Toward a Transpersonal Ecology*, 246). Thus the need for a new paradigm for environmental activism, one that might speak in accents uninflected either by traditional economics or by the tradition of plunder that so thoroughly characterizes Western civilization's relationship with wild nature. In *The Lost Grizzlies,* Bass suggests the outlines of such a new development, along with some more human reasons to implement it:

> It was from the loss of wildness, the loss of vigor, that all the rest of our country's bleeding social ills accelerated. It will take generations to fix these ills, but if we can help change attitudes, we might be able to get there just ahead of the train wreck—might be able to protect the last roadless areas and begin to repair those places that have been harmed. And if we can help change attitudes toward the land, all the other wrongs of domination (rather than caretaking) in society might reveal a pattern, a model to follow, so we can turn things around. (196)

Such a change of attitude, though, will not come from traditional approaches to the wild. The "small good places" that still harbor wildness, Bass writes, "need and deserve our reverence" (*Lost Grizzlies,* 156). What is also needed, though Bass does not say so directly, is some means of comprehending nature—wild nature—as somehow magical, a term he uses to describe "a place that still retains all of its graceful fitted parts" (*Brown Dog of the Yaak,* 37). Such magic has, in fact, been an increasing presence in Bass's nonfiction, as he seeks to articulate his vision in advocating the preservation of wildness.

Bass is insistent on the magic he sees as inherent both in wild places—including his home in Montana, which, he writes, "lies in a seam of magic uniqueness" ("Kootenai Five," 62)—and in wild species—especially large predators. And although Bass is most prominently identified with the Yaak Valley, arguing in books like *Winter* and *The Book of Yaak* to preserve the valley's wildness, his natural histories (*The Ninemile Wolves, The Lost Grizzlies,* and *The New Wolves*) all explore themes of wildness as represented by large predators, which he describes as "canaries in the coal mine [who] will tell how far down the land . . . really is" (*New Wolves,* 61–62). These predators occupy "the top of the pyramid" in the wild;

thus their successful return to the wild means that "[w]e must also repair the base of the pyramid" (*Lost Grizzlies,* 72). David Abram notes that the role of "traditional magic" in Nepal is "balancing the [human] community's relation to the surrounding land" (*Spell of the Sensuous,* 7). Thus magic requires a *complete* system, which is how Bass conjoins his thoughts of magic with his understanding of the land. For as Aldo Leopold noted half a century ago, without the megafauna at the top of the food pyramid, the land itself can never be complete. Without the wolf, without the grizzly, the land is not truly wild: without them, the land is truncated, incomplete; there is no magic. And where there is no magic there can be no healing.

The metonymous connection between wolf and wildness is a central theme in *The Ninemile Wolves,* which chronicles the return of a wolf pack to its ancestral territory in western Montana, much to the surprise of biologists and displeasure of some local ranchers. Bass is generally not physically present in this book (which is unusual in his nonfiction works), preferring to let the wolves, and those humans concerned with their welfare, hold the stage. But while he operates primarily as a reporter, he cannot help being drawn into the wolves' lives, a "rich" story that "can begin anywhere. . . . You can start with biology, or politics, or you can start with family, with loyalty, and even with the mystic-tinged edges of fate, which is where I choose to begin" (4). Though they might prefer to roam the lowlands where food is abundant, Bass continues, "I like to think of the wolves hanging back in the woods, up in the mountains, *longing* for the river bottoms, but too wild, too smart, to descend" (6). In such moments, Bass recognizes something special in these wolves, a "spirituality and mystique—mystic, mystery, myth," pointing out that "there's something *extra* inside them—not just something we place on them, but something extra internal, some kind of fire" (137).[3] Like an Old Testament prophet, he bears witness for Ninemile's new wolves. Although Bass himself is highly nonreligious in any conventional sense, the biblical connotations in *The Ninemile Wolves* are clear; to know that the Ninemile Valley is able to harbor such wildness is, he argues, "as if God himself were to reveal himself: not his work, but his *self*" (147).

Bass takes his witnessing further into the realm of wonder in *The Lost Grizzlies.* He accompanies Doug Peacock and students from the Round River Conservation Studies program in search of evidence that grizzlies still live in the San Juan Mountains of southwestern Colorado, where, according to the conventional wisdom, they have been extinct for decades. The mountains abound with the mystery of wild places, he notes. John Hay, writing of his own home territory on Cape Cod, suggests that his own work "is not just 'natural history' . . . unless you are also willing to call it 'natural mystery'" (*Nature's Year,* 196). Hay is not expressly writing *about* wonder—as I believe Bass does. Yet his argument for an expanded sense of what "nature writing" can do stems from his lifelong recognition of the same wonder in the presence of wildness that Bass finds in the Colorado mountains, where mystery (a term he uses interchangeably with "magic" and "wonder") "is as real and necessary a component of these mountains as are the tangible elements of bears, rocks, sun, trees, water, ferns" (*Lost Grizzlies,* 124–25). Like Hay, Bass recognizes that this sense of wonder must become integrated with those "tangible elements" if we are to preserve the mountains and all they contain.

Such an integration may provide a source for wonder as it leads to human efforts to replenish those elements of wild nature diminished through human actions. Certainly, there is an increased reference to, and involvement in, the magic of wildness in Bass's recent natural history essay, *The New Wolves.* He writes as part of the team working to restore the Mexican gray wolf to its ancestral territory in the American Southwest, a task complicated by the limited number of genetically pure gray wolves remaining, who have been raised for generations in captivity. This genetic strain of wildness has been waiting for the time when such a return would become possible. Bass worries that they may be too far removed from the wild to "remember" how to be wild animals. But to the credit of those responsible for the reintroduction, he reports, the wolves remember their inherent wildness upon their release in Arizona's Blue Mountains.

Echoing John Hay's belief that "[w]here the mystery is, may be the reality" (*Nature's Year,* 193), Bass argues forcefully that "the earth needs wolves for balance" (*New Wolves,* 6–7). For even beyond the importance of the wolves' individual existence, their return to the Southwest "will deepen the mystery of this beautiful red land, causing us to pay more attention to it and to tomorrow, and less to ourselves" (61). But for all its significance, the inherent mystery of wildness seems beyond understanding either by traditional science or by contemporary culture. Though he is increasingly taken by a sense of wonder in the wild, Bass remains hesitant to speak of such spiritual qualities. Yet in the wild, he writes, he finds his "resistance to the sacred is slipping" (*Lost Grizzlies,* 108). So despite any residual resistance he presses on, recognizing, in words that echo Thomas Moore, that the wild habitat he seeks to protect for grizzlies and wolves is also "[t]he shrinking wild habitat of the soul" (*Lost Grizzlies,* 44). Ultimately, I believe, it is this "wild habitat" that serves as Bass's real subject: a wild habitat of both the human soul and the "more-than-human world."[4]

Bass generally echoes Wendell Berry's suspicion of the reductionism in much of science, which both writers feel can often be inimical to wild habitats in its tendency to envision the earth and its inhabitants as insensate objects best fit for exploitation. But "[e]very place on earth has a consciousness," Bass suggests in *The Lost Grizzlies,* "an awareness of being that is the sum of its existence" (149). In a recent article published in *Orion,* he writes of "the shared sense of power" that he finds in wild places ("Raccoons of Yaak," 23), a power that diminishes as old-growth forests are replaced by faster-growing, genetically enhanced trees. "What is the difference in value," he asks, "between a tree that took 40 years to get big and one that took 120 years? Is there a reduction of the magic? Of course there is. Can we measure it? Probably not—but by god we'd better consider it" ("Raccoons of Yaak," 23).

Bass acknowledges that "nature writers and activists could be attaching themselves to issues [such as] racial inequalities, gender inequalities, [or] worker-employer inequalities." But those cultural inequities, he suggests, are overlaid upon the environment. He questions the assertion that nature writers are "lost children, writing instead about salamanders and ferns and mountain ranges of light and shadow, and about the profound movements our hearts undertake when we enter wild places," then replies that nature writers and activists are not lost as their work is "close to the bedrock . . . of human existence" (*Brown Dog of the Yaak,* 65). "Wildness," writes John Hay, "takes such care of wildness that it must always be the earth's criterion of health" (*Immortal Wilderness,* 144).

A few years ago, at the second ASLE Conference in Missoula, Montana,[5] Bass gave a reading that he could not finish. Shortly before the end of the story, he broke into tears and rushed out of the lecture hall, leaving the stunned audience in silence. During the reading, I noticed a spider dangling by a single thread from the high ceiling. The spider and about three feet of its thread were spotlighted by one of the stage lights; I doubt that either Bass or most of the audience could see either spider or thread. The spider rose and fell on its own schedule, quite oblivious to the mass human presence in the hall; but in watching it during Bass's reading I could not help thinking of the image of the spider in Jonathan Edwards's "Sinners in the Hands of an Angry God": "The God that holds you over the pit of hell, much as one holds a spider... over the fire, abhors you, and is dreadfully provoked" (97). For Edwards the provocation was in his parishioners' sinning against the dictates of the Puritan faith; Bass for his part is equally concerned about his own audience's "provocations," especially the wasting of wildness, whether in the Yaak Valley or elsewhere. Bass is no Puritan (though in some of his work he recalls the jeremiad tendencies of Edwards); but he does have his own faith, one no less intense than Edwards's Puritanism: a faith that rises, as Thomas Moore suggests, "directly out of the human encounter with the natural world" ("Mystic Clouds," 32).

Bass began his efforts on behalf of the Yaak with a reliance on the logic of science; he provided lists of Yaak's inhabitants and cited the numerous biological imperatives favoring a wild Yaak. But as his faith in that mode of thinking dimmed, he shifted his emphasis to another kind of faith, one emerging from his relationship with the natural world. Like Edwards, whose religious faith never wavered even as he incorporated the precepts of Enlightenment science, Bass retains both new and old paradigms in his relationship with nature. Edwards's work, whether by intention or not, led toward the work of later natural historians such as William Bartram, Henry David Thoreau, and John Muir, who would articulate through the means of scientific description a world in which faith remains crucial. Bass, operating within that venerable tradition, emerges from the scientific orientation of contemporary Western culture to find a faith based in the reality that science can never fully describe.

Some cultural critics, however, question the very existence of that reality on which Bass builds his faith. Arguing that what we call wilderness is not bedrock at all, but a mere artifact of language and desire, for instance, William Cronon questions the accuracy of Thoreau's famous assessment of wildness ("Trouble with Wilderness," 471). "Wilderness hides its unnaturalness behind a mask that is all the more beguiling because it seems so natural," Cronon argues (472). Though he "celebrate[s] with others who love the wilderness the beauty and power of the things it contains," he argues that the idea of wilderness "is entirely a cultural invention" (472). His "principal objection" to the term is that "wilderness tends to privilege some parts of nature at the expense of others" (491).

But while Cronon is suspicious of wilderness, Bass would counter that wildness (which he argues—following the lead of such advocates as

Thoreau, Muir, and Leopold—is the principal component of wilderness) *is* important. Furthermore, it may be necessary to "privilege" places that still retain their wildness, not at the expense of other places (as Cronon suggests), but rather to ensure that we attend to them before they become as tamed and civilized—as managed and controlled—as the places that Cronon fears such wilderness advocacy will overlook. Bass, in essence, makes the argument that the wild is and ought to be a special case; while it may be *practical* to give priority to human needs in an already human-controlled environment, he argues that to do so in wild places "would involve a diminishing of a significant force in the world, that it would slow the earth's potential and cripple our own species' ability to live with force" (*Ninemile Wolves,* 139–40).

Cronon believes that the idea of wilderness "encourages us to believe that we are separate from nature" and thus "is likely to reinforce environmentally irresponsible behavior" ("Trouble with Wilderness," 492). Bass, though, does believe in wilderness and yet is also entirely certain that we are very much *not* "separate from nature." We are part of the natural world, surely; and the wild part of us, like the wild part of the rest of the natural world, is both endangered and necessary for our continued health. What Cronon does not see, and what Bass makes abundantly clear, is the distinction between that which is wild and that which is not.

"The romantic legacy," Cronon writes, "means that wilderness is more a state of mind than a fact of nature"; he goes on to argue that the concept "gets us into trouble only if we imagine that this experience of wonder and otherness is limited to the remote corners of the planet, or that it somehow depends on pristine landscapes that we ourselves do not inhabit" ("Trouble with Wilderness," 493, 494). Ironically, he illustrates his point with the example of a tree in a garden, which, he argues, is "no less worthy of our awe and respect" than is the tree in an old-growth forest (494). In his focus on the individual, Cronon recalls the difficulty Annie Dillard encountered in her own confrontation with wildness in *Pilgrim at Tinker Creek.* Dillard imagined that her God was dedicated to each individual; she retreated from nature when she discovered that "[e]volution loves death more than it loves you or me" (*Pilgrim at Tinker Creek,* 176).

In essence, what Dillard retreated from was really the absence of control, just as it is for Cronon when he argues for the equivalence of the wild and the domestic tree. For it may be accurate to say that an individual tree in one's garden is as valuable as an individual tree in an old-growth forest; but, as Bass points out, the old-growth forest is more than just a stand of trees. It is also a repository of knowledge, holding elements of wonder and mystery that are inherent in wildness and are thus unavailable to the tree in the garden, however much we may wish to respect it. Unlike Cronon, Bass sees both the forest and the trees. His "allegiance," he writes, "is with complete landscapes" (*New Wolves*, 126); Cronon's argument bypasses the forest for its components as he argues implicitly that all landscapes, no matter how mediated, are equal.

Cronon's motivations are not antienvironmental, I should hasten to acknowledge. He stresses throughout his argument the importance of respectful and sustainable relations with the natural world. What he misses, unfortunately, is Bass's understanding that the natural world depends upon wildness for its vitality. By arguing that wilderness is a human construct that we create and thus control, Cronon gives credence, albeit unwittingly, to societal management of natural systems—and not all such management is as scrupulously respectful of natural systems as Cronon is.

While Bass argues for a hands-off approach to wild places, building no new roads into roadless areas and clearcutting no more old-growth forests, Daniel Botkin has argued that such an approach is based on "old assumptions and old myths" about the way nature operates and that environmental degradation is too extreme to be remedied by leaving nature to itself (*Discordant Harmonies*, 5). Botkin believes that wilderness is best preserved by directly "managing natural resources and enhancing the quality of our environment" (13). Like Cronon, he thinks that whatever we do to "manage" nature—so long as we act responsibly—should be acceptable. Bass, however, is strenuously opposed to the idea of human control over the natural world, which he fears will "diminish" the sense of wonder that he sees as virtually synonymous with wildness.

In partial response to the argument generated by Cronon, J. Baird Callicott and Michael P. Nelson suggest a "utopian" solution to the dilemma posed by their own belief that wilderness "as envisioned by Muir and his successors" does not exist. "Conservation philosophy," they write, "is presently . . . in a state of doubt and confusion" (*Great New Wilderness Debate*, 20). In arguing that we must "get beyond the received wilderness idea," they propose a solution that includes "scientifically selected, designed, managed, and interconnected biodiversity reserves" (20). But while this is certainly an admirable idea, it can also lead to the sort of "islanding" effect noted by David Quammen in his recent book *The Song of the Dodo*.

Islands, Quammen writes, present "a simplified ecosystem, almost a caricature of nature's full complexity" (*Song*, 19). But while naturally occurring islands can be a boon to biologists ("Darwin was a biogeographer before he was an evolutionist," Quammen writes [18]), the "islands" formed by carving up forests for logging are highly unnatural, allowing inhabitant species no opportunity to adapt to truncated circumstances. Quammen describes the biological danger of creating islands of habitat. An actual island is a system with its own equilibrium—one always in flux but not dependent upon the constant infusion of random individuals from the outside to maintain species integrity. In larger systems, Bass's "complete landscapes" for instance, this danger no longer applies: species evolve with the expectation of such infusions, which guard against genetic drift, inbreeding, and susceptibility to various diseases. "Locally rare species," Quammen points out, "tend to be continually wandering in from larger landscapes" (393). But if islanding occurs, those individuals are no longer able to "wander in"; species are thus more prone to extinction.

Among the useful analytical tools that Quammen offers is the distinction between a "sample" and an "isolate," which he derives from the work of Frank Preston. A "sample" is a segment of a larger bio-unit, "part of a continuous ecosystem that is larger and richer than itself" (405). He contrasts this with the "isolate," a self-sufficient area that is not part of a larger bio-unit (392–93). Recent discoveries in island biogeography indicate that the determining factor in species isolation is not the distance between populations of a particular species, but the ability of those diverse populations to *bridge* that distance. That is, an individual of a species must be able to cross the space between viable habitats if otherwise isolated communities of that species are to remain healthy. Quammen calls the sort of habitat fragmentation caused by current logging practices—the practices Bass argues against—"ominous," a "phenomenon . . . known by various labels, one of which is ecosystem decay" (440).

Similarly, Bass writes that it might be "a fairly easy act to 'create' or protect or 'set aside' a single wilderness, but if we do not give it our respect, we have not fixed or even approached fixing the problem" (*Lost Grizzlies*, 156). Besides, as Donald M. Waller points out, islanding can "enhance opportunities for the weedy and often exotic species that increasingly dominate our landscapes, further displacing many native species." Such conditions, if left unchecked, "will surely be catastrophic" ("Getting Back to the Right Nature," 553–54). This catastrophe is what Bass hopes to avert with his work, especially with respect to his adopted home in the Yaak Valley. The valley's magic is contingent upon its ability to offer a complete biological corridor of wildness between Canada and the western United States, and the encircling clearcuts, he argues, clearly inhibit that completeness.

Cronon's argument that "the wilderness idea" itself is a romantic notion—that it is a product of wishful thinking—relies on a no less wishful belief that our culture would be willing to accept setasides as suggested by Callicott and Nelson. News reports about the reintroduction of wolves to Yellowstone and to the Southwest (the process Bass describes in *The New Wolves*) give some indication of the sort of opposition to restoration efforts that often arises. Jim Zumbo, writing in *Outdoor Life,* cites the political opposition of Wyoming senators Alan Simpson and Malcolm Wallop to the reestablishment of wolves in Yellowstone ("Wolf Wars," 81). He quotes Simpson as acknowledging his "distaste for the whole thing" (the return of wolves), along with his fear of the effect predators might have on the state's "hunting harvest" (81). Local hunting interests indeed fear a slippery slope: if wolves are allowed to become established in the area, there will never be any effort to control them, no matter what damage they do.

Associated Press journalist Tim Molloy, writing on the wolves whose reintroduction Bass chronicles in *The New Wolves,* notes the objections of one local rancher, LaMar Clark, who fears that "the wolves threaten families, cattle, deer and other prey" in the area of the reintroduction ("It's Man vs. Wolves," 2A). Other locals speak of their "fear [that] they could lose their ranching rights" to wolf populations (2A). Barbara Marks, whose family has been in the area since 1891, argues that she—as a local resident—ought to know better than the federal government what's good for her land (2A). Echoing claims by locals that feds are "cramming it [wolf reintroduction] down our throats" and that the efforts show "disregard for the concerns of the public" ("Plans to Reintroduce Wolves," B12), Marks argues that "the tax dollars [used to reintroduce the wolves] have been flushed down the toilet" (Murr, "Deadly Days," 34).

Given the intensity of local opposition, how could we expect either individuals or social structures opposed to environmental protection to accept any proposal for wildlife preserves or restoration? What seems to be missing from such proposals is an effort to channel the discussion away from momentary self-interest and into a broader vision that recognizes wildness itself as truly essential.

Through his recognition of nature's sacrality, Bass seeks to establish the basis for such a broader vision. Though he draws increasing attention to it, he knows that in Western culture sacrality is generally understood in terms of traditional churches. In *Winter,* though, Bass writes that he is "so tired of churches [he] could roar," calling a visiting missionary who asks what church he belongs to "dangerous" (101). When he later asks, "Why would anyone come into church and kill all of the grizzlies?" (*Lost Grizzlies,* 149), he distinguishes between the missionaries' "dangerous" interior church and the exterior church of the woods and mountains, recalling Emerson's recognition that formal, traditional religion is an unsatisfactory way to address matters of the soul. In his essay "The Lord's Supper" (1832), Emerson writes that the true role of Jesus is "to redeem us from a formal religion, and teach us to seek our well-being in the formation of the soul" (22, 24). In "The Divinity School Address" (1838), he elaborates this point, since traditional religion prevents "the exploration of the moral nature of man," and suggests that "it is already beginning to indicate character and religion to withdraw from religious meetings" (111, 112). Bass's evocation of a natural sacrality evinces a clearly Emersonian exploration of morality found in nature.

Bass is always passionate about the need for environmental preservation; but, as Warwick Fox has pointed out, no true environmental reform can be possible without addressing the very human tendency toward self-interest. Fox describes what he calls a "transpersonal ecology," noting that most attempts to change behavior and attitudes toward the natural world are based on "moral injunctions," which, he argues, are flawed since they seek to impose a particular morality (*Toward a Transpersonal Ecology,* 243). But, as Bass has discovered, neither the logic of preservation nor any moral blandishments about our responsibility toward other species have been effective in changing environmental attitudes, whether toward the Yaak in particular or toward wildness in general.

Just as Bass realizes that we need to develop a new paradigm for conservation, Fox suggests that the necessary method should be one that "*invites* the readers' interest rather than . . . *demands* the reader's compliance" (243; Fox's emphasis). "Rather than dealing with moral *injunctions,*" he suggests,

> transpersonal ecologists are therefore inclined far more to what might be referred to as experiential *invitations:* readers or listeners are invited to experience themselves as intimately bound up with the world around them, to such an extent that it becomes more or less impossible to *refrain* from wider identification. (244–45)

Fox does not mean to suggest that he becomes either the tree in Cronon's garden or the one in Bass's woods, but rather that he shares with both of them "a single unfolding reality" (232). By learning to identify the tree with the "me," he continues, we become less able, or at least less willing, to accept damage to the tree. In this context we might see Bass as looking for a means by which we might identify our own sense of self with the "single unfolding reality" of the Yaak and therefore become unable or unwilling to countenance further damage to that valley.

Fox refers to this move as "transpersonalization,"[6] but how, and by what means, might so radical a shift in our own self-identification be accomplished? It is easy to see that neither you nor I are wolves, bears, or even ichneumon wasps. By virtue of our individual and separately distinguishable bodies we are each physically *separate* entities.[7]

Rather than in the physical realm, which seems ineffective as a place to envision the transpersonalization of the self, Bass locates his own identification with wildness in his sense of wonder, where notions of separation are perhaps less certain, less convincing.[8] His own process of identification with wildness began with his initial season in Montana, when he recognized that the owls and coyotes around his home "catch mice the way I gather wood. We're all close, we're all tied together" (*Winter,* 36). "I felt like I'd waited all my life," he continues, "to peel off my city ways, city life, and get into the woods—molting, like an insect or a snake" (160).

But the sense of identification with the Yaak that Bass experiences is only part of his process. He also begins to merge his own sensibility with that of the animals whose lives he studies. He writes, for instance, that *The Lost Grizzlies* "is a story of bears and mountains, and yet everything is connected somehow: my friends and family and the woods" (181). Arguing not just for preservation but for restoration of wildness, he points out that the reintroduction of wolves to an ecosystem presents "a chance to let a swaying balance be struck: not just for wolves, but for humans, too. . . . to have the balance the majority of people claim to long for, it must be struck by the wolves as much as by the people. The wolves must have some say in defining it, or it will not be valid" (*Ninemile Wolves,* 10). The wolves "remind us of ourselves on our better days, our best days. They teach us splendidly about the overriding force of nature, too—about the way we've managed to suppress and ignore it in ourselves, or judge it" (39).

The transpersonal identification, which begins as a turn inward, turns back toward the natural world and its inherent wonder as Bass writes of humans and wolves as "brothers in the hunt [but] brothers in something else, too. I am convinced that it has something to do with internal fire, soul, and the creation and pursuit of mystery" (*Ninemile Wolves,* 140). Although he acknowledges that "[a] man is not a bear, and a bear is not a man," Bass recognizes that some readers might still accuse him of anthropomorphizing when he points out that "there is definitely a mixing going on, a merging" between himself and the bears, or that "to the eye of God and to the spirit of those mountains, man is nearly indistinguishable from bear, and that it is more than metaphor to say that we may as well be looking for ourselves" (*Lost Grizzlies,* 43, 99). Yet, he argues, "in some respects, it seems bend-over-backwards ridiculous *not* to, for if a wolf does not have a spirit, then what animal, ourselves included, can be said to have one?" (*Ninemile Wolves,* 131). Bass's "mixing and merging" with wild species results, I believe, not from a physical identification with wolf or bear, but from a sense of that spirit, just as his transpersonal turn inward is not an egocentric turn toward his individual self but a turn of the spirit—or rather a turn *to* the spirit—that inhabits all species.

The spirit inhabiting both wolves and bears also suggests to Bass that "magic" continues to exist in those places still wild enough to support these predators. Returning to the core of his activism, he writes of his fear that our society is "running out of the thing that once sustained us: a certain spirit and imagination upon the land, and certain stories told to us by that land" (*New Wolves,* 121); he has come to believe that this spirit and these stories are what comprise the wonder he sees in wildness.

With increasing focus on that wonder, Bass begins to see it as a "resonance . . . that washed, as if in an echo, through us" ("Raccoons of Yaak," 23). Given the dissonance so often felt between science and the type of faith Bass articulates, it may be ironic to read resonance as a concept best understood through the discipline of atomic physics. In *First You Build a Cloud* science writer K. C. Cole describes resonance as a property of atomic vibrations, which determines such things as "the difference between the visible and invisible, between transparent and opaque" (169). In his recognition of Yaak's resonance, Bass is trying to render the valley's wonder "visible" to a very different sort of layperson.

Where resonance to Cole is a specifically physical concept (as might be expected in a work on physics), Bass uses the term more figuratively when he speaks of the resonance of wildness. Yet perhaps the scientist and the artist are not so far apart as they first might seem: for Cole and Bass share an understanding of resonance as a means of differentiation, whether of physical or metaphysical properties. Cole writes of resonance as a measuring tool, while Bass cites its presence in his call for a new form of science—a nonreductionary science—that will be able to measure the "resonance" of the Yaak's magic, the deep sense of wonder that Bass frequently notes as a characteristic of wildness. Stephen Jay Gould recently argued that the integration of carefully articulated "science" and "religion"—which we might see as the domains of, respectively, the physical and the metaphysical—is essential to the creation of Wisdom in "the fullness of life."[9] Cole writes that "a scientific understanding of nature can deepen the awe, expand the sense of mystery" (*First You Build a Cloud,* 69). And it is in Bass's sense of that mystery and wonder, I believe, that the two modes—the physical and the metaphysical—can achieve the successful integration that Gould calls for.

All of nature resonates. But since, as Cole notes, much of the physical universe is invisible to our physical senses, it may well be that nature has other qualities whose resonance our conscious senses cannot register, like the so-called dark matter that is said to represent most of the universe's mass. The quark, to take another of Cole's examples, was completely unknown until its existence was first postulated and then sought out by scientists. Just so, Bass asks that both science and the culture that encompasses it begin to consider the possibility that what he calls wonder is both real and tangible. Recognition of wonder—of what Thoreau calls "the subtle magnetism in nature" ("Walking," 104)—as inherent in wildness might be understood as a response to the perceived resonance of those wild places: a shared vibration by which, were we to become aware of and attuned to it, we might achieve the wider sense of identification necessary for environmental preservation.

The idea of wonder as means of both identification with and advocacy for wildness is crucial to any understanding of Bass's recent work. He uses wonder both to advocate for wilderness preservation and as the goal in saving both wild places and wild species. But he is clear about his priorities: "I'm not aware of worshipping individual animals or species. My affinity, my allegiance, is with complete landscapes, with wild places," he writes in *The New Wolves* (126). The presence of grizzlies in the San Juans, that is to say, is not as important to him as knowing that the region retains sufficient wildness that they *could* live there. Nor is his advocacy of wonder limited entirely to the more-than-human world; he is as adamant about its importance to the human spirit as to wildness. Finding proof that grizzlies live in the San Juans, he writes, is "not quite like trying to prove God's existence—if there's mud or snow, a grizzly will at least leave tracks—but beyond that, it's almost the same" (*Lost Grizzlies,* 28).

The search for grizzlies, like the reintroduction of wolves (whether "accidental" as in *The Ninemile Wolves* or orchestrated as in *The New Wolves*), is not primarily about human needs, beyond, perhaps, the human need for the wonder that such animals give us. Although it is crucial to know that "no matter how chaotic things get in cities, there still exists in the wilderness a system of logic and grace," wild places "do not exist for this reason—they were here before us and they will, of course, outlast us—but it cannot be denied or ignored that certain places can recharge and cleanse the spirit, can wash away the befouled crust of unhealthy impulses and alienations we've accumulated" (*Lost Grizzlies,* 69).

Environmental activism, writes Thomas Moore, "has to be rooted in the concerns of the soul" ("Ecology," 144). Matters of the spirit, especially when left to dogmatic traditions of the sort that Bass labels "dangerous," readily lend themselves to abstraction. This is the issue Moore highlights with his invocation of a "natural spirituality" that "rises directly out of the human encounter with the natural world" ("Mystic Clouds," 32). By advocating wonder as a feature of wildness and arguing its importance *to human society and human individuals,* Bass has located the means to the transpersonal identification that Warwick Fox calls for, between the human and the more-than-human world. The wonder Bass experiences is the sort of faith Moore describes, one derived from Bass's prolonged interactions with wild places and wild species. Fenton Johnson, writing in *Harper's Magazine,* distinguishes between belief and faith: he links the former with the sort of dogma that Bass calls dangerous; the latter is "the essential virtue of science, and likewise of any religion that is not self-deception" ("Beyond Belief," 40). Faith, Johnson continues, attends to "one's place in and responsibility to the workings of the great order" (52).

Bass has combined the characteristics of science (which we see in his close observation and analysis of the natural world) with those of faith to develop his call for a scientific exploration of the notion of wonder. Thus we see in his work the integration of the two domains, a process that Gould argues will lead to wisdom. By wisely advancing the idea of "Wonder" in his advocacy for wildness, Bass offers a new form of argument no longer dependent on evocation either of loss or of anger and no longer devoid of hope. He has, in effect, added a corollary to Thoreau's famous maxim: "In wonder is the preservation of wildness."

Notes

1. In his essay "The Literature of Loss," Bass defines wildness as "that part of the world that I could have no hope of controlling" (76).

2. Bass has periodically sent out mass-mailings (including one to the membership list of the Association for the Study of Literature and Environment) calling for help in protecting the Yaak. He has also distributed such letters at some of his public readings.

3. Bass's phrasing suggests a connection to the famous "green fire" that Aldo Leopold notes in a wolf's eye in "Thinking Like a Mountain" (*Sand County Almanac,* 129–33). The events in that essay mark the beginning of Leopold's shift toward the conservation of wildness, a movement followed by Bass and many other contemporary nature writers.

4. The phrase is from David Abram, who also argues that "we are human only in contact, and conviviality, with what is not human" (*Spell of the Sensuous,* ix).

5. Bass's reading of "Fiber" occurred on Saturday morning, 19 July 1997, at the second biennial conference of the Association for the Study of Literature and Environment (ASLE), 17–19 July 1997, at the University of Montana, Missoula. The reading was published as *Fiber* by the University of Georgia Press in 1998.

6. Fox uses the prefix *trans-* to indicate several convergent meanings: "beyond" and "changing thoroughly" (as in "transcend"). "In general," he writes, "the most convenient way of capturing these senses of *trans-* is simply to employ the word *beyond*" (*Toward a Transpersonal Ecology,* 198). Thus the term "transpersonalization" represents a move or understanding beyond the human.

7. I do not mean by this that "humans are separate from nature," as the saying goes, but only that we are each—in a purely physical sense—distinct amid all other physical entities, as is every other life form.

8. I refer here to Bass's identification with wildness, not to wildness itself. One holds, perhaps, wildness in the mind as one holds a baseball in the hand: for both wildness and the baseball have presence external to the mind or the hand that holds them.

9. This argument is at the center of Gould's book *Rocks of Ages: Science and Religion in the Fullness of Life;* the phrase "fullness of life" appears only in the book's subtitle and not in the text itself.

Works Cited

Abram, David. *The Spell of the Sensuous: Perception and Language in a More-Than-Human World.* New York: Vintage, 1996.

Bass, Rick. *The Book of Yaak.* Boston: Houghton Mifflin, 1996.

———. *Brown Dog of the Yaak: Essays in Art and Activism.* Minneapolis: Milkweed, 1999.

———. *Fiber.* Athens: University of Georgia Press, 1998.

———. "The Kootenai Five." *Whole Terrain* 7 (1998/99): 62–65.

———. Letter mass-mailed to ASLE membership, dated 17 December 1993.

———. Letter mass-mailed to ASLE membership, dated 21 December 1994.

———. Letter to author, dated 10 April 1994.

———. "The Literature of Loss." *Manõa* 4:2 (Fall 1992): 75–76.

———. *The Lost Grizzlies: A Search for Survivors in the Wilderness of Colorado.* Boston: Houghton Mifflin, 1995.

———. *The New Wolves: The Return of the Mexican Wolf to the American Southwest.* New York: Lyons Press, 1998.

———. *The Ninemile Wolves* (1992). New York: Ballantine, 1993.

———. "The Raccoons of Yaak." *Orion* 18:2 (Spring 1999): 18–27.

———. *Winter: Notes from Montana.* Boston: Houghton Mifflin, 1991.

Botkin, Daniel B. *Discordant Harmonies: A New Ecology for the Twenty-first Century.* New York: Oxford, 1990.

Callicott, J. Baird, and Michael P. Nelson, eds. *The Great New Wilderness Debate.* Athens: University of Georgia Press, 1998.

Cole, K. C. *First You Build a Cloud.* San Diego: Harcourt Brace, 1999.

Cronon, William. "The Trouble with Wilderness, or, Getting Back to the Wrong Nature." In *The Great New Wilderness Debate,* ed. J. Baird Callicott and Michael P. Nelson, 471–97. Athens: University of Georgia Press, 1998.

Dillard, Annie. "Living Like Weasels." In *Teaching a Stone to Talk: Expeditions and Encounters,* 29–34. New York: HarperPerennial, 1982.

———. *Pilgrim at Tinker Creek.* New York: Harper's Magazine Press, 1974.

Edwards, Jonathan. "Sinners in the Hands of an Angry God." In *A Jonathan Edwards Reader,* ed. Harry S. Stout and Kenneth P. Minkema, 89–105. New Haven: Yale University Press, 1995.

Emerson, Ralph Waldo. "The Divinity School Address." In *Selections from Ralph Waldo Emerson,* ed. Stephen E. Whicher, 100–116. Boston: Houghton Mifflin, 1957.

———. "The Lord's Supper." In *Miscellanies by Ralph Waldo Emerson,* 1–25. Boston: Houghton Mifflin, 1890.

Fox, Warwick. *Toward a Transpersonal Ecology: Developing New Foundations for Environmentalism* (1990). Albany: SUNY Press, 1995.

Gould, Stephen Jay. *Rocks of Ages: Science and Religion in the Fullness of Life*. New York: Ballantine, 1999.

Hay, John. *The Immortal Wilderness*. New York: Norton, 1987.

———. *Nature's Year: The Seasons of Cape Cod*. Garden City, N.Y.: Doubleday, 1961.

Johnson, Fenton. "Beyond Belief: A Skeptic Searches for an American Faith." *Harper's Magazine* (September 1998): 39–54.

Leopold, Aldo. *A Sand County Almanac and Sketches Here and There* (1949). New York: Oxford University Press, 1987.

Maslow, Abraham. *Religions, Values, and Peak-Experiences* (1964). New York: Viking, 1970.

Molloy, Tim. "It's Man vs. Wolves on Public Land." *Reno Gazette-Journal,* 22 November 1998, 2A.

Moore, Thomas. "Ecology: Sacred Homemaking." In *The Soul of Nature: Celebrating the Spirit of the Earth,* ed. Michael Tobias and Georgianne Cowan, 137–44. New York: Plume, 1996.

———. "Mystic Clouds and Natural Spirituality." *Orion* 16:3 (Summer 1997): 30–33.

Murr, Andrew. "Deadly Days for Wolves." *Newsweek,* 30 November 1998, 34.

"Plans to Reintroduce Wolves Draw Fire." *Salt Lake Tribune,* 7 October 1994, B12.

Quammen, David. *The Song of the Dodo: Island Biogeography in an Age of Extinction*. New York: Scribner, 1996.

Raymo, Chet. *Skeptics and True Believers: The Exhilarating Connection between Science and Religion*. New York: Walker & Company, 1998.

Slovic, Scott. "Rick Bass: A Portrait." In *Brown Dog of the Yaak: Essays in Art and Activism,* by Rick Bass, 123–37. Minneapolis: Milkweed, 1999.

Thoreau, Henry David. "Walking" (1862). In *Natural History Essays,* 93–136. Salt Lake City: Peregrine Smith, 1980.

Waller, Donald M. "Getting Back to the Right Nature: A Reply to Cronon's 'The Trouble with Wilderness.'" In *The Great New Wilderness Debate,* ed. J. Baird Callicott and Michael P. Nelson, 540–67. Athens: University of Georgia Press, 1998.

Weltzien, O. Alan. *Rick Bass*. Western Writers Series. Boise: Boise State University Press, 1998.

Wolf, Tom. "What Price for the Howl of the Wolf?" *Los Angeles Times,* 5 February 1995, M1, M6.

Zumbo, Jim. "Wolf Wars." *Outdoor Life* 193:2 (February 1994): 59–61, 81–84.

The Space between Text and Action

Redefining Nature Writing through the Work of Rick Bass and John McPhee

Diana L. Ashe

> *I went home and fell asleep immediately and dreamed not of wood ducks and alligators but of house subcommittees and legislative battles waged over clean air and western wilderness areas.*
>
> Rick Bass, *Wild to the Heart* (37)

The genre of nature writing, though well-represented in anthologies and college courses, is in the midst of a major identity crisis: purists of the form define the genre narrowly enough to exclude many of the most well-known and influential contemporary writers about the natural world. Complicating the issue further, many of these writers refuse to be associated with the term "nature writer," perceiving the label as a stigma. What we are left with, then, is a prolific and significant group of writers who write about nature but disregard the nature-writing genre and a group of purists of nature writing who neither attempt nor accept innovations in the genre.

Richard Mabey, editor of *The Oxford Book of Nature Writing*, remarks that "what strikes one most forcibly is the common ground in nature writing. From the earliest times, the same themes have been persistently returned to: nature's profusion and profligacy, the mysteries of migration, the magnanimity of adaptation, the cycle of the seasons" (ix). While the selections he anthologized certainly hold true to this definition, only a small handful of the hundreds of passages were written after 1975, though the collection was published in 1995. The twenty years between Mabey's anthology and Annie Dillard's Pulitzer Prize–winning *Pilgrim at Tinker*

Creek, published in 1975, brought an astounding volume of writing about nature, but little of it has fit Mabey's definition.

Peter Fritzell, in *Nature Writing and America: Essays upon a Cultural Type,* offers a more inclusive definition of "'nature writing' and 'nature books'—personal narratives of experiences in or with 'nature,' as we say, semi-scientific accounts of individual animals or species, records of travel in 'wildlands,' stories of meditative residence in the not-so-wild, field guides, guides to nature study, and various kinds of how-to books, including even guides to legislation and political action" (37). Fritzell underscores the difficulty of trying to locate the complete scope of the genre, saying that "[n]o more than the bookstores or the Library of Congress have we as devotees of nature writing been able to systematize our readings or our ruminations about them" (37). And while he is amenable to contemporary nature writing and writers, even singling out Barry Lopez in his list of exemplars of the genre and quoting Edward Abbey, he saves his highest praise for Annie Dillard, saying that "no book of recent vintage comes closer than *Pilgrim at Tinker Creek* to capturing (and, hence, clarifying) the underlying heritage of American nature writing . . . none comes closer to the often divisive and occasionally enlivening experience of trying to land oneself in America" (219). Unfortunately, the "underlying heritage of American nature writing" is a legacy that Dillard and many of her contemporaries would rather not accept.

While they are constantly and consistently associated with nature writing, many (if not most) of today's writers-about-nature want nothing of the title. A shift in motive has occurred since the 1962 publication of Rachel Carson's *Silent Spring*—just two years before the passing of the Wilderness Act, which, Lawrence Buell contends, "marked the full-fledged emergence of environmentalism as a topic of public concern in America" (*Environmental Imagination,* 10). With environmentalism gaining mass appeal, nature writing exhibited a shift in motive toward activism and away from reflection. This new trend revolutionized the genre, bringing in more, and more diverse, writers who write in more diverse ways for a more diverse readership. Finding the designation of nature writing too limiting, contemporary writers have simultaneously expanded and denied the genre, all the while clinging to its most honored pioneers.

That contemporary nature writing is in such a state of conceptual disarray is unsurprising, considering the lack of consensus as to its beginnings. Peter Fritzell offers a time-line diagram of the development of the genre, entitled "Diachronic view of nature writing," that spans the centuries from 300 B.C. through A.D. 1900 (*Nature Writing*, 80). By 1900 Fritzell indicates strains of nature writing in nature poetry, pastoral literature, autobiography, rural literature, natural history, and "Linnean systematic biology." What happens after 1900, though, is not so clear. John A. Murray, editor of the Sierra Club's American Nature Writing Series, tells us that the term "nature writing" itself is relatively recent and "generally is said to begin with the works of Henry David Thoreau. Most scholars of the field consider nature writing to include all literary works that take nature as a theme" (*Sierra Club*, vii). Daniel G. Payne, in *Voices in the Wilderness: American Nature Writing and Environmental Politics*, disagrees, contending that "American nature writing has existed ever since European explorers began describing the 'New World'—and even long before that, if Native American oral traditions are taken into account" (1). Buell argues that "American environmental nonfiction predates Thoreau by a longer span than he predates us," reaching back to John Smith's histories of the colonies in 1632 (*Environmental Imagination*, 397–98).

Contemporary Environmental Advocates: Resisting the "Nature Writer" Label

In *The Environmental Imagination* Buell traces some of the reasons why authors might be hesitant to associate themselves with nature writing. "[T]he serious pursuit of natural history, from its premodern origins in the late Renaissance, has often been considered somewhat 'grotesque.' Field naturalists in the early republic were widely seen as eccentric misfits. . . . Thoreau repeatedly notes that his neighbors thought his preoccupation with nature absurd" (104–5). He quotes English biographer Henry Salt as saying that the general public, by the end of the 1800s, thought of the naturalist as "a lunatic at large." Even Charles Darwin's father felt "that naturalism was a useless profession" (105). Buell also describes the struggle that Rachel Carson underwent before she published *Silent Spring*, having to surrender to her editors' "middlebrow nature book decorums" (292). Even Buell himself contends with the genre's reputation in praising two of its masterpieces, Barry Lopez's *Arctic Dreams* and William Least Heat-Moon's *PrairyErth:* "No apology whatsoever needs to be made for these works on the score of belonging to a 'minor' genre like 'nature writing.' In point of thematic and formal sophistication, they fully equal the classics of American autobiography and narrative fiction. If their stature is not recognized for awhile, and it probably won't be, that is because we have not learned how to read them" (270). And Buell chooses against the label in his own scholarship, preferring "'environmental nonfiction' or 'environmental prose' to 'nature writing,' which is restrictive both in its implied identification of 'nature' as the writer's exclusive field of environmental vision and in its tendency to exclude borderline cases like eclectic travel and autobiographical and sermonic material" (429).

For all of these reasons and perhaps a few more, many of the most often cited figures in studies of nature writing simply reject the label for their own work. Payne confronts this issue in *Voices in the Wilderness,* explaining that he uses the term "nature writers" "reluctantly, fully aware of the deficiencies of the term," and adding that Barry Lopez and Edward Abbey are among those who "have complained, with considerable justification, about being relegated to that category." The reason for the reluctance of Payne, Lopez, and Abbey to embrace the genre, according to Payne, is that nature writing "today encompasses far more than just natural history, and . . . because we are only beginning to realize that humankind and nature are inextricably linked, both ethically and ecologically, 'nature,' in all its forms, is the theme for our age and one that should not be dismissed as simply the province of 'nature writers'" (6). Payne emphasizes the nuance in the word "relegated" to convey lesser importance, rather than unbiased taxonomy, and plays on the word "province" to insinuate that he perhaps sees the natural history version of nature writing as provincial. Abbey's resistance to the nature writing label can be at least partially attributed to his often contrary persona, but his words on the subject do offer some insight. In the preface to the twentieth anniversary edition of *Desert Solitaire,* Abbey muses: "Even my novels are sometimes classified as nature writing! . . . I never wanted to be anything but a writer, period. An author. A creator of fictions and essays, sometimes poems" (quoted in Murray, *Sierra Club,* 116). Abbey seems to be resisting any qualifiers or limitations at all on his writing, not necessarily finding fault with nature writing in particular.

The purists of "the province of nature writing" hesitate to invite Edward Abbey into their realm, to any extent beyond *Desert Solitaire,* but Barry Lopez they would miss. Unfortunately, this voluntary attrition in the forces of self-identified nature writers takes its toll from more rarefied circles, too. Annie Dillard's *Pilgrim at Tinker Creek* has been labeled "a natural history essay, an environmentalist lyric, and a naturalist autobiography," which (considering her Pulitzer Prize) led to Dillard being considered perhaps our most renowned living nature writer (Smith, *Annie Dillard*, 42). However, Dillard's biographer, Linda L. Smith, claims that while she is often compared "with such twentieth century nature writers as Loren Eiseley, Rachel Carson, Edward Abbey, Aldo Leopold, and John Muir," she "is not primarily a nature writer. In fact, nature takes a progressively lesser role in her work after *Pilgrim at Tinker Creek*. Even if we look only at this, her first book, we still see many differences between it and the work of those typically considered twentieth-century nature writers" (42). Smith cites Dillard's Christianity and her "concern with aesthetics" as evidence of her status as an outsider to nature writing and supports her assessment with Dillard's own words from a 1981 interview: "There's usually a bit of nature in what I write, but I don't consider myself a nature writer either. Weirdly, I would consider myself a fiction writer who's dealt mostly with non-fiction. . . . Its content is the world" (42). Evidencing a bit of snobbery about the form and making a questionable claim, Smith places Dillard on a higher artistic plane than that occupied by nature writing; she argues that the role of nature in *Pilgrim at Tinker Creek* is "the means, art as the end. It is the presence of such an intention . . . that marks the difference between nature writing and literature" (43).

Reviewer Don Scheese would take issue with Smith's idea that Christianity separates Dillard's work from nature writing: "Nature writers, by their very calling, are fundamentally engaged with matters of metaphysics. . . . Annie Dillard's overt religious orientation and purpose recall an earlier era when natural historians such as John Ray and William Paley wrote primarily to prove the existence of God; natural history and natural theology, we are reminded, were once synonymous" (Review, 197). Again we see hierarchy at play; Smith is making a value judgment against nature writing, without apparently being aware of its origins, that places it somewhat lower than literature, art, or religion. Scheese disallows Dillard's protests by noticing the components of the nature writer in everything she does: "As in all her works, she is fascinated by the ways people interact with the land, how they shape and are shaped by the natural environment" (193). His judgment of Dillard may offer the clearest definition of a nature writer that we have yet encountered.

As they distance themselves from nature writing, though, these writers choose to identify themselves instead with forms: Abbey with fiction, essays, and poetry and Dillard with nonfiction. John McPhee's biographer, Michael Pearson, picks up on Dillard's preference, describing McPhee as a writer of literary nonfiction and taking care to explain in a separate chapter McPhee's connection to that form. Echoing Fritzell's lament, Pearson reminds us that "volumes of McPhee's work are scattered all over the library, under call numbers for Recreation, Military Science, Education, Nature, and elsewhere" (*John McPhee,* 13). Buell reiterates the multiform nature of this kind of writing: "In this book I have repeatedly referred to 'environmental nonfiction' as an entity, whereas nothing is more striking than its variegated character. . . . [*Walden*] can be read as a poem, a novel, an autobiography, a travel narrative, a sermon, a treatise. Sometimes the text positively flaunts its diversity, fragmenting into a multigeneric collage" (*Environmental Imagination,* 397). While "nonfiction" certainly describes much of McPhee's and Dillard's work, the term is both too specific and too general to describe what these writers share with Carson, Lopez, Abbey, Bass, and Thoreau—too specific because many of these writers also write stories, poetry, novels, etc., and too general because they also share more in common than fact-based narratives. Edwin Black might argue that these writers see only the internal characteristics of their own work, rather than seeing the web of related works: "Genre refers to the place of the thing in the universe and to its generation as an adaptive and relational entity. Form refers to the constitution and individuality of the thing and to its formation as an entity sufficiently autonomous as to be identifiable. Taken together, the words 'genre' and 'form' are complementary in that 'genre' refers to external relations and 'form' refers to internal relations" (*Rhetorical Questions,* 98).

John McPhee, for example, "has become the most effective literary advocate for environmentalism," but resists the label of nature writer, like so many of his peers (Pearson, *John McPhee,* 22). "He has said, 'I've written about nature and it is terribly important to me,' but he bristles at being defined simply as a nature writer. . . . Although not all nature writers are environmentalists, it is as if he senses that the term 'nature writer' can often be aligned with the word 'polemist'" (100). McPhee's resistance echoes Payne's and Abbey's notion that nature writing is a limitation, a label that puts a writer down as "simply" concerned with nature. The word "polemist" also resonates strongly with the judgments of other nature writers and scholars. Murray mentions "the jeremiads and polemics of just about every nature essayist of our time" (*Sierra*

Club, 17); Edward Abbey "succinctly characterize[s] his own polemical approach" (Payne, *Voices*, 153); Pearson claims that McPhee "is not known as a polemicist or a philosopher" (*John McPhee*, 21); and reviewer William Rueckert calls Rick Bass's *The Ninemile Wolves* an "often polemical account" (Review, 199). In the same review he tells us that *The Ninemile Wolves* is "not just another piece of nature writing in praise of 'wild nature,' nor is it a fanatical (or sentimental) animal-rights tract" (201). These comments reveal the two labels that almost every contemporary environmentalist fears: on the one hand, "just" a nature writer or, on the other, a fanatical polemicist.

Rick Bass and John McPhee challenge these dismissive labels from opposite ends of the spectrum of contemporary environmental advocacy discourse. Bass's very personal writing arises from his own life and is often desperate in tone, making him an easy target for the "polemicist" accusation. McPhee's journalistic writing arises from situations he has created and remains almost neutral in tone, making it seem viable to consider him "just a nature writer." Because both of them balance a carefully honed ethos and an environmentalist agenda, these labels are absurdly reductive. Bass and McPhee are also inarguably influential figures in the genre, so any theory that hopes to help nature writing encompass environmental advocacy discourse must include both writers.

Rick Bass: Using Ethos to Avoid the "Polemicist" Label

Since *The Deer Pasture* (1985), Bass's writing has been associated with both the nature writing tradition headed by Thoreau and the activist spur of that tradition associated with Edward Abbey and his milder sympathizers. Through short stories, novellas, a novel, essays, and literary nonfiction, Bass considers and reconsiders the place and role of humans in nature. However, he takes up this question with an increasing sense of exigence, a developing urgency about the imbalance of human and natural cycles. Bass's essays have always been very personal; readers can even follow the development of his relationship with his wife as it progresses from book to book. His fiction offers the same personal style.

With *The Ninemile Wolves* (1992), though, Bass explores the possibility of literary nonfiction to deliver a "feisty, often polemical account of the return of wolves to the Ninemile Valley... after a sixty-year absence" (Rueckert, Review, 199). With an impassioned plea, Bass presses the implications of the wolves' predicament onto readers:

> I have come away from following the Ninemile wolves convinced that to diminish their lives would be wicked; that it would involve a diminishing of a significant force in the world, that it would slow the earth's potential and cripple our own species' ability to live with force; that without the Ninemile wolves, and other wolves in the Rockies there would be a brown-out, to extend the metaphor of electricity that the power would dim, and the bright lights of potential—of strength in the world—would grow dimmer. (139–40)

Bass increases the urgency of this message a few short paragraphs later, daring his readers: "You've come too far in this story to turn away now, when I start talking crazy like this. You can't turn away. We have to follow" (140). This "highly charged moral and ontological language" occurs again and again in *The Ninemile Wolves,* bringing the imperative of action into the realm of literary nonfiction (Rueckert, Review, 199).

Bass does not take up this direct approach again in *The Lost Grizzlies* (1995), but does continue with some of the techniques he started in *The Ninemile Wolves,* including pondering the fate of the grizzlies in a very personal and conversational style and asking a few direct and pointed questions of his readers. *The Lost Grizzlies* also follows *The Ninemile Wolves* by offering contact information for readers who choose to get involved with the issues at hand, his stated goal in both books.

This space between text and action is where Bass voices his greatest frustration in *The Book of Yaak* in 1996. Acknowledging the special magic of writing fiction, he laments in his introduction that "[t]his book is not like that. It's a sourcebook, a handbook, a weapon of the heart. To a literary writer, it's a sin, to ask something of the reader, rather than to give; and to know the end, to know your agenda, from the very start, rather than discovering it along the way, or at the end itself" (xiii). Stepping outside the understood boundaries of his customary genres is something he wants us to believe that he has been forced to do, something he can only do out of genuine desperation. His excuse for this transgression comes immediately: "My valley is on fire—my valley is burning. It has been on fire for over twenty years. These essays—these pleas to act to save it—it's all I know how to do. I don't know if a book can help protect a valley, and the people who live in that valley. I know that a book can harm these things . . ." (xiii).

With these words, Bass opens his 190-page plea to rescue the valley, to get some attention for it from legislators but not from tourists, to spur his readers to act for his cause. He is self-conscious about his choice to shed literary trappings for plaintive begging, realizing both the potential for failure and the potential for bringing harm to the Yaak Valley along with the attention. As Fritzell reminds us, "In this business of nature and nature writing in America, there is a great desire to cry out, to warn and forewarn as well as to celebrate—but there is also a great desire to be silent" (*Nature Writing*, 295). In addition to the risk of drawing too much attention to a place that should remain unnoticed and untouched, Bass is also painfully aware of the possibility of alienating readers with the banality of his arguments: "I shiver, for these are the same words—the precise words—one finds in the third-class mailings for every other so-just cause at home and abroad" (xiv).

The Book of Yaak shares an identity crisis that so many works of environmental advocacy share, with its use of the jeremiad preventing a comfortable fit in the category of literary nonfiction. Bass himself hesitates to place the book into any framework, because his motivations and his experience writing it are so different: "I'm not writing this like any of my other books—certainly not like my novel. This is not really a book. This is instead an artifact of the woods, like a chunk of rhyolite, a shed deer antler, a bear skull, a heron feather" (xiv). Without an automatic frame in which to view *The Book of Yaak,* Bass and his reader are both unsettled from the very first page—and he makes sure that no feeling of comfort (which he fears will result in complacency) will settle over his readers.

To convey or, better, to transfer his overwhelming sense of urgency about the destruction of the Yaak Valley, Bass painstakingly protects his own ethos as he works to protect this rich and diverse natural area. *The Book of Yaak* self-consciously breaks literary taboos that he deems in his introduction "a sin": he directly addresses his reader, begs that reader to take action for his cause, and offers no surprises, instead revealing his intentions in his introduction (xiii). Because Bass is painfully aware of these transgressions, he must never let his readers lose their identification with him and his way of life. The careful balancing of his ethos depends upon two overriding strategies: first, to paint the situation as dire enough to justify his transgressions; and, second, to paint himself as a reluctant messenger of the valley, beset with misgivings and conflicting impulses.

To set up the Yaak Valley's tragic losses and impending doom, Bass likens it to a house on fire, allowing him to illustrate both the dire situation at hand and his own panic: "If your home were burning, for instance, would you grab a bucket of water to pour on it, or would you step back and write a poem about it?" (10). The urgency of the house on fire is amplified because it is not just any house; it is "your home," where the reader lives, that is burning. Bass heightens the tension of this situation by imposing realistic time limits on the valley, comparing the potential lifespan of a literary work about the valley to the potential lifespan of the valley itself: "And yet, what good does it do that great novel to extend so far into the future—forty years, say—if the place about which it was written vanished, oh, thirty-five, thirty-six, thirty-seven years ago?" (10).

Enemies that threaten the valley are quickly identified: the paper companies that press Congress for more logging roads to access more wilderness to clear-cut more virgin forests; members of Congress who vote on these measures under this pressure without, apparently, reading any of the hundreds of letters that Bass and his comrades-in-arms send them; and, perhaps worst of all, the U.S. Forest Service, the sworn protector of forests that is portrayed as a pawn to "Big Timber" interests (xiv). Exposing these groups' shroud of "secret scandal," Bass warns us that "[e]very day in Montana, and the West, is big industry's Rip-Off Day. They're stripping public resources, public lands, faster than they can recover" (xvi). Lest he allow himself to be easily dismissed as an extremist, he assures readers that his demands are few: he would like "the last few roadless areas in this still-wild valley to remain that way" (xv) and to dedicate the McIntire/Mt. Henry Conservation Reserve to "use exclusively by sustainable, small-scale loggers, rather than continuing to let the international companies work it" (25). He is even careful to spell out his views, claiming that he is "not 'against' logging—though I am against any more clearcuts in the valley. Too often the opposition paints tree-huggers such as myself into total obstructionists" (xv).

Once Bass has readers convinced that the situation is indeed a travesty of justice and a tragedy of incalculable proportions (not to mention that he has already planted the notion that despite the strident nature of his appeals he himself is a reasonable and principled man), he devotes a few short essays to describing the place and the people who brave its extreme conditions. In case readers are lulled into a reverie, Bass tells a bitter tale of former actors, an elderly couple, who had done so much for the valley that the Montana representative to Congress and several activist organizations proposed a minor protection bill that would be named for the elderly couple. In retaliation for the bill, which failed, the letters "H," "A," and "C" were carved in exaggerated scale into the mountain opposite the couple's home. The letters came from the local slogan "Don't hack the Yaak" (25–26, 43–44). The tone of his retelling of these events reinforces one of Bass's early assessments of the Yaak Valley predicament: that it is "the story of a quick buck unraveling the hope for a sustainable future" (xv). Perhaps the most powerful statistic he uses is delivered in an offhand manner, as though it were something that no one even bothers to think about: "Never mind that if, say, every piece of merchantable timber in the 7,000 acre Grizzly Peak country were cut, it would only provide the mill in Libby with two or three weeks of timber" (25). Adding more statistics and interview quotes, Bass supplies readers with ample justification for his intensity, juxtaposing the enduring value of the roadless areas with the fleeting potential for financial gain from clearcuts.

With the valley's predicament and antagonists identified in his account, Bass worries. He worries about flora and fauna, about interdependence and fragile cycles, about islands of wilderness cut off from one another, about his own role in the developing events. He debates the art versus activism dilemma at length and repeatedly, adding to his own ethos as an author concerned with both his responsibility to his readers' needs and his responsibility to his valley (and to the well-being of the entire planet). It is easy to settle this dispute; the needs of the planet must override those of his readers, but Bass makes sure to share his rationalizations often enough that readers never lose sight of his higher purpose.

> Art is incredibly important to me—fiction, especially. But there are thousands of fiction writers in the world, and only one Yaak. It would certainly not cause the earth to pause on its axis if I never wrote another story again. I don't think there was ever any writer about whom that could be said. . . . On the other hand, if a thing like the wilderness of Yaak were to be lost—(10)

Here he is reinforced as an artist, humbled as a writer, and justified as a crusader all at once.

Bass dramatizes the intensity of the struggle between his desire to be both artist and activist by using a metaphor of electrical power, which also serves to embody the very force of human manipulation of resources that the entire book is fighting: "Sometimes panic would spike deep within me—electrical charges of fear registering off the scale—and I would want to abandon all art and spend all my time in advocacy. I still believed in art, but art seemed utterly extravagant in the face of what was happening" (10). Electricity here is menacing, a force that cannot be controlled or measured by human scales, and serves as a striking juxtaposition to the word "art," which seems all the more diminutive when surrounded by these powerful "large" words. Bass further laments the effects of the Yaak Valley on his disposition as he frets about an audience he "ambushed" by begging them to take action on behalf of the Yaak Valley (68). In so doing, he has managed to shift the responsibility for his admittedly unorthodox writing style onto the Yaak. He quotes Thoreau and Leopold freely to get his readers to see the larger picture in conservation, placing himself squarely in the tradition of the most well-known and respected writers about nature (72–73). With this move, readers might well assume that Thoreau and Leopold, too, would have been inspired and driven by their dearest beliefs being defeated in the Yaak Valley.

Bass offers further explanation for his unusual style when he speaks of the need to write about the Yaak Valley as a set of physical symptoms, clearly as unavoidable as breathing. He pieces these together like a story within the Yaak story, starting with his natural tendency toward fiction: "For a while, I'll think that's the way to save a place—to write a pretty story about it, a pretty book—and so I'll change to fit that rhythm and belief, as if I'm in some cycle I do not understand but am nonetheless attentive to" (89). Bass reminds us that the imperative of saving the Yaak overpowers fiction then overpowers him, too. "Later on in the year—for three or four months—I will then find myself trying to do both: art in the morning and hard-core activism in the afternoons and evenings. . . . And then I'll wonder why my eyes drift crookedly, why I sometimes find myself staring at the sun, or why I feel off-balance" (90). This reference to a lack of balance hearkens back to his earlier fears about the chaos of modern society: "And as order and logic become increasingly lost to our senses, I'm certain that these things—art, and the wilderness—are critical to stabilizing the troubling tilt, the world's uneasiness, that we can all feel with every nerve of our senses, but which we still cannot name"

(11). So it is Bass's sensitivity to the predicament of the natural world that impels him toward polemical writing.

In several places Bass's frustration breaks through, compelling him to demand of his reader, "Am I explaining it clearly? Is anyone please angry enough to write a letter? To write five letters, or five hundred?" (122). "Some nights my heart pounds so hard in anger that in the morning when I wake up it is sore, as if it has been rubbing against my ribs—as if it has worn a place in them as smooth as the stones beneath a waterfall" (66). Even in his anger, Bass displays a sense of physical attachment to the issue, his own responsibility, his potential for failure, and his ultimate powerlessness to affect the situation. His physical attachment plays itself out in the vehemence of his writing; he expresses the situation with the same force that it uses to impress itself upon him. By the end of the book Bass is hoping to find an end to the intensity of the situation and his feelings, but again is stuck: "I have to make peace with my art and my anger, with our lives and their brevity—and yet, for me, it still involves fighting, and I will never give any of this up willingly, nor do I understand how any of us can" (173). He also manages to implicate all of us in his angry moments and his reflections on them; the fact that he blames himself allows readers enough breathing room to adopt his anger and frustration without taking more blame than he does.

Bass's last strategy for excluding himself from potentially negative judgments for his polemicism in *The Book of Yaak* (and thus perhaps excluding his argument itself from condemnation) involves placing himself as an involuntary participant in the process, as though by loving the Yaak Valley and simultaneously loving to write he would inevitably write this very book in this very way. Bass associates himself irrevocably with his chosen profession by asserting that "[w]riting—like the other arts—is not a hobby, but a way of living—a way, in the words of nature writing scholar Scott Slovic, of 'being in the world'" (90). As a writer, then, he must live this way, be in the world this way, and thus write about the Yaak in this way. His pure intentions are repeated, with an even more sympathetic motive, as Bass assures his readers that "I never meant to get into it this deep. I meant only to live in these quiet green woods and live a life of poetry—to take hikes, to read books, to lie in meadows with a bit of gold straw in my mouth and watch the clouds, and life, go by" (102). By the time we reach this point, we are convinced that Bass is doing his reluctant duty in writing for the Yaak Valley; his motivations arise from his love of nature, and he feels he has no choice but to write this message. And if the onus is on Bass to take up his pen, then the onus is also on his readers to do the same.

Another way to present Bass's struggles throughout *The Book of Yaak* is in terms of Kenneth Burke's pentad, which sheds light on the motives behind his stance. As the title reveals, Bass emphasizes scene, particularly the determinative power of scene, in *The Book of Yaak*. His fear, articulated again and again, is that the diminishing of wilderness necessitates a diminishing of the prospects of humankind. Hand in hand with this notion is Burke's scene-act ratio, in which "there is complicit in the quality of a scene the quality of the action that is to take place within it. . . . the act will be consistent with the scene" (*A Grammar of Motives,* 6–7). Since Bass sees reverence for wilderness as the highest human virtue, he fears the effect on our virtues (and the acts that result) without wilderness to revere; a diminished wilderness is a diminished humanity. This diminished humanity is seen through the scene-act ratio, which sees human potential through place; in Bass's view, the future of Americans without wilderness is already debased by its dislocation from pure nature.

In expressing these fears, Bass brings us through the stages that Burke has identified as the dramatistic process: in rejecting art in favor of advocacy, Bass experiences pollution; in articulating his fears and misgivings about the demands he makes on his reader, he voices his guilt. Purification comes for Bass through the mortification of the labors involved in writing both the book itself and the hundreds of letters for the same cause and through blaming his pollution on the wrongs of Congress, the Forest Service, and the timber industry. Bass's redemption comes through the release of his book; he has passed his burden on to others, making a convincing case that he has suffered sufficiently under its weight and will continue to do so. His pollution (unlike that of the Yaak Valley itself) has been redeemed, and we cannot blame him for the eventual fate of the valley.

John McPhee: Using Ethos to Avoid Being "Just" a Nature Writer

In stark contrast to Rick Bass's unabashed pleadings, John McPhee manages to write volumes in favor of environmental causes without ever explicitly advocating anything himself. A writer for the *New Yorker* since 1963, McPhee "is not generally prone to making political pronouncements in conversation or in his writing" (Pearson, *John McPhee,* 21). We count him among the greatest of the living writers of environmental discourse, though, because "the majority of McPhee's books focus on nature, on the most serious questions that face us regarding preservation versus development, on the balance between human expectation and responsibility in the natural world. Many of his stories are centered in wilderness areas, and quite a few of his profiles recount the lives of naturalists, environmentalists, and rural dwellers" (100). Pearson takes note of McPhee's often hidden personal views about the subjects he explores: "even when he writes about the environment in a political context, as he does in *Encounters with the Archdruid, Coming into the Country,* and at times, *The Pine Barrens,* he offers no simple solutions to problems and appears to take no sides. He is a storyteller..." (22). In telling his nonfiction stories, though, McPhee dramatizes the height and width and depth of environmental issues and the startling dimensions of environmental fragility.

McPhee's strategy, at its most basic, is to allow the people and the places he profiles to speak for themselves. In the introduction to *Outcroppings,* the 1988 coffee-table collection of his writing alongside Tom Till's photographs, McPhee describes in a rare reflective moment how he made the transition from writing primarily about sports to writing about environmental concerns. Seeking a new subject that would "raise the ante" to a new level of complexity, he "tacked to the wall a piece of paper that presented as a large enigmatic fraction the letters ABC over D. The A and the B and the C were meant to be people, each separately presented in... relationship with D. At that point, I had no idea what the subject would be, let alone what people would be involved" (2). McPhee concedes that "[t]his is no way to go about developing a piece of writing—to start with a structural concept and then look around for a theme" (2). He chose that theme just after 1968, because "[t]hose letters went up on the wall in the early days of the ecologic uplift, when the environmental movement was gathering strength. That seemed to be an obvious choice for a theme" (3). Even in retrospect, McPhee does not reveal his own feelings about the environmental movement. Instead, he traces his interest in nature to a Vermont camp of his youth and a geology teacher at Deerfield Academy. He describes himself as "caught up" in landscapes and admits to some wonder at geological phenomena but is never passionate or even explicit about his own opinions on conservation issues (3–5).

Encounters with the Archdruid grew out of McPhee's alphabetical fraction, pitting David Brower, the first executive director of the Sierra

Club, "the most unrelenting fighter for conservation in the world," against three successive and highly successful opponents: a miner, a developer, and a dam-builder (87). Each nemesis brings an impressive title to the meetings that McPhee has arranged in appropriate wilderness (or former wilderness) areas. With Charles Park, who combines teaching mineralogy at Stanford University with decades of corporate success in mines, McPhee and Brower travel to the Glacier Peak Wilderness, which is threatened by copper-mining interests. With Charles E. Fraser, the developer of Hilton Head Island, McPhee and Brower go to Georgia's Cumberland Island, three thousand acres of which Fraser has just purchased from Carnegie heirs. And with Floyd Dominy, United States commissioner of reclamation and a lifelong dam-builder, McPhee and Brower raft down the Colorado River, which has been (and will continue to be) defended by Brower and dammed by Dominy.

The oppositions in each episode of the three-part book are fierce and complex: while Brower is passionate about conservation, he is also amenable to reasonable use; while each of his enemies is openly antagonistic toward environmentalists (or "druids," as Fraser calls them), each is reverent in some way about wilderness and able to make some concessions. These individuals offer McPhee the opportunity to create stunningly parallel outings, so that his original "ABC over D" fraction is perfectly balanced. As each encounter unfolds, McPhee offers extended descriptions of the contenders and their motivations and positions, set against a backdrop of natural phenomena and human bickering about it. That bickering runs parallel, too: each debate finds some measure of common ground, and each finds no comforting resolution for Brower.

Each of the men who serve as the A, B, and C in McPhee's structural numerator is surprisingly three-dimensional. Defying stereotypes that normally accompany advocates of development and "progress," these men guide their lives by their own brands of respect for nature. Besides the nature-lovers' groups to which Park belongs, for example, we find out that he "knows what he is looking at in wild country." McPhee even says of Park, "I have never spent time with anyone who was more aware of the natural world," implicating Brower by omission; the miner's relationship with wilderness, then, is stronger than that of the man who wants to rescue it (67).

Developer Charles Fraser's history of protecting wildlife is long and varied, making him an especially tricky opponent for Brower. When he began developing Hilton Head in 1957, he was concerned about the alligators, "so he fed them great hunks of raw beef to lull them into acceptance of his bulldozers. The alligators swallowed it. They live now in water hazards and other artificial ponds throughout Fraser's Sea Pines Plantation" (88). Carefully planning his development around what he saw as the most valuable aspects of its wilderness, "Charles Fraser worked in summer with the timbering teams and successfully urged that no cutting be done in oceanfront stands of virgin pine" (90). More extravagantly, "Fraser spent fifty thousand dollars to save one live oak when he built a seawall for a harbor he had dredged," and "he has legally committed himself to leave twenty-five per cent of the plantation in its natural state" (91–92). To supplement his own description of Fraser, McPhee offers long verbatim exchanges of comments about him from other, often unidentified sources. These commentators portray Fraser in every possible role, each one contradicting the next: "He is a visionary young man who has learned that conservation can pay." "Conservation to Charlie means, in great part, that Charlie should not be bitten by a mosquito." "If you're going to have a developer, I'm all for Fraser. Unplanned development would spoil it" (100–101). Without making any explicit judgments of his own, McPhee exposes his readers to the controversy, and the complexity, that Fraser brings to the potential development of Cumberland Island.

Lifelong dam-builder Floyd Dominy shares a similar ethic with Park and Fraser; he believes that natural resources, and nature itself, can and should be manipulated for the "greater good" of the human race. As a county agent in Wyoming during the Great Drought of the 1930s, Dominy saw that nature "is a pretty cruel animal" (156). He immediately set about learning to tame it by building dams and providing water where nature chose not to. In those desperate times, "Dominy and the ranchers and farmers built a thousand dams in one year, and when they finished there wasn't a thirsty cow from Jew Jake's Saloon to the Montana border" (158). Once in Washington with the Bureau of Reclamation, Dominy kept building bigger and bigger dams, but did not do so indiscriminately: "He had given crucial testimony against the proposed Rampart Dam, on the Yukon River, arguing that it was too much for Alaska's foreseeable needs" (170). Trimming excesses from the Bureau of Reclamation's payroll and operations, and priding himself on the numbers of people who get power, water, and recreational use from the lakes he created, Dominy took to bureaucracy as keenly, and as skillfully, as to water.

As the denominator of McPhee's structural fraction, the "D," David Brower likewise has some distinctions readers might not expect. Besides having more children than his convictions allow, he lives in a redwood house in the Berkeley Hills (47–48). McPhee quips: "I had once heard a man in an audience in Scarsdale tell Brower that to be consistent with his philosophy he should wear a skin and live in a cave" (47). Later in the book, Brower, who has been the first to reach the summit of a good number of mountains in his many years exploring the wilderness, sits out the riding of rapids at Upset Rapid, prompting Floyd Dominy to exclaim: "The great outdoorsman standing safely on dry land wearing a... life-jacket!" (231). Brower manages to redeem himself in the end by standing in the raft over Lava Falls, an even more threatening rapid (243–45).

Besides describing each of the players in the successive dramas that he has staged, McPhee recounts their conversation, often alternating soliloquies more than reciprocal conversations. In these we find intense and well-informed debates, a great deal of intractable dispute, and an occasional glimmer of hope for consensus. Brower reaches consensus with each of his adversaries to some degree, and those moments of identification, which grow out of the complexity and integrity of each of the men involved, remind us of the true extent of their fundamental differences.

In "Part 1: A Mountain," common ground between David Brower and miner extraordinaire Charles Park, who also happens to be a member of the Cactus and Succulent Society and the American Ornithologists Union, is sparse. In the course of their hikes, they manage to share views about the importance of population control (though Park has three children and Brower four) and the wastefulness of moon exploration (42, 62). Park even offers a possible legislative remedy to help bridge the gap between miners' rights and conservationists' interests, in the form of changes in the 1872 federal law that gives miners complete rights over public lands, including timber and development, once they gain a patented claim. McPhee does not, however, let his readers know whether or how Brower responded to this idea (55). Once the hikers reach Image Lake, Park is even more disturbed than Brower by the number of campers already there (70).

Every square inch of common ground, though, merely underscores the vastness of the areas in which they vehemently disagree. The two combatants manage to fill a good portion of seventy-five pages with their sometimes angry debates over wilderness and mining issues, neither one of them even approaching conciliation. In the end of their encounter, their opinions are just as opposed as they have always been:

> "I just feel sorry for all you people who don't know what these mountains are good for," Brower said.
> "What are they good for?" I said.
> "Berries," said Brower.
> And Park said, "Copper." (75)

This impasse in part 1 is followed by a minor conservationist victory in "Part 2: An Island." By the time they have settled in for the night on Cumberland Island, Brower and Fraser are playing a sort of game in which Fraser asks, "Suppose you were the dictator and were under no financial pressure whatever. How do you think this island ought to be used in the last years of this century?" (119). As Brower responds to each specific question, Fraser negotiates with him until they reach some level of consensus. At the end of this discussion Fraser concedes that "[t]he Brower Plan is economically sound. . . . I could live within the constraints imposed by the Brower dictatorship" (123). Ironically, instead of creating a major recreation and housing development, Fraser was "in the end to be the catalyst that converted Cumberland Island from a private enclave to a national reserve" (149). His holdings were sold to the National Park Foundation, with enough funding from the Andrew Mellon Foundation to buy the rest of the island from its owners. Even this victory, though, comes off as another impasse: "there could be no victory for Cumberland Island. The Frasers of the world might create their blended landscapes, the Park Service its Yosemites. Either way, or both ways, no one was ever to be as free on that wild beach in the future as we had been that day" (150).

Brower does not manage to find so much common ground with Floyd Dominy but shares with him a modicum of mutual respect—for a moment or two. Their mutually adversarial stance before their rafting trip is recounted by Dominy: "Dave Brower hates my guts. Why? Because I've got guts. I've tangled with Dave Brower for many years" (168). Once they set out, though, they settle "into a kind of routine: once a day they tear each other in half and the rest of the time they are pals" (174). Their arguments are indeed venomous, prompting McPhee to borrow terminology from boxing to describe their verbal sparring (203–4).

In the middle of this recounting of their travels and quibbles, McPhee inserts another montage of quotes about one of the adversaries. This time, it is Brower whose name is being bandied about, in an insurrection of sorts that results in his ouster as executive director of the Sierra Club, which he built in membership "from seven thousand to seventy-seven thousand" (209). McPhee shapes the buzz at the San Francisco meeting of the Sierra Club's board of directors into an echo of that surrounding Charles Fraser upon his acquisition of the Cumberland Island real estate: "He is a great practitioner of brinkmanship, and this time he went too far." "I will say this: I prefer Dave's vices to the virtues of his enemies." "He was the most effective single force in the conservation effort in his country. And still is" (211–13). Once brought to the floor, the motion to accept Brower's (forced) resignation is quickly approved, ten to five. McPhee transports his readers almost immediately back to the rafting trip, a jarring leap from a defeated Brower in the board room to a still-contentious Brower in the river.

Now, though, Brower is faced with a spectacle as frightening as the San Francisco board meeting: the raft is quickly approaching the deadly Upset Rapid, and he is rapidly becoming more upset. His argument with Dominy heats up until debate becomes bickering: "'Oh, for Christ's sake, Dave, be rational.' 'Oh, for Christ's sake, Floyd, *you* be rational'" (222–23). Brower reminds all of his fellow rafters that the river they are enjoying is designated to become what he calls "Lake Dominy," and the confounded reactions cause a change in the atmosphere (225). After this moment Brower and Dominy seem to understand the other better, if only temporarily: "Over the drinks, Brower tells him, 'I will come out of this trip different from when I came in. I am not in favor of dams, but I am in favor of Dominy. I can see what you have meant to the Bureau, and I am worried about what is going to happen there someday without you'" (238). In response to this offering, Dominy returns Brower's generosity: "Up to this point, Dave, we've won a few and we've lost a few—each of us. Each of us. Each of us. God damn it, everything Dave Brower does is O.K.—tonight" (239).

The conciliatory mood does not last long; on the very next page, Brower tells Dominy that "[p]utting water in the Cathedral of the Desert was like urinating in the crypt of St. Peter's." Dominy's response, which can only be called a diatribe, includes claims like "I'm a greater conservationist than you are, by far. I do things. I make things available to man. . . . You conservationists are phony outdoorsmen" (240). For the final challenge of the trip, Lava Falls, Brower surprises his fellow rafters by staying in the boat, and Dominy tries once again to make it through dangerous rapids with a lit cigar. On the other side of the falls, Brower offers what for McPhee's readers will be his parting shot: "The foot of Lava Falls would be two hundred and twenty-five feet beneath the surface of Lake Dominy." In response, "Dominy said nothing. He just sat there, drawing on a wet, dead cigar. Ten minutes later, however, in the dry and baking Arizona air, he struck a match and lighted the cigar again" (245). This final standoff repeats and reinforces one of Brower's mantras, the fact that conservationists do not have real victories, because they can be attacked again at any time, and the moment they lose a battle it is lost forever.

The final standoff and its message are reminders, too, that McPhee's own views are implicit in every sentence, though explicit in few places. His presence is noticeable in the latter, which paint a quiet but consistent picture. Aside from functional uses, like telling readers who walked with whom, McPhee rarely uses first-person pronouns. In a playful moment, though, he teases Brower about his stance against mining in the Glacier Peak Wilderness. Holding up a large rock rich with copper, McPhee shouts, "Dave, look at this! Look at this rock! Don't you think it would be a crime against society not to take this copper out of here?" (54). After describing the beauty of the Cascades, McPhee offers a quote from an absent friend in lieu of an opinion of his own: "I was remembering the words of a friend of mine in the National Park Service, who had once said to me, 'The Glacier Park Wilderness is probably the most beautiful piece of country we've got. Mining copper there would be like hitting a pretty girl in the face with a shovel. It would be like strip-mining in the Garden of Eden'" (10). Once the hikers reach Image Lake, McPhee laments the surprising number of campers they find there: "Objectively, the reflection was all it was said to be. But a 'No Vacancy' sign seemed to hang in the air over the lake" (59). While these statements do reveal something about McPhee's position, they are few and far between.

Instead of direct statements, though, McPhee communicates his ideas throughout *Encounters with the Archdruid*. Brower, after all, is the common denominator, the simultaneous hero and antihero whose battles cover the span of all three of his opponents' battles and then some. By design, he is three times more significant than any of his adversaries, who do not even spill over into another section of the book. They are dealt with, and Brower and McPhee move on. McPhee refers to many other trips he has taken with Brower, places they have explored together outside of the tight structure of this book. And McPhee's repetition of several themes and devices around Brower does more than help tie the encounters together. Brower's constant use of his Sierra Club cup to get fresh water shows his loyalty and faith in the organization that loses faith in him. His equally frequent lament that conservationists have no real victories underscores his endurance for his cause, his undaunted pursuit of the impossible. By showing Brower in this way, McPhee renders him heroic and endorses his heroism.

Most powerfully of all, McPhee takes a stand merely by creating this book. While he does not make emotional claims to the subject matter, he does it a great service by giving it this unique treatment. To arrange these meetings in context between passionate and well-matched adversaries defies the shortcuts so frequently taken in environmental debate. According to Nancy Walter Coppola, "language features often used in environmental discourse can prompt mindless responses. For example, use of oppositional pairs such as 'logger/tree hugger' or 'environmentalist/developer' triggers a predetermined bias. Reliance on these potent symbols short-circuits our thinking and creates dysfunctional communication and a simplistic response to environmental problems" ("Rhetorical Analysis," 11). McPhee does not allow these cases, or these men, to be reduced to debates over progress versus conservation or jobs versus vistas. Instead, he takes those empowered to act into the places in dispute together. And perhaps McPhee harbors some hope, along with his readers, that by arranging these encounters breakthroughs will be made and understandings reached. He is careful to adopt Brower's hesitance to celebrate; each episode ends in some sort of impasse, which is really all Brower needs. Because the land is always subject to further assault, an impasse in one dispute affords him the time to fight another enemy in another battle.

John McPhee's motives are understated in *Encounters with the Archdruid,* but applying Burke's pentad to the book offers another way to assess them. Though his methods differ sharply from those of Rick Bass, McPhee also privileges scene. While Bass puts himself in the privileged position as rhetor, McPhee posits David Brower as something of a co-agent, with Charles Park, Charles Fraser, and Floyd Dominy as counter-agents. Scene, rather than remaining background or setting, becomes a manifestation of the purpose of these encounters and the agency by which McPhee brought these agents together. Brower and his counteragents espouse pragmatic agency, concerning themselves with the means necessary to achieve their respective purposes (whether those means are drilling for minerals, planning for new developments, damming rivers for water and recreation, or protesting for the cause of the wilderness).

To follow McPhee through the dramatistic process here proves elusive; he has so carefully separated himself from the book that he disappears behind his subjects. His purpose is clear (to set powerful agents in opposition); his scenes are powerful (a series of threatened natural wonders), his agents appropriate (all of them have the power to change or protect these scenes), his agency viable (trips to the scenes in question), and the acts genuine (the encounters and resulting debates are intense and sincere).

McPhee puts his agent, David Brower, through the dramatistic process three times in *Encounters with the Archdruid;* because he has positioned Brower as the primary rhetor, his process is clear. Brower has long since rejected the traditional hierarchy, is polluted by his radical nature, and resists his guilt by devoting himself passionately to his cause and placing blame on his counteragents (and their sympathizers). Through this mortification and victimage, Brower receives glimmers of redemption in the moments when he reaches mutual respect or agreement with his counteragents. In a larger sense, he is redeemed by having McPhee create this book around him and his single-minded devotion to his cause. Brower functions as an idealized agent for McPhee, representing the passionate advocate that McPhee the journalist chooses not to be himself. McPhee is redeemed, then, by the recognition that this book and the encounters themselves have opened up new questions and new possibilities for the resolution of seemingly intractable environmental debates. As his biographer says, "The question he asks in *Coming to the Country*—'What will be the fate of this land?'—could well serve as an epigraph for the majority of his work" (Pearson, *John McPhee,* 22–23).

Reconciling the Extremes of Environmental Advocacy Writing

The shift from Rick Bass's prose to John McPhee's is a startling one; it is hard to imagine a higher contrast between any two authors who write in order to raise awareness of and effect change in environmental issues. While Bass's motive is always explicit, McPhee manages to hide his behind a well-orchestrated set of circumstances and agents. In determining that these two writers share a motive, though, we necessarily assign them to share a genre. But which one? They are both uncomfortable with being called nature writers, and their writing does not reflect the pastoral themes and natural history usually associated with nature writing. Indeed, both of them center their books around intractable human conflict rather than migration patterns or mating calls.

Bill Karis and M. Jimmie Killingsworth endorse the idea that "we have reached a crossroads in environmental communication, where groups are trapped in the stale strategies of an outmoded rhetoric, and that it is part of the work we face as rhetorical scholars to discover new language and new approaches that more adequately lead us to a more widely accepted understanding of nature and a more generally engaging course of political and technical action" ("Guest Editors' Column," 6). I would argue in this case that the writers are not trapped at all; they are innovating and capitalizing on every new development in the health of our environment, taking advantage of the social changes that have brought environmental causes to a more prominent place in the public's attention. It is the rhetorical scholars who are trapped in this instance: the category most widely accepted by the public is the one most often rejected by writers and scholars alike. And we have no ready replacements, no system for interpreting the emergent genre as a whole. The changes in writing about the environment have occurred over only the last fifty years or fewer and promise to proliferate. The importance of genre study right now "lies with the overt mixing, blurring and shifting of cultural forms that characterizes late-capitalist cultures and economies. . . . the processes of textual hybridization are accelerated under fast capitalism and a globalized economy" (Luke, "Series Editor's Preface," viii). Interestingly, these are the same forces cited as accelerating both environmental degradation and environmental awareness.

The writing being done today struggles with many of the same issues, but takes on bigger battles than nature writing. It is not nature writing; rather than being writing about nature, it is writing for, or even on behalf of, nature. John Murray informs his readers in *The Sierra Club Nature Writing Handbook* that nature writers have "a dual responsibility: to educate their readers about the processes of nature and to entertain them with a memorable story along the way" (95). To bring this purpose into the realm of environmental advocacy discourse, I would add: "to change their actions or thinking about environmental policy." But while

"Edward Abbey may be justified in his assertion that it isn't enough merely to write about nature anymore—now one must take direct action to protect it—there is something to be said, even from a modern political perspective, for a writer who can simply convey a love of nature to others" (Payne, *Voices,* 3).

The good news is that this third purpose seems to be working. According to Payne, "Perhaps the most remarkable aspect of environmental reform in American politics is the extent to which it is driven by nature writers. Rarely in American political discourse have writers been so instrumental in molding public opinion . . . and the extent to which nature writers have influenced environmental reform . . . may well be unprecedented in American politics" (*Voices,* 3). When writers like Rick Bass and John McPhee frame their narratives around specific, situated environmental battles, we can be sure that more letters will be written to decision-makers, more developments, mines, and dams will be protested (and, perhaps more importantly, more of them will be understood), and more readers will be transformed into activists. For rhetorical scholars, this means that "if nature writers are to influence the debate over the environment in a meaningful way, they must continue to expand their audience, to reach out beyond the committed core of sympathizers who are already predisposed to nature writing and environmental reform" (Payne, *Voices,* 174). The onus is on this "committed core of sympathizers" to reach mainstream audiences more effectively, because, as Payne contends, it is "in the mainstream of American culture that today's nature writers will find the greatest rhetorical challenges and political opportunities, and it is there that the fate of environmental reform will be decided" (*Voices,* 174). If Payne's predictions hold true, then today's nature writers will continue to deliver the greatest rhetorical challenges to scholars of environmental advocacy discourse.

Works Cited

Bass, Rick. *The Book of Yaak.* Boston: Houghton Mifflin, 1996.

———. *The Ninemile Wolves.* Livingston, Mont.: Clark City Press, 1992.

———. *Wild to the Heart.* New York: W. W. Norton, 1987.

Black, Edwin. *Rhetorical Questions: Studies of Public Discourse.* Chicago: University of Chicago Press, 1992.

Buell, Lawrence. *The Environmental Imagination: Thoreau, Nature Writing, and the Formation of American Culture.* Cambridge, Mass.: Belknap, 1995.

Burke, Kenneth. *A Grammar of Motives.* Berkeley: University of California Press, 1969.

Coppola, Nancy Walters. "Rhetorical Analysis of Stakeholders in Environmental Communication: A Model." *Technical Communication Quarterly* 6:1 (1997): 9–24.

Fritzell, Peter A. *Nature Writing and America: Essays upon a Cultural Type.* Ames: Iowa State University Press, 1990.

Hightower, Elizabeth. Review of *The Book of Yaak,* by Rick Bass. *Preservation* 33:1 (1997): 95–96.

Karis, Bill, and M. Jimmie Killingsworth. "Guest Editors' Column." *Technical Communication Quarterly* 6:1 (1997): 5–7.

Killingsworth, M. J., and Michael K. Gilbertson. *Signs, Genres, and Communities in Technical Communication.* Amityville, N.Y.: Baywood, 1992.

Killingsworth, M. Jimmie, and Jacqueline Palmer. *Ecospeak: Rhetoric and Environmental Politics in America.* Carbondale: Southern Illinois University Press, 1992.

Luke, Allan. "Series Editor's Preface." In *Genre and the New Rhetoric,* ed. Aviva Freedman and Peter Medway, vii–xi. London: Taylor & Francis, 1994.

Mabey, Richard, ed. *The Oxford Book of Nature Writing.* Oxford: Oxford University Press, 1995.

McPhee, John. *Encounters with the Archdruid.* New York: Farrar, Straus & Giroux, 1971.

———. *Outcroppings.* Salt Lake City: Peregrine Smith Books, 1988.

Murray, John A. *The Sierra Club Nature Writing Handbook: A Creative Guide.* San Francisco: Sierra Club Books, 1995.

Payne, Daniel G. *Voices in the Wilderness: American Nature Writing and Environmental Politics.* Hanover, N.H.: University Press of New England, 1996.

Pearson, Michael. *John McPhee.* New York: Twayne Publishers, 1997.

Rueckert, William H. Review of *The Ninemile Wolves,* by Rick Bass. *Georgia Review* 47 (1993): 199–202.

Scheese, Don. Review of *The Living,* by Annie Dillard. *Georgia Review* 47 (1993): 193–97.

Smith, Linda L. *Annie Dillard.* New York: Twayne Publishers, 1991.

Unmasking the Self

Rick Bass as Ecojournalist

Gregory L. Morris

Early in his critical study *Nature Writing and America*, Peter Fritzell considers the ways in which American nature writers have traditionally positioned themselves—and the Self—in relation to the natural world they seek to describe. Most American nature writers, Fritzell contends,

> have been unable or unwilling to cast either their own needs and impulses or the underlying terms of their inherited culture (much less their own phrasings) into critical or biotic perspective—and not surprisingly. For the kinds of self-consciousness that typify and define the *best* American nature writing require a tolerance for ambiguity that is very difficult to sustain—a dedication to paradox, and even an occasional delight in uncertainty, that can be extremely unsettling. (16)

Fritzell clearly privileges the work of writers—Thoreau, Dillard, John Janovy—who take the especially long, hard look at the difficult interplay between human desire and nonhuman existence, who often consider the various psychodramas played out by the human traveling through the nonhuman world.

Fritzell goes on to consider how this veering from the Self has implications for subject matter and form within the genre, noting that most American nature writers have turned "toward one form or another of conventionally disciplined science, and away from the potentially exhausting effects of self-consciousness—away from self . . . and toward their nonhuman others" (17). Most American nature writers, he argues, "have written what are largely 'undramatic' works, works not so much of interrogation or inquiry (and certainly not of introspection) as works of identification, information, and appreciation, works that establish and assert rather than doubt or question, works of explication rather than complication" (17). For Fritzell, then, the predominant narrative glance of most American nature writers has been outward and not inward, with writers seeking forms that pursue "explication rather than complication." The Self, it seems, gives way to the Other in the economy of American nature writing.

However, one writer who has managed to place the Self in high perspective against the natural world—one writer who is supremely self-conscious—is Rick Bass. Seeking to center the Self, rather than to erase it, Bass—particularly in his nonfiction—consistently considers the ambiguities and the paradoxes of his own relation to the natural world. This self-centering maneuver is especially evident in his work in ecojournalism, a sort of subgenre of naturalist nonfiction and perhaps one of those forms that allows for the kind of "interrogation or inquiry" that Fritzell considers so valuable and rare.

Bass, of course, is a writer who works in several genres, who is accustomed to adopting various narrative guises. Though he is perhaps best known as a fiction writer and has worked a lot of different nonfictional ground (the personal essay and memoir, the political essay) Bass has done successful and conscientious work as an ecojournalist too. Indeed, as he himself has acknowledged, the impulse in his nonfiction writing has been more and more toward journalism; as he described it to Bill Stobb in an interview: "Fiction is, for me, almost totally a place of the imagination but, increasingly, my non-fiction is less essayistic and more journalistic in dealing with those issues which are so critical to my home and places I love in the West and in the world" ("Wild into the Word," 99). Bass makes some interesting distinctions here, of course—between imaginative and nonimaginative narrative, between form and need—but of particular interest, I think, is his conscious identification of his work as journalism, which becomes here a sort of narrative middle ground upon which he can travel between imagination and exposition, between complication and explication. On this broad, planar narrative surface, Bass can cast his eye in several directions—looking inward and outward—and speak as both Object and Subject.

At the same time, of course, Bass also quite self-consciously casts himself as a journalist and acknowledges that specific, peculiar narrative stance and voice. Yet I would contend that in his journalistic work he just as self-consciously subverts that stance, modifies and disguises that voice. In assuming the role of journalist—and particularly the role of *eco*journalist—Bass also assumes a sort of writerly and political privilege, playing fast and loose with narrative guise. It is a role, in fact, with which he seems profoundly uneasy and from which he seeks to escape. In his book *Green Ink: An Introduction to Environmental Journalism*, Michael Frome distinguishes between green journalism and "just-plain journalism":

> Environmental journalism differs from traditional journalism. It plays by a set of rules based on a consciousness different from the dominant in modern American society. It is more than a way of reporting and writing, but a way of living, of looking at the world, and at oneself. It starts with a concept of social service, gives voice to struggle and demand, and comes across with honesty, credibility, and purpose. It almost always involves somehow, somewhere, risk and sacrifice. (21)

The nature of this "risk and sacrifice" becomes clearer in Bass's works of ecojournalism, as he injects doses of his own "desire" into the narrative equations. Part of what he self-consciously risks is the loss of his own authority; as he collapses, time after time, the writer and the narrator into the dominant "I" in these works, Bass risks the sacrifice of a clear narrative position from which to observe and to report. The confusion is purposeful, I think; feeling a very real tension between reporter and imaginative writer and feeling an overriding allegiance to story—Bass, in the end, is a storyteller above all—he moves loosely among narrative roles, drops one mask and assumes another in pursuit of the core of his story. Perhaps more importantly, Bass makes his way into the realm of the authentically self-conscious writer, allowing the nonhuman object of his study to become (in Fritzell's words) "the overt sign of the desiring human" (*Nature Writing*, 24).

This sort of problematic traversal of narrative territory is best exemplified in Bass's three major works of green journalism. In his two "wolf books"—*The Ninemile Wolves* (1992) and *The New Wolves* (1998)—he is slightly less subjective, less full of what Fritzell calls "psychobiotic self-interest" (29). These books are more objective and scientific and range more distantly beyond Self, as Bass considers a greater plurality of voices not his own or of his own devising. In his "bear book," *The Lost Grizzlies* (1995), he perfects his technique of narrative fluidity and powerfully demonstrates the tendencies of desire as it operates within his ecojournalistic text. It is in *The Lost Grizzlies,* too, that Bass comes to exult in mystery, ultimately finding grace in a resolute indeterminacy.

The Ninemile Wolves, ostensibly a study of the wolf reintroduction program in northwest Montana from 1989 to 1991, occupies a variety of generic positions. With its origins in an article written (as Bass has said) "on assignment" for *Outside* magazine, *The Ninemile Wolves* evolved into a book-length work described in its subtitle as "an essay" and identified in a critical article by Terrell Dixon as a "journalistic narrative" ("Rick Bass," 85). Bass himself explained his authorial purpose this way to Scott Slovic:

> The reason I wrote the book was to honor loss. These wolves have fought valiantly for survival in this day and age, and they've come up short several times, but they always did what it took at the last instant to at least keep one of their members alive and to stay in the world. And I wanted to make sure that was not forgotten, I wanted to put it down for the record and get all the facts right and all the dates. I wanted to have everything right so that . . . it just seemed almost obscene to let it escape into something less than memory or something less than honor. What they did was a thing of amazing integrity, amazing force, amazing power, amazing passion, and I did it for the wolves, but I also realize now that they gave quite a gift to our own culture, if we would just listen to that story. (23)

Bass's self-analysis reveals a wonderful, curious mixture of the reportorial and the memorial. His desire to "honor loss" necessitates a particular concomitant desire to "have everything right": form decidedly follows function here, but just what is that form?

What is clear is that Bass is a writer. What is not so clear here and in these other works is what *type* of writer he is. As I've said before, Bass is a writer preeminently concerned with story—both his story and that told by the nonhuman creatures in his story. He is a writer with a story—or more frequently stories—to discover and to tell, and as a writer/journalist he weaves these stories into a net or mesh of interrelated narratives, each with its separate value and significance and each with its separate (and competing) narrative impulse or argument. Ultimately, though, Bass invests some of those stories—and thereby privileges those stories—with a certain holiness and integrity.

Among these several narrative guises, within *The Ninemile Wolves* Bass most consistently and most wittingly adopts the storytelling role of the journalist, so that story swings into reportage; at a number of points in his narrative, Bass identifies himself not only as a journalist but as one who has conscientiously worked within this tradition and who is aware of its limitations and drawbacks. When he has to call a U.S. Fish and Wildlife Service biologist named Mike Jimenez, Bass laments: "He sounded blue, almost heartbroken, when I got him on the phone, and who could have been otherwise? It's the part of journalism I dislike most: talking to the accident victim, the grieved" (126). As a working journalist, Bass assumes a sort of objectivity: he is the observer, emotionally immune, bringing back the story. But Bass is anything but immune; he is afflicted with—*con*flicted with—desire, and his narrative is pervasively inflected with that same desire. Again thinking of Mike Jimenez, he writes: "It's clearly his dark night of the soul as a wildlife biologist, and as a journalist I've picked this unlucky night to reach him, and as someone who wants wolves in the woods, and who doesn't enjoy other people being unhappy... Well, I wish I'd called on another night" (127). Here we see (at least) the dual nature of Bass's narrative identity: he is the reporter telling a story of the wolves and he is the desirous believer telling the story of what *he* wants—what he wants to believe, what he wants to hear.

Bass makes no bones of his desire, makes no attempt to hide the fact that he wishes his story to shape itself in a certain way. The phrase "I want" echoes throughout *The Ninemile Wolves* ("I want to hold off...," "I want to believe...," "I want to hear..."), reminding us of his other narrative impulse: that of the writer, the poet. While Bass claims a sort of (eco-)journalistic privilege and consciousness, he also embraces his role as an imaginative writer; he is Rick Bass the artist, the poet (and not the scientist). Such an identity grants him a kind of license—he becomes the licentious storyteller, free to work his will (it seems) on the stuff of his narrative: "I can say what I want to say. I gave up my science badge a long time ago" (4). The one narrative stance Bass resists taking in *The Ninemile Wolves* is that of the scientist, for to adopt such a stance would mean also adopting a particularly scientific way of thought and would run counter to his imaginative impulse.

At the same time, however, whenever Bass lapses into "thinking like a wolf," or wondering about the inner lives of wolves, he recognizes his "failure" and takes himself to task: "I'm thinking like a poet. I'm thinking foolishly, stupidly" (101). Bass calls this "doing his poet thing," and it stands in constant opposition to his "journalist thing." This conflict and competition among impulses—journalistic, artistic, scientific—points as well to another source of Bass's narrative identity crisis. Again, Bass has been thinking like a poet, wondering about the workings of the wolf's brain:

> It's easy to say that's goofy-talk, and ridiculous—but looking at that skull, the wolf's brain seemed no larger than a pea. And yet they exhibit such intelligence, such an ability to learn, respond and react. Where does it come from? Of course a poet will say there's a spirit within them, a force much greater than the sum, the weight, of that tiny brain resting slightly behind and above the terrible jaws. There's something missing, unaccounted for, in the equation. I *have* to call it spirit. And I believe the biologists feel it too—even if their duty won't let them admit it. I believe that when it is cold and dark out and they hear the wolves' howls and they are alone, that they anthropomorphize like mad; if that's what you call believing yourself no more or no less than, but equal to, another creature in the woods. I have to believe that even for the biologists there are moments when science strips away, and there is only bare mystery. (132)

Bass finds himself having to negotiate between various discourses—the "goofy-talk" of the poet and the "straight-talk" of the scientist—to arrive at his own brand of ecojournalistic discourse, a compelling and compelled discourse full of mystery and passion. It is a proximating discourse as well, bringing Bass close to his subject, making him "one of the pack." According to Michael Frome, such passion and proximity are part of the appropriate green discourse: "But passion counts: it makes the difference and should not be repressed or inhibited" (*Green Ink*, 34). Bass, in effect, transforms himself—shapeshifts—into the compulsive witness, having to tell his story, as cracked and as mystical as it (and he) may sound. He admits his stake in the story, affirms his investment in its worth both as teller of that story and as participant in that story. Having reached the end of that story, Bass declares:

> I have come away from following the Ninemile wolves convinced that to diminish their lives would be wicked; that it would involve a diminishing of a significant force in the world, that it would slow the

> earth's potential and cripple our own species' ability to live with force; that without the Ninemile wolves, and other wolves in the Rockies there would be a brown-out, to extend the metaphor of electricity; that the power would dim, and the bright lights of potential—of strength in the world—would grow dimmer.
>
> We are "brothers in the hunt" . . . but I think we are brothers in something else, too. I am convinced that it has something to do with internal fire, soul, and the creation and pursuit of mystery.
>
> You've come too far in this story to turn away now, when I start talking crazy like this. You can't turn away. We have to follow.
>
> But the more there is of this kind of talk, the more the wolves shy away, slide away. They're not behind us; they're out in front. We're following. (139–40)

Like all cracked storytellers, Bass draws us—his compelled readers—into the narrative experience, expanding the weave of this story-net. We must listen as he must tell. But is this the appropriate journalistic relationship, this extended manipulation of the reader into engagement, involvement? Neither writer nor reader is effaced; instead, we become part of the story—or of one of the stories—Bass is telling. We, too, are foregrounded. We, too, become one of the pack. We, too, are initiated into the mystery and the knowledge with which this story is imbued.

A similar concern with story inheres in Bass's second wolf book, *The New Wolves: The Return of the Mexican Wolf to the American Southwest.* Once again, the centered story is the wolf-story, a narrative that possesses a kind of physicality and weight—Bass calls it his "story-mass" (84)—and that provides the dramatic structure for his manipulations as ecojournalist. This story details the reintroduction of the Mexican wolf into New Mexico and Arizona and, like his Ninemile story, collects a variety of alternative narratives and voices in the course of its telling. Dominant among these voices, however, is again the voice of Rick Bass, an unabashed presence within his own tale. This story is suffused with his personality and becomes as much a story of his role within this place and the story of this place as of the wolves themselves.

But one of the problems Bass faces in relating this story is accommodating himself to this new, essentially alien place. Admittedly more at "home" in Montana, in the Yaak Valley, Bass must reconcile himself to the biotic and political facts of New Mexico and the Southwest:

> I love deep forests and snowy mountains—they seem to fit some space within me—and so perhaps it is totally my personal paranoia expressing itself when I imagine wolves on sun-hot rocks in 115-degree temperatures, paws bleeding, existing on lizards and the last decade's cow dung, gathered in one last small pack and glaring at one another, panting, heavy radio collars around their necks, wishing mightily they were back in the St. Louis Zoo. But wolves possess what biologists call a "plasticity," meaning, among other things, that they've been here a hell of a lot longer than we have. As long as we don't start killing them again, there's a chance they can recover.
>
> Perhaps it's only my blood's unfamiliarity with the earth's language down in this part of the world that causes me such concern for the wolves. I'm more comfortable with the language of wolverines, larch trees, spruce, marten. (9–10)

As displaced storyteller, Bass must orient himself to the natural, the linguistic, and (by implication) the spiritual topography of this world. Indeed, he must learn a new language, rooted in the blood as much as in the word. He must develop an appropriate discourse for his study, one that fits the situation—its geography, its politics—as well as his own narrative nature.

However, one of the central tensions in *The New Wolves* resides in Bass's own uncertainty about his narratorial identity, for he never comfortably situates himself either as journalist or as storyteller. At one place in the book, he remarks: "It's tempting at this point for either a journalist or a storyteller to spend some time detailing the decades-long struggles of the individuals who, in the beginning, were almost the sole supporters of Mexican wolves" (89). Bass clearly sees himself operating between these two narrative positions, constantly exchanging masks as he moves through the biological and political detail of his story, playing with the identities of each. He is still the desirous believer that he was in *The Ninemile Wolves;* the same strainings of desire and want are heard throughout this narrative; "I want to believe" eventually becomes a kind of mantra for Bass. He thinks hard about what he "wants to be doing" (53); he is "nervous" about the circumstance of the wolves, and he "worries": "I worry that a thing—an invisible thing—is somehow fading from them; and that once it begins leaving them, it can go fast" (45).

Bass also worries about the loss of his journalistic objectivity as he involves himself more and more in the complexities of the wolf-world: "Slowly, irresistibly, I find myself being drawn out into that most dangerous, vulnerable, and indefensible of positions, hope. I tell myself once again to stay objective, and to never lose sight of the bottom line, the one-sentence description of this project: our government *is going to take captive, semi-domestic Mexican wolves and turn them out into a landscape vastly reduced in ecological health*" (99–100). By this time, one wonders if Bass is being entirely serious in his desire (yet another variety of desire!) for objectivity, or if such objectivity is a necessary element in his ecojournalism—or if ecojournalism itself is not a unique brand of storytelling. The palpable interest Bass evinces in his "story-mass," the way in which he makes an aesthetic of his green vision, demands a redefined narrative stance. By force of his own imaginings, he shapes a specific kind of eco-narrative in which observations precipitate desire, ambiguity, and complication—all of which eventually merges with the Self that is Rick Bass.

Bass's hope, of course, is wrapped securely round with his own need: his need to believe in the possibility of reintroduction, his need to understand the psychology of wolfness, his need for wilderness. In truth, Bass's discovered language is shaped by this rhetoric of need. At the same time, however, his optimism is mitigated by his own self-doubt. He worries, for instance, that he is being "naive" (98) in his expressions of desire. Moreover, much as in *Fiber,* Bass here worries that he falls short of the radical act, that his reportage and his storytelling fail to evoke the kind of change of consciousness and condition that the wilderness demands. Is radicalism, asks Bass, an option no longer available to us?: "I wonder: are we having radicalism bred out of us? What does it say for us when the idea of having one hundred Mexican wolves free in the world again is deemed radical?" (91).

In the end, Bass seems to storytell himself right out of his journalistic stance, distancing himself from "the press" and locating himself somehow and somewhere apart from that particular narrative voice. Even early in his work, he objectifies the press as something of which he is not a part and criticizes it for the perspective it takes on the stories it chooses to tell (84). And later Bass effectively abdicates his journalistic role (135), seeing himself as someone (or something) other than a journalist. He never quite reconciles himself to the uneasy stance of the reporting eye, or not at least to the type of vision required by that eye. Too much desire, too much want, and too much belief in myth and mystery shade that vision for Bass to claim identity as a journalist. Perhaps he simply wants to know too much.

This desire for knowledge is just one of the several desires that impress themselves upon Bass's third, and perhaps most interesting and complex, book of ecojournalism, *The Lost Grizzlies.* Part of the book's complexity comes from its participation in a sort of "conversation" with two other writers—Doug Peacock and David Petersen—and their respective bear-books: *Grizzly Years: In Search of the American Wilderness* (1990) and *Ghost Grizzlies* (1995). Both Peacock and Petersen appear as characters in Bass's story, taking part in the search for grizzly evidence in the San Juan Mountains; and they both write of that experience in their own books. What develops is a polyphonic account of the same event: all three writers tell at once the same story and a different story, with their intertextuality deepening the ambiguities already inherent in that story.

But *The Lost Grizzlies* is also complex because, of the three Bass books considered here, it is the work most thoroughly awash with its author's desires. And chief among them—the centering belief of the work and of Bass's effort—is the desire to *believe:* more specifically, the desire to believe in the persistence of the grizzly in the San Juans: "I want to believe they're still down there. I want to find them" (6). This need to confirm the bears' existence originates, like most desires, in the heart of Rick Bass: "I drift south, driving through the night. I wouldn't travel this far if there wasn't that spot, that place in my heart, that vacancy waiting to fill up with belief" (9). The heart is an unabashed, unequivocating presence in this book, guiding Bass in his search for the story, for the bear; the heart also complicates and confuses that search, casting uncertainty upon the nature of the exercise, as he realizes:

> Are we making this search for the bear or for ourselves? There is a huge difference, I know that much. A man is not a bear, and a bear is not a man, but there is definitely a mixing going on, a merging. Some days it feels like this search is for the bear, and other days it feels like it is for people, for the heart of our own species. We could just as well be searching for a cure to one small kind of cancer, or for a lost hymn. We could be up on the Canadian line, going over into the Canadian Rockies. We could be down in Mexico, in the Sierra del Nido, the Sierra

> Madre. Why here? Why in the middle of the country, the square-ass middle of the Rockies, dead center between Houston and Kalispell? It has something to do with a centering, with the concept of heart. (43)

This notion of centering, of getting to the heart(s) of things, colors the book with a kind of romantic spirituality—the same sort of spirituality we have seen traces of in *The Ninemile Wolves* and *The New Wolves.* In *The Lost Grizzlies,* however, we are almost overwhelmed by the spiritual impulse that beats through the heart of the story and of its author. Rick Bass, even while he is searching for bears, searches for aspects of himself.

Nor does Bass shy away from the consciousness and the expression of this search, as he narratively foregrounds this construction (and deconstruction) of his identity. At one point, he admits to having retreated to the mountains in order to "hide," to remove himself from one world in order to discover himself in another. At another point, Bass notes how the search for bears effectively reshapes his own physical nature and offers a kind of masculine renewal: "Each step, each second we're breathing this new air, is getting us ready for our trip, and it's pleasant to think that our bodies are changing rapidly, that we're becoming new men" (25). There is something specifically masculine about *The Lost Grizzlies,* as Bass and others (predominantly men) use the bear-quest to refashion their own masculine identities. According to Bass, an essential, elemental Self lies at the "heart" of each of the searchers, a Self that is somehow to be authenticated through a relationship with the bear; to get to that core-Self, layers of external identity must be stripped away: "How many layers must we take off, how much of the other part of our lives must we shed, before the bears will show themselves?" (41). With those layers of identity removed, what Bass may well find is pure, unadulterated desire.

As such a desire-filled writer, Bass here once again suffers from a conflicted writerly heart and an authorial double-consciousness. Though supremely aware of the Self, he remains uncertain of the nature of the specific Self that writes. Indeed, simply being a writer—whether a writer of fiction or of journalism—seems to interfere with the very consummation of Bass's desire, as he recognizes:

> In fiction, you want to get as close to your story as you can, but in nonfiction, in real life, you're better served if you doubt everything, revere almost nothing, and always protect your heart. It's a fine thing

> to say, *Yes, yes, the mountains were preparing us before opening their secrets to us, for revealing the bear,* but the wary journalist, the careful predator, can't go pursuing every twig crack in the woods, every surge of the heart. If everything's sacred, then the world itself is sacred. To a journalist, however, it is in a story's best interest if only certain moments are sacred. (108)

This is a clear and dramatic expression of Bass's creative dilemma, as the tensions of style and purpose and vision involve themselves in the mystery of the heart. Suddenly, the journalist casts himself as predator, pursuing story and spirit and the heart of the world, but always wary of indulging "every surge of the heart." Even the mechanics of writing—or at least of journalistic recording and reporting of experience—become nuisances and impediments; as Bass scribbles notes on scraps of paper or on the palm of his hand, he directly disrupts the nature of the experience for those such as Doug Peacock who want nothing mediating or sullying that experience. And at one point "the wary journalist"—the "predator" in one imagining of the identity—becomes in another conception the outsider, the undesired (though desiring) observer and witness; the object of another's suspicions, Bass describes "the social leprosy, the stigma, of my being a journalist" (109), again confirming the uneasy identity he professes. This outsider identity, however, may very well serve a specific strategy, as O. Alan Weltzien has noted: "Bass avoids excessive preachiness by playing out a paradox: the fact that he is an interested amateur and writer rather than . . . [an] expert, an outsider rather than an insider, validates his knowledge claims" (*Rick Bass,* 31). While Weltzien is writing here of Bass's technique in *The Ninemile Wolves,* I believe his insight also helps frame our understanding of Bass's placement within the text of *The Lost Grizzlies*—and within the general territory of his journalism: Bass repeatedly exploits his journalistic identity in order to work the worlds of both "truth" and "fact." Shifts in identity ultimately permit shifts in the kinds of knowledge claims that he wishes to make in his work.

Of course, maneuvering through such identity shifts makes the maintenance of a distinct identity problematic for Bass, as notions of the Self continually separate and merge throughout *The Lost Grizzlies.* It is especially interesting that (as mentioned above) the journalist is figured at one point as "predator," for one of the identities Bass seems to want to assume is that of the bear itself. This desire for transformation originates in Bass's relationship with Doug Peacock, whom he invests with a unique physical and spiritual quality, an inherent wildness, a certain "bear-ness." Bass wakes one morning of the search: "I'm up at first light. The wind's rushing harder than ever, but Peacock's already out on the cliff, motionless, swathed in his sleeping bag, and I know that once again, for the moment, I am seeing the bear" (50). Peacock has preternatural abilities—bearish abilities—that place him in close, close relation to the bear; Bass seeks this kinship for himself, seeks to emulate Peacock and thereby to become more bear than Bass, more prey than predator. If Bass cannot be the bear, then he will become Peacock. This, too, is an impossibility.

And Bass perceives the danger posed by becoming bear—and Peacock—to his story even as he sees its advantages. As always, he understands the ambiguities of his writerly relation to the natural world:

> Dutifully, I make notes in my little spiral memo book. It occurs to me that in trying to inventory and measure magic, all of the luster is lost. The rip of the falcon's wings is muted, the dive-bombing of the moment becomes stale. Perhaps I should throw down pen and paper and run hard into the woods like one of the bears—ripping and clawing at a hollow log and consuming ants and grubs and the rich mulch of the earth. In abandoning the story, I might end up seeing more, and learning more.
>
> You would think that the writer, the predator, would have a way to see everything, to catch all movement. But now it strikes me, in the presence of Peacock and Big George and Dennis, that perhaps the way of prey, not predator, is the way to see the most—with the wide eyes and heart of a deer, rather than the tunnel vision of the wolf, the bear, the fox, the journalist. (116–17)

As always, Bass is working on the writerly equation, on achieving the most advantageous and appropriate perspective, on exercising the clearest kind of vision. As the earlier quoted description of Peacock-in-the-morning suggests, Bass—despite his journalistic professions—inevitably falls back upon the imagination and the imaginative act to inscribe the magic that is, for Bass, the bear. By enlisting the imagination, he finds a certain proximity to the bear and to his imposed identity as prey; at some point, he makes the indirect connection—"I imagine I am a bear" (158)—but the imaginative act alone fails to transform Bass into the animal he seeks. This is because, I think, his imagination is warped by desire, by greed, by overwhelmingly wanting belief in the grizzly's existence. At one point in the search, Bass grows impatient, corrupt with desire: "But after a while I can't wait. Those bears ran uphill. I want to find sign. I want more. . . . If that peak above us was the grizzlies' haunt in the sixties, then perhaps it is still their haunt now. Two plus two equals four, I think greedily, wanting still more sign, more bear" (154). Bear scat achieves a kind of religious significance for Bass, standing as relic and signifier of the spirituality he pursues. His dissatisfaction, however, works a slow, dark magic on the "wild habitat of the soul" and manifests itself in the inexplicable bodily sickness that comes upon him seemingly out of nowhere. This sickness clouds and distorts his vision, confusing Bass as both journalist and bear. It also constricts his heart, which for Bass is a central mode and organ of belief; instinct and intuition and the hintings of desire comprise this mountain epistemology. However, his greed and desire serve only to warp this way of knowing and keep him from revelation and the mystic encounter.

We see the dominating presence of mystery and spirit in the third section of *The Lost Grizzlies,* "Teeth of Heaven," wherein Bass succumbs willingly and selflessly to the mystery. This giving-in process begins with the admission of other stories into the central bear-Bass story—"This is a story of bears and mountains, and yet everything is connected somehow: my friends and family and the woods" (181)—and with broadening the weave of the narrative net. In this final section, and on this final walk up the mountain, Bass again identifies himself as a journalist—one of three journalists on the trip ("all these *journalists!*"); accompanied by David Petersen, he now and again feels the burden and weight of that identity. Bass is patently discomfited by his journalistic role and by the restrictions it implies for his imagination and heart as he negotiates the magical landscape of the San Juans. The old conflicts return: to trust the understandings of blood or brain, to see with the eyes of prey or predator, to seek distance or proximity, to release the Self or to feed the hunger of the Self. Clarity remains elusive.

But revelation—the mystical moment—does present itself to Bass eventually on this mountain and on this third quest. Moreover, that revelation comes with the same kinds of conflicted vision and ambiguity that have beset him from the beginning of his pursuit. Bass finally *sees* the bear—a grizzly—in all of its great fullness: "An awe, a reverence, nearly takes seed, the idea that here on this highest reach of mountain a bear can live to reach such an immense size. But the reverence flees immediately; obscured by my desire for escape and safety as I look for a tree to climb, my heart in my throat" (214). The irony, of course, is that Bass has only *seen* the bear and true to his human nature he finds himself needing—well, more: "I want *more*. . . . I want to hold something. I want to have my picture, anyone's picture, taken next to the bear. I want the bear to return from the woods, loll in the meadows, roll over on its back and say, Okay, the jig's up, here I am" (216–17). Bass-as-journalist wants proof; vision and mystical experience suddenly demand evidence, documentation, confirmation.

Bass's postvisionary condition is fraught with doubt, desire, and wonder. At one point he responds:

> It was a magical experience, but like a Puritan, despite all my fond celebrations of the importance of mystery, I realize that I am afraid of it, afraid of mystery and magic. I do not think the bear—Old Grandfather, Illustrious Master, Honey Paw—revealed himself to me. I think the mountain revealed the bear to me. (218)

Bass approaches mystery and its truth and then retreats from that truth. Yet always the essence of the mystery is couched in terms of his own identity; Bass finds himself somehow unworthy of the vision: "I came in prepared never to see the bear, never to find sign. I came in prepared to be protected by failure, to admit loss. In no way that I can think of did I do anything to warrant the mountain revealing its true power to me" (219). I have to think that he is being a bit less than genuine here in his claim to have anticipated failure and loss and in his implied belief that he has successfully kept his desire at bay. But the revelation does serve as a test of that desire, his profound need to see a bear being measured against the uncertain reality of his sighting.

Bass does seem totally invested in the mystical experience and in the change it works upon his nature. The revelation illuminates for him the deep spirituality of the world. Even as he pursues the bear, becomes again the "predator," Bass embraces a new identity despite the undefined power that accompanies it:

> The utter holiness of being alive and part of such a system, the holiness of being allowed to be a lichen within the system—I'm not normally a cheery person, but here on the chalk-rubble slope, tucked into my little lunch cave, I find myself grinning, then laughing at how

> tenuously alive I am. To hell with electricity, with sizzling nerve endings and mispronounced words. I want to learn a new language anyway, the language of breathing forests, the language of further mystery. (219)

Bass again is moved by desire—by the writerly desire for a "new language . . . the language of further mystery." This is not the rhetoric of the journalist, but of the poet. It is the vocabulary of risk. The power of Bass's revelation—a revelation that "was not for scientists . . . but for me"—grants him "the beginning of a new perception" (225), a new way of envisioning his position in the larger landscape and of describing that position. From the bear-gift Bass fashions a new identity "as a tender disciple to mystery"—he becomes a religious witness, a teller of the sacred story.

But the transformation proves only temporary or at least incomplete. Even as Bass makes his way down the mountain, he acknowledges himself as a journalist, suggesting that he still suffers from conflicted desire and belief, or perhaps from a new pure, desire-filled belief. Writing in that "new language of mystery," Bass concludes his self/bear-study:

> Only a handful of grizzlies still exist, in Colorado and in a few other wild places in the West. They move around as a band, and at other times alone. Hounded by history, they often come out only at night. They skirt the high lakes above the tree line, their fur rippling, their muscles rolling. Heaven is in their teeth.
>
> We must learn to love them. We have forgotten how to love them. Like all of us, they will not be here forever.
>
> Bears? What bears? (239)

We end with questions (though Bass follows with an epilogue that seems to offer more testimony to the bears' existence) and with runic, mystic professions. With what language and what vocabulary can we understand the meaning of the claim: "Heaven is in their teeth"? Bass's declaration of love for the bears and for their wildness is a declaration of self-love as well and a final statement of his own desire for proximity. At the center of his story are the bears—but what bears? What is left but Rick Bass, the desiring witness, the ecojournalistic and ecoprophetic voice crying in the Colorado wilderness? Perhaps it is Bass who remains tantalizingly lost amid the welter of desire and belief.

I would suggest that Rick Bass is one of those writers of whom Peter Fritzell speaks in the passage quoted at the beginning of this essay. In the three works studied here, and especially in *The Lost Grizzlies,* Bass confronts the Self in its difficult, often ambiguous and paradoxical relation to the natural world. For him, that Self is often a writerly Self seeking identity and identification; and often that search falls short of complete success, largely because of the persistent, bewildering operations of human desire within the nonhuman world. Reconciliation remains elusive, even in the light of—or perhaps because of—revelation. Like Bass, we remain incomplete. We, too, want more: more of the mystery and more physical verification of the mystery. Like Bass, we simply want to believe.

Works Cited

Bass, Rick. *The Lost Grizzlies: A Search for Survivors in the Wilderness of Colorado.* Boston: Houghton Mifflin, 1995.

———. *The New Wolves: The Return of the Mexican Wolf to the American Southwest.* New York: Lyons Press, 1998.

———. *The Ninemile Wolves: An Essay.* Livingston, Mont.: Clark City Press, 1992; New York: Ballantine, 1993.

Dixon, Terrell F. "Rick Bass." In *American Nature Writers,* ed. John Elder, vol. 1, 75–88. 2 vols. New York: Scribner's, 1996.

Fritzell, Peter A. *Nature Writing and America: Essays upon a Cultural Type.* Ames: Iowa State University Press, 1990.

Frome, Michael. *Green Ink: An Introduction to Environmental Journalism.* Salt Lake City: University of Utah Press, 1998.

Peacock, Doug. *Grizzly Years: In Search of the American Wilderness.* New York: Henry Holt, 1990.

Petersen, David. *Ghost Grizzlies.* New York: Henry Holt, 1995.

Slovic, Scott. "A Paint Brush in One Hand and a Bucket of Water in the Other: Nature Writing and the Politics of Wilderness: An Interview with Rick Bass." *Weber Studies* 11 (Fall 1994): 11–29.

Stobb, Bill. "The Wild into the Word: An Interview with Rick Bass." *Interdisciplinary Studies in Literature and Environment* 5:2 (Summer 1998): 9–104.

Weltzien, O. Alan. *Rick Bass.* Boise: Boise State University Press, 1998.

Thinking Like a Wolf

The Narrative Evolution of The Ninemile Wolves

HENRY HARRINGTON

BEFORE RICK BASS showed up in the Ninemile Valley, thirty miles west of Missoula, most residents of western Montana were well aware of the presence of a new pack of wolves there. Beginning on August 12, 1990, Sherry Devlin, the environmental reporter for the *Missoulian,* filed a series of articles, some short, some feature-length, on the tribulations of these wolves that had unexpectedly turned up to live and breed in a community of mostly small, marginal cattle ranches unaccustomed to the company of this particular predator for fifty years. By the time Bass's book appeared in 1992, Devlin had already written twenty-four articles for the regional daily newspaper, and thirteen more were to follow. The first two dozen articles frame the story Bass tells, but his story is not the same as Devlin's.

The difference between the two stories lies in the fact that Devlin's turns on the *presence* of wolves in the Ninemile Valley, viewed from a distance, while Bass's paradoxically turns on their *absence,* in which he participates. Devlin's story, as it unfolded over the years, was primarily a story of transgression and occupation—wolves showing up where they did not belong, doing things they should not have done, being punished but nonetheless persevering. The subject of Devlin's story remains the wolves: their presence is mapped by *conceptual* space and reported through distinctions between near and far, domestic and wild, that were as familiar to her readers as to her sources. Although she makes a discernible shift in her point of view, achieved largely by the selection of sources and quotations, from describing the wolves as transgressors to describing them as sympathetic residents of the valley, direct encounters with the wolves continue to occur within this conceptual space. Bass's narrator begins his story in the space that Devlin describes, but he takes up a liminal position in relation to it that radically changes the story. History becomes *his* story. In this *perceptual* space, centered on Bass in the Ninemile Valley, the wolf never appears, but nonetheless functions as the object of sublime transcendence from the human "self" that fills Devlin's conceptual space.

Although the main reason that Bass never encountered the Ninemile wolves was probably the haste in which he wrote the book (a bit over a year, I reckon, though it is difficult to tell because he is often working with material that appeared in print earlier and elsewhere), the lacunae create some interesting tensions in the narrative. They mark the inclusion in the narrative of a significant failure, a gap in the continuity of Bass's personal history of "what really happened" to the Ninemile wolves. As I shall try to describe later, this gap ends up serving what, using Jim Cheney's term, I shall call the "postmodern sublime" experience of "thinking like a wolf."[1] At the crux of the narrative, Bass fails to cross the threshold of transcendence that would take him once and for all out of himself to a higher "self," to the level of a seer. Later in the narrative, as he was finishing the book, "a pack of three to five wolves showed up in [Bass's] own valley," and he tries to contradict this earlier failure, appearing at the final hour donning the mantle of a prophet like Ishmael in *Moby Dick,* looking directly on the face of God, as if "God himself were to reveal himself: not in his work, but his *self.*"[2] But this accidental experience occurs in the narrative almost as an afterthought and after he has left the Ninemile Valley, where failure, not success, holds sway.

Bass's failure to see the subject of his book is like the wolf deaths that punctuate the story of the wolves: "It'll break your heart if you follow this story too closely, and for too long, with too much passion. It's never going to end. At least, I hope it doesn't ever end. But as long as there are roads and humans moving up and down those roads [putting the wolves in danger], there are going to be bleak, bleak moments, again and again" (143). These are not "natural" deaths, part of the natural cycle of generation and corruption, but deaths that interrupt and may even eradicate that natural cycle, similar to the effect of Bass's failure on the progress of his "story." These "bleak moments" of absence and death are disquieting, dark places in the natural progress of a narrative that one would never mistake for Ishmael's.

Sherry Devlin once told me that the Ninemile wolves story really had two beginnings, and it was not until well into the series that she went to the "first" beginning, the appearance of the wolves in the valley. Her first *Missoulian* story (12 August 1990) begins, as it were, *in medias res* with the killing of Shirley and Fred Hager's elderly, stroke-weakened dog by a male wolf trying to raise a litter of pups on his own after his mate was shot. In good journalistic fashion, Devlin sets up the human conflict between the locals, "almost all of whom," as Fred Hager says, "[have] a dog," and the U.S. Fish and Wildlife Service (USFWS), charged with the protection of wolves under the federal Endangered Species Act. The conflict manifests itself as a contest between binary opposites—high and low, government and private, excess and decorum, inside and outside. Speaking the "high" language of a government biologist from outside the valley, Ed Bangs, the wolf recovery manager for the USFWS, explains the incident in terms of behavioral pattern: "Wolves are very territorial. . . . They do not distinguish between dogs and other wolves when it comes to perceiving threats [to their territory]." Devlin quotes Shirley Hager speaking in "low," colloquial language informed by an outraged sense of propriety: "I very much object to those wolves being in our valley now. . . . We've been going along with the federal wolf people. But not now. That wolf just came in and jumped on our dog and killed it."

In Devlin's first article on the Ninemile wolves, the dog is as important as the wolf. Dogs make terrific sentimental copy in America. Americans love dogs as companions, "man's best friend." For people like the Hagers, dogs and food are simply and unequivocally antithetical categories. But not for wolves; wolves kill dogs—for territory and for food. When the Hagers leave the dog behind to go to a potluck dinner, the wolf kills or "jumps on" the dog to protect his territory for his pups and, by implication, to enjoy his own potluck of dog. Not only have the wolves shown up in a valley where they have not "belonged" for fifty years, but the death of the dog marks a serious transgression of the space that bounds the Hagers' social existence. The aged dog had no practical or economic value for the Hagers, and yet they cared deeply for it.

The contours of the social space in which the Hagers reside are complex, involving people, the land, and animals in a system of social semiotics, but the space nonetheless would have been familiar to most readers of the *Missoulian,* who live in their own homes surrounded by mountainous national wilderness areas and forests. Englishman Edmund Leach has provided a scheme for unpacking the semiotics of the Hagers' space in "Anthropological Aspects of Language: Animal Categories and Verbal Abuse," a great essay on the use of animals as social categories of thought. Leach maintains that we are bounded by three sets of relations—kinship, topographical, and animal; because all three "discriminate areas of social space in terms of 'distance from Ego (self),'" there is a direct connection between these sets.[3] In other words, the way we talk about animals allows us to make statements about people and the land and vice versa. Simplified, Leach's relationships can be laid out schematically as follows ("Anthropological Aspects," 36–37):

(a)	Self	Sister/Brother	Cousin	Neighbor	Stranger	*KINSHIP*
(b)	Self	House	Farm	Field	Far	*TOPOGRAPHY*
(c)	Self	Pet	Livestock	Game	Wild Animal	*ANIMALS*

Because these sets are homologous, "sibling," "house," and "pet" are symbolic transformations of one another, and so are "stranger," "far," and "wild animal" (36–37).

To the Hagers, their dog might just as well have been their house or one of their immediate family; if Leach is right, and I think he is, the wolf's transgression in killing the dog is fundamentally not unlike the wolves' transgression in the *Three Little Pigs* (blowing the house down) or *Little Red Riding Hood* (eating grandmother). Symbolically, these are all the same transgression committed by a "wild animal" that comes as a "stranger" from "far." No wonder Fred Hager would say: "The idea of wolves sounds great. But when they do what they do, we realize that we cannot live with a pack of wolves. It is foolish to even try."

The key to Leach's table is the "self," which anchors all three sets—kinship, topography, and animals—but what does he mean by "self"? Without doubt, it is a human self, which makes Leach's schema unapologetically anthropocentric. And, implicitly, the self is located at the center of a generic agricultural milieu. Though few of its residents make their living solely from agriculture (the growing season there is short and the land poor yet expensive because of its views and proximity to Missoula and Frenchtown, the site of a large Stone Container pulp mill), that pastoralist self fits the Ninemile Valley. For this self, the topography fans out to "house . . . farm . . . field . . . far." But if this self is not a rural inhabitant but a government biologist, for example, operating far from home (Bangs had been brought in from Alaska for the wolf reintroduction program in Montana), working in a federal bureaucracy, the topographical order of the schema is disturbed; indeed, for such a self, "house" becomes "far" and the orders of not just the topographical set but the kinship and animal sets, too, are inverted. Ed Bangs is a stranger in a strange land, closer in his job, at least, to the wolves than to the residents of the Ninemile Valley.

By a similar token, Leach's schema cannot easily be applied to the author of these stories, because in her objectivity as a good journalist Devlin is invisible, reporting values created in the social spaces of both Ninemile Valley residents and government strangers. The map showing the movements of the wolves that accompanies her 14 October 1990 story derives from this disembodied point of view.

This is the *conceptual space* in which the differing social spaces that Leach's schema describes conflict. Literally, it is a view from above; not geography but the eye of the journalist/cartographer centers the map. As a cultural sign, the map describes the way in which a diverse territory made up of private forests, Indian reservations, a national forest, farms, a resort town, a city, and mountain valleys is turned into a homogeneous ethnos in which wolves wander. The power of such a form of writing (and maps are a form of writing) is that it can assume a normative role in establishing a spatial order for solving political problems of the one and the many, problems like wolves in humanly populated western Montana.[4] The *Missoulian* map, however, is included to illustrate not so much the representation of space as the space of representation—representation of the social space of Devlin's story of the Ninemile wolves.

In Leach's schema of social space the end terms of each of the three sets—self/stranger, self/far, self/wild animal—are stabilized by their opposition to each other. In Devlin's first story the opposition between the "self" and the "wild animal" dominates, even though the biologists' version of the opposition is present. Taken at face value, it is a story about the death of a dog. Within the Hagers' social space the wolf is a transgressor, a stranger come from afar, threatening the family and the house. But in Devlin's subsequent stories we move into an area of ambiguity where the laws of incest and the boundaries of ownership become

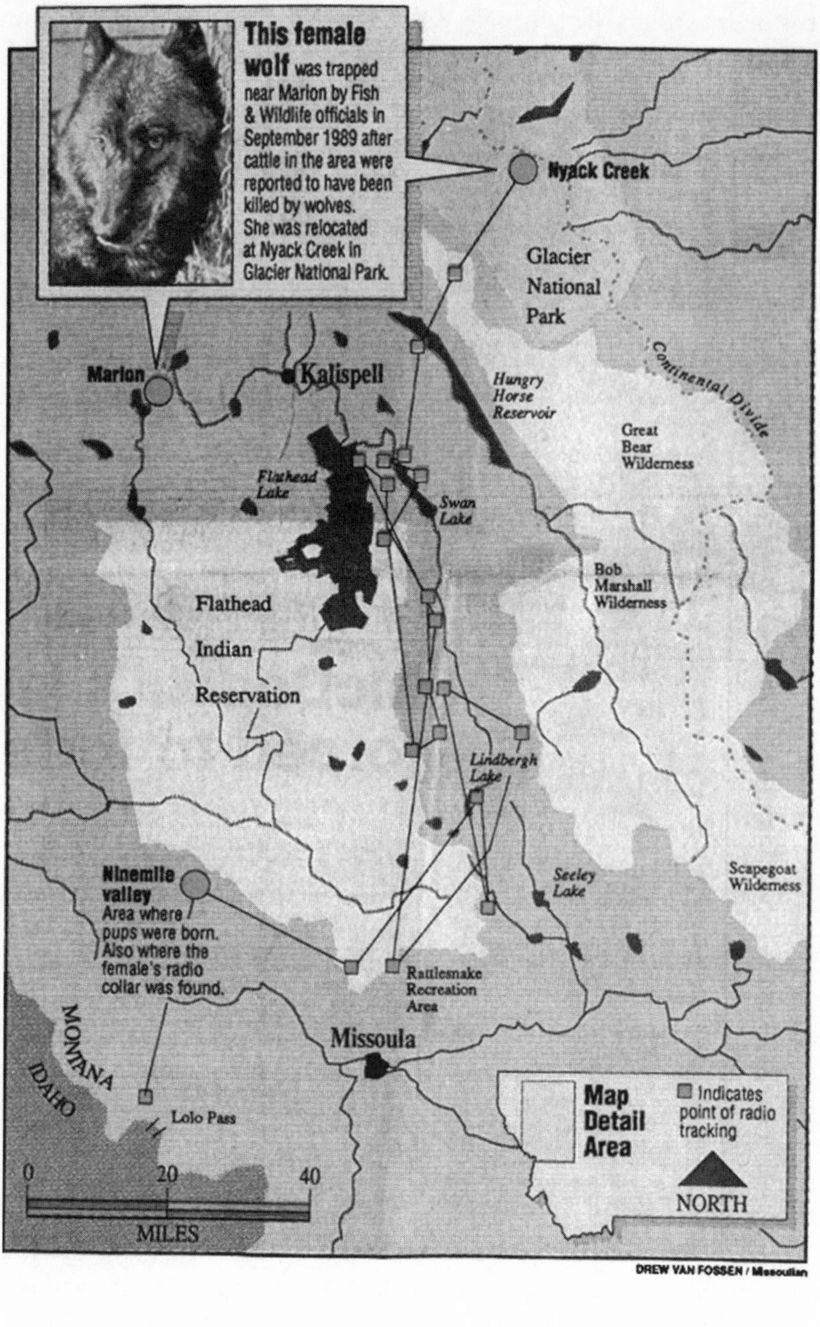

This female wolf was trapped near Marion by Fish & Wildlife officials in September 1989 after cattle in the area were reported to have been killed by wolves. She was relocated at Nyack Creek in Glacier National Park.

Nyack Creek
Glacier National Park
Continental Divide
Marion
Kalispell
Hungry Horse Reservoir
Great Bear Wilderness
Flathead Lake
Swan Lake
Bob Marshall Wilderness
Flathead Indian Reservation
Lindbergh Lake
Seeley Lake
Scapegoat Wilderness

Ninemile valley
Area where pups were born. Also where the female's radio collar was found.

Rattlesnake Recreation Area
Missoula
MONTANA
IDAHO
Lolo Pass
0 20 40
MILES
Map Detail Area
Indicates point of radio tracking
NORTH

DREW VAN FOSSEN / Missoulian

less clear. In this area the transgressions of the wolves take on an aura of heroic perseverance, occasionally compromised by tragic slips but always within the conceptual space defined by the invisible, objective reporter.

The turning point in Devlin's series seems to be in the 14 October 1990 feature-length article, where the highway death of the transgressing male wolf is reported in the context of a complete chronology taking *Missoulian* readers back to the "first" beginning of the story, when a pack of Northern Rocky Mountain wolves migrated from Alberta into Glacier National Park in 1985. In this article the attention shifts to the six orphan pups, who have to be fed in such a way as to nurture their predatory instincts so that they can survive on their own as adults. During the period in which they had to be cared for, the pups were themselves possible (illegal) prey for hunters. Devlin in fact wrote two articles primarily to alert the public to their presence in the Ninemile Valley and to warn indirectly of the consequences of killing these particular federally protected animals.

The climax of this episode in the Ninemile wolves story occurred in a 27 December 1990 article in which Mike Jimenez, the biologist in charge of feeding the pups, is quoted as announcing that the wolves had just killed their first deer: "They did it just like wolves do it. They're in business." Biologically, perhaps they were in business as wild animals, but the implication of the quotation is that they're still not "really" wolves. For Devlin's readers these wolves now occupied an ambiguous zone between "pet" and "wild animal," confusing major oppositions and coordinates in Leach's cultural grid. To keep our social space orderly, we do as Devlin did: we persuade ourselves that *P* and *P~* are wholly distinct and impose a taboo on any consideration of the overlap area common to both circles. Leach himself has a Venn diagram to describe this ambiguous, tabooed position into which the Ninemile wolves moved ("Anthropological Aspects," 45):

P	Both P and P~	P~
man	man-animal	not man
(not animal)	("pets")	(animal)
TAME	GAME	WILD
(friendly)	(friendly/hostile)	(hostile)

The wolf pups, unlike their parents, belong to the overlapping set "Both P and P~." In this set, the distinctions between *me* and *it* are no longer so clear cut. And so, predictably, the wolves no longer inhabited distant forests, but the "field" of "neighbors," specifically, the field of the Thisted brothers. The wolf pups were being fed deer, shot and carried for them from the Metcalf Wildlife Refuge in the Bitterroot Valley fifty miles away, during the same season when the deer hunters were out and were possibly hunting the pups. The pups were *almost,* but not quite, tame, fed by Mike Jimenez, and observed daily from the Thisted brothers' picture window playing and chasing grasshoppers and gophers; and they were *almost,* but not quite, prey to be eaten like the deer and elk that more commonly appeared through the same window.

Even when the grown wolf pups, now a year old, wandered onto a Dixon farm (over the mountain range to the north of the Ninemile Valley) and killed a steer belonging to Carrie Priddy and her brother Ed, their deeds were reported differently than those of their unequivocally wild parents. They "got nervous [out of their familiar valley]," according to Ed Bangs in the 1 April 1991 *Missoulian* article, and "made a bad decision." There is, of course, a difference between killing a steer and killing a pet dog, clearly registered in Leach's schema; "livestock" occupy the middle zone between the primary animal opposition of "self" and "wild animal." In fact, the difference shows up in the way the kill was redressed: as an economic loss made up by a cash payment from Defenders of Wildlife and, as a relocation problem, by removing the wolves from the area. Symbolically, the steer's death is equivalent to an insured shed burning down—an accidental and regrettable loss, not an act of malevolence (that is, "they made a mistake"). Even more indicative of the Ninemile wolves' new status in Devlin's story is her report on 2 November 1991 that one of the pups had been shot. "'A hunter didn't shoot this Ninemile wolf. That person was a criminal with a gun,'" said Ed Bangs. The wolf was where it belonged (more or less). The "criminal" transgressor was a human being, who became the "stranger" from "far" away.

This is the story that Rick Bass intercepted, a story of transgressing wolves that ended up belonging to the Ninemile Valley. "I remember reading about [the big gray male, the loner, . . . left to raise the pups by himself] in the newspaper almost every day that summer" (*Ninemile Wolves,* 37). But he redefines the conflict that Devlin developed, between those officially charged with the reintroduction of wolves to Montana and their supporters and the residents of Montana who perceived a threat from the wolves, into a moral fable: "The [people] who are 'for' wolves, they have an agenda: wilderness, and freedom for predators, for prey, for everything. The ones who are 'against' wolves have an agenda: they've got vested financial interests. It's about money—more and more money for them" (4).

Within this contest, Bass regards himself as a "'for' wolves" kind of guy—a radical freedom fighter traveling with wolves. Adopting this persona gives him artistic license to "begin [the story] anywhere" (4) and tell it in a style that bounces from high to low, wildlife biologist to foot-shuffling tag-along, "telling my truth and what I feel" (*Missoulian*, 7 June 1992). The phrase "my truth," thrown back at those who might criticize him for "anthropomorphizing" wolves, suggests that Bass's is a different truth from that of both the residents and the biologists, who form the principal social dichotomy in the *Missoulian* series. And that "truth" derives from a "self" free from the taint of filthy lucre; that is, Bass nurses the fiction that he is not grounded in the capitalist economy that supports both the professional biologists and the farmers.

On the surface, it would seem that Bass is operating from an inverted version of Leach's scheme, possessor of a "self" quite close to the biologists' and Devlin's (by the end of her series of articles). Though he lives in a Montana valley, his home is far away; he is a stranger to the Ninemile Valley and not a rancher. But Bass is clearly reluctant to identify himself with the biologists. "I can say what I want to say," he writes at the beginning of the book. "I gave up my science badge a long time ago" (4). Commenting elsewhere on his dislike of using radio collars, one of the key tracking methods available to wolf biologists, he explains his reluctance in terms of preserving the "mystery" of wolves that is lost with the kind of knowledge and control of which the radio collars are symptomatic: "Just behind the collar are trappers, helicopters, computers—*knowledge*, instead of mystery" (94). The "self" that Bass tries to develop in the course of his book is indeed similar to those of Ed Bangs and Mike Jimenez, the biologist who worked with Sherry Devlin, because they do not "act and preach automation and data" (51). However, with the invocation of the wolf's "mystery," Bass clearly wants to go beyond that "self" and the "knowledge" that even the "pure unencumbered biology" (83) of Bangs and Jimenez affords.

The wolves' "mystery" inheres in the wild. And the wild in this book is an altogether different kind of space from the conceptual space developed by Devlin and emblematized by her map of the wolves' movement. If one concentrates on the zigzagging line describing the wolf's movement on that map, drawn with data provided by radio collars, it yields a spatial analogy for the kind of "political maze" (31) in which the Marion wolf pack, from which the alpha female of the Ninemile Valley pack migrated, became trapped; it is an expression of the "web" that Bass uses to describe the restrictions on both wolves and people throughout the book. In this other, wild, unmapped and unmappable space, which I shall call *perceptual space,* social relations depend less on the oppositions and sets of relationships that Leach describes than on a discovery of freedom "for predators, for prey, for everything."

To conceive of space in these terms of freedom "from" and freedom "for," Bass has to do for the Ninemile Valley what Aldo Leopold did in *A Sand County Almanac* for the New Mexico mountain, where the death of a wolf provided the occasion for the chapter "Thinking Like a Mountain." Like Leopold, Bass has to define his space and its inhabitants in terms of lived experience, of perception, rather than in terms of resource management. Thus, in writing about the view from the Thisted brothers' house, Bass creates a recessional space that moves outward toward not just the space of "stranger . . . far . . . wild animal," as the rationalist, structuralist Leach would have it, but toward *myth:* "They've got that huge bay window, and below their house, the pasture, and then the woods, and the river, and beyond that, the great mythic-looking mountain" (57). The wolves come over the mountain out of this region of myth into the Ninemile Valley.

Throughout most of the narrative, Bass remains in a liminal position, like the Thisted brothers watching from the picture window, in relation to this mythic space. Eventually, however, like Leopold in *A Sand County Almanac,* he has his epiphanic moment in which he finds himself immersed in this space. And like Leopold's, Bass's epiphany turns on the experience of identifying with the wolf he pursues. This moment comes in chapter nine, which begins with the announcement: "It was time—March 1991—for me to go into the woods and see where these four pups were hanging out." Once in "the woods," he signals his participation in the mythic space of the wolves with heightened language: "They're wandering, weaving. Mike [Jimenez] stops and picks up an ancient elk skull beneath a tree, the wolves' tracks having turned to pass right over it. It's moldy and green with old lichens, gone, gone . . ." (114). The dramatic disorder of this space, its unpredictable juxtaposition of life and death, its gloomy reinforcement of mutability, is prototypically pre-sublime. Participation in such a space precludes not only the distant and aloof position that Devlin adopted toward her subjects, but also a position within Leach's social space, bounded by dichotomies that would compromise his freedom.

Meanwhile, deep into his book, the reader must suddenly come to terms with the fact that Bass has no firsthand knowledge of the Ninemile wolves or even the "mystery" of wolves beyond a glimpse of wolves near his home in the Yaak Valley. Indeed, he's almost childishly pleased when the "G-men" agree to take him out into the "woods" for the first time: "Although Jimenez and Joe Fontaine had been dodging such media requests all winter—'Take me out to see where the wolves live'—they capitulated [to Bass's request]; I got to ride along in the police car, so to speak" (94). Simply accompanying the biologists into the forests of the Ninemile, however, would do no more than ground the narrator's authority in a junior G-man's "self," an amateur biologist, closer to the wolves perhaps than to people; this, in fact, is how he has grounded his authority up to this point. But such bogus authority would do little to instate or preserve the wolves' "mystery" in the narrative or, frankly, to prop up the narrator's position as an inspired renegade who "gave up [his] science badge a long time ago." Bass's narrative strategy depends upon *erasing* the line dividing "self" from "wild animal". He must, in other words, approximate the experience of Aldo Leopold looking in "the fierce fire dying in [the wolf's] eyes."[5]

To do this without appearing to upstage his biologist guides, Bass must grant at least one of them the experience of "thinking like a wolf." Mike Jimenez is the obvious choice, for he fed the pups and was Devlin's primary informant: looking for ravens and other signs of wolf presence, the narrator describes Jimenez as "thinking like a wolf at that moment: that he's trying to get a handle on things. He's not *theorizing,* but just watching, and waiting. Which, as I understand it, is exactly how a wolf hunts" (101). So the episode is set up as the narrator's initiation by Jimenez into transcending the dichotomies that underpin Leach's schema, ceasing to be a human "self" and thinking like a wolf.

What the narrative promises, then, is something very much like a "sublime" moment of transcendence founded upon the experience of what David Abram would call the "more-than-human" wolf.[6] For the past 200 years, this experience of the sublime has been recorded by a variety of writers of European descent in a variety of contexts, but all these writers seem to share a common sequence of moments, triggered by perception of the sublime object, leading up to the moment of transcendence.[7] Bass's narrative follows this sequence laid out by his Romantic predecessors, but with a "postmodern" outcome.

The first phase in the experience of the sublime occurs as an encounter with a sublime other—a scene, an event, or an object—whose distinguishing attribute is sensory obscurity, an obscurity that separates it from the everyday realm of order and rational limits. Considered within the body of American nature writing, one of the odd things about *The Ninemile Wolves* is that its narrator never does see a wolf in the Ninemile Valley. How different from Leopold's encounter with a wolf whom he has hunted! But the spiritual trajectory of Bass's and Leopold's experience is the same. Considered within the tradition of the sublime, however, this lacuna actually serves the sublime experience by enhancing its mystery and moving the narrator beyond conscious thought. For Leopold, listening to the howl of the wolf, the "meaning" of that howl remains "hidden" to one unable to "think like a mountain" (*Sand County Almanac,* 129). Similarly, Bass, confronted with the wolves' absence, remarks that "without realizing I'm doing it, I'm slowly, subconsciously forming an opinion [about the wolves]" (113). Following close upon the sense that he is beginning to apprehend the wolves intuitively comes a kind of confusion characteristic of the sublime in which the narrator's mind becomes aware of its inability to grasp the other and a feeling of alienation from the natural world: "My instinct won't [shut off], and even though my logic tells me it's an impossible task [to determine the number of absent, invisible wolves], the other part is still trying to sort it out" (113).

Two centuries ago this spiritual passage might have led the narrator to a condition in which his mind, conscious of this alienation between his logic and intuition, between himself as a human and as a part of nature, becomes aware of its freedom from the sensory world and transcends it. But Bass is in pursuit not of disembodiment but of "the recuperation of the incarnate, sensorial dimension of experience" (Abrams, *Spell,* 65), etiolated in humans but still strong in wolves. Jim Cheney has reintroduced this dimension, substituting embodied for disembodied transcendence, as a character of the "postmodern sublime."[8] Indeed, *The Ninemile Wolves* is a much better example of the "postmodern sublime" than some of the ones that Cheney selects, because Bass so clearly accepts and approves the possibility of the "animal" within us.

Cheney has been criticized by Mick Smith and others for regressively upholding Jean-Jacques Rousseau's myth of an unfallen, Arcadian nature,[9] and much the same criticism could be leveled at Bass, who identifies the wolves' return with the chance to redress Europeans' treatment of Indians (!): "This time we'll be able to find out if human nature, and our politics, have changed—metamorphosed, perhaps, into something more advanced—or if at the base our politics are still those of Indian killers" (9). But behind remarks like these and behind Cheney's idea of a "postmodern sublime" lies a desire to ground human nature in something beyond the "self" that organizes and defines the limits of our everyday experience of the world—beyond the divisions and dichotomies from which Leach's social space is created.

Earlier in the episode in the woods, the narrator describes Jimenez's actions in the field looking for ravens and other signs of wolf presence as if he was "thinking like a wolf at that moment"; by the end of it the narrator, too, is thinking like a wolf: "The woods air is full of where they were—though I can only feel it, can smell nothing. I want to hear ravens, up ahead. I want to smell a kill" (113). This is the key moment in the book, the one upon which Bass's authority as spokesman for the Ninemile wolves rests, and the one that marks him as having "metamorphosed" into "something more advanced" than his nature-dominating, Indian-killing ancestors. Paradoxically, "more advanced" human nature looks atavistic as Bass identifies with the wolf he pursues. Though the narrative does not develop in this direction, this could be the foundational moment for a human metamorphosis into a werewolf. It is an uneasy moment and does not last long. The spell is broken when Joe Fontaine rejoins the narrator and Jimenez with the question "Did you guys bring a sandwich?" (114). At that instant, the narrator is reminded of his own, human body—"Saliva sprays against the roof of my mouth. My feet are cold"—and he "become[s] human again—all human, leaving any hopes for wolves behind [me]" (114, 115).

The disharmony created by the intrusion of cold feet and sandwiches into the narrative just as the narrator's transcendence seems assured reestablishes the incommensurability and discontinuity between the sublime object—the wolf—and the narrator. Traditionally the sublime "ought" to evoke transcendence that leads to political freedom, precisely the end that Bass pursues; but this interpretation has always idealized the sublime experience, glossing over the possibilities of resistance or loss. The emotions associated with the sublime (which Edmund Burke subsumes under fear, but which Immanuel Kant transmutes to a negative pleasure) are not easy to live with. If one uses Burke as a model,

Bass is engaged in an act of self-preservation, signaled comically by the saliva spraying against the roof of his mouth. But, odd as it seems, given the fearsome reputation of wolves, there is precious little fear in his sublime experience (partly, I suspect, because he never imagines himself the object of *their* attention). So another explanation, embedded in something like embarrassment, is required to explain Bass's falling away from transcendence.

The low comedy of introducing the subject of sandwiches into a narrative about the pursuit of one of the great predators of the American West suggests that Bass is uncomfortable with the point at which he has arrived. It may be that his discomfort comes simply from the return of an ironic consciousness that registers the apparent absurdity of a late-twentieth-century journalist wanting to "smell a kill" in the classic manner of grade-B werewolf movies; but I think there is another motive in play here that goes to a problem that has haunted the sublime as it haunts the "postmodern sublime." From its eighteenth-century origins, privilege has been latent in the sublime. Kant posited universal accessibility for the sublime, and followers like William Wordsworth and Percy Bysshe Shelley theoretically subscribed to this idealism that anyone could have the experience. But looking over its history, there is little evidence that the sublime has functioned so democratically. Instead, a special category of individuals with propensities and opportunities not available to the common person experience the sublime. This comes through clearly in Bass's book. Alone among "journalists," Bass is granted a trip into the wolves' forest with perhaps the only guide who could lead him to the sublime, and he has the experience. But, just as clearly, Bass (with Wordsworth, Shelley, and Kant) wishes that he were not so privileged; that is, he wishes that more people could have the experience that he does of "thinking like a wolf."

The book vacillates right up to the very end on this subject, when Bass recounts a story told to him by an environmentalist friend about a fat dentist (in this book human fat is a sure measure of alienation from nature) with "gold tinged fingers" who was hunting Alaskan wolves from an airplane. The environmentalist telling the story is deeply disturbed that the fat dentist "was so *close* to understanding," in other words, was so close to the sublime, but failed to attain it. "He had almost seen it, [his friend said]: just by the way he was talking, the awe in his voice and eyes" as the dentist described leaning over the wolf with his gun. But, finally, the fat dentist *did not* understand (161). Bass almost certainly means the story to illustrate the potential for *anyone,* even a flying, fat hunter who makes his living inflicting pain, to become free and "one of the pack," but the story can also be read another way. Only certain people, under certain circumstances, predisposed in a certain way can understand what Bass and his friend understand. It is, in other words, a rare and privileged experience, available to an exclusive community called "environmentalist."

The problem with this exclusivity, given the hortatory character of the book, is that it provides little ground upon which to base hope for the restoration and preservation of wolves in the West. Furthermore, the experience that binds this community of environmentalists is impossible to sustain. Eventually, cold feet and hunger will precipitate the return to a human "self" and the reinstitution of taboos against blood lust. It is at this level of cold feet and taboos, just as much or perhaps more than at the level of sublime transcendence, that common humanity operates in the West that Bass describes, leaving the reader doubtfully wavering between the fact of the everyday and the illusive possibility of the sublime.

Although discomfiting, this position is characteristic of "contextualizing" that occurs in the "postmodern sublime." Put simply, Bass ends up abandoning any pretense of philosophical coherence such as the older sublime might afford. There is little evidence of an abstract understanding that cuts through differences in individual experiences characteristic both of the discourses of the nineteenth-century sublime and, surprisingly, of modern ecology. Though he cites a number of ecological accounts of the value of wolves in the Montana ecosystem in the course of the book and allows them to *inform* his position, Bass ends up trying to create a new mythos around the possibility of thinking like wolves.

If I am interpreting the book correctly, then, Bass is trying to solve the problem of privilege inherent in the sublime by backing away from the experience, almost as if he were embarrassed by it, and rejoining the muddle of everyday existence. In *The Ninemile Wolves,* neither ecology nor sublime transcendence can be counted on to clarify the muddle or fill the gaps left by unsighted and killed wolves. If there is a problem with Bass's approach to the muddle and the possibility of thinking like wolves, it is that he never fully disengages from anthropocentrism, even as he approaches sublime transcendence. It is always Bass and other people doing the looking at and for wolves. Because they are absent from his experience, the Ninemile wolves are never described as looking back at him, smelling him, sensing him; but they might have been, even though he did not encounter them. Had he seriously entertained the possibility of being seen by the unseen wolves, the problem of privilege might have assumed a different shape.

Strange though it is to European ways of seeing and thinking, but common to aboriginal ways, the wolves may not have meant him to see them. In 1996 my daughter Emily worked for Mike Jimenez, who was trying to finish up collecting data on the movements of the Ninemile wolves for his Ph.D. dissertation in wildlife biology at the University of Montana. For three months she tracked the Ninemile wolves day and night using radio telemetry as well as traditional tracking methods, never seeing one of them until the last day of work in late August. Not seeing them was an important part of her brief, Jimenez's theory being that the sight of her might affect the wolves' movements. On that last day, however, as she was sitting in her truck taking a break on the edge of the road, there appeared, to her amazement, three wolves. They played within a few feet of her for twenty minutes or so, untroubled, but watching her watch them. Though a trained biologist, she thinks it possible at least that somehow they knew she was leaving their trail and that they had come to say goodbye. What a fine thing it would be, and I think Rick Bass would agree, to live in a country where we might join the wolves on the horizon of our consciousness where the self fades into thinking like a wolf or being thought of by a wolf.

Notes

1. Jim Cheney, "Postmodern Environmental Ethics: Ethics as Bioregional Narrative," *Environmental Ethics* 11:2 (1989): 117–34.

2. Rick Bass, *The Ninemile Wolves* (New York: Ballantine Books, 1993), 147.

3. Edmund Leach, "Anthropological Aspects of Language: Animal Categories and Verbal Abuse," in *New Directions in the Study of Language*, ed. E. H. Lenneberg (Cambridge, Mass.: MIT Press, 1964), 36.

4. See, for example, William Boelhower, "Inventing America: A Model of Cartographic Semiosis," *Word and Image: A Journal of Verbal/Visual Enquiry* 4:2 (April–June 1988): 475–97.

5. Aldo Leopold, *A Sand County Almanac and Sketches Here and There* (New York: Oxford University Press, 1987), 130.

6. David Abram, *The Spell of the Sensuous: Perception and Language in a More-Than-Human World* (New York: Pantheon Books, 1996).

7. See Edmund Burke, *A Philosophical Enquiry into the Origin of Our Ideas of the Sublime and the Beautiful*, ed. James T. Baldwin (Notre Dame: University

of Notre Dame Press, 1968); Immanuel Kant, *The Critique of Judgment,* trans. James Creed Meredith (Oxford: Clarendon Press, 1952, 1978); and Friedrich von Schiller, *Naive and Sentimental Poetry and On the Sublime,* trans. Julius A. Elias (New York: Ungar, 1966).

8. Cheney, "Postmodern Environmental Ethics," 117.

9. See Mick Smith, "Cheney and the Myth of the Postmodern," *Environmental Ethics* 15:1 (1993): 3–18; and Jonathan Bordo, "Ecological Peril, Modern Technology and the Post-Modern Sublime," in *Shadow of Spirit: Postmodernism and Religion*, ed. Phillipa Berry (London: Routledge, 1992).

"Too Damn Close"

Thresholds and Their Maintenance in Rick Bass's Work

RICHARD KERRIDGE

THERE IS A RECURRING paradox in Rick Bass's writing. He wants to enter wild places and encounter the rarest creatures, yet he also wants these places and creatures to remain unknown, on the far side of a threshold. He does not wish the strange and rarely glimpsed to be transmuted into the familiar and thoroughly known. Because any encounter will begin to initiate this transmutation, Bass seeks only the briefest meetings: the most momentary intersections of separate worlds. For him the most fascinating places are those that refuse to yield themselves up, retaining their mystery, their deep hinterland, and continuing to offer frontier experiences, visitations, and encounters in what anthropologists call "liminal" space.

He dislikes, for example, the radio collars that biologists place on wild creatures. For Bass there is a sense of loss in always being able to know where these creatures are:

> I'm not much on radio collars, though it doesn't really matter what my thoughts are. I understand that they can be used, like anything, with discretion or without discretion. The wolves I've seen in the wild have not had radio collars, and I'm glad for it. I've seen grizzly bears with and without radio collars and seeing a grizzly with a collar does nothing for me; seeing one *without* does everything. Just behind the collar are trappers, helicopters, computers—*knowledge,* instead of mystery. (*Ninemile Wolves,* 91–92)

This surveillance may, Bass concedes, be benign. Often the collars are for the animals' protection. But surveillance it is. It may deny the animal nothing, but it denies us the experience of being taken by surprise. An animal in a collar is an animal whose movements may be tracked, intercepted, controlled. To Bass such surveillance is yet another encroachment on the wilderness, demystifying it and proclaiming its transformation into commodified spectacle, available on demand. A wolf or grizzly wearing a collar bears the mark of human manipulation. However fearsome the animal, the encounter with it cannot quite seem to be an encounter with elemental wildness. Someone has too clearly been there before, and the creature does not confront us as an emissary from unknown territory. The frontier experience is diminished.

Bass is not as purist about this as I am making him seem. As the quotation shows, he is willing to be pragmatic, but it is a duty that hurts and is always accompanied by urgent regret. The forms of environmental management that protect wild nature are also threats to its essential wildness. In compensation Bass must reassert this wildness and define it against those very forms of control. This is the dialectic that gives his writing its characteristic surges of energy. I want to explore that dialectic here, but also to suggest that it tends to produce a polarization between the wild and the controlled that drives them too far apart and becomes too categorical in its demarcation of space.

The Ninemile Wolves (1992) celebrates two forces in tension with each other: the heroic efforts of environmentalists to manage and secure the wolves' recovery, and the wolves' independence: their indomitable capacity to evade and exceed control. The implicit suggestion is that if the wolves did not retain this aura of irreducible wildness the environmentalists' efforts, even if materially successful, would be a cultural and spiritual failure. In protecting the wolves the environmentalists would have rendered them domestic and familiar; and thus, though the animals themselves might survive and prosper, their *meaning* would be in danger of extinction. The parts of that mythic meaning that inspire the fear and hatred that drives the persecution of wolves must be dispelled, but other parts—those that give the wolf its glamour—must be preserved. The wolf should cease to be seen as menacing, but continue to be seen as disconcertingly and gloriously wild. The balance is delicate.

The book's preeminent heroes are the elusive border-crossing pioneer-wolves that began, in 1989, to reinhabit the Montana valleys. Above all, there is the alpha female "with a heart like a furnace" (29), who, having been tranquilized, captured, collared, and relocated to Glacier National Park, immediately left the park and ran a hundred and fifty miles before making contact with another migrant wolf, hitherto undetected. "Wolves," says Bass, "have a lovely way of coming out of the woodwork" (33). Radio collars would deprive them of this knack of taking us by surprise. All forms of management and monitoring threaten to rob the encounter with wildness of its thrill; or, if the thrill remains, it will be inauthentic and simulated, clearly obtained by pretense and contrivance.

Like Bill McKibben in *The End of Nature,* Bass fears the loss of "nature" as a source of authenticity as much as he fears the loss of actual places and creatures. He campaigns passionately for the preservation of roadless areas of wilderness, especially in the Yaak Valley where he lives. This is not only to save the forests from physical destruction by clearcutting, but also to keep them unknown, unopened. He wants them to be vast in proportion to the walker, who alone can enter them; and he wants them to be full of hidden places.

Bass's ideal is the kind of deep acquaintance with place that comes from inhabitation rather than analytical study. In a characteristic Romantic paradox, he writes with intense self-consciousness as one standing at the threshold of immanence, yearning for the relinquishment of self-consciousness that would come as he was drawn across that threshold. Book after book recounts Bass's devotion of a large part of his life to the effort to become an inhabitant of the Yaak. Describing the valley, he makes the declaration of a lover crossing a threshold into deeper loving attention: "I don't know why I love it more each year" (*Brown Dog of the Yaak,* 54). Leaving the valley is almost a desertion: "Cold autumn stars are shining down when I leave my wooded valley of Yaak. . . . I love my deep forest of Yaak, love the sanctuary it provides, but Doug, although a new friend, is already a dear one—a teacher and a guide—and so I head South" (*Lost Grizzlies,* 5).

Bass wants to know the Yaak as inhabitant and lover, but if necessary he is prepared also to know it encyclopedically. In his campaign of advocacy, he lists the place's component creatures: "wolves, grizzlies, woodland caribou, sturgeon and giant owls and eagles . . . cedars, hemlock, spruce, fir, pine, aspen, ash, alder, tamarack" (*Book of Yaak,* 14). Taking such an inventory involves standing back and attempting to sum the place up or see it whole. This position of survey is distant from the kind of experience that might come from belonging to the valley and being integrated into its complex ecosystem. Bass strives to make these two perspectives compatible, and especially to avoid compromising the second. Having made his inventory, he is concerned to show how the creatures listed may still take the walker in the forest by surprise. He is interested in the shock of recognition when a rare creature is encountered and in the instant of seeing that creature before identifying it. Names, as we shall see, are often delayed in Bass's narratives: description of the creature comes first.

This is a familiar device in writers influenced by Viktor Shklovsky's account of how art may defamiliarize objects to which we have become habituated—in the 1970s "Martian" school of British poets, for example. In Bass, however, it is a naturalized device, used to evoke a moment of perception prior to recognition, and implicitly to privilege that moment. Turning from his inventory, Bass replaces himself in the valley, putting himself at hazard and coming upon the valley's creatures unexpectedly. A grizzly is suddenly revealed by a turn in the trail (*Book of Yaak,* 56). A mountain lion rushes out of the woods in pursuit of Bass's dog (*Brown Dog of the Yaak,* 30). With each encounter the Yaak reveals a little more of itself: each is a sign of potential, promising further revelations. And each vanishing—the wolves and grizzlies retreating into remote hinterlands, the dog's unexplained disappearance from Bass's yard one afternoon—reaffirms the place's mystery, its status as threshold.

This is nature writing in the tradition of the Romantic sublime, in which to venture into the wild is to come nearer to the presence of God or its secular equivalent. The rarest places, hardest to reach, are the closest to the domain of the ineffable; to exhaust these places by opening up their innermost recesses and mapping their entirety is to banish this ineffability. If the place has been explored to its furthest limit, there remains no threshold from which the protagonist falls back in awe, unable to cross because doing so would mean being transformed into something beyond communication. In Paul Hamilton's description, the characteristic move of the Romantic sublime is that it "recasts failures of understanding as the successful symbolic expression of something greater than understanding" (Larrissy, *Romanticism,* 13).

William Wordsworth in Book VI of *The Prelude* (1805 text, ll. 488–640) provides a famous archetype. The poet and his companions climb an Alpine pass in order to cross from France into Italy but lose the path, only regaining their bearings when the highest point is already behind them. They meet a peasant, who tells them they have already crossed the Alps. At the time of passing the highest point they had no consciousness of doing so; thus are they saved from an experience that might represent a completion of knowledge of that landscape and therefore an end to its capacity to offer the sublime. The poem's speaker, the older Wordsworth looking back on this experience, reflects that "our destiny, our nature, and our home / Is with infinitude, and only there" (538–39). He recounts how, descending the gorge after discovering their error, he felt an increasing sickness and pressure associated with a sense of the disparity between the visible surface of the landscape and the infinite processes at work within it. Relief from this feeling was found only through an appeal to all-inclusive abstractions: "the types and symbols of Eternity" (571).

In Wordsworth's narrative a providential accident prevents the traveler from exhausting the landscape's potential for the sublime. Similar necessary failures occur frequently in Bass's work. *The Lost Grizzlies* (1995) tells the story of three attempts, between 1990 and 1993, to discover with certainty that there were still grizzly bears in the Colorado mountains, where they had been declared extinct since the 1970s. As Bass admits (95), the quest is ambiguous, since the best chance of survival for any remaining grizzlies may lie in remaining undiscovered. In achieving its end, the expedition may endanger the thing it craves: a neat materialization of the characteristic paradox of quest literature. Added to this is Bass's familiar paradox. He wants to find the bears, but not to familiarize them: not to convert them into something thoroughly known. Desire is aroused by that which is rumored and remote, and is brought to a pitch of excitement by the proximity of the still-invisible object. The moment when that object comes into view is the climax and the beginning of anticlimax. At that point begins the familiarization of the desired thing, its conversion from rare to common.

A strong influence on this book, given explicit homage (40), is Peter Matthiessen's *The Snow Leopard* (1978), the narrative of another search for a rare mountain-creature. Famously, perhaps providentially, Matthiessen does not have to face the problem of anticlimax because he never sees the snow leopard, though there are several charged moments when he feels he is about to see it. The leopard provides a never-to-be-reached threshold that draws the traveler on. The word never becomes flesh. Matthiessen's other search is for his recently dead wife. At times the snow leopard seems to represent her, in its refusal to materialize and in the diffuse yet constant presence that is maintained because the leopard is not pinned to a particular place and time. Matthiessen's ability to accept its nonappearance signals a new stage of his bereavement.

Bass does eventually see a grizzly, however, and therefore has to find a different technique to avoid the conversion of the longed-for thing into a familiar thing. He uses an absent center. When he sees the bear he does not recognize it or does not dare to know what it is. He has just noticed the uneasy behavior of some deer:

> A great wind-weathered fallen fir-tree lies on its side halfway between me and the skittery does, which are now only thirty yards away. When I am ten yards from that fallen tree—which I am all but ignoring, focusing on the deer—a creature leaps up from behind it, seemingly right in my face, a brown creature with great hunched shoulders. It's a bear with a big head, and for the smallest fraction of time our eyes meet. (214)

The word "bear" is delayed for a sentence, and the all-important word "grizzly" comes two pages later, long after the bear has gone. Once the animal is absent, it can be named. Only minutes after the sighting it has already withdrawn into the realm of uncertainty and is thus protected from loss of mystique. Did he really see it? Believing he did becomes, as he descends the trail, more and more an act of faith:

> . . . I'm convinced that was how I was able to get so unnaturally close to the bear.
>
> Which I believe was—is—a grizzly. (216)
>
> I saw a bear. I believe it was a grizzly. (218)
>
> I am so rattled by the sanctity and strangeness of the encounter that I continue to try and construct in my mind ways for it *not* to have been a bear—for it to have been a figment of my imagination, the hallucinatory tremblings of an aneurysm, perhaps. The Blue Spark Special. Are the things we see and feel real? Aren't they as real as rock? We *are* still alive, still sensate, aren't we?
>
> It *was* a bear, a lunging, fleeing, giant bear. (218–19)

The question of whether he really met a grizzly provokes a series of questions about the reliability of his perception, as if what he has seen is incompatible with normal possibility; as if his meeting, on the mountaintop, was with God. The three sections of the book are entitled "The Fall," "Revelation," and "Teeth of Heaven."

From the beginning, the searchers' approach to bear territory has been marked by stages of initiation. Moving from suburbs into foothills, they pass through a series of zones, each of which increases their sense of separation from the urban and domestic. In the outer circles of wildness they are depressed by litter and the mere presence of hikers. Farther in, they enter a high meadow reached only by descending a dangerous rock chimney. Such a place should be pristine, but to their dismay they find a hunter's glove, possibly dropped from the air. This small out-of-place object, abruptly appearing from another world without initiation, has the power of a taint or defilement. What they thought of as wild space suddenly is not. "I look at him as if to say, We did not get far enough in" (58). A similar uncanniness attends objects from the wild that are encountered in urban space—particularly a bear's head, perhaps a grizzly's, in a town bar (75–77). By insisting that boundaries should not be easy to cross, the writing strives to establish a strict duality between wild and familiar spaces.

"We did not get far enough in." Distance, in or out, becomes a preoccupation. Another meeting with a grizzly, in *The Book of Yaak* (1996), elicits the repeated exclamation, "Too close; too damn close . . . We were all too damn close" (56–57). Getting too close could mean death for the man or for the bear. In *The Lost Grizzlies* the paradox, again, is that if the searchers succeed in establishing that grizzlies are present, they will then argue that the animals should be approached as little as possible. "If we find the bears—*when* we find them—we must turn our backs and walk away" (56). Once contacted, the grizzlies are to remain positioned as wild and unfamiliar, beyond the threshold.

"Liminality" as a concept in anthropology, first introduced by Arnold van Gennep, was given extensive definition by Victor Turner in *The Ritual Process* (1969) and *Dramas, Fields and Metaphors* (1974). Liminality, in this context, is a process connected with rites of passage. The initiates, often moving from childhood to adulthood, are ritually separated from their place in the social structure. They then pass through a liminal zone, a space "that has few or none of the attributes of the past or coming state" (*Ritual Process,* 94), before undergoing a rite of return and reincorporation into the social structure, in their new identity. Each stage, each *limen* or threshold, in this departure and return will be marked by ritual. In some societies, the liminal zone for young men is a period spent outside the community, with other male initiates, in wild nature. Turner describes this zone as "open and unspecialized, a spring of pure possibility as well as the immediate realization of release from day-to-day structural necessities and obligations" (*Dramas, Fields and Metaphors,* 202). David Trotter, in *The Making of the Reader* (1984), has applied this concept to Romantic poetry, in which liminality becomes secular and individual. Wordsworth's special attention to vagrants, travelers, and beggars as well as his poetic narratives of excursion into wild landscape and return are identified by Trotter with the desire to move in and out of liminal space.

In *The Lost Grizzlies,* the thresholds of this space—the various stages of entry and withdrawal—register in marks and traces that indicate that either humans or bears have recently been present: two worlds at a point of intersection. The grizzlies' proximity becomes tangible in a number of signs: spoor, claw-marks, skulls, bedding-litter, hairs, scats (excrement). Absence vies with presence in the aura of these objects, which the explorers make into totems. The signs are at first equivocal and later more certain, until, on the penultimate expedition, the party gets near enough to hear the warning teeth-clicking of a group of bears, which still do not show themselves (151). After Bass has finally seen his bear, its receding presence also is marked by traces. Bass finds three huge scats, still moist, which he carries back for identification (221–22). Each scat is a tablet brought down from the mountain, a token of the bear and a reclaimed portion of the abject, which Bass is prepared to handle with the intimacy he was unable to extend to the animal itself.

The desire of Bass's expedition to encounter these rare creatures is flirtatious. The men want to see the bear, but they want seeing it to be difficult, to be promised and denied, to be anticipated and remembered rather than held in the present. Intermediary objects, things that have touched the bear, are caressed and examined with an intensity generated by the absence of the animal itself, still distant across the threshold. The reasons for all this are eminently practical, but also providential, in that they allow the thresholds to be maintained.

When Bass visits Romania to watch brown bears, as he recounts in his essay "Creatures of the Dictator," he encounters a different problem. The bears have been familiarized by the practice of luring them into the open with baits. The baiting draws the bears in close to a hunting lodge from which the dictator Nicolae Ceausescu, recently overthrown and executed, used to shoot them. Habituated to the baiting, they now move in predictable ways. The encounter with a bear is thus deprived of its status as a chance meeting between two creatures moving independently; it loses its mystery and is no longer an intersection of two separate worlds.

Bass says, "I am almost unable to look at the bears—it feels pornographic" ("Creatures of the Dictator," 140). The bears have been brought across the threshold, into the zone of the familiar and controlled:

> I'm not even as upset about the fact that the bears are being shot, for once, as I am about the method: the incredible steps that have been taken to avoid an engagement with nature. We could be anywhere, I think—it doesn't have to be in Romania, at the edge of the old, crumbling Communist empire. We could be at a game farm in California, Texas or Illinois, in a hunting blind—a shooting gallery—set up for some rich industrialist to come and do their thing. (139–40)

The wild ceases to be space marked off from that of the community. These bears, lured up close, are as uncanny as the stuffed grizzly-head in a town bar in *The Lost Grizzlies.* Bass's desire is to find a new source of liminal mystery, and in "Creatures of the Dictator" he achieves this in two ways. One involves his baffled sense of proximity to the murderous violence of Ceausescu's regime and its overthrow. He is close in time to these terrible events and stands on the same ground (a refrain in the essay is that the soil has been soaked and soaked with blood), yet his own safety divides him from them absolutely. They become a powerfully absent presence. At the beginning of the essay, he speculates that "perhaps, underground, all the flesh has not finished rotting off of Nicolae Ceausescu's skull" (123): a vision in which the penetrating scrutiny of scientific materialism combines with gothic terror. His imagined ability to look closely at Ceausescu's skull in its secret place underground gives a glimpse of the process of familiarization and demystification that would occur if the skull were available for forensic examination. Since the moment is imaginary, however, that process is abruptly foreclosed, and instead we are given the excitement of standing at a threshold we are unable to cross. We are safe, but can feel the proximity of something measurelessly terrible. The threshold here is between subjectivity and mortality. Bass's sensation is similar to that felt by Wordsworth in Book X of *The Prelude,* when he visits Paris only a month after the September massacres:

> . . . the fear gone by
> Press'd on me almost like a fear to come;
> I thought of those September Massacres,
> Divided from me by a little month,
> And felt and touch'd them, a substantial dread. (ll. 62–66)

Bass's other method of restoring a sense of threshold and mystery, and of escaping the feeling of degradation that fills Ceausescu's hunting lodge, is to attempt to discover whether his Romanian guide, Weber, secretly loves the bears. Weber is an expert who seems thoroughly worldly in his involvement in the system's compromises and who professes a detached scientific rationalism. "It's classic Communism, I think smugly. . . . Still, it becomes my goal to try and get Weber to admit that, yes, he loves the bear" ("Creature of the Dictator," 130). Weber will not make the admission explicitly, but Bass's observation of him provides signs enough for a moment of release. As Weber watches a bear:

> . . . he leans forward quickly, lips moving, mumbling to himself; as if this is the first bear he has ever seen.
>
> He loves the grizzlies. (140)

If the bears are the object of a lover's gaze, this will do something to move them back across the threshold, enabling them to elude familiarity and mastery.

I hope it is clear from my account that I admire these effects in Bass's writing. I want to conclude with a note of reservation, however, from the perspective of an English ecocritic in a land without large areas of wilderness, a land in which even a walk into the mountains will not carry you farther than a few hours from roads and habitation. If English enthusiasts for nature are to retain any version of the Romantic sublime, it will be a sense of the sublime felt in close proximity to the familiar and the instrumental; the long initiatory preparation will not be possible. One recourse for English nature writing, traditionally, has been what the poet and critic Jeremy Hooker has called "ditch vision": the focus upon small margins, interstices, and micro-worlds. Hooker points out that "the feeling for particulars in a localized nature and for places with a human scale, as distinct from the sublimity of wilderness, has been strong in English writers since Gilbert White" ("Ditch Vision," 26). Nature writing that focuses on places with a human scale is likely to resist drawing clear boundaries between wild territory and familiar territory, in favor of a more complicated mixture in which the wild is to be found in the midst of the ordinary and vice versa.

The nature poetry of Ted Hughes, for example, provides an interesting point of comparison with Bass. Hughes, I will suggest, adopts similar strategies to Bass but draws his boundaries in very different places.

To Bass, a wolf or grizzly wearing a radio collar, or a bear lured in close by a bait, is beginning to lose its aura and is perhaps halfway to being a domestic animal. But in Hughes's poem "The Bull Moses," which first appeared in his collection *Lupercal* (1960), a farm animal (albeit an imposing one) provides a threshold encounter not so distant from the liminal effects of *The Lost Grizzlies.* A child is hoisted up to see over the door of the bull's stall, so that something normally hidden, something excitingly powerful and dangerous, can be glimpsed. The hiddenness of the animal intensifies the child's desire to see it. If it were easy to see—if the gaze could hold it steadily—its aura would begin to disperse. The poem re-enchants the bull by setting imaginary walls and thresholds around it, in addition to the material walls that are there to restrain this dangerous animal. Hughes's speaker—who seems to be the adult poet looking back at this childhood moment—sees all these walls as marking a line between two worlds. The bull, huge yet barely distinct in the darkness, is "Something come up there onto the brink of the gulf, / Hadn't heard of the world, too deep in itself to be called to" (*New Selected Poems,* 32). Much the way that spoor and scats mark the edges of the grizzlies' world, the threshold of the bull's is marked by changing states of moisture in the steam of his breath and the "ammoniac reek" of his urine.

Hughes re-enchants an animal that has, in material practice, been thoroughly appropriated for the purposes of industrial farming. He aligns this bull with generations of wild bulls and implicitly with ancient traditions of bull-worship. The encounter is dramatized as a pause. The child is held at the edge, just short of being thrust or dropped into another world, and the speaker, remembering this moment from childhood, gazes raptly across the threshold at something immanent and barely remembered. The bull comes to signify animal instinctiveness and authenticity. More specifically, he signifies a primal masculinity, imprisoned, minotaur-like, in a deep cell. Because the bull still possesses these qualities, while the speaker, full of Romantic self-consciousness, feels alienated from them, the bull inhabits a different world. The poem presents the bull's power not as defeated and imprisoned but as latent and intact. In the completeness of his dreamy immersion he seems impervious to our world, untouchable by it. People make scarcely more impression on his consciousness than the fly at which he swings his muzzle. His docility is seen as a mysteriously deep self-absorption.

But what is missing—what the poem disavows—is knowledge of the agricultural practices that have domesticated the bull and reduced him to docility. In the second half of the twentieth century these practices became further and further removed from the traditional husbandry that can be seen as at least allowing nature some space. Most notably excluded from the poem is the industrial perspective that sees cattle as production-line commodities, measuring them in terms of carcass weight, udder conformation, and so forth. It is true that Hughes's poem seems to recall an event in his own childhood—in the 1930s or early 1940s, before the industrialization of farming in Britain in the postwar decades produced the "factory farm." It is also true that Hughes later expressed public disquiet, in the preface to *Moortown Diary* (1989) and elsewhere, about many aspects of modern intensive agriculture. But by 1960 the industrialization was well under way, and "The Bull Moses" does not include markers to indicate that its events belong to a specific historical period, nor acknowledgment of its role as a mediator of the world of farms to a wider community. Since the 1960s Hughes's poetry has been consistently popular and has frequently been set for study in schools (he is one of a small number of contemporary poets named in the National Curriculum for students aged 14–16). His work has played a major part in the literary representation of farming in the era of industrial agriculture. In that preface to *Moortown Diary,* he describes the part of Devon where he bought a farm with his second wife as a secret, unviolated enclave:

> Buried in their deep valleys, in undateable cob-walled farms hidden not only from the rest of England but even from each other, connected by the inexplicable, Devonshire, high-banked, deep-cut lanes that are more like a defence-maze of burrows, these old Devonians lived in a time of their own. It was common to hear visitors say: "Everything here's in another century!" (*Moortown Diary,* viii)

Deep valleys, walls, banks, lanes, mazes, burrows: the emphasis again is on thresholds and boundaries that mark this secret place off from the outside world. The disaster Hughes proceeds to deplore is the penetration of these boundaries by modernity in the malign form of intensive, industrialized agricultural practices. His implicit wish is to find a way of sealing the boundaries again. The *Moortown Diary* poems were first published, without the preface, as *Moortown* in 1979. The narrative-sequence of poems *Gaudete* (1977), written at much the same time, is also concerned with the power of these thresholds. Set in a village near an Artificial Insemination Centre that markets the semen of bulls, it recounts a disturbing eruption of the sacred-primitive into a modern farming community.

The problem is that these boundaries make for dramatic confrontations, as forces from either side cross abruptly and uncannily into the other, but not for elaborate and pragmatic negotiations. And, apart from these occasional eruptions, the maintenance of the boundaries produces separate worlds that coexist without disturbing each other. In "The Bull Moses," Hughes is able to keep the bull mysterious, deep in its separate sphere, by means of a disavowal of knowledge of what will happen to the bull—hence the reversions to a relatively preindustrial past and to the child's viewpoint. Industrial processing involves a profoundly demystifying intimacy with the animal's body, which is dismantled and converted into various derivative products: semen, tallow, gelatin. What, for Hughes, is the relationship between these ways of seeing cattle and the ways we find in his poem? We might assume the two views to be incompatible. But Hughes does not force the conflict. He finds no place for the industrial discourses in his poem; they come into no collision with the mythic and Romantic ways of seeing the bull that interest him.

In effect, the two discourses coexist, each occupying its demarcated cultural space, safely invisible to the other and therefore untroubled by the other, as if Hughes and the farming industry have simply agreed to use the animal in different ways. Hughes uses the same animal but uses a part of it that is surplus to industrial requirements. The child or poet visiting the farm does not disturb its operation. And in recent years the commodification of old-fashioned farming methods, displayed to tourists on farm visits, has become a familiar part of the "heritage" industry. In his disavowal, in such poems as "The Bull Moses," of knowledge of the industrial context—in his simulation of the child's innocent and spontaneous viewpoint—Hughes also denies himself any explicit recognition that his own work may be a commodity in a similar industry.

Both Hughes and Bass are drawing boundaries that separate the wild from the domesticated, the mysterious from the familiar. Living in the American West, Bass is able to differentiate wilderness from urban or agricultural space much more clearly than Hughes, for whom the boundaries are less physical and have more to do with different ways of seeing. Bass would have difficulty, I think, in accepting that a domesticated animal, so much under the control of industrial agriculture, could yet be the object of this kind of wonder. His view would seem to be closer to that of land-ethic theorist J. Baird Callicott, who argues that farm animals, while deserving of humane treatment, have been carried too far from wildness and must belong in a different category than wild animals ("Animal

Liberation," 52–53). Yet both Bass and Hughes make demarcations that erase the context of what they describe. Their differences mask a similarity.

In Bass's case that context includes the work done to maintain "wildernesses" and to contrive effects of "nature." He is willing to accept the necessity of such expedients as radio collars only as long as they are seen as sacrifices for the sake of protecting the wildness that is their opposite:

> It's not the wolves who are captured and collared or injected with xeno-dye who get the break, however. Those are the ones who sacrifice, who give the break, by being studied, to the ones who aren't studied. (*Ninemile Wolves*, 93)

In contrast, Stephen Budiansky argues that "to have nature be 'natural' requires constant human intrusion" (*Nature's Keepers*, 16). Budiansky sets out this case in detail, citing many instances of local ecosystems maintained only by constant interventionist management. He rejects McKibben's contention that to manage nature, to know it penetratingly enough to predict and manipulate its behavior, is to leave it devoid of the kinds of meaning that make it "nature." For Budiansky, "many artificial landscapes are both ecologically important and aesthetically pleasing" (119). His approach is not, primarily, literary; he does not give an account of how the Romantic sublime may be re-created in the midst of artifice. Yet his implicit argument is that this should be possible, and if he did not approve of much else in Hughes, he would probably applaud Hughes's willingness to move the frontier of wildness into the middle of the farm. The belief that to achieve the sublime by deliberate arrangement is to render it inauthentic rests, for Budiansky, on a willful ignorance about the already contrived nature of most landscapes: as, for a poststructuralist, it might rest on a refusal to see the culturally mediated nature of the experience. My reservation about Bass's insistence on the sacredness and remoteness of thresholds is that he keeps the zones so separate as to diminish the capacity of one practice, one discourse, to criticize others.

Note

A version of part of this article appeared in Richard Kerridge, "Ecologies of Desire: Travel Writing and Nature Writing as Travelogue," in Steve Clark, ed., *Travel Writing and Empire*, 164–82 (London: Zed Books, 1999).

Works Cited

Bass, Rick. *The Book of Yaak*. Boston: Houghton Mifflin, 1996.
———. *Brown Dog of the Yaak*. Minneapolis: Milkweed Editions, 1999.
———. "Creatures of the Dictator." In John A. Murray, ed., *American Nature Writing* 1995, 123–44. San Francisco: Sierra Club Books, 1995.
———. *The Lost Grizzlies*. Boston: Houghton Mifflin, 1995.
———. *The Ninemile Wolves* (1992). New York: Ballantine, 1993.
Budiansky, Stephen. *Nature's Keepers: The New Science of Nature Management*. London: Phoenix, 1995.
Callicott, J. Baird. "Animal Liberation: A Triangular Affair." In Eugene C. Hargrave, ed., *The Animal Rights/Environmental Ethics Debate*, 37–69. Albany: SUNY Press, 1992.
Hooker, Jeremy. "Ditch Vision." *Powys Journal* 9 (1999): 14–29.
Hughes, Ted. *Moortown*. London: Faber and Faber, 1979.
———. *Moortown Diary*. London: Faber and Faber, 1989.
———. *New Selected Poems* 1957–1994. London: Faber and Faber, 1995.
Larrissy, Edward, ed. *Romanticism and Postmodernism*. Cambridge: Cambridge University Press, 1999.
Matthiessen, Peter. *The Snow Leopard* (1978). London: Vintage, 1998.
McKibben, Bill. *The End of Nature*. Harmondsworth: Viking Penguin, 1990.
Trotter, David. *The Making of the Reader*. Basingstoke: Macmillan, 1984.
Turner, Victor. *Dramas, Fields and Metaphors*. Ithaca: Cornell University Press, 1974.
———. *The Ritual Process* (1969). New York: Aldine de Gruyter, 1995.
Wordsworth, William. *The Prelude or Growth of a Poet's Mind* (1805). Oxford: Oxford University Press, 1970.

Can a Book Protect a Valley?

Rick Bass and the Dilemmas of Literary Environmental Advocacy

KARLA ARMBRUSTER

> *This book is . . . a sourcebook, a handbook, a weapon of the heart. To a literary writer, it's a sin, to ask something of the reader, rather than to give; and to know the end, to know your agenda, from the very start, rather than discovering it along the way, or at the end itself.*
>
> *My valley is on fire—my valley is burning. It has been on fire for over twenty years. These essays—these pleas to act to save it—it's all I know how to do.*
>
> Rick Bass, *The Book of Yaak*

ALTHOUGH RICK BASS is best known as a writer, and especially as a writer engaged with issues of nature and wildness, increasingly he is becoming identified as a committed environmental activist as well. In particular, he has turned his energies toward saving the Yaak Valley in northwest Montana, his home since 1987, from further clearcut logging. While his fight to save the valley has made use of more traditional political "weapons," such as a campaign of letters to Congress, the cornerstones of his efforts to date are four books of literary nonfiction—*Winter: Notes from Montana, The Book of Yaak, Fiber,* and *Brown Dog of the Yaak: Essays on Art and Activism*—and roughly fifty magazine and newspaper articles about the Yaak. In using his writing as a form of activism for the place he loves, Bass is engaged in what I would describe as literary environmental advocacy: the practice of using literary writing to speak for nature in opposition to prevailing cultural ideologies that sanction the domination, manipulation, and destruction of the nonhuman world.

A tradition of literary environmental advocacy can be found among American writers at least as far back as Thoreau, who began his 1862 essay "Walking" by proclaiming:

> I wish to speak a word for Nature, for absolute freedom and wildness, as contrasted with a freedom and culture merely civil,—to regard man as an inhabitant, or a part and parcel of Nature, rather than a member of society. I wish to make an extreme statement, if so I may make an emphatic one, for there are enough champions of civilization: the minister, and the school-committee, and every one of you will take care of that. (49)

While writers like Thoreau and Bass who "speak a word for Nature" in defiance of prevailing cultural norms are often also described as "nature writers," I see an important difference between the broad category of nature writing and the more specific, though sometimes overlapping, category of literary environmental advocacy. Nature writing is generally understood as literary nonfiction that reflects some combination of the traditions of science, natural history, and personal narrative and interpretation.[1] In their focus on relationships between humans and the rest of nature, writers who adopt the stance of environmental advocacy often draw on these same traditions, but they are further distinguished by their emphasis on the ethical implications of the relationships they see between humans and the rest of nature. In other words, they take the overtly political stance that humans are interconnected with the rest of nature, that humans are no more inherently valuable to the whole than any other part of nature, and that Western culture should adapt its values and practices to reflect such beliefs. While much of what we traditionally consider nature writing relies heavily upon what Scott Slovic has termed the "rhapsodic" mode, which celebrates the wonder and beauty of the natural world, works of literary environmental advocacy are much more likely to engage in what he calls "the jeremiad," an explicit warning or critique designed to persuade an audience to change its perspective ("Epistemology," 84–85).

Most writers in the tradition of literary environmental advocacy have combined their literary efforts at advocacy with more traditional political activism. Significantly, Thoreau's commitment to speaking a word for Nature at least once went beyond the strictly literary to the verge of the political, beyond general proclamations such as his statement in "Walking" to a specific public call for action. As Daniel G. Payne documents in *Voices in the Wilderness: American Nature Writing and Environmental Politics,* Thoreau delivered his essay "Chesuncook," which ends with an impassioned argument for public forest preserves, as a lecture to the Concord Lyceum in 1853. The essay went on to reach a much larger audience when it was published by the *Atlantic Monthly* in 1858.

As the cultural sense of urgency about environmental degradation has grown since Thoreau's time, so has the number of writers who have felt compelled to argue for environmental reform.[2] As Payne demonstrates, just a few decades after Thoreau's death John Muir began successfully building on the groundwork that Thoreau and other writers had laid, becoming the first American writer to "effectively combine esthetic, ecological, economic, and ethical rationales into a persuasive polemic for political change" (*Voices,* 2). By the time of his death in the early twentieth century, Muir's combination of passionate literary nonfiction and tireless public activism had helped to support major conservation legislation and the creation of at least three national parks. Subsequent writers who followed Muir's path of literary and political advocacy include Aldo Leopold, who proclaimed the value of wildlife and the complex ecology of "the land organism" in scientific, public, and literary/philosophical forums;[3] Rachel Carson, who moved from the indirect advocacy of celebratory works of nature writing like *The Sea around Us* to the direct call for action of *Silent Spring,* which alerted the entire nation to the dangers of the misuse and overuse of pesticides; and Terry Tempest Williams, whose lyrical writing about the Utah landscape and the abuse that it—along with its residents—has suffered is complemented by her public activism. In his book, Payne testifies to the powerful effect writers such as these have had on the history of environmental reform in the United States, writing that "[p]erhaps the most remarkable aspect of environmental reform in American politics is the extent to which it has been driven by nature writers" (*Voices,* 3).

The number of books, essays, and articles that Bass has written on behalf of the Yaak suggests that on some level he holds on to the hope that a potent combination of literary and political advocacy can still catalyze significant environmental reform, that a book can save a valley—his valley, to be specific. In "The Blood Root of Yaak," he writes: "Somehow, I remain convinced that words—the immeasurable, untrackable power of them—can save the immeasurable diversity and magic of the Yaak" (16). His writing about the Yaak, while driven by this conviction, is also notable for the extent to which it dwells upon the difficulties and dangers inherent in literary environmental advocacy. He sets this tone in the introduction to *The Book of Yaak*, beginning with his concerns about what it means to write such a book: "I shiver, as I write this. I'm shivering because it's winter in my windowless unheated rat-shed of a writing cabin. I'm shivering because I'm so nakedly, openly, revealing the earned secrets of my valley—places and things I know, which the valley—the Yaak—has entrusted to me" (xiii). The stance of speaking for nature that Bass takes is one that few writers or readers substantively question, presumably because they assume that if nonhuman nature is to be protected from the ravages of human societies, some human being must persuade others to respect the natural world's rights, interests, and integrity. While it is clear that the natural world sorely needs its human advocates and that these advocates can be effective, environmental advocacy is nevertheless a risky and complex undertaking. In his books about the Yaak, Bass demonstrates a self-reflexive concern with both the ethical and practical implications of his own environmental advocacy found in few other works in the same vein.

In doing so, Bass echoes recent discussions within feminist and postcolonial theory as well as anthropology that emphasize the problems involved in advocacy or "speaking for others."[4] While these particular debates have focused on certain people speaking for other, less privileged groups of humans, many of the issues they raise can be extrapolated to human advocates speaking for natural others. In particular, when people such as Bass speak for nature, they risk misunderstanding the needs of the natural place or system they are representing and thus they risk misrepresenting it; consequently, it is important that they examine their motivations for speaking and their relationship to the place, species, or other entities they wish to represent. There is also always the danger that their advocacy will result in human beliefs or behaviors that are ultimately more harmful than helpful; as Linda Alcoff explains in "The Problem of Speaking for Others," the danger of unintended consequences means that it is crucial for advocates to "analyze the probable or actual effects of the words on the discursive and material context" (26). And, of course, there exists the very real possibility that their advocacy just won't make enough of a difference to accomplish their purposes.

The potential for advocacy to go awry or otherwise fail to achieve its goals stems from several interrelated factors: the limits of an advocate's knowledge of the people, place, or other entities that he or she is speaking for; the slipperiness of language, which may not be interpreted as the advocate intends; the gap between comprehension and action, which may leave the audience moved by the advocate's words but still reluctant to act; and the power of the complex cultural forces the advocate is up against, forces that may even affect the advocate's own motivations and approach. While no advocate can avoid and overcome all the risks arising from these factors, those who are conscious of the various ways their acts of advocacy can be weakened, undermined, or turned against them have the best chance of avoiding such outcomes. Thus, Bass's pervasive concern with the ways his advocacy might go wrong may actually improve his chances of avoiding or mitigating the very problems that so preoccupy him.

Ultimately, Bass's writing about the Yaak reveals an ongoing negotiation between his fears about the problems inherent in advocacy and his desperate need to speak in the valley's defense before it is too late. In this essay, I explore this negotiation and what the issues Bass raises might mean for the discourse of literary environmental advocacy in general: How does a writer reach the point of making a commitment to advocacy for a place, even at great spiritual or artistic cost? How does a writer best establish the authority to speak for a natural place, minimizing the possibility of misrepresenting the needs of the place or misusing the stance of advocacy for professional gain or moral self-satisfaction? How does a writer predict the ways in which his or her efforts at advocacy might go awry, resulting in decisions or behaviors that might ultimately harm the place he or she is trying to protect? And finally, how does a writer reconcile the demands of advocacy with the demands of art? Overall, I argue that Bass's awareness of these issues allows him to address them in ways that strengthen the impact of his writing, both as activism and as art.

The Move from Art to Activism

Scott Slovic notes in "Rick Bass: A Portrait" that "[i]t is possible to chart Bass's own progress from bewilderment and discomfort to love, and eventually to fierce protectiveness by reading his series of books about Montana and the Yaak that begins with *Winter*" (131). In addition to chronicling Bass's changing relationship with the valley, these four books also delve deeply into his fundamental concerns about art, activism, and relationship to place. Bass's own relationship to the place he is trying to save began in 1987, when he moved to the unusual wild valley in the northwest corner of Montana called the Yaak. Originally a petroleum geologist, he had begun to make a name for himself as a writer with *The Deer Pasture* (1985), "Where the Sea Used to Be" (1987), and "Wild to the Heart" (1987). Several years after moving to the Yaak, he published a book of literary nonfiction called *Winter: Notes from Montana* (1991), which was, in his words, "about falling in love with [the] valley" (*Book of Yaak*, 2).

In learning to love the valley, though, Bass also learned to fear for its future: clearcut logging was rapidly encroaching on its last wild and roadless areas. Very quickly, he set about trying to save the place he loved—specifically, he began the campaign to preserve the remaining roadless areas in the Yaak as official wilderness. His series of books about the Yaak demonstrates a sense of urgency about achieving this goal that climaxes with *Fiber* and falls back into a more reflective, though still committed and impassioned, approach in *Brown Dog of the Yaak*. In *Winter*, Bass seems to be working primarily in a rhapsodic mode of nature writing: he describes his first winter in the Yaak as a kind of initiation into the place and repeatedly expresses his desire to see the isolated valley as a sanctuary where he can "hide out" from civilization, including its assaults on nature. But even in this first book, he is unable or unwilling to avert his gaze from the clearcutting he sees going on in the Yaak and the damage it causes: erosion of soil, silt-choked streams, and loss of wildlife habitat. He shows himself struggling to suppress the anger he feels at this damage, representing such feelings as fundamentally in conflict with the book's purpose: "I don't mean to rant. I'm trying to keep this polite, low-key, respectful. Quiet. Falling snow. But inside, I rage" (39).

In *The Book of Yaak* (1996), published five years later, Bass has clearly moved far past the "polite, low-key, respectful" mode. In this collection of essays he forcefully demonstrates his profound knowledge and love of the Yaak not only through rhapsodic passages that celebrate the valley's wildness and diversity but also through jeremiads on the forces threatening that wildness and diversity, his determination to preserve it, and his alternating moods of hope and despair about the possibility of doing so. Significantly, Bass sent a copy of this book to the office of every United States congressperson. In *The Book of Yaak* he explains that while *Winter* was about "falling in love with, and learning to fit a place," this book is about the second part of the cycle, "the giving back, after so much taking" (2).

This sense of cycles, and of the importance of giving back, becomes an even more important theme in *Fiber* (1998). While constructed as fiction—at least for its first forty-two pages—*Fiber* is a loosely autobiographical first-person account by a narrator who moves to the Yaak as an artist after a previous life as a geologist and what he calls a "taker." He describes moving from art into a third life of activism and finally into a fourth stage in which he devotes himself to the more "real" activities of selective logging and "hid[ing] deep in the woods and learn[ing] the names of vanishing things, in silent, stubborn protest" (41). Ultimately, the book acts out its narrator's movement from art to the real by breaking out of the fictional mode at the beginning of the fourth and final section, which begins with the proclamation: "There is, of course, no story" and then denies key aspects of the narrative up to that point: "no broken law back in Louisiana, no warrant. . . . I am no fugitive, other than from myself" (45). Bass goes on to describe the plight of the Yaak and entreat readers to help save it—a plea reinforced by the section on "What You Can Do" following the acknowledgments at the end of the book. The book's title, *Fiber,* further emphasizes the importance of the real by drawing our attention to the very material the book is made from.

In *Brown Dog of the Yaak: Essays on Art and Activism,* Bass provides his most direct and detailed exploration of all three of the topics mentioned in the title: art, activism, and his dog Colter, a German shorthaired pointer with "a bomb in his heart," who "burned brightly" in his passion and talent for tracking and pointing grouse. Because Colter inexplicably disappeared one day from Bass's home in the Yaak, this book is a tribute to him—and, by extension, to the Yaak Valley, which produced him and, Bass believes, "carved and sculpted" him during the four years of his life before he vanished. Although he never explicitly connects the loss of his dog with the potential loss of the valley's wildness, his grief over losing Colter is woven throughout the book and functions almost as a foreshadowing of the grief that may still come: "What is vanishing? How do we measure wildness, and decide what needs preserving, both in reality, as well as in story, in shadow? . . . What happens when the durable things fall away, one by one, then two by two? What kind of stories do we tell, as we are falling? And how do we live our lives?" (25).

Bass's admiration for Colter's spirit and his fearless and focused pursuit of his one passion—birds—leads him into discussions of his own passions for art and for the Yaak Valley, and how the second compels him to activism, which takes him away from the first. Throughout the book he comes back again and again to the image of Colter tracking grouse, rushing "like a dervish, left and right, . . . back and forth, as if crossing some burning river, his eyes glowing like candles all the while" (3). In this pattern of casting right and left, Bass finds a model for balancing his need to experience the real wildness of the landscape with the need to create art that communicates the "shadow" of that experience—activities that he represents as potentially irreconcilable in *Fiber.* He also moves past the despair over activism he expresses in *Fiber,* ultimately concluding that activism is a debt that must be paid if either wildness or the art that springs from it is to remain possible.

The Authority to Speak

As feminist and postcolonial critics have insisted for a number of years, the ethical and political legitimacy of any act of advocacy—not to mention the accuracy with which an advocate represents the perspective of those for whom he or she speaks—is tied up with the ways an advocate establishes the authority to speak. In the case of a literary environmental advocate such as Bass, the question becomes how he establishes his authority to speak for the Yaak, to claim as he does in *The Book of Yaak* that his text is "not really a book. . . . [but] instead an artifact of the woods, like a chunk of rhyolite, a shed deer antler, a bear skull, a heron feather" (xiv). Bass is quite self-conscious of his role as advocate, pointing out that he is "advocating for a voiceless thing" (46) and that when he visits his congressional representatives he sees himself as sent by "[t]he bears and wolves. . . . I was speaking for them" (105). Perhaps because of this level of consciousness, Bass seems to have carefully thought through and negotiated a number of the most crucial issues that can affect an advocate's ethical and political authority to speak.

Environmental writers often claim the authority to speak for natural areas by representing themselves as authentic inhabitants of the place in question. Of course, establishing this kind of authenticity is a subjective business, but several criteria can be used to evaluate the relationship the writer claims to have with the place. One is simply how long the advocate has lived in the place—and this is something that many scholars of environmental literature take very seriously.[5] However, I believe that the quality of the time spent is equally as important as the number of years, and so the fact that Bass has lived in the Yaak just under fifteen years does not seem to disqualify him from acting as a legitimate advocate.

It is Bass's deep knowledge of the valley's landscape, plants, animals, and human inhabitants that more firmly establishes him as a legitimate advocate in my view. Virtually all his works on the Yaak, whether they are books, articles, or letters, include some kind of catalogue of the names of the valley's rare, endangered, threatened, or sensitive species, ranging from charismatic megafauna such as the grizzly bear and the gray wolf to little-known plants such as the maidenhair spleenwort and the water howellia. Bass's knowledge of these species extends far beyond their names, however; when the narrator of *Fiber* explains that "[t]here are seventy-six species of rare and endangered plants in this forest . . . and I know them all, each in both its flowering and dormant state" (31), he expresses an intimate knowledge gained through firsthand experience and attentiveness that Bass demonstrates in his other books as well. In *The Book of Yaak,* for example, he writes of a state of intimacy that one can achieve only through this kind of lived experience: "As the winter deepens . . . each day, if you are deep into the rhythm of your place, you can feel the deer coming down off the mountains in the night, moving lower and lower into the valley" (12). But most striking, perhaps, is the place where the narrator of *Fiber* compares his current depth of knowledge to the lack of knowledge he possessed when he first moved to the area (and Bass's other works suggest that this comparison applies to the author as well); almost in disbelief, he remembers the time when

> I did not know the names of the things that I was walking past, or the cycles of the forests, or the comings and goings, lives and deaths, the migrations, of the animals. At night, hiking home after I'd traveled too far or been gone too long, I did not know the names of things by their scent alone, as I passed by them in the darkness. (24)

Importantly, Bass does not represent his intimate relationship with the Yaak as one-sided, between knower and known, subject and object, but rather as deeply reciprocal. The narrator of *Fiber* enacts this kind of reciprocity by consciously and carefully shaping and changing the landscape through his selective logging, but also remaining open to the ways the place shapes him: as he explains, "I am trying to let the land tell me who and what I am—trying to let it pace and direct me, until it is as if I have become part of it" (8). In *Brown Dog of the Yaak,* Bass suggests that he and the other residents of the Yaak participate in such a dialectical relationship with their place: "There is an age-old dynamic of give-and-take—of people sculpting a place, like a nest to live in, and of the land sculpting, creating, our soapy-soft selves—our lives, our cultures, and even, perhaps, our souls" (44). Throughout his writing about the Yaak, he demonstrates a deep sense of humility in regard to the landscape and its nonhuman residents, a humility that is reminiscent of what Gary Snyder has called the "etiquette of freedom," a standard of behavior based on the knowledge that humans are inextricably part of natural systems. Knowing this means recognizing real danger and understanding when a fellow creature has granted you a favor, as Bass demonstrates in *The Book of Yaak* when he describes leaving a mountain after encountering a grizzly bear: "That was how I left the mountain—grateful, more than grateful, for having seen the tracks—and for the bear having heard me coming and having moved slowly away from me, rather than toward me. I knew it was very important not to overstay" (52).

For Bass, a commitment to reciprocity also takes the form of wanting to give something back to the place that has given him so much, the place that he describes in *The Book of Yaak* as having taught him "why and how to live" (173). Of course, his efforts to protect the Yaak are one of the things he gives; I think the narrator in *Fiber* speaks for Bass when he says, "And perhaps this is where the activism came from, after the storytelling—the desire to defend a land that defended me. The desire to give, for once, after a lifetime of taking" (17). I find Bass's commitment to this kind of reciprocity the most convincing evidence that he can legitimately speak for the Yaak, for it suggests that he is truly a part of the place, not just its representative—that there is an underlying truth to the narrator's claim in *Fiber* that his very self is inextricable from the valley: "They can never get me. They would have to get the land itself" (36).

In *The Rediscovery of North America,* Barry Lopez asserts that a true sense of place includes the obligation "to develop a hard and focused anger at what continues to be done to the land not so that people can survive, but so that a relatively few people can amass wealth" (42). Bass's reciprocity with the Yaak clearly includes this kind of anger; in *The Book of Yaak* he explains that "as [the Yaak] became my home, the wounds that were being inflicted upon it—the insults—became my own" (6). Perhaps the strongest expression of his anger at these wounds—and of his frustration that his efforts at advocacy seem so often to go unheard—occurs in the later, nonfictional portion of *Fiber,* in which he attacks art, the left, the right, the Sierra Club, the Nature Conservancy, and even the reader. As he describes it, he is "a snarling wolverine, snapping illogically at everything in my pain, snapping at everyone" (50). While he realizes that such anger is not always effective, it does reveal the depth of his commitment and, perhaps, fuel it as well—ultimately, for him, calling a place home means being willing to defend it, no matter the cost to himself.

For Bass, one of the major costs of activism or advocacy is the damage it can do to his art, as I will discuss later in this essay. He begins to explore the contradictions between art and activism in *The Book of Yaak,* expressing a sense in the passage that begins this essay that using writing for activist purposes is actually a sin from a writer's perspective, a transgression that, as he suggests in "The Blood Root of Yaak," may require him "to sell [his] artistic soul" (17). The narrator in *Fiber* responds to this dilemma by giving up art in order to pursue his third life of activism (though Bass weaves in a suggestion that the narrator can never completely leave any of his lives behind). However, it is in *Brown Dog* that Bass most directly elaborates on the dangers of activism to the artist, expressing his fears that "the violence, the bottomlessness, of activism. . . . will consume us" (68–69) and that it might destroy "the inner peace that can otherwise make art, or a life lived, fruitful" (81). In the end, though, his debt to the place that inspires and nourishes his art is more powerful than his fears about the costs of activism, and so he concludes that he must simply hope it can be done: "pulling activism on a sled or stoneboat behind you, while chasing art" (71).

Another factor that affects an advocate's authority is where he or she locates the impetus to speak—in innocence or in complicity. One danger in speaking for others—including a natural place—is the temptation of believing that speaking for those others means that you are innocent of any complicity in the forces threatening or harming them. An advocate's belief in his or her innocence can be dangerous, often leading to an overly simplistic sense of who is responsible for environmental threats. As feminist critic Linda Alcoff explains, "the practice of speaking for others is often born of a desire for mastery, to privilege oneself as the one who more correctly understands the truth about another's situation or as one who can champion a just cause and thus achieve glory and praise" (29). All too often, environmental advocates view themselves as champions of this sort, locating the sources of environmental damage outside themselves and failing to examine their own relationships to the forces creating the evils they challenge.

Bass, however, sees his obligation to speak for the Yaak as growing out of his complicity in the forces working to harm it, writing in *The Book of Yaak* that "[w]e are all complicit. Shareholders pour gallons of fuel into the maw of the beast, but as consumers, we are almost constantly, daily, checking the oil and changing the wipers. . . . It is our very complicity that gives us the right—the responsibility—not to be silent, but to speak up" (162). Similarly, Bass is careful not to paint the Yaak's problem in terms of loggers versus environmentalists or jobs versus trees and wildlife, explaining that "I am not 'against' logging—though I am against any more clearcuts in the valley. Too often the opposition paints tree huggers such as myself into total obstructionists" (xiv). By seeing the environmentally sound possibilities of logging if practiced on a sustainable scale and acknowledging how even environmentalists contribute to environmental problems, Bass avoids a simplistic, black-and-white version of the situation that would rule out compromise and inevitably end in a stalemate between holier-than-thou environmentalists and the loggers they would see as enemies.

Any act of advocacy rests on an implicit or explicit assumption that the one being spoken for cannot speak and be heard within arenas of power—thus making the act of advocacy necessary. This is certainly true of advocacy for nonhuman entities such as the Yaak, which are unable to speak in human language at all. As Bass explained in an interview, "I know that with any group of individuals that are voiceless, it's easier to manipulate and abuse them, a lot easier to control them, if you keep them voiceless and don't acknowledge their right to exist in the world and their right to have responses to the world" (Stobb, "Wild," 101). Bass conveys this sense that he is speaking for those who cannot speak for themselves throughout his writing about the Yaak, even referring to the valley and its rare and endangered species as "voiceless" at several points.[6]

While it is necessary that human advocates like Bass bring the rights and responses of natural entities to the attention of those who might otherwise ignore them, there is also a danger when advocates assume that they know everything about the entities for whom they speak and that they must do everything for them, overlooking the ways in which those entities are powerful in their own right and ignoring the wisdom they might provide about their own situations. Postcolonial critic Gayatri Spivak has pointed out the difficulties that First World feminists encounter when trying to obtain information about the rest of the world's women in order to speak for them, objecting to the fact that they so often fall back on "a colonialist theory of most efficient information retrieval" (*In Other Worlds,* 179). Like these feminists, advocates who seek to speak for nature must remember to "listen"—at least metaphorically—to what the natural place has to say, to learn from it, and to be aware of the ways the place can and does help itself. As Barry Lopez explains in *The Rediscovery of North America,* "When we enter the landscape to learn something, we are obligated . . . to pay attention rather than constantly to pose questions. To approach the land as we would approach a person, by opening an intelligent conversation. . . . We will always be rewarded if we give the land credit for more than we imagine" (36–37).

In his writing about the Yaak, Bass certainly takes on the role of defender and advocate of the place, but he also represents the ways that the place itself is powerful, sustaining him, teaching him, and collaborating in his efforts. He often characterizes the landscape as setting the terms of what Lopez might call the conversation between them. In *Winter* he emphasizes that "[t]his valley, this landscape, has the option of taking me or rejecting me. I don't have any say in the decision" (67–68). The narrator of *Fiber* recognizes this same power in the valley when he describes being shaped by the Yaak, explaining that "any landscape of significance, of power—whether dramatic or understated—will alter us, if we let it" (4). In addition, Bass also represents the valley as contributing to its own defense in certain ways. In *The Book of Yaak,* for example, he exults when the spring muds prevent logging trucks from running for six weeks. He also describes the way he relies on the Yaak to work its magic on the important politicians and businessmen he and his friend Tim take on flyfishing trips in the area; only once the Yaak has done its part do he and Tim hit the visitors up for letters to Congress. In *Fiber* he even presents the valley as speaking for itself in its own way, through "the eloquence of . . . silence" (51), a silence that one can understand only if one is very much immersed in the place.

While recognizing and listening to the wisdom of the natural place itself plays an important part in establishing writers as legitimate advocates for nature, it is just as crucial that they recognize and listen to the ideas of the people who live in those places. While some of Bass's writing about the Yaak, such as *Fiber,* touches very little on the other people with whom he shares the valley, in other works he makes clear that he does consider them an important part of the place. In *Winter,* for instance, he emphasizes that gaining the acceptance of his neighbors is a crucial aspect of his initiation into the valley. In *The Book of Yaak* and *The Brown Dog of the Yaak* he often writes about his friends and neighbors in the area: people "who trap, who tan hides, who try to log small green slip sales; those who build log and frame homes, who fix small engines, who hunt and garden, who teach, who guide hunters and fishermen, who write, who plant trees, who tend bar, who preach, who raise sled dogs and bird dogs" (*Book of Yaak,* 24). He emphasizes that all of the roughly 150 residents deliberately sought out the wildness and isolation of the Yaak and that many depend on that wildness for their livelihoods. He admits that they don't all agree on everything but suggests that they nonetheless form a real community, bound by their shared love of the place: "A fierce pride develops—a pride of self and place—and even an ornery pride and appreciation for your neighbors; even for those whose politics or values you might disagree with 100 percent" (*Brown Dog,* 43). He represents himself as open to the questions and concerns of those who disagree with him as well, explaining that he participates in an organization called the Yaak Valley Forest Council, which is made up of residents of the area with diverse backgrounds and opinions who have come together to work out a way to preserve the place that they all value.

The Effects of Advocacy

Clearly, the legitimacy of an advocate's authority to speak holds not only the ethical implications I have discussed, but also practical ones; someone who lacks sufficient knowledge of a natural place and its residents, or who speaks primarily for his or her own advancement or sense of moral authority, risks speaking in a way that misrepresents the place and its interests. However, many other factors can also affect the ultimate success of an act of advocacy. As the history of any movement for reform will illustrate, even the best-informed and best-intentioned efforts at advocacy can go awry in innumerable ways—and this is not surprising, since these efforts are by their very nature up against immensely powerful prevailing ideologies and norms. The power of these ideologies and norms to recontain or subvert even the most radical discourse cannot be overestimated: witness the degree to which corporate America has already coopted the discourse of environmentalism. Bass's writing about the Yaak is shot through with an awareness of all the ways in which his efforts to protect it might go wrong; as he confesses in *The Book of Yaak*, "I don't know if a book can help protect a valley, and the people who live in that valley. I know that a book can harm these things" (xiii). While there is no way to assure the success of his advocacy for the Yaak, Bass's realization and occasional straightforward discussion of the many ways his efforts might be undermined may work to avert at least some unintended consequences.

In the late nineteenth century conservationists such as Gifford Pinchot and preservationists such as John Muir parted ways over whether natural areas should be set aside as reserves for human uses such as logging or left alone, preserved for inspirational and recreational purposes but also for the inherent value of their wildness.[7] Today environmental ethicists still debate whether we should value nature instrumentally, as a mean to human ends, or intrinsically, as something valuable in and of itself.[8] For activists like Bass, though, the effectiveness as well as the philosophical implications of arguments for nature's value must be taken into account. In the short run, it seems that focusing on a particular place's instrumental value, such as arguing that we should preserve the rainforests because of the potential pharmaceuticals we can glean from their yet-undiscovered or unexamined species, would be more effective with public and politicians alike. However, many environmental thinkers (including Aldo Leopold in the first half of this century) have worried that this approach leaves many places and species—those without demonstrable value to humans—unprotected and that it fails to challenge the underlying ideology that nature has no inherent value.[9]

Interestingly, Bass's approach to establishing the value of the Yaak circumvents the dichotomy between these two approaches, arguing for its value to humans (albeit in noneconomic terms) and larger natural processes but also making clear that, for him, the "magic" of the place is inherently valuable. All his arguments stem from his sense of the valley's biological uniqueness, diversity, and wildness—qualities that he sees as interdependent. As a mixture of the wetter, lower-elevation Pacific Northwest landscape and that of the northern Rockies, he argues, the Yaak is ecologically unlike any other place. He considers it significant that so many rare species hang on in the valley despite the assaults of logging roads and clearcuts; he has a favorite theory that the animals and plants of the

Yaak—many of them representing endangered species—are genetically important because they are "survivors." For example, he sees the area's grizzlies as possessing "the invaluable, immeasurable genes of survivors. . . . They're not roadside park grizzlies, but the real thing, raw as a secret, shifting and flowing through time, and through the forest: never seen" (*Brown Dog*, 29). While he calls this theory "goofy" in *The Book of Yaak*, he also reports that a biologist agrees with him (80). Even more importantly, Bass points out, the Yaak is in a geographical position that allows the genes of its species to travel to other potentially wild places; in *Fiber* he describes it as a "genetic pipeline to funnel its wild creatures and their strange, magical blood down into Yellowstone and Bitterroot country. . . . It can still resurrect wildness" (47).

As this last passage suggests, for Bass, the diversity of the Yaak is intricately bound up with its wildness. Leaving the valley alone, leaving it wild, will help its diversity of plants and animals persist, he argues; conversely, the valley's very diversity is one thing that marks it as wild. In one sense, Bass's appeal to biodiversity is instrumental, pointing out how the Yaak's diversity can enrich that of other areas; however, this contribution to larger natural processes will benefit not just humans but entire ecosystems and all the species that depend upon them as well. And Bass makes it clear that, for him, the valley's wildness is an intrinsic source of value, explaining that its diversity "contains more power than the sum of its parts. . . . I believe magic in a landscape can be that simple: a place that still retains all of its graceful fitted parts" (*Brown Dog*, 36–37). This magic is something he continually marvels at, and he sees it as the result of a process that transcends human concerns: "after we are gone, I know that nature will keep weaving, and that it will be beautiful" (*Book of Yaak*, 47).

The valley's magical diversity and beauty are inherently worth preserving for Bass, but he understands that this argument may not persuade others: "If action cannot be roused on behalf of the handful of wolves hanging on in the Yaak Valley" or on behalf of the grizzlies, caribou, bull-trout, orchids and moonworts, sedges and swans, he muses, "perhaps action can be roused by anger at what is being done to you, in secret. . . . the story of the quick buck unraveling the hope for a sustainable future" (*Book of Yaak*, xv). This charge that the destruction of places like the Yaak is a vast crime being perpetrated upon the American public rests upon Bass's conviction that the Yaak does contain something of value to all of us. "We need wildness to protect us from ourselves," he explains. "We need wilderness to buffer this dark lost-gyroscopic tumble that democracy, top-heavy with big business and leaning precariously over rot, has entered" (*Book of Yaak,* xv). He argues that saving the Yaak can serve as a challenge to American culture at large, a way to prove that we haven't been completely corrupted by consumerism and that we can still acknowledge the value of a wild place; as he puts it, the Yaak is "a place to save—a place to exercise our strength and compassion—that last little bit that the advertisers have not yet been able to breed, or condition, out of us" (xiv). The wild, roadless areas of the Yaak are producing something more than "just timber," he argues in *Brown Dog* (121): their forests are more than crops of fiber to be harvested like corn or wheat because "what is produced from those untouched gardens is invisible, immaterial, immeasurable—though just as important, and just as nourishing" (44).

Another pitfall of environmental advocacy is the risk that a place or species can be saved only at the expense of other places or species—a point of view bolstered by the political realities of advocacy work, and perhaps most famously by the example of David Brower's successful campaign to block the construction of a dam on the upper Colorado at Echo Park (inside Dinosaur National Monument). Brower, the executive director of the Sierra Club at the time, later bitterly regretted agreeing not to protest the building of the now widely reviled Glen Canyon Dam as part of the final settlement over the Echo Park dam.[10] While these tradeoffs may be unavoidable at times, it is important for advocates to see beyond the ways in which they and their causes may compete with others so that they can focus on the roots of the problems that they all share. Bass sounds as though he might be falling into the trap of pitting the Yaak's interests against those of other wild places when he accuses President Clinton of "trading the currency of the Yaak's wildness for votes and red rock" (46) in the last section of *Fiber.* However, he seems to critique the idea of trading one place's protection for another's when he wonders, in a 1998 editorial in the *New York Times,* "what kind of citizen could stand in a roadless area and be soothed by the seemingly endless sweep of forested blue ridges and yet know that this forest's protection had been bought by the continued liquidation of the Tongass and the Pacific Northwest?" ("What Our National Forests Need"). He acknowledges that all places are equally important to those who love them in *The Book of Yaak:* "I know you have similar stories—identical stories—about [other] places . . . about every place that's loved" (90).

Another controversial issue that can affect the outcome of any act of environmental advocacy is how the concept of "protection" is defined. Some environmentalists feel the best form of protection is to keep an area free of any human use or interaction, but this concept, which lies at the heart of the U.S. legal definition of wilderness, has come under a great deal of attack lately.[11] As environmental historian William Cronon has argued, the very idea that wilderness is or should be pristine and unused by human beings reproduces the human/nature dualism that so many scholars have identified as one of the roots of the environmental crisis. When we assume that nature is at its best when we leave it alone, Cronon explains, "We thereby leave ourselves little hope of discovering what an ethical, sustainable, *honorable* human place in nature might actually look like" ("Trouble with Wilderness," 81).

Interestingly, Bass does not exactly make the argument that the Yaak should be left free from human use. Although his goal is to have its last wild and roadless areas designated as official wilderness, which would drastically minimize human activity within its boundaries, he asks this only because it is the one way to ensure that clearcut logging will not occur. In *The Book of Yaak* he describes the plan he would prefer, which would be to designate the Yaak forests for sustainable, small-scale logging by local people, who would then deliver the wood to local, value-added industries, such as cabinetmakers, thus, as he puts it, making "that tree last for days rather than seconds" (110). Why retain logging, even in this form? As he explains, "I see too much play in the Rockies these days, and not enough work" (68).[12] In *Brown Dog of the Yaak* he elaborates further: "I *want* logging to continue up here, to help this place keep its identity and rough character. But if the forests are lost, we'll lose even logging" (49). Of course, the narrator in *Fiber* practices sustainable, small-scale logging, though he is unable to sell to local industries. Significantly, it is through his work as a logger that he comes into a deeper knowledge and experience of the rhythms of the place where he lives. Thus, Bass presents sustainable work in nature as a way to learn, to gain respect, to become connected to the nonhuman aspects of a place; for example, in *Fiber* he shows the narrator "reading" the rings of a log to learn about the life of the tree he has cut: "Here is where it reached the canopy and was then able to put more of its energy into width and girth than height" (38). Through such passages, Bass seems to be making an argument that there are positive ways for humans to interact with nature, ways that benefit both by building a sustainable and intimate relationship between them.

Another major concern of environmental advocates—and Bass is no exception—is that their statements of advocacy will draw undue attention to the places they care about and perhaps damage them by attracting excessive tourism. The classic example is Arches National Park in eastern Utah, made famous through Edward Abbey's *Desert Solitaire* and, at least in the eyes of some wilderness buffs, ruined by the admiring crowds who have made pilgrimages to visit it after reading the book. In a 1994 interview, Bass seems unconcerned about bringing tourists to the Yaak since he feels it is not a conventionally attractive place, and he has faith that if they do come, "they will be touched by the land and behave in such a way that will not bring it harm and in fact will be inspired to fight their hearts out for it" (Slovic, "Paint Brush," 20). In *The Book of Yaak,* he seems more concerned about potential tourists and their impacts, joking that he is "tempted to tell [his readers] that Yaak is the Kootenai word for carp, or leech, or 'place of certain diarrhea'" (124). On a more serious note, he warns readers that "it is not a place to come to. It is a place to save" (xiv). This issue takes a back seat in *Fiber,* perhaps because the narrator claims to have abandoned advocacy, but it is a real and pressing one. Not only can advocacy-driven tourism dramatically alter the place that is written about, but it can discourage readers from finding the value in the places they live by encouraging them to seek out landscapes similar to those they read about. Ultimately, writers like Bass often gamble that publicizing their places will be worth the risk. Through his awareness of this issue, and his willingness to confront it directly, Bass employs a strategy seemingly designed to inspire readers to act to save the Yaak without encouraging them to visit it.

Art and Advocacy

Bass is certainly not the first literary environmental advocate to note and lament the draining effects of activism: in his case, the ways in which the demands of advocacy take him away from his twin passions—writing fiction and experiencing the wildness of the Yaak firsthand—and lead to what he calls "brittleness." But what is unusual is his recurring sense that the aims and methods of art and of advocacy may be ultimately incompatible. As he indicates in the passage from *The Book of Yaak* that begins this essay, he believes that art—in his case, fiction—gives something to its readers, while activism asks something from them. In addition, he experiences art as taking the artist somewhere new and mysterious; in activism, by contrast, the activist knows the goal from the very beginning. Despite the ways in which Bass sees activism as contrasting and even undermining art, his overriding need to effect political change keeps drawing him back to activism despite the costs and keeps him constantly questioning the effects of everything he does on the place he loves.

Bass's sense that art and advocacy are incompatible is most pronounced in *Fiber*, where the narrator claims to have rejected his second life as an artist for a third of advocacy or activism. This narrator abandons art because he feels it cannot make a significant difference in the world, asking: "What story, what painting, does one offer up to refute Bosnia, Somalia, the Holocaust, Chechnya, China, Afghanistan, or Washington D.C.? . . . Some of us fall out and write letters to Congress, not novels" (40–41). Ultimately, though, this narrator finds activism unsatisfactory as well, describing activists as blinking "on and off like fireflies made drowsy over pesticide meadows" (42). Instead he rejects even activism for what he calls "something real" (21)—a life of physical labor that brings him into deeper and deeper intimacy with the woods that he loves, an intimacy so powerful that he compares its growth to "sinking deeper into the earth" (25). Activists become "frayed by stress and the imbalance of the fight," he points out, so they move on: "Some of us raise children, others raise gardens. Some of us hide deep in the woods and learn the names of vanishing things, in silent, stubborn protest" (41).

However, the narrator's "lives" need not be viewed as the completely disconnected stages he sometimes suggests they are. Interestingly, his new life in contact with the "real" maintains certain affinities with a life devoted to art. He compares the process of selecting which trees he will cut to selecting notes of music: "As one falls or is removed, others will rise, and with each cut I'm aware of this. Art is selectivity—that which you choose to put in a story—and it's what you choose to leave out, too. This new life is still a kind of music, a kind of art, but it is so much more real and physical and immediate" (18). Ultimately, he suggests he has not left his old lives behind but only added new layers to his identity with each new endeavor; as he points out over and over, the processes by which both natural systems and human beings change over time are complex, fluid, and recursive: "Perhaps one reason none of us knows what's inside the heart or core of anything is that it's always changing: that things are always moving in a wave, or along an arc, and that the presence of one thing or one way of being indicates only that soon another will be summoned to replace it, as the night carves out the next day" (17). He also suggests that art itself is equally complex; just as he cannot know how much his old identities as taker, artist, and activist remain part of him, he claims, "neither you nor I can really be sure of how much of any story is fiction, or art, and how much of it is activism" (4). Most importantly, he even hopes that his new life in touch with the "real" can somehow function as activism, working to undermine the cultural forces threatening his place:

> I try to select only the densest, heaviest blown-down logs from the old forests of darkness, and I try to envision them, after their passage to Idaho, or Texas, or wherever they go, as standing staunch and strong within their individual houses' frameworks. I picture houses and homes getting stronger one at a time—one board at a time—as they feed on my magical forest, and then I imagine those strong homes raising strong families, and that they will act like cells or cores scattered across the country—like little stars or satellites—that will help shore up the awful sagging national erosions here at century's end. (20–21)

But with the break from fiction into nonfiction in the fourth section of the book when "the story falls away" (45), Bass seems to reject not only the "one board at a time" theory of saving the country or saving the Yaak but also the efficacy of art as a way to make a difference, insisting that "storytelling . . . has gotten so damned weak and safe" (45) that it cannot save anything. He suggests a similar disillusionment with activism when he recounts the dismal political situation in which "the left has vanished" (45) and embattled natural places like the Yaak are the losers for it. Ultimately, he expresses a deep sense of frustration with both art and advocacy, a frustration about having to ask over and over again for something that seems so right and obviously necessary to him. This frustration doubtless grows from his unavoidable dependence on others—and on his readers in particular—to take action in response to his message of advocacy. Bass's readers are the ones with the power to help save or destroy his valley, a valley they have probably never seen, and it is precisely the limits of his own power to move them to action that produce the frustration and desperation he reveals in the last section of *Fiber.* In that section Bass emphasizes his dependence on his readers by first rejecting it, snapping that "if you think I'm going to say *please* after what they've already done to this landscape, you can think again" (49), and later deciding that he must say "please" after all—but still with a strong note of resentment mixed in. "I am saying please," he writes, "at the same time that I am saying, in my human way, fuck you" (50).

Despite the frustration with activism that Bass displays in *Fiber,* his final words—"Somebody please help" (51)—reveal the desperate desire to save the Yaak that seems always to bring him back to advocacy, despite its dangers and costs. In both *The Book of Yaak* and *Brown Dog of the Yaak,* Bass also comes back to the necessity of advocacy, but in these works he strikes a more hopeful stance and represents art, activism, and the love of a place as even more necessarily interdependent. In all these books, his basic dilemma is that his activism saps the time and energy he would rather put into the "real" experience of his place and into his art—and yet both the place and the art that grows out of it are in danger, thus leading him back to the necessity of activism and advocacy.

While Bass's commitment to art is evident in passages such as the one that begins this essay, he also consistently demonstrates a deep humility about the ways in which his writing is indebted to the "real" world that it strives to represent, and often to the Yaak in particular. In *Brown Dog of the Yaak,* he emphasizes how crucial it is "that you try always to remember that the subject is more important, or more powerful, than the shadow of the subject, which is your artistic treatment of the thing" (13). For Bass, the subject of his art is inevitably found in its opposite: the physical world. As he explains, "[s]urely memories, and stories, require stones, boulders, trees" (8). In fact, he goes so far as to suggest that the measure of art is how well it approximates or evokes the "real" world that inspired it: "Stories *almost* become alive as they more closely approach the thing after which they are modeled" (111). Ultimately, he gives the natural world the credit for any greatness found in his books about it: "when we come back with shining objects, it is not we who were brilliant but the places to which we traveled" (14). In *The Book of Yaak* he claims that art can be seen simply as "one of the spillover effects, one of the indicators of the richness of a place" (37).

As Bass points out in *Brown Dog of the Yaak,* this kind of relationship between art and a natural place might lead to the hope that the place can be immortalized through a work of literature—its beauty and spirit captured for all time, immune to clearcuts or any other damage. Nonetheless, he is adamant that art cannot substitute for the place that inspires it, that it is only the shadow of its subject. But can a work of art help to preserve a place? Certainly, as he acknowledges in *The Book of Yaak,* "[a] great work of fiction can become a cornerstone in the literature of a place" (10) and "[a]rt can be its own sort of advocacy for place" (93). However, it takes time for literature to inspire action, if it ever does; as he explains, "what good does it do that great novel to extend so far into the future—forty years, say—if the place about which it was written vanished, oh, thirty-five, thirty-six, thirty-seven years ago?" (10). Bass's fear is that works of art about a place will wind up as nothing more than "little cages of words and stick-letters, approximations and models of that vanishing world above and below, and all around" (*Brown Dog,* 37).

In his case, Bass feels that the stakes are too high to rely on art alone; as he sees it, "I am not afraid of failing at a short story—at a work of fiction. But I am afraid of failing the valley; and I am afraid of failing my neighbors, my friends and my community" (*Book of Yaak,* 188). Thus, despite the dangers and costs, he sometimes must set aside the fiction he loves and engage in more straightforward advocacy and activism: "You've got to step in and do both. The vanishing wilderness might be able to tolerate a few slackers who traffic, who indulge, in nothing but pure art. . . . [but] you'd better deliver the goods, if you love a thing but choose to take the long path away from it" (*Brown Dog,* 78). While Bass is always wary of the ways in which activism can drain his energies and leave him "brittle," in both *Brown Dog* and an essay titled "The Blood Root of Yaak" he holds out the hope that some pattern for sustaining both art and activism over the long haul can be found in nature. In "Blood Root" in particular, he writes of the "subtle, less dramatic patterns that we might look to for faith in the notion of persistence, as both artists and activists, stories in which a little bit of work at a thing, every day, decides an outcome: the cow elk grazing steadily, conserving her energy late in the fall to earn the extra pounds of fat that will carry her through winter" (12).

Supporting Bass's hope that art and activism can be kept in balance is his recognition that they come from the same root. In *Brown Dog* he asks: "Art, or activism? They shadow one another; they destroy one another: but they share the same inescapable, irreducible bedrock fuel—passion" (118). Certainly, passion has characterized Bass's fiction as well as his nonfiction and other works of advocacy for the Yaak. And this passion is at its heart a passion for a place and for a way of life in that place. Because of the ultimate value Bass puts on that place and way of life—both for himself and for the other people and animals with whom he shares the valley—he has persisted in speaking out for them, again and again, in spite of the risks, difficulties, and costs of which he is so well aware. In his passion and his focus, Bass is like his brown dog Colter, who caused an inexplicable lightness of heart in people who watched him track grouse: "He was a witness, an ambassador. As I think we all are—as we cannot avoid being—for the place where we come from, the place where we live" (48). And in his remarkable awareness of the complex and dangerous nature of his undertaking, he increases the effectiveness of his advocacy both as environmental activism and—despite his own protestations—as literary art.

Notes

1. See Fritzell, *Nature Writing and America;* Lyon, "Part I: A History"; and Murray, *The Sierra Club Nature Writing Handbook,* for definitions of nature writing.

2. See Brooks, *Speaking for Nature;* and Nash, *The Rights of Nature,* for discussions of the increasing prevalence and cultural impact of advocates who argue for the value and rights of nonhuman nature.

3. See Ulman, "'Thinking Like a Mountain,'" on the scope of Leopold's advocacy.

4. See Alcoff, "The Problem of Speaking for Others"; Spivak, "Can the Subaltern Speak?"; and Roof and Wiegman, eds., *Who Can Speak?*

5. For an example, see the discussion of *Fiber*—which Bass read before its publication at the 1997 Association for the Study of Literature and Environment (ASLE) Conference—that took place on the ASLE listserv in July and August 1997: http://www.asle.umn.edu/discuss/discuss.html.

6. See *The Book of Yaak,* p. 46, and letter from Rick Bass to "Friends of and Letter-Writers for the Yaak Valley."

7. See Nash, *Wilderness and the American Mind.*

8. See Proctor, "Whose Nature?" for just one discussion of this issue.

9. See Aldo Leopold, "The Land Ethic."

10. See Helvarg, *The War against the Greens,* 56, for further discussion of this tradeoff.

11. See the Wilderness Act of 1964 for this definition.

12. See White, "'Are You an Environmentalist?'" on the issue of environmentalism, leisure, and work.

Works Cited

Alcoff, Linda. "The Problem of Speaking for Others." *Cultural Critique* (Winter 1991–92): 5–32.
Bass, Rick. "The Blood Root of Yaak." *Orion Afield* 1, no. 1 (Fall 1997): 12–17.
———. *The Book of Yaak*. Boston: Houghton Mifflin, 1996.
———. *Brown Dog of the Yaak: Essays on Art and Activism*. Ed. Scott Slovic. Minneapolis: Milkweed, 1999.
———. *Fiber.* Athens: University of Georgia Press, 1998.
———. Letter to "Friends of and Letter-Writers for the Yaak Valley." 15 February 1997. Found on "Don't Hack the Yaak" web site: http://www.geocities.com/RainForest/Vines/5054/direc.htm.
———. "What Our National Forests Need." *New York Times,* 16 January 1998, late ed., A25.
———. *Winter: Notes from Montana*. Boston: Houghton Mifflin/Seymour Lawrence, 1991.
Brooks, Paul. *Speaking for Nature: How Literary Naturalists from Henry Thoreau to Rachel Carson Have Shaped America*. San Francisco: Sierra Club, 1980.
Cronon, William. "The Trouble with Wilderness, or Getting Back to the Wrong Nature." In *Uncommon Ground: Toward Reinventing Nature,* ed. William Cronon, 69–90. New York: Norton, 1995/96.
Fritzell, Peter. *Nature Writing and America: Essays upon a Cultural Type*. Ames: Iowa State University Press, 1990.
Helvarg, David. *The War against the Greens: The "Wise Use" Movement, the New Right, and Anti-Environmental Violence*. San Francisco: Sierra Club Books, 1994.
Leopold, Aldo. "The Land Ethic." In *A Sand County Almanac with Essays on Conservation from Round River,* 237–64. New York: Ballantine, 1966.
Lopez, Barry. *The Rediscovery of North America*. New York: Vintage–Random House, 1992.
Lyon, Thomas J. "Part I: A History." In *This Incomperable Lande: A Book of American Nature Writing,* ed. Thomas J. Lyon, 3–91. New York: Penguin, 1989.
Murray, John. *The Sierra Club Nature Writing Handbook*. San Francisco: Sierra Club, 1995.
Nash, Roderick. *The Rights of Nature: A History of Environmental Ethics*. Madison: University of Wisconsin Press, 1989.
———. *Wilderness and the American Mind*. 3rd ed. New Haven and London: Yale University Press, 1982.
Payne, Daniel G. *Voices in the Wilderness: American Nature Writing and Environmental Politics*. Hanover, N.H.: University Press of New England, 1996.

Proctor, James D. "Whose Nature? The Contested Moral Terrain of Ancient Forests." In *Uncommon Ground: Toward Reinventing Nature,* ed. William Cronon, 269–97. New York: Norton, 1995/96.

Roof, Judith, and Robyn Wiegman, eds. *Who Can Speak?: Authority and Critical Identity.* Urbana and Chicago: University of Illinois Press, 1995.

Slovic, Scott. "Epistemology and Politics in American Nature Writing: Embedded Rhetoric and Discrete Rhetoric." In *Green Culture: Environmental Rhetoric in Contemporary America,* ed. Carl G. Herndl and Stuart G. Brown, 82–110. Madison: University of Wisconsin Press, 1996.

———. "A Paint Brush in One Hand and a Bucket of Water in the Other: Nature Writing and the Politics of Wilderness: An Interview with Rick Bass." *Weber Studies* 11 (Fall 1994): 11–29.

———. "Rick Bass: A Portrait." In *Brown Dog of the Yaak: Essays on Art and Activism,* ed. Scott Slovic, 123–37. Minneapolis: Milkweed, 1999.

Snyder, Gary. "The Etiquette of Freedom." In *The Practice of the Wild.* San Francisco: North Point Press, 1990.

Spivak, Gayatri Chakravorty. "Can the Subaltern Speak?" In *Marxism and Interpretation of Culture,* ed. Cary Nelson and Lawrence Grossberg, 271–313. Urbana: University of Illinois Press, 1988.

———. *In Other Worlds: Essays in Cultural Politics.* New York: Methuen, 1987.

Stobb, Bill. "The Wild into the Word: An Interview with Rick Bass." *ISLE: Interdisciplinary Studies in Literature and Environment* 5:2 (Summer 1998): 97–104.

Thoreau, Henry David. "Walking" (1862). In *Civil Disobedience and Other Essays,* 49–74. New York: Dover, 1993.

Ulman, H. Lewis. "'Thinking Like a Mountain': Persona, Ethos, and Judgment in American Nature Writing." In *Green Culture: Environmental Rhetoric in Contemporary America,* ed. Carl G. Herndl and Stuart G. Brown, 46–81. Madison: University of Wisconsin Press, 1996.

White, Richard. "'Are You an Environmentalist, or Do You Work for a Living?': Work and Nature." In *Uncommon Ground: Toward Reinventing Nature,* ed. William Cronon, 171–85. New York: Norton, 1995/96.

The Wilderness Act of 1964. In *The Great New Wilderness Debate,* ed. J. Baird Callicot and Michael P. Nelson, 120–30. Athens: University of Georgia Press, 1998.

Jeremiad, Elegy, and the Yaak

Rick Bass and the Aesthetics of Anger and Grief

MICHAEL P. BRANCH

> *I do separate in my mind, totally, the didactic or political writings from art. It's hard to do, but I try. [Merging the political and the aesthetic is] like merging gas and flame. I don't have that possibility and I think it's an incredible danger—it can lure you really close to the edge, and I'm in no way tempted to pursue it further. I already have pushed it about as far as I care to.*
>
> Rick Bass (Slovic, "A Paint Brush in One Hand and a Bucket of Water in the Other," 26)

> *Art, or activism? They shadow one another; they destroy one another: but they share the same inescapable, irreducible, bedrock fuel—passion. Love, or fury. Love, and fury. They will always be near one another, in an artist's heart . . . and for me, there just came a point one day where I was spending too much energy trying to keep the two apart. It seemed artificial, unnatural, brittle, to have two similar passions, sharing the same rootstock—a reaction against injustice and disrespect—and yet to exclude or excise one of them from my life, for the sake of another, did not feel true or healthy. I would rather fail at both than be disloyal to one, even if succeeding at the other.*
>
> Rick Bass, *Brown Dog of the Yaak* (118)

Part I. Neurotic on the Subject: Rick Bass and the Challenge of Literary Activism

The activist is the artist's ashes. And what awaits the activist's ashes: peace?

Rick Bass, *Fiber* (42)

In discussing the tension between writing as art and writing as advocacy, Bass confesses that "it's fairly well established that I'm pretty much neurotic on the subject" (*Brown Dog,* 106). However, in the five years between his 1994 statement that he assiduously avoids the explosive combination of art and activism (in the first epigraph above) and his 1999 assertion that art and activism are inseparable manifestations of his deepest personal and literary passions (in the second epigraph above), his energy and his writing have been increasingly devoted to the activist project of winning wilderness protection for the remaining roadless cores in the biodiverse but heavily logged Yaak, his home valley in northwestern Montana. Indeed, in these few years he has written hundreds of letters, scores of magazine and newspaper articles, and three books—*The Book of Yaak* (1996), *Fiber* (1998), and *Brown Dog of the Yaak: Essays on Art and Activism* (1999)—that celebrate the Yaak, decry its mistreatment, and ask readers to help protect the valley by joining a letter-writing campaign on its behalf.

As Bass has shifted from fiction toward nonfiction, from art toward advocacy, and from the ranging landscapes of Texas, the South, and the West toward the home landscape of the Yaak, he has also raised important questions about the dynamic relationship between the aesthetic and ethical imperatives of nature writing. While environmental literature has for centuries braided literary artistry with a concern for the natural world, the blistering urgency of Bass's sometimes single-minded devotion to the Yaak is now "forcing the issue" by causing readers to consider just how much environmental invective they will accept in the nature writing they choose to read. Bass's recent work invites us to reconsider the relationship of art to activism since this work not only illustrates but also interrogates that relationship. Because Bass's struggle to reconcile the artist and activist elements of his own identity is central to *The Book of Yaak, Fiber,* and *Brown Dog of the Yaak,* these books can help us to think about what we expect of nature writers and what we will allow them to expect of us.

If Rick Bass is "neurotic on the subject" of the proper relationship between art and activism in environmental literature, I would argue that his readers—and readers of contemporary American nature writing generally—are even more so. Recent reviews of the three Yaak books mentioned above are particularly revealing in their deeply divided responses to Bass's energetic preservationist rhetoric.

In one camp are the reviewers—who presumably represent a substantial group of Bass's readers—who not only accept but embrace the forceful and repeated message that the Yaak must be saved. Writing in the *Utne Reader,* for example, Hugh Delehanty is unequivocal in calling *The Book of Yaak* "[a] beautifully written plea to save . . . one of the last great wild places in the United States" (84). In her review of *Fiber,* Mary Sojourner declares that "[I]f I were rich, I would give this book to every burned-out activist I know," and she concludes her review in words that echo Bass's own pleading conclusion to *Fiber:* "Please read it. Please" (32). Like Delehanty and Sojourner, many readers of Bass's Yaak books admire what they view as the hard-hitting truth of his environmental call to arms.

In the opposite camp are reviewers—who, again, surely represent some larger group of Bass's readers—who are impatient, disappointed, even frustrated with Bass as polemicist. In his equivocal review of *The Book of Yaak* in the *New York Times Book Review,* Peter M. Leschak complains that Bass "wants you to support efforts to protect the ecosystem of northwestern Montana's Yaak Valley without being welcomed there at all. Stay away, he urges, just write letters of appeal and protest to Congress, the United States Forest Service and the timber companies" (31). In a vitriolic dismissal of *Fiber,* Stephen J. Lyons objects that "I wanted to read Rick Bass and instead I got William Bennett: a weak narrative and a thin scolding on American culture. . . . [Bass is] angry and frustrated, full of loss for landscape, and filled with hatred for the federal government and the corporate world. In the words of one of my journalism professors, 'We're killing trees for this?' Sadly yes. Save the Yaak, certainly, but do it in spite of this book" (32). Like Leschak and Lyons, then, at least some readers of the Yaak books find what they view as Bass's shrillness detrimental to the quality of his work.

The largest camp of reviewers, though, consists of those representing readers who admire Bass's activist passion but specifically question the literary merits of his endeavor—a questioning that he himself engages in on occasion. Reviewing *The Book of Yaak* in *Outside,* for example, Miles

Harvey concludes that "[i]t's not great literature, but it is effective agit-prop that will no doubt inspire readers to send their own zealous letters to Capitol Hill" (100). In a lengthy review published in the *Los Angeles Times Book Review,* Pam Houston explains that while it is "not [Bass's] most crafted book so far," *The Book of Yaak* "is perhaps his most passionate. It is raw with emotion and meant to be . . ." (8). Reviewers' mixed feelings about Bass's blending of narrative and advocacy are perhaps best expressed by Mary Paumier Jones, who, in her review of *Brown Dog of the Yaak,* comments ingenuously that "[r]eading about Colter [the dog of the book's title] and the Yaak is more fun than reading about activism," but nevertheless praises the overall project of the book (88).

For his own part, Bass clearly cares less about opinions regarding his literary prowess than he does about the central goal of inspiring readers to help him save his endangered valley. Here, for example, are the words with which he concludes *Brown Dog of the Yaak:* "I don't care if you read my books. I don't care if someone says nice things about them, or mean ones. I've heard plenty of both, and it's just words, wind-drifted and gone-past. But please, save the last roadless areas in the Yaak. This valley—the Yaak, and its remaining interior wildness—is the shape of magic. This valley has more to give than just timber" (121). As a contribution to the Milkweed Editions Credo Series, *Brown Dog of the Yaak* is intended to reflect its author's deepest beliefs and convictions, particularly as those beliefs inform and inspire his work. It is telling that Bass's deepest belief about his own writing is that it is less important than the subject it aims to represent and defend. "[I]n that frantic violence of activism, I can rarely view anything these days save through the monocle of the Yaak," he admits. "It is like pulling a plow when instead you want to be ice skating. No writer, no artist, wants to be Johnny One-Note. But for the Yaak I would gladly be Johnny Zero-Note. I would trade any book for one hundred seventy-five thousand acres of wilderness. . . . Warblers, elk music, starlight on the fur of sleeping wolves, wild trout—I would trade a book for that" (*Brown Dog,* 87).

Because readers and reviewers appear so unusually—and so interestingly—conflicted regarding the accomplishment of what I will call Bass's "Yaak-tivist" books, I want to inquire into what our conflicted reaction to these books suggests about our implicit expectations for American environmental writing at the millennium. Most readers seem to feel a genuine admiration for Bass's passion and for his willingness to fight for the place he loves. Readers also appear to understand the ecological importance of such fights, and they are often quick to note that we need people of strength and conviction to be champions for wilderness. In addition, many readers appreciate that Bass stands not for the abstraction of "the environment," but for a particular place where he lives and to which he is entirely committed. In short, readers generally appreciate his ethical project.

However, even readers who do not find themselves impatient with Bass's highly charged activist rhetoric seem to doubt whether the artistic value of the Yaak-tivist books is not compromised by the stridency of the political message they promote. While this reaction is perhaps partly attributable to an entrenched skepticism in literary studies regarding the "literariness" of creative nonfiction—a genre that carries its insecurities in its name (since it is unnecessary to add "creative" to modify "poetry" or "drama," for example)—readers also have a deeper suspicion about the artistic value of advocacy; while "imaginative literature" retains the scent of immortality, writing with an explicit political agenda often strikes readers as circumscribed or ephemeral.

Finally, the overall impression one gets from both positive and negative evaluators of the Yaak-tivist books is that Bass has made his audience uncomfortable. The unmitigated zeal of the author, the alternately frenetic and digressive movements of his prose, the sledgehammer urgency of his message, the openness of his expressions of anger, the thinly veiled heartbreak that lies beneath his rage—all these the reader finds disconcerting and would perhaps as soon avoid, the way we always wish to avoid anger and pain if we can.

What ultimately characterizes the discomforting effect of these books, however, is that their author directly and repeatedly asks his readers for help—he asks them not only to *think* something, or even to *feel* something, but actually to *do* something. We are accustomed to nature writers who exhort us, in general ways, to love the land, to behave responsibly toward it, to respect its nonhuman inhabitants, and to cultivate and honor our connections to place. Indeed, we not only tolerate but virtually require such messages of our environmental writers. But while Bass does all these things, and beautifully, he also grabs us by the collar and insists that we *do* something, and quick: "Am I explaining it clearly?" he demands. "Is anyone please angry enough to write a letter? To write fifty letters, or five hundred? It is a civil war, and if they have no honor for the land, then how can you expect them to have honor or respect for you?" (*Book of Yaak*, 112). Unlike most writing that travels as "literature,"

Bass's directly challenging prose aggressively insists that we account for ourselves—that we either do something to help or admit that we are willing simply to watch while the remarkable wilderness Bass describes is lost forever.

Extreme by what we might call the normative standards of literary behavior, Bass's rage, his grief, and his pleas for help may strike some readers not only as "unliterary" but also as simply too close for comfort—as involving and perhaps even implicating us in a problem that we would perhaps rather read about without being asked to help solve. In the following pages I consider what seem to me the primary dynamics of Bass's disconcerting approach and suggest several literary contexts within which this approach might be more fully understood. By examining the relationship of the Yaak-tivist books to the jeremiad and to the elegy, two venerable literary historical traditions to which I believe these books contribute, I wish to suggest not only that Bass's recent work is literary but that it is perhaps more so than we care to admit.

Part II. Love and Fury: The Aesthetics of Anger

I am saying please, at the same time that I am saying, in my human way, fuck you.

Rick Bass, *Fiber* (50)

In celebrating the life and work of Edward Abbey in a eulogy published shortly after Abbey's death in 1989, Edward Hoagland wrote that what is needed in contemporary environmental writing is "honesty, a pair of eyes and a dollop of fortitude to spit the truth out, not genuflecting to Emersonian optimism, or journalistic traditions of staying deadpan, or the saccharine pressures of magazine editors who want their readers to feel good." Hoagland then imagines righteous ghosts chastising nature writers of our own day for their unwillingness to speak angrily about the environmental damage visible everywhere around them: "Thoreau would be raging with grief in these 1980's. *Where were you when the world burned? Get mad, for a change, for heaven's sake!*" ("Edward Abbey," 44). It was to Abbey's credit, Hoagland asserts, that "no one will ever wonder what he saw as the world burned. He said it; he didn't sweeten it or blink at it or water it down or hope the web of catastrophes might just go away" (45).

Clearly akin to Abbey in his rage and in the directness of his charges against the environmental conflagration to which he bears witness, Rick Bass has written that reading Abbey's *The Monkey Wrench Gang* in 1976 was for him a "crossing over" into a life of passion and anger on behalf of the natural world. Before reading Abbey, he writes, "I hadn't yet learned, or felt, passion—not the passion of defense, the passion of anger, of a back-to-the-wall fight. . . . a call to arms and night fury," and an attendant call to protect "the shrinking wild habitat of the soul of which we've been made guardians" ("Crossing Over," 23). With each passing year of his literary career, however, Bass appears increasingly devoted not only to the passion for art, but also to the passion of anger and the fight. "There's a civil war in the West," he said in a 1994 interview, "and it's a scandal, I think, that exceeds any in our nation's history since slavery. It encourages brutality, it encourages domination, it encourages in the short term everything that is destructive to the thing that matters most to us, which is the future" (Slovic, "Paint Brush," 28).

For Bass personally, the front lines of what he has repeatedly characterized as an environmental "civil war" are in the trenches of the Yaak itself, his home valley, where a number of endangered flora and fauna are waging a losing battle against extinction in the last remaining roadless cores of a once unbroken wilderness now shattered by decades of excessive corporate logging. In his recent work, he speculates openly about the divergence of his own artistic and activist paths, often implying that his shift from art toward activism has been more a matter of compulsion than of preference. "I should have seen how easy it would be to slide from a simple love for this valley into the full flame of obsession," he writes in *The Book of Yaak*. "I never meant to get into [activism] this deep. I only meant to live in these quiet green woods and live a life of poetry . . ." (101, 102).

Despite this avowed preference for a life of art, Bass often characterizes art as a luxury that he can no longer fully afford. In "20515 House, 20510 Senate"—so titled to remind readers to whom their expressions of concern about the fate of the Yaak should be addressed—and again in *The Book of Yaak*, Bass uses one particularly lucid example to dramatize his own changing priorities: "I still believed in art, but art seemed utterly extravagant in the face of what was happening. If your home were burning, for instance, would you grab a bucket of water to pour on it, or would you step back and write a poem about it?" (*Book of Yaak*, 10). In comparable passages throughout his recent work, Bass characterizes his literary activism not as a calculated preference, but rather as an emergency response to an urgent situation. In *Brown Dog of the Yaak,* he explains his view that literary art is the "beautiful shadow" of the physical world that it attempts to represent and from which it draws inspiration (17). If the natural world burns—and the image of environmental destruction as a sweeping holocaust is one that Bass invokes repeatedly—the light of creativity and attention will have nothing to strike, and nothing of sufficient importance will remain to cast the long, rich shadow that we know as literary art. "I will write about the fairy slipper, the Calypso orchid, later. First we must save them," he writes ("20515 House," 5). Or, as an image from *Fiber* contends, "[t]he activist is the emergency-room doctor trying to perform critical surgery on the artist" (42). As the multiple personae of *Fiber* suggest, the artist and the activist are mutually dependent parts of the same person—a complex and often conflicted person who has come to believe that if the activist persona fails to protect the ecological integrity of the natural world, the artist persona will be bereft of the most important subject of artistic celebration.

In his struggle to save the last roadless cores of the Yaak, to negotiate between the demands of his artist and activist selves, to conduct an ambitious letter-writing campaign to Congress, to maintain hope in the face of incipient despair, and to fight the injustice of cut-and-run corporate logging, Rick Bass has become angry indeed. "Waterfall," the shortest and among the most powerful and revealing chapters in *The Book of Yaak,* reads, in its entirety:

> Some nights my heart pounds so hard in anger that in the morning when I wake up it is sore, as if it has been rubbing against my ribs—as if it has worn a place in them as smooth as the stones beneath a waterfall. Sometimes a calm, smooth, placid expression can harbor more fury than an angular, twisted one. And sometimes serenity can harbor more power than anger or even fury. I know that and I'm trying to get there—to peace, and its powers—but I just don't seem to be able to. The river keeps falling. The sound of it, in my ears. (66)

Like a waterfall, Bass's anger is powerful and at the same time absolutely natural, uncalculated, inevitable. Far from being an abstract, intellectualized objection to forestry policy, his fury is an immediate and involuntary response to local conditions that threaten his home. If the author of the Yaak-tivist books seems a wounded animal fighting to protect its burrow, nest, or den against invasion and destruction, it is because he is precisely that. Like any animal whose habitat is threatened, Bass responds by using the tools—the defenses—that are most natural to him. "My valley is on fire—my valley is burning," he writes. "These essays—these pleas to act to save it—it's all I know how to do" (*Book of Yaak*, xiii). And Bass's anger occasionally manifests itself in attacks that are typical of any trapped or suffering animal, as he admits in likening himself to "a snarling wolverine, snapping illogically at everything in my pain, snapping at everyone . . ." (*Fiber*, 50).

Ours is a culture that tends to discourage open expressions of anger, instead favoring and often requiring the more "focused" or "constructive" expressions of discontent that depend upon energetic repression and that tend to fit comfortably into institutionalized structures of social power and communication. Although American history is replete with events so morally repugnant that anger would seem not only an acceptable but an absolutely necessary response, it is very often the case that angry people, however just their cause—and one thinks of such famously angry Americans as the framers of the Constitution, dispossessed Native Americans, escaped slaves and their abolitionist advocates, and activists for racial equality and civil rights—are perceived as embarrassing, offensive, or dangerous. As a culture, it would seem that we have often been more concerned about good behavior than about justice, and we have frequently resisted those whose ethical concerns have compelled them to behave in ways that make us uncomfortable.

Though we are frequently more devoted to denying or displacing anger than to understanding and redressing its often legitimate causes, it must be said that anger is a primary engine of cultural change and that it has often proven an indispensable tool in the service of social justice. As Cardinal Manning once wrote, "[a]nger is the executive power of justice" (Marcus, "Art and Anger," 70). And if William Blake was correct that "[t]he tigers of wrath are wiser than the horses of instruction," we also might have reason to believe that anger contains and can reveal genuine insight as well as raw passion (Sonnenfeld, "Pathology of Anger," 419). Considering it from a sociobiological point of view, we must also assume that if anger were not a useful and adaptive trait it would have been selected out of us ages ago—as each one of us well knows it has not. According to social scientists who study the phenomenon, anger is an emotion that, like any other human emotion, may be pathological, benign, or creative, depending upon its manifestation. Often, though, anger is an effective protective response that prepares us for the "fight or flight" reactions so closely linked to self-preservation (Allcorn, *Anger in the Workplace,* 21). Indeed, research shows that in a majority of cases expressions of anger result in beneficial rather than harmful consequences not only for the person who is angry, but also for the person who is the target of that anger (Kassinove, *Anger Disorders,* 25). Given the important cultural, biological, and social functions of anger, we might have more reason to fear the *repression* than the *expression* of an emotion possessing "motivational value which, at the minimum, contributes to sustaining oneself and, in a more general sense, contributes to creativity and hard work" (Allcorn, *Anger in the Workplace,* 41).

While the anger that often drives the Yaak-tivist books has alienated some reviewers, who speculate that Bass's "shrill" tone has compromised the literary value of his work, there is in fact deep precedent for the importance and value of anger in American literary art. Among the earliest and most enduring American literary forms is the jeremiad, which depends upon anger for its generic structure, lyrical force, and social valence. Originally referring specifically to seventeenth- and early-eighteenth-century sermons in which backslidden Puritan congregations were chastised for their wickedness, this remarkably adaptable rhetorical form has been perennially reinvented and remains prevalent in American religious, political, and social discourse today.

The basic structural and rhetorical elements of the jeremiad are as follows: it castigates readers for some failure, usually moral or ethical in nature; it uses this criticism to persuade readers to consider the dire consequences of this failure, if continued, and therefore urges them to mend their ways; it is a ritualistic form that attempts to reunify a community and reaffirm the community's values or purpose; though critical in nature, it ultimately attempts a renewal that will result in new hope (Opie and Elliot, "Tracking the Elusive Jeremiad," 10). In colonial America the jeremiad was variously used to inspire rededication to religious aims, to reunify congregations and local communities around common goals, and to bolster hope and faith during times of trial, when the fabric of the community was strained by internal or external threats. The jeremiad unquestionably *moved* people—not only moved them to reexamine and adjust their behavior but, with its sheer moral and rhetorical force, moved them to roll and moan in the aisles of the churches where the sensuous, imaginative, blistering prophecies of the jeremiad fell upon them like scalding rain.

While the providential ideology of Puritan theocrats may strike many of us as narrow or even hypocritical, the jeremiad remains a venerable American rhetorical form that has been employed by many sorts of Americans to advance many sorts of causes. During the eighteenth century, patriot polemicists such as Patrick Henry, Samuel Adams, and Thomas Paine used a nationalist form of the jeremiad to chastise loyalists and doubters and to persuade them to work for the bright future of an independent American republic. During the nineteenth century, abolitionists such as John Brown, William Lloyd Garrison, and Harriet Beecher Stowe rebuked the nation for its complacent adherence to the brutal injustices of slavery and prophesied that God's wrath would fall upon those who refused to join the righteous cause of emancipation. During the twentieth century, the jeremiad was used effectively by Martin Luther King, Jr., Malcolm X, and Stokeley Carmichael, who insisted that "one nation, under God" would exist only when a radical restructuring of American laws and values ushered in a new age of racial equality and justice for all.

The American literary tradition, which has from the beginning navigated a course that parallels and crosses the stream of American political life, is also replete with jeremiadic writing. From Jonathan Edwards's "Sinners in the Hands of an Angry God" (1741) to Thomas Paine's *Common Sense* (1776) to Henry Thoreau's "Civil Disobedience" (1849) to Upton Sinclair's *The Jungle* (1906) to Allen Ginsberg's "Howl" (1956), expressions of rage and outrage have punctuated the nation's literary history and have been offered in every possible literary genre, from the sermon, political pamphlet, and essay to the novel, poem, and song. Any anthology of American literature will contain an ample share of what Albert Sonnenfeld has called "ireful prophets," who write to raise our awareness and, if necessary, to "bludgeon us out of the tepid waters of our complacency" ("Pathology of Anger," 409, 418). In recent decades anger has been a crucial component in American literature treating the Vietnam conflict, countercultural youth movements, women's rights, racial equality, addiction and alcoholism, homosexuality and homophobia, AIDS, mental health, and urban violence. As African-American playwright Amiri Baraka said of his work in a 1964 interview, "if it sounds like anger maybe that's good" (Stone, "If It's Anger," 8). And it *has* been good that American literature has often sounded like anger, for angry writers have been effective advocates for social change and distinguished contributors to the richness and diversity of the nation's literary tradition.

Of course it was the "city on the hill" that Puritans such as John Winthrop wanted to protect and revitalize through use of the scathing rhetorical form of the jeremiad. Since the mid-nineteenth century, however, the jeremiad has also been used by writers working to protect and revitalize not the city but rather the hill—the endangered American environments that have so long been the province and concern of the American literary artists we now call nature writers. Think, for example, of the vituperative, accusatory rhetoric of Henry Thoreau's *Walden,* in which the venal materialism of American culture is blasted in the interests of promoting ethical and aesthetic regard for nature. "It is very evident what mean and sneaking lives many of you live," writes Thoreau to his quietly desperate readers (49). Despite Thoreau's angry and incisive rhetoric—and at least in part *because* of it—*Walden* continues to be considered a literary classic even by those whom it disconcerts.

Or think of John Muir, whose published writing increasingly tended toward environmental polemic as he neared the end of his life. In his famous battle to save the Hetch Hetchy Valley from damming, for example, Muir raged against "[t]hese temple destroyers, devotees of ravaging commercialism, [who] seem to have a perfect contempt for Nature, and, instead of lifting their eyes to the God of the mountains, lift them to the Almighty Dollar" (*Yosemite,* 196–97). Muir's Calvinist upbringing well qualified him to handle the jeremiad, and he was often unsparing in his willingness to predict not only the loss of wildness but also the wrath of God for those who took what he depicted as the Devil's side in an epic battle between Good and Evil. Despite this penchant for invective—and again, I suggest, in large part *because* of it—Muir is widely celebrated as having been among the most accomplished American literary proponents for wilderness.

Or, closer to our own historical moment, consider the many nature writers who have used anger or wrath—and/or the related concepts of judgment or sin—as a rhetorical weapon in battles to preserve endangered landscapes or the war to inspire the broad cultural changes upon which an environmentally sustainable American society must ultimately depend. Although any number of such books can be cited, a list of prominent examples might include Rachel Carson's *Silent Spring* (1962), Edward Abbey's *The Monkey Wrench Gang* (1975), Terry Tempest Williams's *Refuge* (1991), and Barry Lopez's *The Rediscovery of North America* (1992). While in these books the judgment of God has typically been replaced by the scientifically demonstrable consequences of our environmental errors, these green jeremiads, while secular, maintain the structure of the traditional jeremiad: they chastise our culture for its environmental sins; urge us to adjust our behavior; reaffirm the importance of health in the extended natural community of which we are a part; reinforce the value of an ethics of respect and affection; and, ultimately, attempt to reinvigorate our hope that it is not too late to avoid the unhappy consequences of the bleak, ecologically impoverished world that they so powerfully envision.

In each of the examples cited above, and of course in many others, the jeremiad has functioned as a structured expression of anger applied in the service of social and/or environmental justice. And while the terms have changed over the past four centuries, the essential structure of the jeremiad as a rhetorical form has remained remarkably stable—and has remained so because it has proven effective in inspiring reexamination of values and motivating efforts toward positive change. Anyone who has read Rick Bass's Yaak-tivist books knows how angry this author is, how that anger has motivated his activism, and how essential that anger is to the often startling and moving narrative dynamics of his prose. A literary Jeremiah of his own place and time, Bass lashes corporations and government for their immoral indifference, decries the exorbitant moral and spiritual costs of the extinction of the wild, and prophetically admonishes us to change course before we awake to a ravaged world, emptied of beauty and integrity. And, like the literary Jeremiahs who preceded him, Bass wants not to depress spirits but to raise consciousness, to revitalize a community of environmental concern, and to envision a new hope that the burning world may be saved before we are left only with ashes—the ashes of the once green forest and the ashes of the artist who is consumed along with it.

Excerpts from one of Bass's many unpublished letters in support of a letter-writing campaign on behalf of the Yaak clearly mirror the structure of the traditional jeremiad:

> For those of you new to the campaign—and it may be one that will last the rest of our lives, but we are too many years into it to back down: they are waiting for us to back down, which is reason in itself to intensify, ever intensify, our efforts. . . . [w]e must make the name *Yaak* well-known, even dreaded, in Congress. . . . We have to do what we can, everything within our grasp, to make this a national campaign, and to stay on the Congress' back, every month, and ride them into

> the ground. . . . [The U.S. Forest Service is] starting to fear justice. . . . [The destruction of the Yaak] is a huge secret sin and it is our responsibility to stop it and I remain convinced that . . . it still lies in our power to stop it. . . . The good news about all this anger is it means we're starting to get to them. ("Yaak Letter," 3–4)

While Bass's devotion to preservation of the Yaak is, as he admits, that of a zealot, it may be worth remembering that zeal is often an indispensable tool for reform. I am reminded of Martin Luther King, Jr.'s response, in his remarkable *Letter from the Birmingham Jail,* to critiques of him as an "extremist": "the question is not whether we will be extremist but what kind of extremist will we be. Will we be extremists for hate or will we be extremists for love?" he asks. "Will we be extremists for the cause of justice? . . . the South, the nation and the world are in dire need of creative extremists" (23).

However "shrill" some readers might find him, Rick Bass is a "creative extremist" who is working within the long, rich, stable, and rather venerable American literary tradition of the jeremiad. The resiliency of this rhetorical form suggests, I think, that American art has long accommodated anger and that social and environmental justice has in fact required it. Far from vitiating American literary works, anger has often been their mainspring. While it is quite true, as Barbara White notes, that the jeremiad has been particularly well adapted to literature that responds to the environmental crisis ("Acts of God," 94–95), Scott Slovic also correctly observes that scholars of nature writing often prefer lyrical, celebratory literary modes, while more political forms of nature writing "evoke the disapproval, even the scorn, of such scholars" ("Epistemology," 86). Unlike scholars of satire, who are accustomed to viewing anger as a "fine art" (Rosenheim, "Anger as a Fine Art," 80), scholars of nature writing too often view advocacy-based literature as aesthetically compromised—"as if," in the words of feminist scholar Jane Marcus, "writing inspired by anger were not worthy of the name of art" ("Art and Anger," 69). "Anger is *not* anathema in art," Marcus contends. "[I]t is a primary source of creative energy" (94). Just as our culture is anxious to avoid or mute upsetting manifestations of anger, it would seem we are likewise anxious to avoid full critical recognition of literature that openly expresses and inspires anger.

The "problem" with the sort of anger we see in Bass's work is not that it is inappropriate, vicious, ineffective, or even "unliterary"; it is, I would suggest, simply that it makes us uncomfortable. Because none of us wishes to deal with people when they are angry, and none of us likes to become angry—and the Yaak-tivist books compel us toward both experiences—reading Bass can be upsetting and heartbreaking. If the goal of literary art is to make us feel happy or *entertained*, in the superficial sense of the word, then Bass has undoubtedly failed us. If, however, we define literary art as a cultural form that combines accomplished writing and powerful sentiment to address vitally important issues, then critical estimates of Bass's unliterary shrillness may reveal more about our own attitudes than they do about the aesthetic weaknesses of his books. Speaking from a literary historical point of view, it may be enough to say that if Bass is angry—and I certainly agree that he is—then he finds himself in extremely good company. Readers find it doubly disconcerting that in addition to exclaiming angrily, in his human way, "Fuck you," he is also pleading, as he does in the final lines of *Fiber,* "Somebody please do this. Somebody please help" (50, 51).

Part III. A Kind of Celebration: The Aesthetics of Grief

> *In the case of a story that recognizes impending loss, that of itself can be, even if in a bittersweet way, a kind of celebration....*
>
> Rick Bass, *Brown Dog of the Yaak* (63)

Rick Bass once characterized nature writing as "the literature of loss" ("Literature," 75), and he has written that as a literary artist "[y]ou have to engage with your beloved, even in the face of impending loss—especially in the face of that loss—as a means of showing honor and respect to the subject" (*Brown Dog,* 72). Thus, the Yaak-tivist books are Bass's attempt to honor the beloved—the lovely yet ravished wilderness of the Yaak Valley itself. And while the anger in these books has often caught the attention of reviewers, the tenor of the Yaak-tivist texts is one more of grief than of rage. Bass's anger, though genuine, seems primarily a means of resisting despair, an attempt to convert what might otherwise be a feeling of paralytic helplessness into a form of creative energy that will lead to protection of the Yaak and other endangered wilderness. As he once observed, "[i]t is a hugely expensive luxury, this holding of hope" (*Brown Dog,* 23).

In Bass's descriptions of the Yaak and his concern for its fate, we see a person who feels the pain of the injuries inflicted upon his home landscape—who experiences a "suffering with" that is at the spiritual and etymological root of the word "compassion" (Macy, "Working," 241). For if Bass's *passion* may be characterized as a kind of *anger,* then his *compassion* must be characterized as a form of *grief.* Speaking of loss of wilderness in his valley, he writes, "I'm not sure at which point I allowed the pain of it to be absorbed by me deeply enough so that I had no choice but to react against it" (*Book of Yaak,* 4). Bass often describes a visceral reaction to the environmental damage that he witnesses on the logged slopes of the Yaak's mountainsides. "Each year, the bare gullies, the gouges of eroding soil, cut deeper and deeper, up on those high-elevation clearcuts: up at the source of wildness," he laments. "I cannot look at them without feeling physically—not emotionally, but physically—the sensation of injury. I cannot shut my feelings out to that numbness any more. I have become too much of this place" (*Book of Yaak,* 155). Elsewhere in *The Book of Yaak,* Bass describes himself as "sickened" by the realization that "what is being done to our home, and to our country, erodes and endangers our capability for joy" (167).

Bass's visceral reaction to environmental damage illustrates important recent findings by environmental psychologists, who are only beginning to appreciate the degree to which human physical, emotional, and psychological well-being is contingent upon the health of natural environments. In various cognate areas of environmental psychology—such as behavioral geography, phenomenological dwelling, place identity, transpersonal psychology, and ecological psychology—research is demonstrating that environmental stresses are felt deeply by those who inhabit damaged landscapes and that excessive stress to natural ecosystems is quick to register as psychological and social stress in the human individuals or communities affected. As Joanna Macy writes, "[w]e are not closed off from the world, but rather are integral components of it, like cells in a larger body. When part of that body is traumatized—in the sufferings of fellow beings, in the pillage of our planet, and even in the violation of future generations—we sense that trauma too" ("Working," 241). Theodore Roszak uses the term "ecological unconscious" to refer to the deep sense in which our psychological and emotional well-being is connected to and contingent upon the health of the natural world we inhabit (*Voice,* 13).

If, as I have argued, anger is too often repressed or transferred, the same might be said of grief—that necessary and potentially revitalizing human emotional, psychological, and spiritual response to loss. Our culture has relatively few productive social rituals by which grief may be expressed, shared, and understood; as with anger, we seem to find grief not only upsetting but also vaguely embarrassing, as if grief were a kind of nakedness from which we feel inadvertently compelled to avert our gaze. Like anger, grief disconcerts us. Beneath this discomfort, of course, is fear—the legitimate fear that there will not be time, solutions, or even tears enough to respond fully to all that we are losing. Grief is a dark place that we are loath to enter because we fear that we will not find our way home from it.

Yet the environmental losses surrounding us are palpable and real, and the repression of our sorrow at this loss often comes at the price of our cultural and individual health. Our physical and ethical well-being requires that we recognize loss—not that we wallow in it, helplessly, but that we express it in order to release the tremendous creative energy it can contain. Indeed, creative grieving is something that nature writers, in particular, must help us to do. Rick Bass observes that "sense of loss is one of the main reasons so many or our finest writers [engage in] 'nature writing'" (*Brown Dog*, 64). As ecologist and chaplain Phyllis Windle writes in "The Ecology of Grief," the movement toward a functional and sustainable environmental ethic will require "passion, commitment, creativity, energy, and concentration." "We shall have none of these," she continues, "if we fail to grieve (alone and with each other) for the magnificent trees, the lovely animals, and the beautiful places that we are losing" (144). Part of Bass's cultural work is to express and thereby help us to reckon what we might call environmental grief—that sadness and sense of loss that necessarily attends the realization that so much diversity, beauty, and mystery is being driven from the world each day. In the Yaak-tivist books Bass wishes to tell "a story that recognizes impending loss," not simply "weeping and lamentation," but a story that "can be, even if in a bittersweet way, a kind of celebration" (*Brown Dog*, 63).

There is a sense in which nature writing might be considered a literature of trauma as well as a literature of hope or of beauty. While critical studies of trauma literature often focus on narratives written by survivors of the atrocities of war, torture, or physical abuse, the critical paradigm used to describe traumatic stress and its artistic expression offers genuine insight into the creative grieving that is at the core of much contemporary nature writing. Survivors of traumatic events typically carry a heavy burden of pain and a poignant sensitivity to loss in their memory and imagination. Whether the stress on the individual is personal or environmental, there is a natural urge to deny or repress the emotions—often emotions of anger and grief—that memories of trauma encode. The acknowledgment of traumatic stress is especially difficult because, biologically speaking, the remembering or imagining of a traumatic event is very much a *reliving* of it, in the sense that the psychobiological response to remembered trauma is extremely similar to that elicited by actual, immediate trauma. In most cases, victims of trauma move through a series of healing stages that includes remembering and acknowledging the trauma, telling stories of the traumatic event, establishing a sense of community with other survivors, and, ultimately, directing the energy released by the healing process to some form of service—often service to other survivors or service to help spare others from comparable suffering (Wilson, *Transformation,* 19; Herman, *Trauma,* 156). In a surprising percentage of cases, reactions to traumatic stress include a state of "hyperarousal" that is often characterized by unusually high levels of motivation and creativity; indeed, art is frequently a productive response to severe environmental stress, as the richness and diversity of the literature of trauma clearly demonstrates (Herman, *Trauma,* 35–36).

Of course, literature that explores the psychosocial and environmental dimensions of loss and grief is much older than what the twentieth century has taught us to call the literature of trauma. Like the jeremiad, a venerable rhetorical form that revitalizes the community by harnessing and expressing anger, the elegy is an even more ancient literary form that, to paraphrase Rick Bass's description of his own project, is centrally concerned with honoring its subject by engaging with the beloved in the face of loss. In particular, the pastoral elegy—which developed in the seventh century B.C. and has been important in Western literature since the time of Theocritus and Virgil—is a form of literary mourning that bears close resemblance to the literary grief that inspires Bass's Yaak-tivist books.

Although the elegy is a traditional and conventional literary form—a well-established cultural formula that instructs us in how to express grief through art—the uses of the elegy have been quite various. Think, for example, of the diversity of styles and subjects addressed by Theocritus's *Idylls* (circa 270 B.C.), Virgil's *Eclogues* (37 B.C.), John Milton's "Lycidas" (1638), Thomas Gray's "Elegy Written in a Country Churchyard" (1751), Percy Bysshe Shelley's "Adonais" (1821), Alfred Lord Tennyson's *In Memoriam* (1850), Walt Whitman's "When Lilacs Last in the Dooryard

Bloom'd" (1865), W. H. Auden's "In Memory of W. B. Yeats" (1940), Thomas Merton's "Elegy for the Monastery Barn" (1957), and Allen Ginsberg's "Kaddish" (1961), and by environmental elegies such as Aldo Leopold's "Marshland Elegy" (1949), James Dickey's "For the Last Wolverine" (1961), W. S. Merwin's "For a Coming Extinction" (1963), Margaret Atwood's "Elegy for the Giant Tortoises" (1976), and Pattiann Rogers's "Eulogy for a Hermit Crab" (1986).

Despite the range of uses to which the form has been put, there remains in the elegy a series of structural elements that includes the following: the writer invokes the muse, identifying the source of artistic inspiration; the natural world joins the writer in mourning the loss of someone or something much beloved; the writer decries the negligence that has allowed the loss to occur; the writer questions the justice of the loss and often "adverts to the corrupt conditions of his own times"; some ritual of mourning, which often includes the placing of flowers or leaves, is conducted; finally, there is an attempt at a summary consolation by which the loss of the beloved might be compensated for (Abrams, *Glossary*, 50–51).

Readers of the Yaak-tivist books may find it useful to imagine these books in terms of the elegiac structure: the muse Bass invokes is the magical wilderness of the Yaak; the natural world shares his mourning in the face of loss, a mourning expressed, for example, in the unanswered mating call of the last surviving woodland caribou bull in the valley (*Book of Yaak*, 77); he repeatedly excoriates the negligence of the timber companies in treating the land irresponsibly and lambastes the U.S. Forest Service for allowing them to do so; he questions the justice of a corrupt economic and political system in which avarice and exploitation prevail over long-term environmental health; he conducts various rituals of mourning for the lost wilderness of the valley, rituals which include the anonymous gifting of timber by the "log fairy" persona in *Fiber* (20) and the ritualistic hike he takes for a sick friend in the concluding chapter of *The Book of Yaak* (174–87); finally, Bass resists easy gestures of consolation but does maintain the hope that, with the reader's help, the wilderness he describes may be saved and the losses already registered atoned for and perhaps ultimately healed.

In his study of the English elegy, Eric Smith writes that "elegy is specifically about what is missing and also about what is more certainly known to have been formerly possessed." It is a literary form that "fundamentally represent[s] a basic life in contact with Nature" and that ultimately asks us to "join in an act of faith" even as it "provokes and disturbs." Because the elegy "will not permit us to leave at the back of our minds the questions which it raises," it is a form that, according to Smith, "can make us uncomfortable both as human beings and as critics" (*By Mourning Toungues,* 2, 5, 3). In his study of the modern elegy, Jahan Ramazani adds that the elegy has become vitally important as Western culture has moved increasingly toward an unhealthy banishment of death and loss from public discourse—a dangerous banishment that he incisively labels "a privatization of grief" (*Poetry,* 15). We need elegists more than ever before, argues Ramazani, because we are forgetting how to grieve creatively. "We need their elegies, however disturbing," he writes, "because our society often sugarcoats mourning in dubious comfort, or retreats from it in embarrassed silence, or pathologizes it" (ix).

Readers of Bass will know how accurately these critical comments on the literary shape, emotional uses, and cultural work of the elegy describe the project of the Yaak-tivist books. Bass does speak of a life in nature, he does mourn loss, and he does, in expressing his sorrow through art, attempt to *publicize*—in the several senses of the word—the often unbearable private weight of grief. In forcing us to see what is being lost in the Yaak, he provokes us; in asking us to recognize the value of what we are losing everywhere in the West, he disconcerts us; by asking us to join a letter-writing campaign on behalf of an endangered place, he requests that we join him in an act of faith—faith in the value of community, democracy, and wilderness. In the first of his remarkable *Duino Elegies,* Rainer Maria Rilke wrote that "beauty is nothing but the beginnings of terror we can hardly bear" (Packard, *Poet's Dictionary,* 50). In *Brown Dog of the Yaak,* Bass writes, "I'm terrified that the loss, the slippage, of even one or two of these elements in the Yaak . . . can lead to a diminution of the magic; a vanishment; a disappearing" (37). At the heart of Bass's elegiac art is advocacy; at the core of his advocacy, anger; at the source of his anger, grief; at the root of his grief, love.

THE ENVIRONMENTAL ELEGIAD: NATURE WRITING AND THE VIRTUES OF DISCOMFORT

We need to be writing a letter a day, all of us, in the way that, as children, we all rose once to say the Pledge of Allegiance.

Rick Bass, "Crossing Over" (21)

Bass has written that the nature writer must honor the beloved in the face of impending loss. It might be said that some form of impending loss compromises the beloved of any contemporary nature writer, though writers respond to this predicament in various ways. Some nature writers choose to ignore the political context that imperils their beloved landscapes, preferring to work primarily within the traditional Romantic mode of lyrical celebration of nature. Others acknowledge threats to the landscapes they describe, but attempt to sidestep such threats to avoid depressing the reader or marring the beauty of their own landscape descriptions. At the other extreme are nature writers whose obsession with loss has blinded them to beauty, displacing celebration of the beloved landscape with an unmitigated dirge, nostalgic and apocalyptic by turns. To understand the difficult choices contemporary nature writers often face, imagine someone you love dying of cancer: one choice is to repress the truth of their condition because the pain of admitting it is too great; another is to be so overcome with anguish, even resentment, at their impending loss that you fail to celebrate and love them while they live. These two choices, understandable but also unfortunate, mirror the approaches many nature writers have taken to the impending loss of the beloved place.

It seems to me that, given the "condition" of American nature writing and the "condition" of many of the landscapes it would represent, the choices described above are no longer adequate. To elide the immediate threats to places in our pronunciations of love for them constitutes, I would argue, a moral and aesthetic failure—a failure to honor the beloved by refusing to engage fully. Conversely, to limit our view of the beloved physical world to the agony inspired by its loss not only is a failure to see beyond ourselves but is also an invitation to despair and its attendant moral paralysis. If nature writing is to perform valuable cultural work—if it is to fully address the exigencies of our historical moment—it must navigate the narrow passage between blithe rhapsodies and orgies of grief.

In urgently expressing an honest response to what he views as the deepest source of his passion and concern, I would argue, Rick Bass has fully discharged what some critics seem to view as his obligation to be "literary." I do not agree with the surprisingly general sense that advocacy-based writing is necessarily less artistically accomplished than other sorts of writing; nor do I hold that writing that powerfully expresses anger or grief is more likely to be ephemeral or artistically compromised than writing that demonstrates what is often viewed as greater "control." On the contrary, literary history suggests that the most important, moving, valuable, timely, and enduring works of literary art are precisely those that discover, tap, and release strong feelings that are repressed or denied by the culture beneath whose surface they simmer. Readers who care about the fate of the land and its creatures must come to terms with anger and grief and must learn to see these feelings as a reservoir of opportunity from which strength and creativity may be drawn. As Thomas Fuller wrote, "[a]nger is one of the sinews of the soul[, and] he that wants it hath a maimed mind" (Marcus, "Art," 70); and, as Charles Darwin observed, "[one] who remains passive when overwhelmed with grief loses [the] best chance of recovering elasticity of mind" (Windle, "Ecology," 137).

In unlocking and exploring the emotions of anger and grief that are induced by environmental loss, Bass uses literary art to heighten our awareness, to inspire us, but also, if necessary, to cause us salutary discomfort. Among the things readers find most uncomfortable about the Yaak-tivist books is their explicit request that the reader become involved in protecting the remaining wilderness of the Yaak by writing letters on its behalf. Each of the three books discusses the need for the reader to contribute to the Yaak letter-writing campaign, and each concludes with a chapter or appendix that is explicitly devoted to telling readers how to help. In engaging the reader directly, and offering specific information about how readers can contribute to the cause of ecosystemic health in this vitally important wilderness corridor, Bass challenges our passivity, provokes us to act on the values we hold, and attacks the ethical inertia that often causes us to choose entertainment over action. I would argue that it is the role of the artist to make us uncomfortable when we stand to learn from discomfort. Like Thoreau, who in *Walden* famously boasted that he wanted to crow loud and long, "if only to wake [his] neighbors up" (128), Bass wants to shake from the slumber of passivity in order that we might have a new opportunity to think, to feel, and, ultimately, to *help*. If being asked to help makes us uncomfortable, as it often does, perhaps this is a salutary discomfort that, like the discomfort of anger or of grief, might lead to something better.

Rick Bass's use of the "elegiad"—if I may offer a neologism to describe the rhetorical shape of the grief and anger so important to the Yaak-tivist books—combines and expresses emotions that are central to the legitimate literary ambitions of nature writers. In his introduction to

Desert Solitaire, Edward Abbey, who well understood both fury and sorrow, explained that "most of what I write about in this book is already gone or going under fast. This is not a travel guide but an elegy. A memorial. You're holding a tombstone in your hands. A bloody rock. Don't drop it on your foot—throw it at something big and glassy" (xiv). Like *Desert Solitaire,* the Yaak-tivist books are intended to celebrate, to rage, and to mourn. They are intended not as entertainments but as literary weapons that, like Abbey's bloody rock, might be launched by caring readers at the glassy face of the injustice that Rick Bass sees devouring the last wilderness of the Yaak. "I have to make peace with my art and my anger, with our lives and their brevity," he writes, "and yet, for me, it still involves fighting, and I will never give any of this up willingly, nor do I understand how any of us can" (*Book of Yaak,* 173).

Works Cited

Abbey, Edward. *Desert Solitaire: A Season in the Wilderness* (1968). New York: Touchstone, 1990.

Abrams, M. H. *A Glossary of Literary Terms.* 6th ed. Fort Worth: Harcourt Brace Jovanovich, 1993.

Allcorn, Seth. *Anger in the Workplace: Understanding the Causes of Violence and Aggression.* Westport, Conn.: Quorum, 1994.

Bass, Rick. *The Book of Yaak.* Boston: Houghton Mifflin, 1996.

———. *Brown Dog of the Yaak: Essays on Art and Activism.* Minneapolis: Milkweed, 1999.

———. "Crossing Over." *Petroglyph* 4 (1992): 17–23.

———. *Fiber.* Athens: University of Georgia Press, 1998.

———. "The Literature of Loss." *Manõa* 4:2 (Fall 1992): 75.

———. "20515 House, 20510 Senate." *American Nature Writing Newsletter* 5:1 (Spring 1993): 3–5.

———. "Yaak Letter." Unpublished letter on behalf of the Yaak Valley letter writing campaign. Troy, Montana, 21 December 1994.

Delehanty, Hugh. Review of *The Book of Yaak. Utne Reader* 80 (March–April 1997): 84.

Harvey, Miles. Review of *The Book of Yaak. Outside* 22:1 (January 1997): 100.

Herman, Judith. *Trauma and Recovery.* New York: BasicBooks, 1992.

Hoagland, Edward. "Edward Abbey: Standing Tough in the Desert." *New York Times Book Review* (7 May 1989), 44–45.

Houston, Pam. Review of *The Book of Yaak. Los Angeles Times Book Review* (26 January 1997), 8.

Jones, Mary Paumier. Review of *Brown Dog of the Yaak: Essays on Art and Activism. Library Journal* 124:12 (July 1999): 88.

Kassinove, Howard. *Anger Disorders: Definition, Diagnosis, and Treatment.* Bristol: Taylor & Francis, 1995.

King, Martin Luther, Jr. *Letter from the Birmingham Jail* (1963). San Francisco: HarperSanFrancisco, 1994.

Leschak, Peter M. Review of *The Book of Yaak. New York Times Book Review,* 1 December 1996, 31.

Lyons, Stephen J. Review of *Fiber. Northern Lights* 14:1 (Winter 1999): 32.

Macy, Joanna. "Working through Environmental Despair." In *Ecopsychology: Restoring the Earth, Healing the Mind,* ed. Theodore Roszak, Mary E. Gomes, and Allen D. Kaner, 240–59. San Francisco: Sierra Club Books, 1995.

Marcus, Jane. "Art and Anger." *Feminist Studies* 4 (1978): 69–98.

Muir, John. *The Yosemite* (1914). San Francisco: Sierra Club Books, 1988.

Opie, John, and Norbert Elliot. "Tracking the Elusive Jeremiad: The Rhetorical Character of American Environmental Discourse." In *The Symbolic Earth: Discourse and Our Creation of the Environment,* ed. James G. Cantrill and Christine L. Oravec, 9–37. Lexington: University Press of Kentucky, 1996.

Packard, William. *The Poet's Dictionary: A Handbook of Prosody and Poetic Devices.* New York: Harper & Row, 1989.

Ramazani, Jahan. *Poetry of Mourning: The Modern Elegy from Hardy to Heaney.* Chicago: University of Chicago Press, 1994.

Rosenheim, Edward, Jr. "Anger as a Fine Art." *College Composition and Communication* 16 (1965): 80–84.

Roszak, Theodore. *The Voice of the Earth: An Exploration of Ecopsychology.* New York: Touchstone, 1992.

Slovic, Scott. "Epistemology and Politics in American Nature Writing: Embedded Rhetoric and Discrete Rhetoric." In *Green Culture: Environmental Rhetoric in Contemporary America,* ed. Carl G. Herndl and Stuart C. Brown, 82–110. Madison: University of Wisconsin Press, 1996.

———. "A Paint Brush in One Hand and a Bucket of Water in the Other: An Interview with Rick Bass." *Weber Studies* 11 (Fall 1994): 11–29.

Smith, Eric. *By Mourning Toungues: Studies in English Elegy.* Ipswich: Boydell, 1977.

Sojourner, Mary. Review of *Fiber. Northern Lights* 14:1 (Winter 1999): 32.

Sonnenfeld, Albert. "The Pathology of Anger: Wrath and Rhetoric." *Romantic Review* 78:4 (November 1987): 405–19.

Stone, Judy. "If It's Anger . . . Maybe That's Good: An Interview with LeRoi Jones." In *Conversations with Amiri Baraka,* 8–11. Jackson: University Press of Mississippi, 1994.

Thoreau, Henry David. *Walden and Civil Disobedience* (1854). New York: Penguin, 1986.

White, Barbara. "Acts of God: Providence, the Jeremiad, and Environmental Crisis." In *Writing the Environment: Ecocriticism and Literature,* ed. Richard Kerridge and Neil Sammells, 91–109. New York: St. Martin's Press, 1998.

Wilson, John P. *Trauma: Transformation and Healing: An Integrative Approach to Theory, Research, and Post-Traumatic Stress Therapy.* New York: Brunner/Mazel, 1989.

Windle, Phyllis. "The Ecology of Grief." In *Ecopsychology: Restoring the Earth, Healing the Mind,* ed. Theodore Roszak, Mary E. Gomes, and Allen D. Kaner, 136–45. San Francisco: Sierra Club Books, 1995.

Fiber

A Post-Pastoral Georgic

Terry Gifford

Not Pastoral, But Georgic

I want to argue that Rick Bass's little book *Fiber* constitutes nothing less than a new literary form: the post-pastoral georgic. I am not sure that I fully understand all of the twists and turns of this short text. Its final sentences in particular still leave me slightly confused in their puzzling shifts of tone. But this very device—sudden shifts of tone—has been the strength of a daring narrative told by an unreliable narrator that achieves what I have come to think of as a slightly flawed masterpiece. That it continues to make me think hard is a tribute to the triumph of art over criticism, of mystery over explanation, of the complexity of the text over any reductive attempt to categorize it. Yet I still want to claim *Fiber* as a new literary form because it might help to demonstrate how this book is a turning point, in my view, away from the current cul-de-sac of American nature writing.

I refer to an awestruck, earnest, and ultimately predictable discourse that lies behind the worst of American nature writing, as it does (and I write from a U.K. perspective) behind the weakest British writing about the countryside. In the final sentences of *Fiber* the discourse of complacent, cozy, firelit, indoor engagement with this story of an environment's urgent crisis seems suspect because it appears to evoke the discourse of the pastoral. Yet, for me, it is in the way that *Fiber*, as a whole, outflanks the pastoral that the originality of its achievement lies. In the United States pastoral literature has an honorable tradition that the Thoreauvian critic Lawrence Buell has described as "counterinstitutional" (*Envi-*

ronmental Imagination, 50) in its positive effects. Indeed, this has also been the achievement of the best European pastorals such as William Shakespeare's *The Winter's Tale* or Thomas Hardy's *The Return of the Native*. Certainly Bass's writing has always featured the classic impulse of the European tradition of pastoral to retreat into nature and return with insights that have moral implications for a mostly urbanized (or, earlier, court) society.

The danger has always been that pastoral literature might sometimes fail to seek or achieve such redeeming insights and become a sentimental discourse of rural escapism. Indeed, it was the American critic Leo Marx who needed to distinguish between what he called "complex and sentimental kinds of pastoralism" (*Machine in the Garden*, 32). Even in the United States, where the pastoral mode is considered to have an integrity that links J. Hector St. John de Crèvecoeur, Henry David Thoreau, John Muir, and Wendell Berry, the verb expresses the danger. To "pastoralize" is to idealize as an Arcadia—a literary construct that acts as a rural retreat from social and environmental realities. It is the predominance in English literature of "sentimental pastoralism" that has led to the term "pastoral" taking on a pejorative use in Britain. I believe it is the American equivalent of this pastoral escapist complacency that Bass has in mind when he says in *Fiber* that today "storytelling has become so damn weak and safe" (45).

As a mode of literary expression, pastoral has, from its beginnings in Greek and Roman literature, involved a certain amount of weakness and safety. For the Greek court in Alexandria, Theocritus wrote the *Idylls* in the third century B.C., supposedly in the voice of the shepherds of his native Sicily. This literary deception has given us the notion of the "idyllic"—an idealization of a life in close contact with nature. It was the Roman poet Virgil, writing two centuries later, who established the location of the pastoral idyll in the literary construct of Arcadia in his *Eclogues*. Of course, Arcadia was an actual place on the Peloponnesus peninsula of Greece, but the idealization of it as the location of a past Golden Age has left us with the construct of a rural place of safety from which to offer a critique of urban life and values. And then idealized rural literature created a continuous tradition of antipastoral correctives that pitched a stark and provocative realism against "sentimental pastoral" from George Crabbe and John Clare in England to Robinson Jeffers and Edward Abbey in the United States.

In contemporary American nature writing much of its storytelling "has become so damn weak and safe" precisely because it can be the formulaic, escapist pastoral that one finds, for example, in the annual anthologies edited by John A. Murray (no longer published by the Sierra Club), in his advice in his *Nature Writing Handbook* to nature writers to "edify and entertain" (95) rather than to challenge and innovate, and in what Leonard M. Scigaj calls the "cushy limbo" of the nature poetry of Robert Haas (*Sustainable Poetry,* 115). As editor of the complete works of John Muir (*John Muir,* 1992 and 1996) I am aware of the strengths of the tradition of American nature writing and of its capacity for thought-provoking advocacy in the hands of Aldo Leopold, Terry Tempest Williams, Gary Snyder, and others. But it seems to me that the distinctly American art form of the first-person anecdotal narrative about epiphanies of connection to landscapes is in danger of becoming repetitious and complacently unoriginal. Perhaps the lack of an American literary criticism possessed of a rigor to distinguish the "sentimental" from the "complex," even after Leo Marx provided a rationale for such rigor as long ago as 1964, has not helped the development of the genre in which Bass has been working. To his credit, he seems to be aware of this himself in his narrator's critique of contemporary storytelling.

One of the ways in which Rick Bass avoids the idealizing traps of the pastoral is to base *Fiber* on the practical work of a man who hauls logs. Indeed, his narrator poses this work against that of storytelling:

> I thought I was made all along for writing short stories, and maybe one day again I will be—as forests recycle through succession—but this landscape has carved and fit me—it is not I who been doing the carving—and I can feel, am aware of, my change, so that now what I best fit doing is hauling logs, one at a time. (17)

Growing like the forest, within the forest, this man has found his fit in this place—the climax forests of the Yaak Valley in northwest Montana, where Bass himself moved to live the life of a writer. The punch-line of this long sentence is the final surprise of "one at a time." This narrator works at hauling logs like an artist,

> choosing for my harvest only the wind-tossed or leaning trees, or the trees that are crowded too close together, or diseased. I try and select individual trees like notes of music. . . . As I choose and select, I listen to that silent music all around me, faint but real, of what I am doing—not imagining, but *doing.* (18–19)

Despite the slightly odd and highly sensitive way this work is conceived here, it is work. Its emphasis is on "not imagining, but *doing*." In this Virgil would recognize not a pastoral, but a georgic discourse. Virgil's *Georgics* (composed 36–29 B.C.) is a poem that serves as a practical guide to vegetable and animal husbandry. This poem has given us the generic name for a literature of rural work in which realism counters any tendencies toward idealization. The narrator of *Fiber* has retreated from art into a world of "things" and "doing." His concern is to know the names of things in the forest as he gets "in pace—once more—with the land" (27). It emerges from the text that his georgic is really that of the gestural politics of an environmentally sensitive oddball logger. But before exploring the unusual work of this narrator, perhaps I ought to explain why I call this contemporary georgic text "post-pastoral."

Post-Pastoral

Lawrence Buell recognizes that classical pastoral form is probably defunct. Rather than taking a narrow classical definition of pastoral, Buell, like Marx, prefers for American literature a broader notion of "pastoralism." Against "the specific set of obsolescent conventions of the eclogue tradition" ("American Pastoral Ideology," 23), Buell claims for pastoralism a continuing essentialism: "pastoralism is a species of cultural equipment that western thought has for more than two millennia been unable to do without" (*Environmental Imagination,* 32). Also like Marx, Buell believes that the "wholly new conception of the precariousness of our relations with nature is bound to bring forth new versions of pastoral" (*Environmental Imagination,* 51). Indeed, Buell might recognize one such in Rick Bass's *Fiber.*

For me, new versions of pastoral that outflank the dangers of the sentimental are best seen as part of a continuity with some of the work of Shakespeare, William Blake, William Wordsworth, Gerard Manley Hopkins, and D. H. Lawrence, for example. Literature that escapes the closed circuit of pastoral and antipastoral discourse, that recognizes the problems of our language unavoidably constructing nature for us, that accepts a continuity between inner and outer nature, and that takes responsibility for our problematic, inescapable relationship with our planet I have come to call "post-pastoral" literature (*Pastoral,* 146–74). Rather than viewing *Fiber* as a new version of pastoral, with all the contemporary problems surrounding the word, I would suggest that the book is best seen as part of the innovative and enlightened tradition of post-pastoral texts in English-speaking literature. I think of this literature as implicitly asking six questions of the reader. I certainly hope to suggest that *Fiber* does this and much more, the "more" being all the other questions, challenges, and mysteries that are embedded within the art itself.

Briefly the six post-pastoral questions that *Fiber* raises in common with other post-pastoral texts might be fleetingly illustrated by a sentence from the text:

1. Can awe lead to humility in our species that might control the hubris of continuous exploitation? "This country—the Yaak Valley . . . [is] like having found the rich dense place you were always looking for" (8–9).
2. What are the implications of recognizing the creative-destructive cycles of the universe of which we are part? " . . . I am sinking deeper and deeper into the old rot of the forest, until soon I'll be waist-deep in the soil—and this is neither delicious nor frightening. It is only a fit" (19).
3. How can we learn to understand the inner by being closer to the outer? "I am trying to let the land tell me who and what I am—trying to let it pace and direct me, until it is as if I have become part of it" (8).
4. If we all live in one ecosystem of diverse cultures, isn't nature culture and culture nature? "The valley cannot ask for anything—can only give—and so like a shell or husk of the valley I am doing the asking" (50).
5. If our evolved consciousness gives us conscience, how should we exercise our responsibilities toward our ecological home? "Somebody help. Please help the Yaak. Put this story in the President's, or Vice President's, hands" (50).
6. How can we best address the fact that our exploitation of our environment has emerged from the same mindset as our exploitation of each other? "We all possess a 'stake' in these public wildlands" (57).

In *Fiber* these questions for the reader are integrated by the writer's artistry into a bold and perhaps risky narrative strategy that might be called "the post-pastoral georgic."

Post-Pastoral Georgic

One of the ways in which Rick Bass has avoided the traps of "sentimental pastoralism" in his writing is by combining hard scientific knowledge with surprising narrative devices that have been called "fresh and strange" (Lowell, *New York Times Book Review,* 11) or "unfamiliar, bizarre" (Weltzien, *Rick Bass,* 23). Indeed his narrative strategy has developed into an exploration of what Terrell Dixon has called "a viable border country" ("Review," 103) between the tame or domesticated (*Brown Dog of the Yaak*) and the wild (*The Lost Grizzlies*), between fiction and nonfiction, between mythic discourse and personal anger, between art and activism. Bass's books and interviews are punctuated by outbursts of frustration at boundaries, whether it is those between "pure biology" and "fiction" (*Ninemile Wolves,* 83) or, as in an essay published the year after *Fiber,* between art and activism: "Wrestle as I will with the question, and try as I might, I cannot separate the two for any longer than a few months at a time—any more than other things in the world can be kept separate" (*Brown Dog of the Yaak,* 113).

The result of this integration of fiction and nonfiction, of biology and personal anger, of art and activism, is the bizarre narrative form of *Fiber.* More than a straightforward georgic, *Fiber* is a book about work that evaluates modes of work—logger/activist, activist/artist—in relation to the crisis of a particular environment. It even implicitly questions the role of the writer himself in producing *The Book of Yaak.* Was this too much the work of the artist—the storyteller—and not enough of the activist? Did it fall into the coziness of the pastoral and fail to do anything practical for the threatened valley itself? Did the earlier book call forth, as it were, a new mode that broke the old forms of American nature writing?

The four books of Virgil's *Georgics* were concerned with how best to work the land for the long-term benefit of both that land and its future husbandry. The delicacy of the husbandry of trees in Book II is millennia away from the crudity of clearcutting the old growth of the Yaak Valley. In *The Georgics,* the characteristic climax-growth woods of different regions are celebrated as independent of human care or harvesting:

> What a joy it is
> To view Cytorus surging with its boxwoods
> And Naryx with its pines! What a joy it is

To look on land beholden to no drag-hoes
Nor any human care! (91)

Fiber is a post-pastoral form of georgic partly because what begins as a working logger's tale becomes one of urging responsibility for our ecological relationships. In this text, consciousness, which since Virgil's time (specifically Lucretius's *De Rerum Natura*) had seemed to be what separated our species from the rest of nature, has been used to attempt to heal that separation. Here the imagination, under the urgent pressure of a specific ecological crisis, has forced a new form of narrative out into our culture. It is a superb example of Gary Snyder's contention that the spirit of Coyote, totem of the shape-shifting capacity of the human imagination, combined with the Bear totem's boldness in "protection of the wild," is what might bring us back into a right relationship with our home, the earth itself (*Place in Space,* 171).

Narrative Strategy

I want to look more closely at the narrative strategy of *Fiber* by referring to my personal first experience of this narrative. It's a rare and exciting moment when you know that you are in the presence of a masterpiece. This gradually became clear to me as I listened to Rick Bass read his new story "Fiber" at the second conference of ASLE (the Association for Studies in Literature and Environment) in 1997. We were in Missoula, Montana, where the Bitterroot River meets the Clark Fork. Since traveling in recent years to the U.S. conferences of ASLE, together with the Community and Environment conferences at the University of Nevada, Reno, and at Weber State University, I'd realized that Rick Bass was a writer that I needed to get to know. I'd bought his two most recent books, *The Book of Yaak* and *The Sky, the Stars, the Wilderness,* and been intrigued as to the next development of a well-known nature writer whose ecological thinking turns toward urgent advocacy in *The Book of Yaak,* but whose lyrical celebration of connectedness in the novellas of the later book raised, for me, the problems of coziness and "safety" in current American nature writing.

As his reading unfolded, in a series of breath-taking narrative twists that surprised the audience, Bass himself seemed to be expressing the frustration of an artist whose form has become too satisfyingly comfortable to change anything, while the clearcutting of old growth forest encroaches upon the very valley he has been enthusiastically celebrating in his recent book *The Book of Yaak*. I suddenly realized that I was hearing a cunning, passionate leap out of the "weak and safe" and into a new literary form.

In *Fiber*, the narrator explains that he is in the fourth phase of his life, which has moved from the "taking" of the geologist, to the creativity of the story writer, to the activist on the run from the law, to the "giving" of his present phase as "the log fairy." He cuts fallen timber for the sawmills, but his best logs he places at night individually in the trucks of sleeping loggers or at the gates of a sawmill. The mystified locals call the unknown person who is doing this "the log fairy." There are early hints that this is to be no ordinary narrative. In the same sentence in which the narrator admits that the boundaries between fiction and reality are blurred, he also points out that the functions of storyteller and activist can be blurred: "Neither you nor I can really be sure of how much of any story is fiction, or art, and how much of it is activism" (4). At the end of the second paragraph of the book, the narrator distances the reader from his narrative by commenting on public responses to his earlier stories: "They would write letters to me then and talk about the characters in those stories as if they were real people, which strangely saddened me" (3).

In this narrative of only fifty small pages, in a book that is beautifully designed and made by the University of Georgia Press, what Bass manages to achieve within the modest scope of four tightly written parts is nothing short of miraculous. *Fiber*, as I have suggested, does perhaps have flaws that I'll examine later—moments of final uncertainty of mode and uncertainty about the role of the illustrations—but it is a narrative that takes huge risks for such a slim volume.

At first, the reader might assume that the runaway of the opening sentence is a romantic who wants to be shaped by this landscape, who knows and respects the trees he is working with, and who is working toward an environmentally attuned future with his wife and children away from "the omnipresent hypercapitalism here at post-consumer century's end" (8). After learning from the mountain forest each day, "back home, in your cabin, your dreams swirl, as if you are still traveling, still walking, even in your sleep, across this blessed landscape, with all its incredible diversity, and the strength that brings" (10). This beautifully orchestrated voice then jumps to admitting, in the same rhythmic phrasing, that back in the first phase of his adult life he took, not just oil as a geologist, but jewelry that he hung on trees, boats that he burned, and cars that he sank. "I would look at my two hands and think, What are these for, if not to take?" There is, he tells us, a warrant out for his arrest.

In his book Bass teases his audience with the difficulty of interpreting this narrator's voice. The autobiographical connection of his oil geologist past, for example, is both a red herring in the development of *this* narrative and very much to the point in terms of Bass's personal development. As I listened to his reading, the voice of the narrator in the story seemed to change. One moment I was listening to a narrator who was a lyrical, learning naturalist: "The shape of the land beneath the forests is like the sluggish waves in an ancient, nearly petrified ocean—the waves of the northern Rockies sliding into the waves of the Pacific Northwest—so that it is like being lost, or like having found the rich dense place you were always looking for" (9).

Then I was listening to a logger narrator who had turned his earlier playful capitalist self into a newly playful "log fairy," an activist of small, theatrical, knowing gestures: "A thing I do sometimes, when I have a log I'm really proud of, is to haul it out and carry it on my back and place it in the road next to some other logger's truck, like a gift" (20).

At the next moment I was listening to a narrator who was a slightly mad environmental activist, starving his family in the backwoods of Montana while he played out a fantasy of his own: "Whenever a new car or truck enters the valley, I run and hide. I scramble to the top of a hill and watch through the trees as it passes. They can never get me. They would have to get the land itself" (36).

It was from a cabin in backwoods Montana that the Unabomber cycled to post the bombs that, during a seventeen-year campaign in the 1970s and 1980s, killed three people and maimed twenty in an attempt to "stop technology." But this narrator is not a Unabomber. He merely hauls logs, although the very restraint of his gestures is intended to be more than puzzling:

> I want to shock and offend. Hauling *logs?* My moderation seems obscene in the face of what is going on on this landscape, and in this country—the things, the misery, for which this country is so much the source, rather than a source of healing or compassion. (41)

The third section of the book ends with a statement of the ineffectiveness of both the activist and the artist. First the artist's work is rendered inadequate to the world crisis in terms that are an echo of Bertolt Brecht's words written in 1938:

> What kind of times are they, when
> To talk about trees is almost a crime
> Because it implies silence about so many horrors? (318)

Bass's narrator says:

> What story, what painting, does one offer up to refute Bosnia, Somalia, the Holocaust, Chechnya, China, Afghanistan, or Washington, D.C.? What story or painting does one offer up or create to counterbalance the ever-increasing sum of our destructions? (40)

The narrator has the belief that natural "rampant beauty will return" once the world's terrors have subsided "like a fire sweeping across the land." But an urgency has both demanded activism and witnessed its ineffectiveness. Bass typically suggests both that the activist needs the artist and that the artist needs the activist. While "activism is becoming the shell, the husk, where art once was," its hollowness suggests that it also needs the imaginative flair, perhaps the communicative originality, of the artist. Meanwhile the artist, especially the nature writer, is a dilettante until rescued by the urgent sense of purpose of the activist. So "the activist is the emergency-room doctor trying to perform critical surgery on the artist" (42).

The final section of this narrative begins with a breathtaking twist: "There is, of course, no story: no broken law back in Louisiana, no warrant, no fairy logs." Because "storytelling has gotten so damn weak and safe," it is inadequate to confront the rape of the Yaak on behalf of an American exploitation of natural resources in which even the Sierra Club, "bastion of radicalism," tactically connives. The Yaak could be the "genetic pipeline" for the regeneration of wilderness in the West, we are told, but the timber company's vice-president sits on the board of directors of the Nature Conservancy's Montana Chapter (48). The timber company, Plum Creek, the narrator tells us, "owns the cork to the bottleneck" of the valley. But there is still time to "do the right thing."

The narrator here becomes defiant: "If you think I'm going to say *please* after what they've already done to this landscape, you can think again." But the narrator of *Fiber,* who by this time at the live reading in Missoula had clearly become the author himself, hears his own voice and realizes what he must sound like. Bass continued reading from the text:

> I recognise the tinny sound of my voice. I know when an edge is crossed, in art: when a story floats or drifts backward or forward, beyond its natural confines. And I understand I am a snarling wolverine, snapping illogically at everything in my pain, snapping at everyone—at fellow artists, and at fellow environmentalists. (49)

At this point in the Missoula reading, Bass was overcome by emotion. An edge had, indeed, been crossed beyond the proud defiance of his own emotional tone. He had to regain his composure in order to speak the following lines from the text:

> I am going to ask for help, after all. I have to ask for help. This valley gives and gives and gives. It has been giving more timber to the country, for the last fifty years, than any other valley in the Lower 48, and still not one acre of it is protected as wilderness. (50)

Apparently some skeptical members of the audience felt that this was a hyped-up "performance" on Bass's part. But I know from public readings myself that you can get affected by your own work when you realize that this audience in particular is reading the emotional subtext while you are speaking. It can be disturbing if you let yourself realize at the time that they may be understanding things about your text that you don't. Many singers have to distance themselves slightly from the emotional content of what they are singing if it is not to overwhelm their ability to perform it. The singer Sting made precisely this point in a TV interview on British television recently: "You can't let yourself think too much about what you are singing or you couldn't sing it." So the backlash of skeptical contributors to the ASLE listserv discussion during the week following the reading, writing in indignation at having been emotionally manipulated by this "false" breakdown of Bass the reader, was really missing the point. It was, in my view, precisely because Bass, a founder member of ASLE, was reading to an ASLE audience that he knew was understanding more of what he was asking for than any other audience. He was asking for help, through his story, in front of the very 400 people in the country most likely to actually help. And this awareness got to him at that tricky moment in his reading when a proud defiance became a vulnerable plea.

Two Flaws in *Fiber*?

By this stage in the narrative, the narrator has made two surprising twists, the first having been the declaration that "There is no story" in the opening of part IV, and the second being the concession that "I am going to ask for help, after all." So the third twist is that, having merged narrator and author in the previous two twists so that we are now convinced that a personal plea is being made by the author (endorsed by his emotional breakdown in the Missoula reading), he writes: "I load the logs slowly into the back of my ragged truck and drive them slowly to the mill in protest" (50).

This immediately suggests that the narrator is still the log fairy or is speaking in the voice of the log fairy. One might put this down to Bass's final playful flourish of strangeness for the reader—his desire to keep the enigma of art active until the end. But the result is misjudged, in my view, because he surely needs the reader to believe that he is serious in his final plea—the fourth twist of the tale—for somebody to "put this story in the President's, or Vice President's, hands." At the end of the book is a list of twelve addresses, headed by that of the U.S. president, to whom the reader is urged to write letters on behalf of the Yaak. My feeling is that one would be inclined to do this only if one was convinced by the author's pleas. But in the book's final lines three enigmas are created with what seems to me to be the intention to distance or confuse the reader. Here, it seems, art is still fighting a rearguard action with advocacy in the narrative's last throes. It is as though the author cannot relinquish the role of the log fairy narrator. The book concludes with these lines after "put this story in the President's, or Vice President's, hands":

> Or read it aloud to one of them by firelight on a snowy evening with a cup of cider within reach, resting on an old wooden table.
>
> The firelight on the spines of books on the shelf flickering as if across the bones or skeletons of things; and outside, on that snowy night, the valley holding tight to the eloquence of a silence I can no longer hear over the roar of my own saw.
>
> Somebody please do this. Somebody please help. (50)

There are three aspects of the story's ending that seem to be at work here to puzzle the reader. The first produces a skepticism, I have discovered, among British readers (which I share myself) about the sentimental coziness of that snowy evening, overloaded as it is with firelight, cider (coyly "within reach"), and that old wooden table (presumably made of timber from the rape of the Yaak's old growth). The second puzzle is the grammar of the next sentence, which is softened to the extent of omitting an active verb. For me, this is not poetic; it is "poesy" (in both senses). Third is the reappearance of the logger's saw in an apparent reversion to the voice of the log fairy. With the provocative perverseness of an Edward Abbey, this logger cannot hear the eloquent silence of this valley. (Is this the Yaak or a different valley in which sits the listening president or vice-president?) It would hardly make sense for Bass himself to be sawing in such a way that he was dead to the valley's eloquence. I could strain to make clever, positive interpretations of these three enigmas in this crucial passage, but that would be to sidestep my suspicion that there is a problem for the reader at the very moment before the final request for the reader's action. There may be a way of understanding Bass's intention, however flawed it might be in execution, as carnivalesque play with conventions and expectations. But a sense of the complexity of elements at work here is indicated by a consideration of what I would nominate as the second possible flaw in *Fiber.*

In his earlier work Rick Bass has undoubtedly been guilty of "sentimental pastoralism" at times. It's hard to celebrate a place or an animal without appearing to be indulgently lyrical. This is a problem shared, of course, by visual artists. The cover painting for *Fiber* by Montana artist Russell Chatham is a moody, even gloomy, antipastoral evocation of forest. But do the woodcuts by Bass's wife, Elizabeth Hughes Bass, that accompany the text tend toward a pastoralization of it? The butterfly that announces part IV of the text and its pulling of the rug from beneath the narrative seems to bear no relation to the tension created for the reader at this point by the story. The prettifying of the text with art cut from wood seems to betray an innocence of the ambiguity of the roles of both art and wood in the text. If it were argued that these images are aware of that ambiguity, they would be read as counterpointing the tensions in the text. On the other hand, they do represent the creative relationship with both wood and place in their mode and content. The woodcuts echo the art that the narrator and his wife "do not talk about anymore" (25) as well as the limitations of their art: "What story or painting does one offer up or create to counterbalance the ever-increasing sum of our destructions?" (40). In fact, the notion of "counterbalance" is visually present in the woodcuts in form and in content. The illustrations include not only evidence of wild creatures but also books, a truck, and a log cut from a stump. Indeed, the first two images in the book are a counterpoint of technique, the white making the image of a fern in the first and the black making an image of a flower in the second. The same trick is played with a paw-print on page 21 and page 25 and with the butterfly on page 26 and page 43. Does the play in the relationship between woodcuts and text do anything other than pastoralize the book as an object? Is the play in this relationship another aspect of carnivalesque risk in *Fiber*?

Carnivalesque Risk

Throughout this narrative Bass has used devices to surprise the reader and unsettle his text. Inevitably, reviewers have already started characterizing the fractured narrative technique of *Fiber* as "postmodern." Certainly Bass has created a classic case of "the unreliable narrator." To catch the spirit of this I have used the word "playful," while showing that it is intended for serious purposes that should lead to readers' actually putting pen to paper on behalf of the Yaak Valley. This is what has come to be called, after M. M. Bakhtin, "carnivalesque" discourse. Bakhtin wrote of what he called "the complex nature of carnival laughter":

> It is, first of all, a festival laughter. Therefore it is not an individual reaction to some isolated "comic" event. Carnival laughter is the laughter of all the people [for example, all people who think they can read a narrative for what it is]. Second, it is universal in scope; it is directed at all and everyone, including the carnival's participants [that is, the author of the narrative]. The entire world is seen in its droll aspect, in its gay relativity [the way a logger could be close to being a log fairy]. Third, this laughter is ambivalent: it is gay, triumphant, and at the same time mocking and deriding. It asserts and denies, it buries and revives. (*Rabelais,* 11–12)

The risk of Bass's "carnivalesque" ambiguity in the final passage of *Fiber* may be intended to act in the manner of the last line of Ted Hughes's epic poem sequence *Cave Birds:* "At the end of the ritual / up comes a goblin." Just when the reader (the witness to the ritual that is art) thought it was all over, another enigma emerges to provoke further thought, even to revive the ritual in a new way: "It asserts and denies, it buries and revives." But the result seems to me to be merely an artistic confusion that will defuse further action on the reader's part.

Discussing good advice for writers from Ernest Hemingway in his latest essay, Bass dismisses the "ten usual rules for writing" and goes on to characterize his own form of narrative risk-taking: "Beyond that, it is all about how far you can leap, how far you can fly—how far you can fall and still come back" (*Brown Dog of the Yaak,* 97).

In *Fiber,* fiction has, in fact, leapt into activism, and, more importantly, the threatened reality of a particular landscape has been served by the flight of this new form of fiction. If Bass has fallen in the final passage of the book, it is retrieved by the passionate, cunning flight of the whole. Like Frenchman Jean Giono's 1953 story *The Man Who Planted Trees,* this is a book that will become a benchmark in the imaginative power of storytelling on behalf of a neglected and abused environment. With *Fiber,* not only has Bass achieved his most profound work to date, but the art of the storyteller has moved on in terms of what the imagination can do for real places.

Works Cited

Bakhtin, M. M. *Rabelais and His World.* Translated by H. Iswolsky. Bloomington: Indiana University Press, 1984.

Brecht, Bertolt. *Poems* 1913–1956. London and New York: Methuen, 1976.

Buell, Lawrence. "American Pastoral Ideology Appraised." *American Literary History* 1:1 (1989): 1–29.

———. *The Environmental Imagination.* Cambridge, Mass.: Harvard University Press, 1995.

Dixon, Terrell F. "Review of *In the Loyal Mountains.*" *Western American Literature* 30 (1995).

Gifford, Terry. *Pastoral.* London and New York: Routledge, 1999.

———, ed. *John Muir: The Eight Wilderness-Discovery Books.* Seattle: Mountaineers Press, 1992.

———, ed. *John Muir: The Life and Letters and Other Writings.* Seattle: Mountaineers Press, 1996.

Giono, Jean. *The Man Who Planted Trees.* London: Harvill, 1995.

Hughes, Ted. *Cave Birds.* London: Faber and Faber, 1978.

Lowell, Susan. *New York Times Book Review,* 5 March 1989.

Marx, Leo. *The Machine in the Garden*. New York: Oxford University Press, 1964.
Murray, John A. *The Sierra Club Nature Writing Handbook*. San Francisco: Sierra Club Books, 1995.
Scigaj, Leonard M. *Sustainable Poetry: Four American Ecopoets*. Lexington: University of Kentucky Press, 1999.
Snyder, Gary. *A Place in Space*. Washington, D.C.: Counterpoint, 1995.
Virgil. *The Georgics*. Translated by L. P. Wilkinson. New York: Viking Penguin, 1982.
Weltzien, O. Alan. *Rick Bass*. Boise: Boise State University Press, 1998.

Sounding the Depths of Rick Bass's Ancient Seas

O. Alan Weltzien

So, now, let us add Moby Dick to our blessing, and step from that. Leviathan is not the biggest fish;—I have heard of Krakens.
Herman Melville to Nathaniel Hawthorne, 17 November 1851

I think we ought to read only the kind of books that wound and stab us. . . . We need the books that affect us like a disaster, that grieve us deeply, like the death of someone we loved more than ourselves, like being banished into forests far from everyone, like a suicide. A book must be the axe for the frozen sea inside us.
Franz Kafka to Oskar Pollak, 27 January 1904

Franz Kafka's arresting definition of reading—and, by extension, writing—has framed the career of Rick Bass. Kafka's figures suggest reading as acutely painful, fundamentally transformative, even self-annihilating. Through his hyperbole we understand that the experience of books should in no way confirm the status quo, but rather should reconstitute identity, however harrowing the process (e.g., the prospect of self-mutilation). His final two metaphors, like a daring seventeenth-century Metaphysical conceit, stab our comfort, promoting the same disruption of sensibility found in the opening sentence of *Metamorphosis*. To paraphrase: reading a book represents an act of violence that unleashes an internal force that might well drown us. Ideally, books disturb and shift our ground and tap our potential as nothing else does. Ideally, reading prompts an experience of self-inundation, a radical baptism, from which a new self possibly emerges. Kafka's remarkable "frozen sea" image has resonated across the twentieth century, taken up by diverse writers including Jim Harrison and, through him, Rick Bass, who tilts and thaws it, in deference to his background in petroleum geology, from "frozen" to "ancient sea." It sustains the idea of the sea as origin of life, universal matrix. Kafka implies as well a troubled state of disconnection; Bass's adaptation stresses the sea as repository of the history of life.

The idea of ancient seas forms an essential credo, if not the primary *idée fixe,* in Bass's career, and close study of it enables us to plot his increasing environmental activism. From the benchmark year 1985, petroleum geology has been both fact and metaphor; *Oil Notes* (1989) makes clear that drilling—paraphrasing W. B. Yeats's rationale for *A Vision*—provides metaphors for writing. Oil drilling, as will be seen, defines writing and reading, but gives greater pause as a metaphor for epistemology and definition of art. Bass, after all, brings an unusual background to environmental writing. His abandonment of petroleum geology as praxis and shift in focus from the ancient seas as resource to the ancient seas as trope measure the awakening and growth of his biocentrism and activism. Bass's career in oil ended in 1985 as his writing career began, both occurring during his larval, pre-Montana life, with *Oil Notes* serving as valediction. If the shift from extraction to stewardship occurred quickly in literal terms, it occurs more slowly in the writing; we witness it in the rise and fall, and inevitable extinction, of Old Dudley Estes, an allegorical Everyconsumer or Ultimate Consumer who exists, however faintly, in the *Fiber* narrator's first life.

Near the beginning of *Basin and Range* (1981), his first excursion into geology, John McPhee reminds us that geology is "a fountain of metaphor" (24) and that there is "more than a little of the humanities in this subject" (25). If Bass grows less interested in oil, his commitment to the "fountain" of geology deepens: *Fiber*'s quasi-autobiographical narrator, for example, finds himself "once again daydreaming about those buried landscapes, and other hidden and invisible things" (*Fiber,* 33). The ancient seas trope provides Bass essential self-definition, and during his career he renounces his predatory attitude without renouncing his allegiance; instead, he orients himself to it more passively, employing it as a mode of instruction and inviting us to adopt it similarly for ourselves. Bass, like McPhee, though to a much lesser extent, becomes a devotee of deep time, and the perspective of deep time instills lessons of biocentrism and humility that writers such as Bass preach and celebrate. In another respect, Kafka's vision of books eliciting sharp, liberating change closely fits the shape of Bass's recent work, specifically his tendency toward propaganda, prodding his readers to act in particular ways to help save the roadless Yaak, for example. Kafka writes to his friend: "If the book we're reading doesn't wake us up with a blow on the head, what are we reading for?" In many respects Bass's fiction echoes his clarion-call ecojournalism, and both descend from Kafka's radical definition of reading and writing.

Oil Notes begins with a double reading reference, as Bass quotes poet-novelist Jim Harrison quoting Kafka about "'freeing the frozen sea inside us'" (1). The paraphrase contains no reference to books or reading. When Bass returns to it at the end of his first entry, he sustains the paraphrase and sets his own microcosm-macrocosm analogy in motion:

> I know where oil is, and I want to try to explain to you what it feels like, how it is, to know this.
>
> I just do not know how to do it—show you—because it is three-dimensional, or even beyond. It is future, undrilled and I am present, knowing. I don't know yet, without drilling, how to bridge that gap.
>
> It is the frozen sea within me. (2)

Finding oil means finding oneself; the quest of locating ancient seas of petroleum is epistemological, and drilling, like writing, bridges from present to future knowledge. This definition of art ironically appropriates Kafka insofar as Bass literalizes the "frozen sea" as oil, preeminent lubricant of the twentieth-century American economic engine and measuring stick of the U.S. lead in global exploitation of fossil fuels. It is ironically fitting, particularly in retrospect, that this son of Texas adopts, for a time, oil as his language for self, the vestment of identity. Bass warms but narrows Kafka's metaphor, reducing and restricting its expansive potential meaning to that of "liquid gold," and shifts its emphasis from reading to writing. He outgrows petroleum geology but certainly not geology, widening the metaphor again but retaining the emphasis upon ancient seas as aesthetic and ethical sourcebook: a prescription for better writing and living in tune with one's immediate physical surroundings.

In *Brown Dog of the Yaak* (1999), Bass quotes Annie Dillard's conviction that writers must always spend extravagantly, spending everything on their work in all stages, then returns—a decade later—to Kafka: "I like what Kafka said, about how a book should be 'the ax for the frozen sea inside us'" (96). The shift from paraphrase to direct quotation confirms his abiding interest in geology as "fountain of metaphor" rather than petroleum geology as fact. His coupling of Dillard with Kafka suggests writing to be as self-consuming and liberating as, in different respects, reading. Too, given the context of Milkweed Editions' Credo Series, of which *Brown Dog* is the first volume, Bass's mention of Kafka's ax is first of all self-referential. After all, through the recent nonfiction he strikes out at his readers'—and admirers'—lethargy and demands action, if not changes in behavior, to resist continued environmental degradation. Insofar as he writes out of anger, for instance, he seeks to create comparable anger and advocacy in the reader. Bringing Kafka's eloquent statement to the oilfields of the South equips Bass with a remarkable figure that defines art and, for himself at least, combines old and new lives. As we follow him from oil pockets through myriad other strata of deep time, we study applications of geology to ecology—for example, the seismic shift from exploitation to stewardship. We also assess the sustained resonances of geology as metaphor in Bass's poetics of reconnection, of living in place. Applying Kafka's ax, then, to several of Bass's books and stories, we plot the divergence of fact from metaphor and the diffusion yet concentration of the ancient seas trope. We leave oil pools but range across deep time, gathering its imagery into a language wherein Bass's aesthetic and ethics become one.

The Ancient Sea as Fact and Metaphor

As already noted, the opening of *Oil Notes* shows Bass appropriating Kafka's "frozen sea" as the ancient sea of fossil fuels. A young man's book, *Oil Notes* conveys, above all, the passion and excitement of hunting oil and proving wells. He tries hard to convince us that "capturing energy is really the most magnificent experience" (109); the book expresses a young engineer's pride and the potential pitfalls attending this addictive career. It celebrates the romance of oil witching. The pride stems from the engineer's unshakable intuition and confidence, just as the addiction manifests itself through the joy of the hunt and uncanny avoidance of dry wells. Though the book chronicles a job and way of life, Bass's analogy between self and earth, between his interiority and potential oil reserves, demonstrates that oil forms the lesser part of his search. His sounding the depths as a metaphor for self-knowledge and the wellsprings of art resounds across American literary history. Bass's drill, like Kafka's ax, glances back to Herman Melville's harpoon, for example, as my first epigraph suggests. Each violent, penetrating tool obviously symbolizes not only a Faustian quest for knowledge, but the sexual nature of that quest and something of the often painful consequences of it. The quest is as idealistic as it is ambivalent, as it modulates so easily into familiar paradigm of conquest. Melville provides the definitive version of the metaphor, and his comparison of the next novel (i.e., the mythical "kraken" and, in fact, the failed *Pierre*) to the just published *Moby Dick*, promising it to Nathaniel Hawthorne as a greater quarry and prize, measures the vault of his literary ambitions. Melville's metaphor lends itself to all manner of neo-Freudian and Jungian speculation, just as Bass's drill lends itself all too easily to the accusative critiques of Annette Kolodny and her ecofeminist daughters.

Contrary to the stereotype of greedy Texas oil drillers, Bass focuses upon the mystery of finding oil and the difficulty in communicating that peculiar combination of experience and intuition to the reader, advising her "that you have to get down under and beyond the mere occupational greed and look into the simplicity, the purity, the sacred part of it—the act, not the results, and yourself—and be aware that it is history, buried" (13). He thus separates himself from the masculinist narrative embodied in the oilfield roughneck or wealthy operator; and the literary career of Old Dudley Estes, whose surname may have been inspired by Texan Billy Sol Estes, records the abandonment of that "master" narrative.

Instead, there is something virginal about the Bass persona, whose holy grail is the Black Warrior Basin, which straddles the north Alabama–north Mississippi state line (26). He romanticizes and animates the basin, describing its wider, northern section's "old buried beaches, Mississippian (Paleozoic) in age," seemingly within hand's reach; farther south, "in that deeper, narrower part of the basin, the sands, five and six thousand feet down, like plunging porpoises, sounding, headed back to deep" (26–27). The driller's "[fifty-foot electronic] tool passes through all that dark mystery of time" (30) as if equipment, the human touch, only assists and completes oil's natural pathway upward. In a quick primer in petroleum geology, Bass likens drilling a proving well to a "child's game," judging it "as daring a rescue as ever there was," when the oil is "home free" (28). This is because, those "plunging porpoises" notwithstanding, oil "always tries to climb higher than it is: moving, like a miner, through and between pinhead spots of porosity, trying to get up to the area of least pressure—back to the earth's surface, where it used to be" (27).

In this first sounding of Bass's novella and novel title, the ancient sea exists, perhaps, more as fact than as metaphor. Certainly the Black Warrior Basin, "darker and more buried and mysterious" (29), remains the focus of his fieldwork in *Oil Notes.* Yet he casts the oil driller as heroic archeologist, returning this treasure trove of buried history—what he originally calls "future, undrilled" (2)—to the present. He bypasses conventional oilfield attitudes and dispositions by concentrating on process, not product, and defining the enterprise in the old language of literary romance. This language deflects writer and reader away from the spectacular economic facts of the oil business to its obscured, disinterested "sacred part" that includes the quest and the self. Bass's achievement in *Oil Notes* and later uses of the ancient seas trope consists in that deflection away from the loud facts and myths of frontier machismo and prodigious wealth swirling about the oil business. His desire of "*entering* the reservoirs" (158), of closing the distance between himself and the Black Warrior Basin, marks the extent of his personal metaphorical appropriation of oil drilling.

Perhaps unsurprisingly, Bass puts his oilfield background to fictional use in 1987, just two years after quitting the business and the very year of his life-changing move to the Yaak Valley of northwest Montana. In "Where the Sea Used to Be," his first published story, we see "the sacred part" of the oil business pitting itself against "the mere occupational greed." The same contest plays itself out in Bass's novel of the same name, wherein the latter is defeated. The fact that he chose to republish the story one decade later as the central panel of the triptych of novellas, *The Sky, the Stars, the Wilderness* (1997), itself published within a year of *Where the Sea Used to Be* (1998), prompts a comparative analysis. Obviously, the novella remains central in Bass's work; equally obviously, it forms a rough draft for the novel that he spent the intervening years rewriting at least six times. Bass himself stresses the differences between story and novel (personal communication, 1998), but they share far more than title, protagonist, and antagonist. In both we study the ancient sea as both fact and metaphor, though the latter takes us "down under and beyond" the former, in the process consuming it. The novel (and other texts) liberates the novella's definition of ancient seas as oil reservoirs. The Black Warrior Basin defines Bass's epistemological quest and thematizes his identity as a writer. Even as it is diffused into the more general imagery of ancient seas, it remains a potent referential language of interiority.

In both novella and novel, Wallis Featherstone represents an authorial surrogate, and again the novel's elaborations of Wallis plot the changed emphases of Bass's career, particularly the emergence of his environmental activism. "Where the Sea Used to Be" presents the first fictional use of the Black Warrior Basin, which forms its essence. In fact, the unnamed basin represents the novella's major force and presence, one greater than Old Dudley, here a relatively benign oil billionaire:

> The basin was an ancient, mysterious, buried dry sea: scooped out deep into the old earth more than three hundred million years ago and then filled slowly with sand, from an old ocean, waves lapping at empty shores—an Age of Sharks, thousands of varieties of sharks in the warm waters in those days—hundreds of miles of empty beaches, a few plants, windy days, warmth, no one to see anything, the most mysterious sea that ever was—and then, slowly the sea had left again, and the dunes, the bays, were covered up by millions and millions of years: swamps first, then deserts, then mountains, then river country, carrying parts of the mountains back down to the same sea, older, further south....
>
> The basin and its history lay hidden, and no one ever knew it was there, and the oil and gas from all its lives and warmth were only two thousand feet below the green and growing things of the present. It had been ten thousand feet below, at one time, but erosion and time were stripping back down, coming back closer to it, as if trying to get back to the old beaches, and those times. (55)

Bass's time-lapse romanticization recapitulates a master narrative from "deep time," which reverberates forward into the present. Couched in superlatives, the ancient sea constitutes Bass's Genesis, a "fabulous" myth of origins described as if it were recoverable—yearning to return to the surface of earth and consciousness, where it used to be. This holy grail gleams and beckons; knower and knowable may converge, and paradise be regained. Later Wallis and his girlfriend, Sara Geohagen (an apt surname), fly and study the land's skin from three miles up; he apprehends, as a gestalt, "where the sea had ended . . . curving and snaking all around, like a serpent, like a thing still, even that day, alive: it seemed to move as they watched it" (70). He dreams about the old beach as if it is exclusively his own, communing like a lover with his private prehuman landscape, a maritime Eden (78–79).

If the ancient sea is an allegory of knowledge, it contains, in outline, an equivalent to the Tree of Knowledge of Good and Evil. Thus Bass adds moral if not theological overtones to his master trope, as though the Book of Genesis were superimposed, however faintly, over geologic history, a plot from Paleozoic time. When Wallis contemplates the Gulf of Mexico, he realizes:

> This was his old ocean, cowardly, on the retreat now: some three hundred miles south of where it had once been, in its greatness, inland, when it was brave: the ocean's great advance northward into a place and country it had never been before, and might never return to. (79)

The romanticization of the ancient sea depends upon the archetypal formula of a golden age (that capitalized "Age of Sharks") succeeded by a long decline and fall, in this case a gravitational one. A tall tale, a fabled myth, and a "brave" ancient sea give way, eventually, to a decidedly unheroic present, a "cowardly... retreat," which, however, holds out the promise of reconnection and recovery of elements of that past. Bass's achievement consists in his reanimating this formula—perhaps our most essential story of origins, our rich legacy of nostalgia—through the language of petroleum geology. After all, "where the sea used to be" points backward and forward, like two-headed Janus, bringing the depths of the past to the surface of the present. The clause promises unity in time and space. The question becomes, what kinds of unity are not only possible but ethical? What manner of reconnection enlarges the human spirit in the paltry present—our geological nanosecond? Paradoxically, sustaining "the sacred part" of the oil business entails moving away from it.

From Resource to Trope

After 1985 Bass left the Black Warrior Basin behind, and though he quits that particular "ancient sea" he returns repeatedly to the trope of ancient seas to solidify his identity as a writer, assess the consequences of the ethics of stewardship, and teach his readers his version of living in place. Recalling Kafka, we can say that Bass grows preoccupied with the ancient sea within, not without. As he repeatedly redrafts his big book that retains his 1987 story title, he demonizes and exorcises Old Dudley. Old Dudley comes to symbolize overproduction and overconsumption in all of us, a parodic extension of that mindset that construes natural resources in terms of short-term human application only. To the extent that the U.S. economic success story across the twentieth century depended upon our disproportionate use of the globe's finite supply of fossil fuels, Old Dudley poses a cautionary tale, a symbol of extraction run amok. In an uncollected story, "The Earth Divers" (1994), Bass presents a draft existing midway between novella and novel. The title affirms that Melvillian epistemological quest discussed earlier; the story, however, parodies that traditional idealism inherent in the notion of sounding the depths, as no earth diving takes place.

In the seven years since his first appearance, Old Dudley has turned into the crude, hateful force that we study at length in the novel. Our attention focuses upon him, his protégé Matthew, and the first-person narrator, the unnamed Wallis, who is a neophyte. There is no mention of ancient seas; instead, Bass keeps us in Houston at oil parties, thereby initiating his Houston-Yaak, city-country polarity in which the former's pollution and towers stand for corporate evil—a redundancy. Many of Old Dudley's repulsive physical traits and behaviors elaborated in the novel first appear in this story, a satire of backbiting, hypocrisy, and drunken revelry. Nonetheless, during the workday the old man and his sidekick teach the tyro "the small corners, the hidden parts of geology I had yet to learn":

> Those were the days—the nights, rather—that I dreamed of wolves. Wolves racing through the woods. The breath of wolves hot on the flanks of their prey... some nights I was the prey.... But other nights I became the wolves, and I'd be right behind the prey, gaining on it. And then some nights I would be upon it, and finally I was beginning to learn hunger again. I learned how to find oil, too. (10)

We have known since *The Deer Pasture* (1985), his first book, that for Bass, as for many who write about hunting and themselves hunt, it gains value primarily as a metaphor for self-discovery. Hunting precedes and resembles oil drilling, though its horizontal motions may seem at odds with the latter's vertical plunges. "The Earth Divers" exists between his two wolf books, *The Ninemile Wolves* (1992) and *The New Wolves* (1998), and by this time he has already developed the character of Mel Estes, the novel's wolf biologist who "hunts" the second Swan Valley wolfpacks without being a predator.

The narrator of "The Earth Divers," a novice Wallis, learns Bass's pride in finding oil celebrated in *Oil Notes;* he delights in his wolflike intuition, his unerring ability to close in upon his goal. But Bass's vision has widened as he shifts his interest away from the climax of deer kill or oil strike and concentrates upon the process of quest. He easily shifts perspective from predator to prey, remarking in *The Lost Grizzlies* (1995), for example, "perhaps the way of prey, not predator, is the way to see the most—with the wide eyes and heart of a deer, rather than the tunnel vision of the wolf, the bear, the fox, the journalist" (116–17). Certainly Bass has outgrown the "tunnel vision" of the oil business, typically stereotyped according to its "mere occupational greed." As his self-education in the Yaak's woods continues, he seems to renounce his earth-diving past even as he has purified it of the dross of praxis and realigned it as a Melvillian epistemological metaphor. The ancient seas, earlier conceived in part as a fossil fuels resource, have become a trope.

At times Bass appears to renounce his former life altogether, as if casting off the ancient seas trope, though this is not the case. In "Getting It Right," his contribution to the *Headwaters: Montana Writers on Water and Wilderness* anthology (1996), he juxtaposes past and future, depths and surface, implying their opposition rather than unity. He glances backward as though bidding farewell to a calling now judged lesser, inferior in some way:

> I used to be a geologist. I guess I still am; it's not a thing that ever leaves you. I still dream of the ancient buried landscapes that I used to map—knowing intimately these places two and three miles below the surface, places I'd never been and would never see. Reaching vertically, drilling holes deep, and dreaming ancient dreams. . . . I spent all my time in the past, mapping the various sizes and distributions of the sand grains of those disintegrated mountains. It was a wonderful culture and I loved it. . . . (6)

But the new life in northwest Montana feels, by contrast, like "the future, right now," and the writer claims to have reoriented himself:

> Under the trance of this land's beauty—not some buried landscape two miles down, but this one, here-and-now—my mind has re-formed itself, sculpted by this land as a glacier sculpts stone, to change from desiring to plunge vertically through the earth to instead wandering

> laterally across it: a 90-degree change, and a turn, a gravitation, toward the future. (6)

Back in *Oil Notes,* oil rather than one's chosen landscape is "future, undrilled," so it would seem Bass makes a sea change and abandons the depths; but he doesn't, since depths and surfaces combine to form the future. The nonfiction Bass persona precisely foreshadows the plot of *Where the Sea Used to Be,* in which the fictive alter ego, Wallis, undergoes his most complete education, throwing over petroleum geology for Mel's wolf biology. But in realigning himself from father to daughter, Wallis does not wholly shed his past. Bass cherishes it, using the temporal perspective of deep time to advance his homilies about biocentric humility and environmental advocacy. A passage from *The Book of Yaak* (1996) exemplifies the recent Bass who combines old and new lives, geology and stewardship. In *Yaak* he quotes Terry Tempest Williams quoting D. H. Lawrence's ideal "blood knowledge," defining thereby the need for a centering rhythm conflating advocacy and "your 'other,' peaceful life" (90–91). *Yaak*'s best statement of this rhythm of taking root echoes Kafka's "frozen sea" and reaffirms Bass's central trope: "the blood rhythms of wilderness which remain in us (as the old seas and oceans remain in us) are declaring, in response to the increasing instability of the outside forces that are working against us, the need for reconnection to rhythms that are stable and natural. . . . We can find these rhythms within ourselves" (13).

The ancient seas trope, earlier an epistemological conceit, now encompasses a personal ethics. The analogy between the earth's interior and one's own remains as strong as ever; Bass's recent fiction and nonfiction further develop it to explicate what I earlier called his poetics of reconnection. It becomes the referential language for the project of introspection that uncovers those "blood rhythms of wilderness." In forming our green self, we take our cue from the myriad rhythms of our chosen topography, assuming new shape from it just as Bass preaches, in several places, that "this landscape has carved and fit me" (*Fiber,* 17). While this prescription for living in place is commonplace among nature writers past and present, Bass's referential language is less so. If the ancient seas imagery constitutes a romanticized master narrative and archetypal golden age formula, as stated earlier, it also articulates a chthonic theme—what William Least Heat-Moon, near the end of his long *PrairyErth,* calls "habitance" or in-dwelling. Living a life somehow rooted in the natural world, even if one dwells in a city, reconciles surfaces with depths and forms a bulwark against terminal despair: a seductive legacy of decline-and-fall nostalgia, which progressive environmental destruction feeds. Bass's metaphorical use of geology points the way and clarifies his shift from a conservationist to a preservationist outlook expressed through the gospel of wilderness.

The Decline and Fall of Old Dudley

In *Basin and Range* as well as the subsequent trio of books that comprise *Annals of the Former World*, John McPhee continually bridges deep time and human time, cross-referencing prehistory and history in an artful dance of chronologies. He quotes several geologists for whom earth time fundamentally redefines their own, and that redefinition illuminates Bass's recommended integration of past and present. Two geologists, for example, ruminate about one million years being the shortest usable unit of deep time:

> "You begin tuning your mind to a time scale that is the planet's time scale. For me, it is almost unconscious now and is a kind of companionship with the earth."
> "If you free yourself from the conventional reactions to a quantity like a million years, you free yourself a bit from the boundaries of human time. And then in a way you do not live at all, but in another way you live forever." (129)

The opening of *Fiber* sustains this merger of geologic and human time scales, using "a thousand years per inch" (3). Such statements express the rationale of Bass's chthonic theme, the best answer to the pressure of our geological nanosecond and the oppressive weight of prehistory. The "long view" entails both self-annihilation and a diffused endurance, a zen Buddhist-like "companionship"; it is, of course, religious. In *Fiber*, to a lesser extent *Brown Dog of the Yaak*, and especially the novel, Bass connects his ancient seas to the "blood rhythms of wilderness" credo to explicate and urge the geologist's long view as ideal.

In these more recent texts, geologic history becomes the reference point for personal history. *Fiber*'s four-part structure and its narrator's recursive use of his earlier three lives both suggest a stratigraphic rather than simple linear definition of the self. At times the narrator talks as if he has shed his earlier lives as geologist, artist, then activist, but other comments pose these as accumulations that together comprise the log fairy narrator. Early in the story, Bass fits Kafka's "frozen sea" to the Yaak, epitome of semiwilderness anywhere: "The shape of the land beneath the forests is like the sluggish waves in an ancient, nearly petrified ocean—the waves of the northern Rockies sliding into the waves of the Pacific Northwest—so that it is like being lost, or like having found the rich dense place you were always looking for" (8–9). This poetic animation of plate tectonics sustains the power of Bass's ancient seas symbolism and detaches it from its earlier connotations of fossil fuels, specifically oil. Its familiar present-tense energy sustains the lost-is-found paradox wherein going down—Bass's fond imagery of descent—is going home to one's truest self, shaped by those "blood rhythms of wilderness."

This paradox describes as well the conceptual climax of *Brown Dog of the Yaak,* when Bass dismisses the apparent differences within that book's four essay subjects, above all his career as both writer and activist, by appealing to "share[d] root stock," "this truth of metaphor," "that place of irreducibility" to which an artist, like a petroleum geologist, "cut[s] down" (119). Clearly his master trope provides him the image of bedrock unity that reconciles opposites, especially his own sense of divided self that *Fiber,* more than any of his other works, dramatizes. It suggests, as well, an optimal mode of integration, since discovering the ancient sea within means incorporating the lessons of geologic time into our own and practicing, as a result, a land ethic based on personal humility and preservation.

In *Fiber,* the narrator's allegorical wife, H/hope—this text's expression of Wallace Stegner's famed dictum, the geography of hope—"is still searching to settle into the rhythms of this place—the fast rhythms on the surface, as well as the slower ones frozen in the rock below" (23). In *Brown Dog,* Bass defines the Yaak as both "very new" and "very old, possessing beneath and within itself a memory more ancient than that of any of the lands now at the surface" (45). If one imitates, in certain respects, one's chosen landscape, then the truest self integrates "slower" and "fast" rhythms, the legacy of ancient seas and surface processes of change—like McPhee's two geologists quoted earlier. How, then, does one discover and sustain the slower rhythms amidst the fast? What does it mean to live according to the earth's time as well as one's own, as if adopting the mindset, absent the training, of professional geologists?

What are the practical consequences of using geologic time as a mode of instruction?

Where the Sea Used to Be elaborates answers to these questions, unsurprisingly suggesting in the process that wilderness rhythms are geologic. The fusion of opposing chronologies, the superimposition of geologic time upon our own, enables Bass to extend that project of introspection deriving from Kafka's analogy between self and earth and Bass's elaborations of it. Contrary to the journalistic Bass of "Getting It Right," *Fiber*'s narrator recognizes that

> some of my old desires are returning, my burrowing or diving tendencies: the pattern of my entering the ground vertically again, as I did when I was drilling for oil; desiring to dive again, as if believing that for every emotion, every object, every landscape on the surface, there is a hidden or corresponding one at depth. (25)

Here the analogy hyperbolically defines allegory as though the earth's interior exists primarily as a system of geologic objective correlative, a Boehmian book below the surface. Bass backs off this exaggerated claim of correspondence, though the narrator sustains the primarily metaphorical value of the ancient seas. Macrocosm informs microcosm: "Maybe someday I will go back to books. Maybe someday I will submerge back into the vanished or invisible world, and will live and breathe theory..." (38). The Melvillian quest resonates without check since "outer" interiors—of seas current or ancient—prefigure inner, those "diving tendencies" marking one's calling as a writer.

By this stage of Bass's career, the ancient seas exist as metaphor, not fact; their basis in fact serves their value as source and symbol of human potential. His separation from the practices and economics of petroleum geology takes the form of his steady exorcism of Old Dudley, who comes to symbolize, like a medieval cardinal sin, American gluttony, emblematized by the Osborne Russell excerpt about the wolverine that serves as epigraph to the novel and is also quoted in *Brown Dog* (61–62). Particularly since *The Book of Yaak*, Bass has preached, along with the need to discover those "blood rhythms of wilderness," the gospel of giving back rather than taking (e.g., *Fiber*, 17); and Old Dudley, or acquisitiveness gone haywire, supremely embodies the self-consuming doom of overconsumption. Looking back upon his first life as geologist, *Fiber*'s narrator judges himself a taker, an indiscriminate thief: "Just the oil, at first, from so deep beneath the ground, and from such a distant past that at the start it did not seem like a taking; but then gradually and increasingly from the surface" (10–11).

This statement more pointedly disavows the "mere occupational greed" of petroleum geology than any other in Bass's career. It certainly condemns, at least to some extent, his past complicity in the oil business and measures his growth beyond it. It also serves moral judgment against Old Dudley, the terms of which the novel works out. *Fiber*'s narrator ruefully admits, "It was as if I was trying to eat the world, or that part of it" (11), and Bass opens the novel by defining Old Dudley with the same Freudian emblem of infantile orality. Bass explicitly condemns American overuse of fossil fuels by linking it with general theft. And in the conservative moral universe of the novel, replete with an ancient but familiar country-city archetype (i.e., Houston is evil; the second Swan Valley, pure), the thief ultimately receives his just deserts as the second Swan Valley's primary season, winter, kills the exploratory drilling project and himself.

As mentioned earlier, the publication of novella and novel within a year of one another, a complex echo, calls for—insists upon—comparative analysis, and "The Earth Divers" helps us plot the demonization of Old Dudley. Contrary to the novella, the novel opens and closes with him, now a subterranean geologic force, an extant remnant of Steven Spielberg's *Jurassic Park* (6), a monster as much as a character who probably belongs in a circle of Dante's Inferno. The beginning defines the passions and obsessions of petroleum geologists in terms of his inescapable force field: his tyrannical control over their obsessions, his absolute rapacity as regards both oil and employees, above all, the hand-picked protégés. Matthew, further developed from "The Earth Divers," forms the novel's cautionary tale for Wallis, a doomed alter ego (e.g., they are both color blind), as Old Dudley destroys him. The novel's opening pages, then, recapitulate Bass's attraction to and thematic use of ancient seas, "that aqueous, other world" (7), but now we construe it through the black hole of Old Dudley, for whom oil, "reassembled from old life into the sour vat of death—was like the old steaming blood of the earth" (9). That master narrative noted in the novella—the presentness of genesis, the romanticization of geologic processes—is replayed in the novel's opening (5), though the business of oil drilling temporarily eclipses it. But the novel defeats that business even as it suggests how we might live by giving back, under the tutelage of the geologic long view.

As in fable, when Wallis crosses the divide separating the second Swan Valley from the rest of the world, he symbolically dies and is reborn, in the process dreaming and "descend[ing] to the safest place in the world" (16). Unsurprisingly, this Wallis, like his earlier avatar (in the novella), dreams of ancient seas and subterranean lands, but now "he imagined that perhaps those old lands were held in place by a quietness and enduringness—a smoothness of fit. The way rain falls, the way snow falls. The way birds sleep. The way lichens grow in red and blue mosaics across damp boulders and old stone walls. The way a log rots" (60). We read the inside according to the outside, interpreting geologic processes according to tangible processes affecting the earth's skin. This Wallis grows beyond, understands more than, the earlier one and combines stages of Bass's career. Furthermore, the titanic processes of genesis have quieted: Bass changes his master narrative by stressing its ecology or "smoothness of fit." This changed emphasis points up his matured understanding of wilderness as both fact and cardinal virtue. "Old lands" and new lands are governed by the same processes, which truth brings the fabled geologic past forward, into our time. *Fiber* repeatedly proclaims that "the old, even when it is buried beneath the new, sometimes rises and surges, pierces through, and reappears" (4)—where the sea used to be, in other words; and that "things are tied together, as the future is linked, like an anchor, to the past" (25). Bass inscribes the idea that the ancient seas are not only ancient.

Mel, antagonist of her father and Wallis's tutor and, later, lover, defines this fictionalized Yaak valley as youthful: "'Everything is the same age up here. . . . Everything is ten thousand years old, and that's that. . . . It's all the same age. It's not an old country. It just feels that way.'" When Wallis reproaches her, as McPhee's geologists might, for deeming ten thousand years a long span, she reproaches him as one of you "city guys": "'You forget how long time can be—four seasons, for instance. You like to compress things, rather than drawing them out. *Attenuating* them'" (45). Wallis's changing dreams and Mel's insistence both proclaim the reciprocity of surfaces and depths and the convergence of geologic time with human time. *Where the Sea Used to Be* in effect draws the ancient seas back to the land's surface by suggesting the intertextuality of both: we understand the valley's present according to its past, and vice versa. Certainly Wallis quits the way of compression and attenuation, slowing down and living according to the valley's pulses—those "blood rhythms of wilderness" recommended to all. Too, reading the novel simulates the "long time" of "four seasons." Above all, it "draw[s] . . . out" the luxurious length of winter: a fictional illustration of those themes adumbrated in *Winter* (1991), now occupying the novel's "Book One" (i.e., more than the first half of the novel) and returning at the close. Winter constitutes the primary seasonal reality, its slowing rhythms imitating the uniformitarianist view—however qualified or discredited by now—of geologic processes. A widened view of seasonal time imitates geologic time and enables character and reader to live according to both chronologies, like McPhee's geologists.

Somehow, winter both obscures and reveals evidences of those ancient seas. The land's skin does intimate the depths, though Wallis, groomed as Matthew's successor, must learn to reread in order to apprehend this truth as he has not before. The narrator of *Fiber* realizes that "the land itself up here is inverted, mysterious, even magical, turning humans, and all else, inside out, in constant turmoil, constant revolution" (40). Wallis knows that in summer,

> he could also climb the cliffs' crevices, could climb like a spider and with his rock hammer could chip the real and physical samples from the cliff walls—ancient petrified oceans frozen to stone and lifted high into the sky so that the world—erosion, weathering, wind, and the clutch of plant-roots—could begin eating at them. (71)

If the past meets the present, it eludes the young prospector who enters this landscape at the outset of its longest season, as though snow obscures—mocks—evidences of Bass's master trope. Snow exemplifies "the world" that nibbles away at the past, in contrast to Old Dudley's baleful, omnivorous appetite with which the novel begins. In the contest between appetites, "the world's" inevitably wins; and to align himself with it rather than with Old Dudley, Wallis twice fails in mapping (geologically) the valley. To learn to reread, Wallis renounces his recent training and adopts the broader Bass view of geology as metaphor.

In the novel's echoing of the novella, we unsurprisingly discover sameness and difference. By the novella's end, Wallis holds both his integrity and independence and his lover: "The only reason he could have two passions rather than one was because he had never ruined the first. It hadn't ever been sold, when asked for" (*The Sky, the Stars, the Wilderness,* 86). The later Wallis, just a bit older and less innocent, knows grief, having loved (Sara—now Susan) and "lost everything" before the novel begins (8). As intimated in "The Earth Divers," under Old Dudley's tutelage he has learned "to read the stories below him . . . almost to the core—losing himself in lands where no one had ever been, or seen, or even imagined; and where certainly there was no such thing as grief" (8). Here sounds the same pride in quest, the same hoped-for original discovery and private communion, seen in *Oil Notes* and "Where the Sea Used to Be." The change, however, marks a greater social communion, even dependency, than Bass staked earlier. The romance plot, the slow convergence of Wallis and Mel, underscores the ancient seas trope, Wallis's claim notwithstanding, as domain of affective as well as imaginative experience (e.g., *Fiber,* 25). To love again, the protagonist studies his dreams and learns to look beyond his geologic maps.

If Wallis reads depths with expertise, Mel, a wolf biologist, reads surfaces with similar expertise. Having just shown Wallis and Helen, Matthew's adoptive mother, her four-seasons "hide" map of wolf movements—and nineteen dry well sites—in the valley, "the most beautiful map Wallis had ever seen" (73), Mel remarks, "'It's more like now I'm reading stories out on the land—stories tucked under the snow, stories running from me, just around the next bend. It still feels like I'm reading'" (75). Yet Mel, a fictional descendant of wolf biologists applauded but sometimes castigated in *The Ninemile Wolves* and *The New Wolves,* must also learn to reread, because scientific knowledge has obscured mystical knowledge, a truer source of wisdom and an applied environmental ethics. Oil geologist and wolf biologist together pose a parable of the limits of quantification. The novel suggests that for both to understand their chosen place they undo their respective expertise and learn to read anew. Wallis, with a perfect track record for locating oil, fails twice with maps, and Mel quits her maps for a new life as teacher and mother. Terry Tempest Williams once told me that she abandoned her life list when she discovered herself to be more interested in individual birds, not more new species (personal communication, 1994). Presumably Mel comes to intuit wolves as do the Eskimo tribes that Barry Lopez studies and celebrates in *Of Wolves and Men.* Once Wallis abandons the search for ancient seas of oil, he knows the ancient seas better and integrates their chronology into his own.

Summarizing the thinking of professional geologists in *Basin and Range,* John McPhee concludes that we remain for the most part imprisoned within our "animal sense of time": "The human mind may not have evolved enough to be able to comprehend deep time. It may only be able to measure it" (127). The dilemma of acute chronological myopia is familiar. *Where the Sea Used to Be* suggests the urgency of the dilemma and a way of "comprehend[ing] deep time" beyond merely "measur[ing] it." Certainly it states that measuring deep time misreads it or at least insufficiently interprets it. Overconsumption of our limited base of fossil fuels within our geological nanosecond misreads the primary homily of deep time, the track record of extinctions (*Basin and Range,* 128). Clearly, Wallis's learning curve in the novel serves as exemplum. For example, following Mel in the woods, noting her silvicultural expertise, he divines a unity of chronologies:

> It was similar to where Wallis went in his maps: the surface, the skin of the world, was no different from its depths. He had known that intuitively. But it was a source of great awe, to realize now that her forest above was like his subterranean oil fields.
>
> He suspected the similarities did not stop there; that if one stretched the time scale out far enough—expanded it—all things, at one point or another—wolves and humans, forests and mountains, dead people and living ones—became similar, and that it was only in the compression of things—the moment—that there appeared to be any significant flutter of individuality. (198)

The disciple has quit the laser single-mindedness of his former mentor, the way of oil drilling. So, too, Bass advocates seeing beyond the "compression" of our lifespans and recognizing, in the earth's long view of which ancient seas serve as token, our miniscule place in time. In the shifted perspective occasioned by deep time, that "flutter of individuality" teaches humility as does nothing else. Bass opens part II of *Fiber* by declaring, through his narrator, his belief in "power": "I like the way continents are always straining to break apart or ride up on and over one another, and I like the way the seedlings in the forest fight and scramble for light" (15). Figuratively speaking, plate tectonics and organic growth, depths and surfaces, Wallis and Mel enact the same language. In this language of "power," human power exemplified by Old Dudley counts for nothing.

Where the Ancient Sea Is

I was once told by a man I'd known through childhood that there were two kinds of geologists: those interested in oil and those interested in rocks. I understood him to mean that the former had sold their souls and weren't really geologists any more. In *Oil Notes,* Bass defines and excoriates "ego-geologists" who pose as being "[a] *leader*—in a profession of men and women who cannot be led, and will not" (135). Old Dudley has served, I believe, as an arch-example of the "ego-geologist" in Bass's literary imagination: a barometer that registers Bass's changing use of his ancient seas trope. Two other texts within *Where the Sea Used to Be* illustrate competitive interpretations of the ancient seas. The more frequent, Old Dudley's journals (i.e., the novel's italicized passages), is suspect and ultimately rejected. These journal entries, bound in old, decrepit leather volumes, constitute "the ancient, loopy ramblings of [a] precocious teenager," "close to what seemed like madness" (49, 51). Bass includes twenty-six entries, all but the last read by Wallis, framed by a preamble-rationale (49–50) and "*a parting word*" (361): some of them are lengthy, including the one opening Book II (283–86). We read, like Wallis, as students of Old Dudley's own ancient sea, witnessing the genesis of a Faustian "ego-geologist." The journals are both a set of wannabe lectures, a personalized course in geology replete with titles and subheadings, and an adolescent autobiography that underscores, above all else, that masculinist paradigm of conquest (e.g., plowing the depths, consuming the earth).

At the beginning of the book Bass acknowledges the scientific source of Old Dudley's journals, Alexander Winchell's *Walks and Talks in the Geological Field* (1886), "from which many of the 'lectures' in this book were adopted." The quotation marks bespeak Bass's ironic view of his antagonist's claims to disciplinary authority and identity as a teacher. At least once, Wallis reads aloud (111–16), but mostly his silence echoes ours, as if this hieroglyphic text, like cryptic strata in a skewed time lapse, requires decoding. With appropriate irony, Bass has Old Dudley reading out loud to Amy, his impregnated woman in the second Swan Valley, "the last brittle journal open to the last page," his own rendition of a Nietzschean Zarathustra (358–61)—and Amy falls asleep (361). Her temporary sleep signifies our surrogate condemnation of the journals with their overweening pride, a perverse pledge to the message of dominion promised in Genesis 1.

In contrast to this devil's text stands another, less frequent but more conspicuously placed. The novel includes two pairs of black-and-white photographs by one Stuart D. Klipper. The reproductions measure approximately 1 inch by 4 inches, the first pair gracing the novel's and

Book I's (1) title pages and the second pair placed on Book II's and the Epilogue's title pages (281, 441). Together they tell the tale of deep time, asserting its primacy over the steep arc of ambition signified by Old Dudley's journals. These are not hieroglyphic. The first photo, which could be the Grand Tetons cathedral group shot from Jackson Lake (looking southwest), displays the sort of scene that nineteenth-century travel narratives, affirming the Burkean aesthetic of sublime and picturesque, sought out and gushed over. A symmetrically arranged local range dominates the photo, with the peaks' snowfields and glaciers backlit, along with cirrus and stratus clouds; the photo's upper half, its radiating streamers of light a descendant of the Luminist tradition, contrasts with the shaded lower half, the shores of a large lake, including peninsulas and a couple of small islands. It's a visual freeze-frame of that master narrative from deep time attractive to Bass and his readers in his earlier evocations of the ancient seas; it's also a romanticized epitome of the Rocky Mountains, an affirmation of uplift.

The second photo replaces the first's dynamic and aesthetic appeal with a far quieter but bigger scene: a frame of calm, limitless sea, its surface slightly wrinkled by small waves, and a dark blend of cirrus clouds in the photo's left hand contrasting with the washed-out white clarity of the right half. It shifts the earlier photo's light-dark contrast by ninety degrees. Together, this visual text recapitulates, in miniature, geologic process including plate tectonics, faulting, uplift, and weathering. It emblematizes deep time, which ironizes—and dismisses—the posturings of human time recorded in Old Dudley's journals. Turning from the first photo to the second, we traverse geologic epochs, if not eras. The former answers Bass's decade-long title and *idée-fixe: this* is where the ancient sea used to be, but if seas come from mountains, mountains come from seas as well. The second photo describes where the ancient sea *is,* as if we imagine southward from New Orleans, with the younger Wallis,

at the novella's end. Current seas contain the shapes and processes of ancient ones, and these shapes and processes lead not to oil and overconsumption but to a personal incorporation of geologic time into our everyday lives.

Bass has explored the ancient seas, both his own and the earth's, thoroughly in his career to date. His diffusion of focus away from oil reserves enables him to use the language of geology, that "fountain of metaphor," to present what I earlier called his poetics of reconnection, of rootedness. The marriage of self and place assumes a chthonic form that integrates time by contextualizing our own into that prized geological long view. In that marriage of chronologies, we apprehend that where the sea used to be is also where it is. Through this sense of double marriage, we each have the best chance to live biocentrically, beyond the prison of our own mortal span.

Works Cited

Bass, Rick. *The Book of Yaak*. Boston: Houghton Mifflin, 1996.

———. *Brown Dog of the Yaak: Essays on Art and Activism*. St. Paul: Milkwood Editions, Credo Series, 1999.

———. *The Deer Pasture*. College Station: Texas A&M University Press, 1985, 1999; New York: W. W. Norton, 1996.

———. "The Earth Divers." *Weber Studies* 11:3 (Fall 1994): 7–10.

———. *Fiber*. Athens: University of Georgia Press, 1998.

———. "Getting It Right." In *Headwaters: Montana Writers on Water and Wilderness*, ed. Annick Smith. Missoula, Mont.: Hellgate Writers, 1996.

———. *The Lost Grizzlies: A Search for Survivors in the Colorado Wilderness*. Boston: Houghton Mifflin, 1995.

———. *The New Wolves*. Toronto: Burford & Lyon, 1998.

———. *The Ninemile Wolves*. Livingston, Mont.: Clark City Press, 1992; New York: Ballantine, 1993.

———. *Oil Notes.* Boston: Houghton Mifflin/Seymour Lawrence, 1989; Dallas: Southern Methodist University Press, 1995.

———. *The Sky, the Stars, the Wilderness.* Boston: Houghton Mifflin, 1997.

———. *Where the Sea Used to Be.* Boston: Houghton Mifflin, 1998.

Gould, Stephen Jay. *Time's Arrow, Time's Cycle: Myth and Metaphor in the Discovery of Geological Time.* Cambridge, Mass.: Harvard University Press, 1987.

Heat-Moon, William Least. *PrairyErth.* Boston: Houghton Mifflin, 1991.

Kafka, Franz. *Letters to Friends, Family, and Editors.* Ed. John Calder. New York: Schoken, 1977, 1978.

Lopez, Barry. *Of Wolves and Men.* New York: Charles Scribner's Sons, 1978.

McPhee, John. *Basin and Range.* New York: Farrar, Straus & Giroux, 1981.

Where the Sea Used to Be

Rick Bass and the Novel of Ecological Education

Terrell F. Dixon

In his 1987 essay "Speaking a Word for Nature," Scott Russell Sanders examines the role of fiction in environmental literature only to ask: "Why is so much recent American fiction so barren?"[1] His investigation, echoing Thoreau's famous introduction, "I wish to speak a word for Nature,"[2] offers the following answer: "What is missing from much recent fiction, I feel, is any sense of nature, any acknowledgment of a nonhuman context."[3] His call for more nature fiction constitutes a contemporary ecocritical milestone in two ways. Simply by assuming the importance of nature fiction, Sanders fosters the ongoing expansion of what ecocriticism considers nature writing; he helps the necessary effort to include novels and short stories as well as poems and essays in what we designate as nature literature. The lack of nature fiction that Sanders finds in the decades preceding his essay is also useful. His essay can serve as a line of demarcation, highlighting by contrast a crucial period in American fiction toward the end of the twentieth century, a time when more and more writers came to see fiction as a way to explore the complexities of our environmental crisis.

This development is manifest in several ways. In the late eighties and the nineties, short story collections such as *The Watch* (1989) and *In the Loyal Mountains* (1995) by Rick Bass, *Cowboys Are My Weakness* (1993) by Pam Houston, *Field Notes: The Grace Note of the Canyon Wren* (1995) by Barry Lopez, and *The Middle of Nowhere: Stories* (1991) by Kent Nelson began to celebrate wildness and its role in preserving the world. The final decade of this last century also produced important novels that looked at environmental questions from another perspective, investigating environmental degradation in our increasingly postnatural landscape. Embodied in such novels as Don DeLillo's *Underworld* (1998), Richard Powers's *Gain* (1998), Jane Smiley's *A Thousand Acres* (1991), and Helen Maria Viramontes's *Under the Feet of Jesus* (1995), what we can call the literature of toxicity occupies a central place in the fiction of *fin-de-siècle* America.

Equally important, however, is another development in end-of-the-century environmental fiction: one that we can call the novel of ecological education. It is easy to see how these times give rise to this type of fiction. Underlying many such specific issues as environmental degradation and the loss of wilderness habitat is a more general and fundamental problem: the lack of knowledge about nature. With the profound and ongoing demographic shift that has transformed America into an urban nation, one where over 80 percent of the population lives in cities, the kind of informal environmental education that was once commonplace has become rare. Very few Americans now grow up with the kind of firsthand knowledge of the natural world that characterized previous generations. As farm populations dwindle and suburban developments occupy previously open spaces, the interaction with the natural world that occurred as a part of growing up in small towns or as a part of daily life in rural areas can no longer be taken for granted. Opportunities for firsthand contact with nature diminish even as the causes for environmental concern multiply. In this situation, literature has begun to take on more of the cultural work of inculcating ecological awareness, of calling attention to and celebrating the nonhuman context of life.

The extraordinary outpouring of important literary nonfiction in the last part of the twentieth century, the work of writers like Annie Dillard, Barry Lopez, Robert Michael Pyle, Scott Russell Sanders, and Ann Zwinger, has constituted one well-known literary response to our environmental situation. The American novel, however, has also begun to make its own distinctive, though less celebrated, contribution, and the novel of ecological education constitutes an important, specific part of this contribution. In fact, with its freedom to build an imaginative framework for its explorations and with a long tradition of the novel of education—the novel that narrates a process of education so that it may, in turn, educate a reading public—on which to draw, the contemporary novel is perhaps uniquely suited for the task of educating the reading public about the importance of ecological education.

This is not to suggest that the contemporary phenomenon that we can call the novel of ecological education is overtly or even especially didactic. The texts that are part of this group, one that includes novels such as Charles Frazier's *Cold Mountain* and Andrea Barrett's *Voyage of the Narwhal,* succeed by creating engaging characters and narratives that also explore the growing environmental concerns of our time. It is most helpful perhaps to see such novels as adaptations of the earlier tradition of the *Bildungsroman,* the novel that traced the early education of its central character, moving from innocence to experience. In contrast, however, to a character like the youthful Pip of *Great Expectations,* who learns to understand the immorality inherent in his culture's false definition of a gentleman, the novel of ecological education focuses on education that occurs later in the protagonist's life and that emphasizes a relearning of the right relationship to the rest of nature. This kind of novel depicts the process whereby those who have already absorbed the prevailing environmental ethos of their culture acquire a different awareness of their world. In a type of novel that is more *Umweltroman* than *Bildungsroman,* these texts trace an adult protagonist's growth into a new, more ecologically viable view of the natural world.

This novel of ecological education takes its thematic direction from the ways in which the environmental movement seeks to reshape traditional Western cultural values. It depicts a shift away from seeing the natural world solely as a resource and from the corollary belief that humans are distanced from and exalted over the rest of nature. In place of these assumptions, the novel of ecological education emphasizes human connectedness to and interdependency with the natural world. The education of the protagonist is measured by growth away from an anthropocentric world view to an ecocentric one, away from a view that privileges the interests of the aggressive and dominant individual to one that features a larger sense of community that includes nonhuman nature. He or she moves away from seeing this nonhuman world in terms of utility and commodification and into a new moral perspective that is based in a grounded reciprocity with nature and that advances the goal of an ecologically sustainable culture.

Along with relearning the right human relationship to the rest of nature that is at the core of the novel of ecological education, there are other concerns that recur with some frequency. These novels tend toward a mistrust of technology, especially when technology is offered as an answer to environmental problems. They tend also to emphasize hands-on outdoor education, seeing the outdoors and actual interaction with nature as much more critical than what takes place in schoolrooms or when reading. It is not that such sources of knowledge are unimportant; in fact, they, like the novels in which they occur, can serve as important guides. The novels do share with Gregory Bateson, however, the strong belief that "the map is not the territory,"[4] that there finally can be no real substitute for the firsthand experience of nature. Probably the most consistent feature of this type of novel, however, is its reevaluation of traditional gender roles. Relearning attitudes toward nature often also involves a corollary relearning of what is the right behavior for the gendered self, and there is great range in how such redefinition of gender roles develops. It can (as in *Cold Mountain*) involve relinquishing the role requirement that women stay separate from nature except through the mediated form of books and journals or supervising the work of others, or it can (as in *Voyage of the Narwhal*) involve relearning the traditional masculine requirement that manhood be proven by the conquest of nature.

Among these recent examples of the novel of ecological education, one where this theme is most intensely felt and most fully developed is Rick Bass's *Where the Sea Used to Be*. Unlike *Cold Mountain* and *Voyage of the Narwhal*, for example, it is not a historical novel. The time of the narrative is roughly contemporary,[5] and this gives an edge of passion and urgency to the text. This novel also differs from other novels in this group in its concentrated geographic and character focus; this novel all takes place within one isolated mountain valley, where its two central figures occupy the same cabin. The narrative structure thus develops from a mutually shaping effect, what the novel calls the "sculpting" of the interactions between characters and the shaping of the valley.[6] And the combined effect of all these features gives this novel's development of ecological education a unique focus and intensity.

Compounding this intensity are two other factors: the author's own attachment to the valley that inspires the novel and his dedicated efforts to protect it from ongoing environmental threats. The second Swan Valley of *Where the Sea Used to Be* is clearly a novelistic version of Rick Bass's beloved Yaak. Imaginative embodiments of the Yaak have, of course, been a familiar part of his fiction, but in this first novel he goes about this process differently. By imagining a second Swan/Yaak Valley, one located in a remote and wilder area behind the more settled first

Swan/Yaak Valley, Bass underlines the high stakes embodied in the novel's central theme of ecological education and also sets the stage for his exploration of how we might learn to protect such wilderness landscapes.

In his construction of this second Swan/Yaak Valley, Bass continues developing an important literary technique, one that plays an increasingly significant part both in his work and in contemporary American environmental writing—a technique that we can call imaginative restoration.[7] In a time when what humans have built prevails more and more over previously natural landscapes, imaginative restoration offers a way for environmental literature to envision and encourage change, to blend the art of literary creation with the inculcation of activism. It thus has become a familiar feature in contemporary nature writing. Imaginative restoration appears at the heart of a variety of environmental narratives that range from the Manhattan short story "The Open Lot" by Barry Lopez, the final chapter of a literary nonfiction narrative about urban nature in Los Angeles, *Sagebrush and Cappuccino* by David Wicinas, to the nonfiction study about suburban Boston *Ceremonial Time: Fifteen Thousand Years on One Square Mile* by John Hanson Mitchell. By figuratively stripping away the built veneer of civilization to envision the natural world that lies several layers of time beneath it, narratives like these invite the reader to imagine restoration in the world outside the text, envision possibilities for restoration in landscapes that might otherwise be seen as beyond ecological hope and given up as lost.

The appeal that this literary technique has for Rick Bass is evident in his numerous experiments with it prior to this novel. The first two stories from his collection *In the Loyal Mountains*, for example, employ imaginative restoration in two very different ways. In the initial story, "The History of Rodney," the restorative theme resides in its setting. Rodney is a former town of sixteen thousand where a dozen people currently live; the area's return to the wild is brought about by a sudden change in the river's course, and the results are seen in the abundance of wild turkeys and huge wild pigs and in the owl that hunts mice in the protagonists' house. "Swamp Boy," the next story, situates restoration within the mind of its young protagonist. He stands in a wetland area of suburban Houston imagining the buffaloes and wolves that fought there three centuries earlier. This second mode of imaginative restoration has grown in importance for Bass over the years. As he writes within a world that is increasingly developed and degraded, the type of change depicted in Rodney—that is, change built on a serendipitous shift away from commerce and development—seems increasingly unlikely. The ability (in both characters and readers) to see beneath what has been built or, in the case of wildlife extirpation, to see beyond what has been taken away becomes increasingly important. Imaginative restoration of the landscape that once was there also serves as one way in which Bass can reconcile his activist and artistic selves. Once readers see the process of imaginative restoration enacted on the page, they can begin to apply this imaginative technique to landscapes important to them. When the positive change of environmental restoration is envisioned in this way, the activist's work for actual change can follow.

Experimentation with imaginative restoration also figures in Bass's longer works of literary nonfiction, those narratives that deal with wilderness preservation, what he calls "the big wild."[8] In *The Lost Grizzlies: A Search for Survivors in the San Juan Wilderness of Colorado,* for example, Doug Peacock, a biologist named Dennis Sizemore, and Bass search for verifiable proof that grizzlies still survive in the San Juan mountains. State biologists say they all have been extirpated, but, as Peacock says, "they have no imagination" (10). The team's arduous search is, from the first, fueled by imagining the bears who could still inhabit this wilderness and how their presence would add both meaning and mystery to this landscape. By the end of the book when Bass does find huge bear scat (later verified by DNA tests as that of a local grizzly), much of this narrative's cultural work has already been done; the reader has been taught to feel the rightness, even the necessity, of the big bears' presence. The possibilities of preserving grizzly habitat in the San Juans have been enhanced by a capacity for imaginative restoration that drives both their search and Bass's narrative.

In *Where the Sea Used to Be,* however, Bass makes his most extensive use yet of imaginative restoration. Situating the novel in an imagined version of a beloved place where the developmental and environmental clocks have somehow been turned back enables him to ask a key environmental question, one crucial both to broader contemporary environmental efforts and for him personally: how can we learn to preserve the landscapes that we love? The precise role of imaginative restoration in this novel thus is to set the stage for the novelistic inquiry into how we can foster wilderness protection. His own act of extended imaginative restoration in creating the second Swan/Yaak Valley is a necessary prelude to the theme of ecological education. With the second Swan Valley in place, the novel can then focus on how we can learn to preserve wilderness.

The answer to this is presented in a complex process of ecological education that begins with the young oilman protagonist entering the second Swan Valley. Wallis has been sent to the valley on a mission from the Houston oilman Old Dudley, and the basis for what Wallis learns is presented within the pronounced differences between the characters of Old Dudley and his daughter, Mel. Old Dudley wants Wallis to study the landscape so that he can construct a map that will find oil, but Wallis's on-site guide to this valley is Mel, a woman who values very different aspects of this landscape than her father. The contrast between old Dudley, the rapacious wolverine-like captain of an extractive industry and a man who wants to eat the world,[9] and Mel, the self-taught naturalist who studies the valley's wolves, structures the contested meaning of this valley and of wilderness in contemporary American culture. It also sets in motion what will become the two-stage ecological education of Wallis.

A hunting scene that occurs just after Wallis enters the valley on Thanksgiving Day initiates the first part of this process. The occasion is the tracking of a wounded deer, one that flees the outdoor feast with a knife in its throat. The lesson is Mel's brief lecture on the etiquette of the wild, instructing valley citizens to behave in ways that respect the thoroughgoing interconnectedness of the valley's ecology.

> "You have to go get that knife. You have to find that deer. There'll be blood on the blade. The coyotes and wolves will lick it, and cut their tongues. The taste of their own blood will excite them and they'll bite harder. They'll cut their tongues off, in their frenzy. There'll be blood everywhere," she said. "They'll be attacking each other. They could all eat each other up, just because of that one knife blade. Go get it. Better hurry." . . . "In the spring the bears would find the carcass," she said. "They'd come gnaw on it and get all cut up. . . . you could wipe out the whole upper part of the food chain single-handedly."[10]

Although Mel, after some initial hesitation, continues to teach Wallis, she seldom again has recourse to such overt instruction. Once Mel sees the battle for the soul of the young geologist taking shape, she deliberately avoids the kind of bullying verbal pressure that characterizes Old Dudley's championing of the oil industry. Mel elects instead to go quietly about her work, modeling her own environmental values for Wallis to observe and emulate.

Interwoven with the novel's tableaus of teaching and learning is the growing mutual attraction of Mel and Wallis. The slowness of their developing relationship is due in part to the equally slow decline of Mel's long relationship with the novel's other central character, Matthew. Unlike Danny the bartender, who has come to the valley out of grief for the toxicity-driven cancer deaths in his family, and unlike Mel, who is drawn to the valley by its wildness, Matthew is one of the few characters fortunate enough to begin life in the valley. After his parents died when he was four, Matthew was adopted by Helen, the presiding spirit of this valley, and grew into an important valley citizen. Although young Matthew has earned respect for his hunting prowess, he is most noted for the creation of a unique wall—one that has come to signify the distinctive ethos of the valley community. In fact, the first thing that Wallis sees on his entry into the valley is this unusual rock wall, one that seems somehow to make the scenery "wilder, as if they were going back in time, back to some time before true fences" (19).

To understand the meaning of Matthew's somewhat mysterious wall, and thus his relationship with Mel and role in the novel, it is helpful to look back at Bass's first full-length book about settling into the Yaak, *Winter: Notes from Montana* (1991). A central theme of that journal narrative is his internal conflict about the right role of fences in his new home. On one hand, there is the still powerful pull of lessons learned in childhood. Trying to close his neighbor Breitenstein's fence, Bass remembers his father's exhortation always to close the fence gap, thereby honoring the Texas tradition of livestock ownership and private property boundaries. On the other hand, there is his competing sense of delight in a somewhat mythical Montana moose, a powerful wild creature who easily runs right through fences, taking them down and dragging them with him, thus simultaneously asserting the rights of the animals who were on the land before the settlers and embodying and exalting the fenceless freedom associated with his new wilderness home.[11]

In *Where the Sea Used to Be,* published some seven years later, the exemplary valley citizenship that is a feature of Matthew's early life is expressed by his building a new kind of wall, one that resolves the fence conflicts featured in *Winter* and that is uniquely suited to the second Swan Valley. Matthew began to build this rock wall when he was seven. By the time he is sixteen, it is twenty miles long and "so beautiful" that other valley residents have started to help him with it. This wall is different from ordinary fences and boundary markers, however: it serves no purpose and sets "no boundaries." It exists instead as "a crafted thing of durability" that pays "homage to the beauty just beyond and above the wall—the mountains themselves" (244).

Matthew's wall also serves as a symbolically instructive paradox. As the seeming oxymoron of a boundary-less wall, it ties to the kind of magical realism found in Rick Bass's earlier short fiction. It also works, however, to appropriate semantically the meaning of a wall, to move away from viewing a wall as an iconic artifact of cultural division, a construction that divides landscape and individual property owners and destroys wilderness wildlife habitat. Instead, Matthew's (and Bass's) new kind of wall serves to echo and express admiration for the natural walls of the valley, to bring the valley together in communal celebration of place and of the resolve to keep that place open. In the autobiographical terms of *Winter*, Matthew's wall shows Bass moving beyond his old ties to Texas private land divisions and into support for undivided wilderness habitat. This boundary-defying wall becomes a structure that signifies Rick Bass's acceptance of the unfenced freedom of wilderness. As the built embodiment of the wilderness freedom found in their isolated valley, the wall is also an important landmark for his characters who live in this second Swan—one that fosters their sense of community. Those interlopers who visit the valley bent on destructive development fail to understand it, but the residents can barely wait for spring to work on it together.

By the time that Wallis enters the valley, however, Matthew has come under the influence of Old Dudley and changed into a "city guy," a man whose job it is to make drilling map after map for Old Dudley. Matthew still returns sporadically to see Helen and Mel, but each trip back to the valley shows him weaker and more detached. As Wallis settles into the valley, Matthew moves farther away from it, leaving Mel alone with his cabin and her work.

This work becomes the most important tool in Mel's resolutely unobtrusive teaching of Wallis. She studies the valley's wolf pack in ways that embody an "ecofeminist curriculum" and that constitute the first stage of what Wallis needs to know.[12] In stark contrast to Old Dudley's unrelenting abuse of the land, of women in general, and of herself in particular, Mel avoids disturbing the valley's ecology and imposing her beliefs on Wallis. Like Martha, the wolf biologist in "Two Deer," Mel wants to preserve "the last sanctuaries" for wild things,[13] and the methodology she develops for her wolf study is in keeping with this. Not only does Mel forgo the intrusive scientific practice of radio collars as tracking aids,[14] but she also constructs her wolf movement maps with a unique tracking method.

> To give the wolves space and respect, she tracked them backward, hoping to avoid giving them the feeling that she was chasing them. She worked backward along their trail, working always two or three days into the past. The maps would look the same anyway as long as she could find the tracks, the story would get told. And as seen from the air the map would look identical, whether she mapped them forward or backward. (69)

This scrupulous care with which Mel gathers her scientific data also shapes her attitude toward the knowledge that she gains. In contrast to the anthropocentric arrogance that permeates Old Dudley's journal and his speeches, Mel acknowledges limits in what she learns and wants. She knows and respects the otherness of the wolves, realizing that for all of her hard work she cannot see the real thing and that she therefore necessarily constructs a logic for their behavior that comes as much from her own mind as from their communications. Unlike her father, Mel sees the interconnectedness of all the life in the valley, and she relates to the valley by being "submissive to it, rather than trying to dominate and consume it" (96). In contrast to her gluttonous father, who wants to dominate and eat the world, Mel's different kind of landscape hunger is infused with her wish to be an interdependent part of it. These attitudes are what Wallis absorbs while working on Old Dudley's oil map and while slowly falling in love with Mel.

At the exact midpoint of this narrative, two important changes occur: the Mel-Wallis relationship accelerates and the ecological education of Wallis enters its second stage. After the first half of the novel features the problems of the larger culture represented in Old Dudley and the potential for change seen in Mel's ecological views, the second half begins with a rapid series of changes. Mel and Wallis finally go out together to view the wolves, and later that evening they become lovers.[15] That same evening Mel announces other important changes. She will extend her resolve not to interfere in the life of the valley one step further by ending her twenty-year wolf tracking and mapping project. Henceforth she will express her regard for the wolves by leaving them alone. Mel changes to a different kind of environmental work by teaching ecology to children at the valley school.

Wallis also changes. He has begun to understand and value Mel's way of being in the world, and he is now ready for the second stage of his ecological education. One crucial part of this is his movement into active, thoughtful engagement with the valley's flora and fauna. The same night that Mel decides to teach school, Wallis initiates his own nature study by examining "a dead bird more carefully than any work of art" (201). Mel formerly had to urge him to leave his map-making and go outdoors, but Wallis now participates in the natural world of the valley and thinks about it. His meditations enable him to see beauty as well as utility in nature—the snowberries in the dead bird's crop, for example, are beautiful despite the fact that they cannot be used as food or in necklaces. The valley's geology, too, becomes notable for its beauty, not just as a potential drilling site. Wallis enjoys learning about wildlife by watching a mother grizzly and cubs at play and by carrying binoculars and a book that help him learn to know birds. The sheer jubilation that migratory birds show at being in this particular wild place convinces him that the animals he is learning to love have an individuality. All of these activities contribute to a newfound pleasure in living each day.

It was Old Dudley and his oil extraction obsession that first sent Wallis to the valley, however, and the strong desire to dominate the land by drilling maintains its fascination for him. As the novel charts the course of a contemporary ecological education, there is tension between the new ecofeminist side of Wallis learned from Mel and the part of himself still enthralled by Old Dudley's aggressive, patriarchal masculinity. This conflict goes deep enough that it does not get resolved in a simple linear forward movement. The difficulty that Wallis will have in leaving behind his own version of Dudley's drilling mentality becomes clear with his second map of the valley—the one that he is certain will find oil. After pleas from others in the valley, his own reflections on what is important about life there, and especially the knowledge that Mel is pregnant, Wallis hides the map. He cannot quite bring himself to destroy it, however, and that lingering attachment has consequences.

Old Dudley finds this map and immediately begins the destructive process of drilling. He brings men into the valley to build a road to the well site (368). These "conquerors" (368) kill deer out of season and destroy the black bear that has become the dying Helen's companion and totem. The drilling activity drives the wolves, those crucial indicators of wilderness health, from the valley. Despite all this evidence of ecological damage, however, the sight of the rig renews in Wallis the old gluttonous desire to dominate and consume nature. By cloaking this hunger in a perverse mockery of spirituality, he momentarily persuades himself to see the rig as "altar" (391) and the taste testing of mud samples as a kind of "communion" (396). He even joins Old Dudley and Matthew in an act of homage to the technological dominance of nature as they form an unholy three-man drilling team.

Change and the confirmation of his ecological progress come with the chance to learn another mode of masculine relationship to nature. An epic elk hunt led by Matthew takes both men away from the well, frees Wallis from this slip back into Old Dudley's obsessive need to dominate and destroy nature, and completes his ecological education. What frees Wallis from this drilling is, significantly, the need to provide for another, more basic and natural form of hunger; they must replace the winter meat supply lost when fire destroyed the smokehouse. This hunt that closes the narrative also parallels the deer-tracking episode that opens it, and the hunt completes his education. Just as Mel's statement of ecological principles and her subsequent modeling of ecological behavior initiate his education, Matthew's instruction in the ecology of the hunt and in an alternative mode of masculine work completes what Wallis needs to know.

This teaching hunt also completes another interwoven narrative thread: the long process whereby Wallis and Matthew trade places. The two characters (each representing a stage in the author's own life) have always had much in common. They were born months apart; they met in Houston, where they both worked finding oil for the same man; and they have loved the same woman.[16] With this hunt, the arcs of their respective lives intersect and complete an exchange of destinations and values. Wallis, who must struggle to remember his Houston office, has been acquiring the ecological knowledge of place that qualifies him for citizenship in the second Swan Valley. He resists Old Dudley's bullying pressure to come back to the city, and his deepening connections to the valley and to Mel make him stronger. Matthew's increasing commitment to Old Dudley's business and detachment from the valley, in contrast, lead him to bouts of self-hatred and depression. His increasing debilitation makes the point that drilling hollows out the men (and the societies that practice it) even as it depletes the earth.

As the last act in their long process of trading places, however, the elk hunt does enable the urbanized Matthew to bequeath his hunting knowledge to Wallis. From the outset, their respective roles in this hunt are clear: Matthew will give "instruction" (408), and Wallis will "pack and learn" (409). Matthew's first lesson is that Wallis must (in contrast to those hunters from outside who hunt from the highway) respect his prey, and that means learning about the territory where the elk live and how they live. Wallis learns how to get the female elk to lead them, over series of days, to the huge bull, how to find grouse as they sleep silhouetted in the bare trees, and how to fire up dead juniper trees to ward off life-threatening hypothermia. When they return with an abundance of elk and deer meat, Matthew has passed on his knowledge to the newest member of the valley's human community and is free to take off for his self-destructive job in Houston. Wallis, with this initiation into ecological manhood,[17] has now developed both sides of his ecological self. His blend of ecofeminist values and traditionally male ecological knowledge qualifies him for full citizenship in the valley.

With this hunt and Wallis's ecological education complete, the novel moves quickly toward closure. The oil well is a dry hole after all, and it seems highly likely that Wallis, like his mentor Mel, will make no more maps; together they will continue to learn the territory. Old Dudley dies, and his last word, "Nothing," speaks to the hollowness of his life. Mel watches carefully as they float his body down the river, making sure he is out of the valley forever and hoping that ten thousand years go by before someone else like him comes to the valley. Matthew, the inheritor of Old Dudley's many oil properties, heads home to Houston.

Where the Sea Used to Be closes with a celebration of ecological community, present and future. Not only does the second Swan/Yaak Valley remain largely undeveloped, with the chief current threats to its wilderness over, but Mel and Wallis also rejoice in the new life that will emerge from "the warm small mound of her stomach" (445). This child, like the other valley children taught by Mel, will grow up in a community that knows and protects the valley.

As an intense, thoughtful, and fully realized novel of ecological education, *Where the Sea Used to Be* constitutes part of an important response to Scott Russell Sanders's call for novels that deal with our relationship to the natural world. The contemporary novel of ecological education, composed of texts that combine celebration of the natural world with attention to how we can build communities that cherish and protect that world, provides a measure of hope about the prospects for ecological change in the new century.

Notes

1. Scott Russell Sanders, "Speaking a Word for Nature," *Michigan Quarterly Review* 25 (Fall 1987): 648–61. This essay is also included in Scott Russell Sanders, *Secrets of the Universe: Scenes from the Journey Home* (Boston: Beacon Press, 1991), 205–27.

2. Henry David Thoreau, "Walking," in *Nature Walking* (Boston: Beacon Press, 1991), 71.

3. Sanders, "Speaking," 649.

4. Bateson provides a complex explanation of the cultural meanings that he attaches to these two terms in *Steps to an Ecology of Mind* (New York: Ballantine Books, 1972), but throughout he argues for the primacy of the experience itself over any abstracted rendition of it.

5. Although the feel of an earlier time does permeate much of this novel, it comes from the relative absence of development and contemporary technology within the valley setting rather than from an actual historical setting.

6. This reciprocal shaping effect of humans with nature, women and men, is a frequent topic for Rick Bass. See, for example, *Brown Dog of the Yaak: Essay on Art and Activism* (Minneapolis: Milkweed, 1999), 41.

7. This term grows out of an environmental literature discussion with Ralph Black. Both William Jordan III in "The Ecology of Walden Woods," in *Thoreau's World and Ours,* ed. Edmund Schofield and Robert Baron (Golden, Colo.: North American Press, 1993), and Laurence Buell in *The Environmental Imagination* (Cambridge, Mass.: Harvard University Press, 1995) make the general observation that imagination has a role to play in restoration, but neither discusses how contemporary ecological literature has begun to develop the literary technique of imaginative restoration as a central part of its environmentalism.

8. Rick Bass, *The Lost Grizzlies: A Search for Survivors in the San Juan Wilderness of Colorado* (Boston: Houghton Mifflin, 1995), 102. Subsequent references to this book are noted parenthetically in the text.

9. It is typical of Old Dudley that, while he mentions this ability to see what was on the landscape in earlier periods, he dismisses it as a mere biomechanical quirk of the human brain.

10. Rick Bass, *Where the Sea Used to Be* (Boston: Houghton Mifflin, 1999), 28. Subsequent references to this book are noted parenthetically in the text.

11. Both crucial scenes take place at the end of *Winter.* See Rick Bass, *Winter: Notes from Montana* (Boston: Houghton Mifflin, 1991), 141–46.

12. This term comes from "Two Deer," an earlier short story in which the characters, actions, and themes clearly are precursors to *Where the Sea Used to Be.* Martha in that story is a wildlife biologist who resembles Mel and explains

to her boyfriend, the narrator, that his work (in this case building roads in the West) is wrong. The story first appeared in the *Paris Review* (Winter 1995–96): 18–33. For discussion of another story that is also an important antecedent to this novel, see the discussion of Bass's first published short story, "Where the Sea Used to Be," in O. Alan Weltzien, *Rick Bass* (Boise, Idaho: Boise State University Press, 1998), 20–21.

13. "Two Deer," 25.

14. Although criticism of the unimaginativeness and intrusiveness of much wildlife biology is embodied in Mel's conduct, it is always implied rather than stated directly; Mel's method here is clearly meant as an improvement over the standard wolf biology procedures of collaring and tracking that Bass criticizes in *The Ninemile Wolves.*

15. Like the road-building narrator in "Two Deer," Wallis's change seems at least to some degree hormonally driven. Wallis, however, would not use a phrase like his: "It was her ass that converted me" (25).

16. The Wallis-Matthew duality clearly embodies two sides of the author's self, his history and his choices, as it comments also on the dilemmas that define American masculinity in its relationship to the natural world.

17. This emphasis on hunting raises a series of cultural issues. Bass clearly joins with such writers as Richard Nelson in the belief that hunting can, and should, be an ecological activity. The hunt has often been constructed in American fiction as a rite of initiation, signifying the growth from boyhood to manhood. What is different in this novel is how Bass carefully presents the hunt as a rite of *ecological* manhood, one that blends ecological values and a traditionally masculine activity. Although some literature, such as many of the pieces included in Pam Houston's edited collection *Women on Hunting* (Hopewell, N.J.: Ecco Press, 1995), conceives of hunting as also being a female activity, this novel clearly posits it as a masculine one; first Matthew and then Wallis will bring meat home to Mel.

Works Cited

Barrett, Andrea. *The Voyage of the Narwhal.* New York: W. W. Norton & Co., 1998.

Bass, Rick. *In the Loyal Mountains.* Boston: Houghton Mifflin, 1995.

———. *The Lost Grizzlies: A Search for Survivors in the Wilderness of Colorado.* Boston: Houghton Mifflin, 1995.

———. *The Ninemile Wolves.* Boston: Houghton Mifflin, 1992.

———. "Two Deer." *Paris Review* 137 (1995): 18–33.

———. *Where the Sea Used to Be.* Boston: Houghton Mifflin, 1998.

Frazier, Charles. *Cold Mountain.* New York: Atlantic Monthly Press, 1997.

Sanders, Scott Russell. "Speaking a Word for Nature." *Michigan Quarterly Review* 26 (Fall 1987): 648–62.

Slovic, Scott. "An Interview with Rick Bass." *Weber Studies: An Interdisciplinary Humanities Journal* 11:3 (Fall 1994): 11–29.

Thoreau, Henry David, and Ralph Waldo Emerson. *Nature. Walking.* Ed. and introduction by John Elder. Boston: Beacon Press, 1991.

Weltzien, O. Alan. *Rick Bass.* Western Writers Series 134. Boise: Boise State University Press, 1998.

Conclusion

Self-Portrait with Dogs

O. Alan Weltzien

Rick Bass's newest book, *Colter* (2000), sustains the eulogy that fuels *Brown Dog of the Yaak* (1999). The earlier book, Bass's *Essays on Art and Activism* (its subtitle), grows out of an obituary impulse stemming from his German shorthair pointer's sudden disappearance and death. The newer book proves that Bass was not yet done with this hunting dog, above all what he means. Its subtitle—*The True Story of the Best Dog I Ever Had*—suggests its popular appeal, as if part of the dime-store novel tradition of earlier generations, and Bass's unabashed sentimentality. Those superlative claims place the book in a familiar, well-worn spot in popular literature (i.e., "man's best friend"), yet Bass brings it off so that, by the end, we feel at least some of his acute loss and lament. Ostensibly the biography of Bass's dog, who disappears in his fourth year just as he approaches his prime, *Colter* works as a love story between hunting "partners," the man always the inferior partner, witnessing a miracle of perfect athleticism wherein the dog is wholly in tune with his quarry and *raison d'être*. This love story does not cloy and somehow transcends cliche, as though the reader, like Bass, serves as religious witness to a sustained state of grace. Through effortless storytelling, sudden pivots into humor, self-deprecation, and fresh, sometimes intense lyricism, Bass persuades the reader to his straightforwardly Romantic, even hagiographic conception. In this idealistic celebration Colter emerges as both holy clown and visible sign of divine joy, a Blakean song of innocence.

Bass avoids mockery and irony so that *Colter* as apotheosis does not backfire, and the dog as ideal embodiment of the Yaak provides us with another self-portrait of the writer. In *Colter*/Colter we plot Bass's ambitions and shortfalls. *Brown Dog* begins by describing "the bomb" in Colter's heart, and Scott Slovic's accompanying "Portrait" begins similarly, fusing the identity of pointer and writer; *Colter* elaborates the analogy so that we again believe the "man's best friend" truism and in the process evaluate Bass's conflicted landscape. To invoke Michael Branch's two rhetorical traditions discussed in this volume, in *Colter*, Bass foregrounds elegy and mutes anger. Unsympathetic readers might accuse Bass of self-indulgence, regarding *Colter* as a turning away from environmental activism, for example. I interpret it as exemplifying Bass's sermon, in *The Book of Yaak* (13), on "the notion that settling-in and stand-making" constitutes our central act of recovery and rebalancing at the industrial twentieth-century's end. How does Bass, a semirecluse ensconced in semiwilderness, persuade his readers, almost all of whom inhabit more crowded precincts, to the intimate connections between wilderness and wildness? The man-dog marriage manifests these connections. Certainly Colter's meteoric rise and tragic murder represent—returning to Scott Slovic's essay, "Politics in American Nature Writing," cited in the introduction—a "conjunction of the dire and the beautiful" (106). Embedded in a passionate love story, such a "conjunction" illustrates that realignment of values, living in place within the natural world however defined, from which activism best emerges. Bass's landscape depends upon a familiar biocentrist ethics: only from enough love does action spring. This ethics resembles Thomas Lyon's conclusion in this volume's opening essay.

Bass readers meet Homer and Ann, his Mississippi-born foundlings, in earlier essays and books, thereby learning his attachment to hunting dogs. *Colter*'s prologue narrates Bass's first look at the last two of a Yaak litter and depicts Colter as the "goofy" runt—a privileged term in Bass's world, repeatedly used to describe Colter. Colter's story turns magical in the sense that the runt morphs into the one extraordinarily gifted dog. By the time Bass unashamedly proclaims that "Colter was one of the greatest bird dogs that ever lived" (136) and then ratchets that up to "Colter was probably the greatest pointer who ever ran" (186), we grant him his panegyric. Colter's sudden disappearance in September and Bass's recovery of the corpse—and discovery that Colter had been shot in the spine near Bass's home—eight months later come as a shock and mark the story as classical American tragedy. Bass celebrates a creature greatly gifted and cut off in his prime. He imagines

Colter still running and hunting, awaiting another rendezvous (173, 187), like the dispersed Ninemile wolfpack from years ago. Also as in *Ninemile Wolves,* Bass anthropomorphizes enthusiastically, calling Colter, the much superior hunting partner, "my boy, my brown boy" (35), "my little man" (51), "the thrashing wild brown man" (60), "the little bomber man" (60).

Colter, quintessence of the Yaak and trained in East Texas, at Jarrett Thompson's Old South Pointer Farm (chapters 1 and 6), overlaps not a little with Bass's own geography and constitutes, in many respects, an idealized projection. This extended essay in self-portraiture is *Colter*'s chief interest, particularly for non–bird hunters. The self-portrait, drawn in an adolescent language of desire, proclaims the value of wildness that Bass extols in all his work. The urgency of that value explains in many ways his equal commitment to his writing life and environmental activism. It spills across fiction and polemical journalism alike.

Bass develops the theme of religious witness central to, for example, *The Lost Grizzlies:*

> Unlike Superman [a subsequent, younger dog], Colter hadn't hunted so much to please me, in those first years, as to please the universe; and even as he began to mature, there was always that feeling, that knowledge, that it was between the bird and him, and that I was merely fortunate enough to get to watch it. (172)

The sacramental theme locates this writer in a tradition of nature writing predating Thoreau. Within that tradition, writing may start and finish with scientific observation, but it consists mainly in the religious experience and lyrical celebration of witnessing. To watch is to participate lovingly, and the fact of observation is raised to a condition of wonder. From that condition issues advocacy.

Bass's writing elevates the man-and-his-dog formula to a state of grace, another theme he sustains. Early on he distinguishes dog owners from others without disparaging the latter, and he insistently puts himself down as a bird hunter (e.g., chapter 13) even as he apologizes for bragging about Colter (e.g., 47). He elaborates the prologue's analogy between Colter and himself, parenthetically noting: "After adolescence . . . he stopped retrieving birds, as if concentrating only on his business, his breeding—the discovering and pointing of them. His higher calling. The brown dog as artist" (xii). He thus glances backward to Colter as exemplum in *Brown Dog* and forward across this book, wherein the writer assesses himself against this species of perfection. This dog symbolizes an optimal balance of nature and culture and distills the wildness that Bass thematizes and prescribes throughout his career. And as quintessence of the Yaak, Colter epitomizes Bass's defense of place. This man-dog relationship provides, along with "The Sky, the Stars, the Wilderness" and *Where the Sea Used to Be,* his strongest statements to date of living in place.

Bass contrasts a story of childhood he has not yet told (chapter 3), or his annual spruce grouse pilgrimage (chapter 7), with stories of Colter's puppyhood (chapter 1) and adolescence (chapters 5–6). Born in the Yaak, Colter is schooled in Texas; born in Texas, Bass is schooled in Utah and, later, the Yaak. They sleep together during their autumn bird hunts east of the Continental Divide in Montana, along the Rocky Mountain Front or in the Missouri (River) Breaks; and on the hunts Bass walks twenty miles while Colter runs a hundred. The clumsy human strides, literally and metaphorically, after canine artistry, always falling short yet always trying to close the distance. Clearly, Colter is more than dog since his name, Bass reminds us, comes from a human of supernatural speed who outran the Blackfeet (35); it evokes his human ancestry and essence ("His glory is in the wide-open throttle, and in the moment," 154). The one artist projects himself into the other as Bass probes the analogy:

> A dog's heart is at least as knowledgeable as his nose and I wonder, as I write, how much he picks up of my rhythms, my emotions from sentence to sentence. I wonder if those silent efforts, word by word and then strings of sentences, carry to him invisibly, like the background saw of some summertime insect—or if he just sleeps. . . .
>
> In the field with him, in the autumn, though, as we move through the light and the shadows, I can hear, sometimes dimly but other days as if with a shouted roar, some of the silent fury and joy passing through his blood as he runs—and I can almost feel it in my own blood. (86–87)

Man and dog stay close in this pair of scenes. In the first, at Bass's writing cabin, site of Colter's eventual burial, he whimsically imagines a transference, a shared artistic vision, the dog's intuitive understanding; in the second, *Colter*'s repeated, quintessential scene, he imagines a shared (after D. H. Lawrence) blood knowledge, his own intuitive understanding. In the first, both are "at rest," the animal sleeping and guarding while the writer works inside the space that defines him; in the second, the animal comes into his own, and the writer tags along. From the beginning, their hearts are on fire together (8). Bass writes at length about his dog's heart as though this animal takes him, over and over, through a door, across a threshold to a new plane. In his childhood reminiscences, which contain many examples of superb writing, he develops this original metaphor to define human-animal relationships:

> These immeasurable bonds we have with animals, and other elemental forces of nature, are like guy-wires attached, invisible and slack, to some huge canvas tent. And over the course of our life, each time we stretch one of the guy wires, it is pulled taut, and the structure of the tent, which represents all our inner identities, is lifted, and we see more clearly the possibility of who we might become—and of how we can fit the world. (24)

The tent of the self is expandable, and we can grow higher and bigger to the extent we realize such "immeasurable bonds" as *Colter* commemorates. In the prologue, Bass announces themes as in an overture: "Hunting with a dog, you go past a certain place in the world, and in yourself... it's like travelling into new country, new territory: some unexplored land, still in this life, but so sensate and crisp as to seem beyond this life" (xiii); "a luminous new country just beyond the borders of the sleeping town" (xiv). In *Colter,* Bass braids this familiar theme with the themes of religious witness and a state of grace; his prized dog constitutes another border country, and with him he repeatedly crosses a liminal space into a landscape of epiphany (e.g., 128–30).

Colter's meteoric rise and sudden disappearance and death are framed by Bass's other dogs: the older generation, Homer and Ann, and a new trio, Superman, Point-Man (both "Colter clones"), and big Indy (epilogue), who imperfectly fill the void. Ann's tragic death and Bass's grief foreshadow Colter's more painful tragedy. In this self-portraiture with dogs, Bass most of all prizes Colter's intensity, which defines his own even as it outdistances it.

Colter sustains common Bass themes—regretting his past modesty in environmental activism (127), being most at home in the woods, the ways in which a particular landscape sculpts a self (19)—but it primarily explores a variant of the latter: "in just a few short years, the dog turns around and sculpts you" (32). One's chosen place, the valley as sculptor (e.g., *Fiber* and *Where the Sea Used to Be*), channels its energies through the hunting dog, and in this reversal Colter signifies soulmate, alter ego, and mentor. On a failed Texas quail hunting trip with his father and some of his friends, Bass, defending Colter's idiosyncrasies, describes himself. He dismisses "tweedy sportsmen" who

> prefer a dog that is more like a robot—a dog that would never, ever bump a bird, not by mistake (even if the dog had to become ever more cautious, gradually lowering its intensity level), and never, by God, on purpose, for the sheer adolescent joy of fucking up. They have spent the last hundred years line-breeding the perfect dog, or so they believe, intent upon all the things a judge can quantify in a trial, but overlooking, decade by decade, the intangible of heart. . . . (137)

He asserts, "I would rather have watched my dog run like the wind, any day, even if it meant passing up a few opportunities at birds" (143–44). Both dog and his elegist, as arch-romantics, subscribe to William Blake's Proverb of Hell: "The Road of Excess Leads to the Palace of Wisdom." Both act goofy and young, occasionally cutting up and fucking up, doing their best to blaze through their days and seasons. *Colter* readers picture not only the dog's pyrotechnics in the field but also his almost-human grin, and that grin, above all, confirms this animal fable's insistent reversals—the brown dog as artist and sculptor of the hunter-writer.

In an article in *Sierra* (September–October 2000), "Man of Two Minds," David James Duncan explores the conflicted landscape of art and activism that is the present volume's subject. Like his friend Rick Bass, Duncan began as a fictionist but started writing nonfiction "out of a sense of betrayal, out of rage over natural systems violated, out of grief for a loved world raped, and out of a craving for justice" (52). Duncan evokes a now-familiar persona, and, unsurprisingly, he profiles Bass, "perhaps the most frenzied activist I've ever met," "a man crazed, every day and all at once, by beauty, violence, grief, and love" (57). In some respects Bass fits the mold of the legendary, recently deceased environmental activist David Brower—John McPhee's "Archdruid" discussed in the present volume by Diana Ashe. According to one obituary article, Brower most recently resigned from the Sierra Club Board in

May 2000—his third resignation since 1985. This article quotes Brower as stating: "'The world is burning and all I hear from [the board] is the music of violins.... The planet is being trashed, but the board has no real sense of urgency. We need to try to save the Earth at least as fast as it's being destroyed.'"

The frenzied activist, like the prophet, risks stridency and unpopularity in devotion to his convictions. But what if the prophet and the psalmist are one, as Thomas Bailey and others in this volume remind us? Earlier in his article, Duncan depicts and salutes the artist's contemplative life as embodied in Thomas Merton, then reveals that it was Bass who sent him "the Merton quote on the activist's self-defeating frenzy." Bass significantly annotated Merton in the margins, "in a scrawl even more frenzied than his letter": "'*Yes. But NO / Can't do it! Not yet. / Now now*'" (57). Bass obviously affirms the artist's life ("*Yes*") but equally affirms its insufficiency ("*But NO*"); the activist exists, however contentiously, alongside the artist. *Colter* is the work of the psalmist, but the prophetic voice lurks within; the eulogy also inscribes the recipe for wildness-wilderness.

With *Colter*, then, Bass brings his earlier three megafauna books home to the self. Given Colter's genetic inheritance, he displays at least some of the magic possessed by Montana and Arizona wolves and Colorado grizzlies. To the extent that this Yaak native epitomizes the place, he reflects some of the conceptual territory Bass stalks in *Winter*, *The Book of Yaak*, *Fiber*, and some other stories. Colter functions as analogy and preternatural other, existing both as alter ego and across an unbridgeable chasm. The writer's desire stems from the tension between these. His story earns a place alongside dog fables such as John Muir's *Stikeen* and Jack London's *Call of the Wild* and *White Fang*. As hagiography, *Colter* provides Bass yet another vocabulary of perfection and desire that both moves and persuades us. This neo-Romantic vocabulary taps the energy of fable to create a love story brimming over with humor and poignancy. It repeatedly enables him to dog Colter to a higher place—what Wordsworth in "Tintern Abbey" calls "the wild heart of things," also the primary home of such a writer as Bass. As mentioned earlier, *Colter*'s basic scene—a man alone with his hunting dog, "keeping up with the heartworks of the dog, and he with yours" (96)—is commonplace, though Bass's sacramental cast is less so: "Though I love to hunt with friends, these parallel, sometimes overlapping lines of grace, where shadow and object merge and become for some moments indistinguishable one from the other, have come only when Colter and I have been alone in the field" (94).

When Bass narrates that essential scene, we achieve a transcendental communion that is richly liminal. *Colter* rises to a series of epiphanic "moments," and within these writer and reader apprehend Wordsworth's credo. The narrative defines and reanimates Bass's idealized union, a temporary ecstasy wherein writer and dog move like "two birds travelling in some graceful drift to some point, some location, known surely to their hearts" (97). The scene occurs away from the Yaak, east of the mountains, in landscapes with few natural borders. They bound in unbounded country—the archetypal Western literary landscape, the unfenced playground (or work site) of the self:

> There is nothing ahead of them but more country—no borders. Everything is behind them: everything. There are two lines of movement—the north-south stride of the hunter and the east-west stitching of the dog—both wanting only one thing, *a bird,* and wanting it so effortlessly and purely that they come the closest they will ever come to shared language. For several minutes they travel across the prairie like that, indistinguishable from one another in heart, in desire—until finally the scent cone is encountered, and the dog must leave that place in time, that striding harmony, and accelerate, supercharged, into his own greater, vaster capability to desire that bird. . . . The hunter feels a charge of excitement as well, but much of it comes from the dog—the shadow, now—rather than the subject itself, *the bird*—and the hunter hurries forward to the completion of things, with the dog dashing and darting now, chasing the bird, running it, trying to capture it as a tornado perhaps tries (in flinging up trees and houses and people) to capture the soil. (95)

Bass's charged prose engenders that "charge of excitement," itself moving like "two birds traveling in some graceful drift." We see the pattern's weave, the geometric union of purpose. Elsewhere, reflecting upon that "shared language" through which a bird hunter repeatedly glimpses perfection, a "middle ground that exists between dog and man," Bass concludes: "My God, it is a real thing, unlike so much else. It is still what it is" (81). This affirmation illustrates that "same, inescapable, irreducible bedrock fuel" of "passion" and "same root-stock" of art and activism defined in *Brown Dog* (118–19) and cited in this volume's epigraphs. It also describes *Colter*'s achievement, a celebration of authenticity and intensity that, repeating Bass, pulls taut a guy wire and lifts the structure of our respective tents so "we see more clearly the possibility of who we might become—and of how we can fit the world" (24).

Works Cited

Bass, Rick. *The Book of Yaak*. Boston: Houghton Mifflin, 1996.

———. *Brown Dog of the Yaak: Essays on Art and Activism*. St. Paul: Milkweed Editions, Credo Series, 1999.

———. *Colter: The True Story of the Best Dog I Ever Had*. Boston: Houghton Mifflin, 2000.

———. *Fiber.* Athens: University of Georgia Press, 1998.

———. *The Lost Grizzlies: A Search for Survivors in the Colorado Wilderness.* Boston: Houghton Mifflin, 1995.

———. *The Ninemile Wolves.* Livingston, Mont.: Clark City Press, 1992; New York: Ballantine, 1993.

———. *The Sky, the Stars, the Wilderness.* Boston: Houghton Mifflin, 1997.

———. *Where The Sea Used To Be*. Boston: Houghton Mifflin, 1998.

———. *Winter: Notes from Montana*. Boston: Houghton Mifflin/Seymour Lawrence, 1991.

Blake, William. "The Marriage of Heaven and Hell." In *The Poetry and Prose of William Blake,* ed. David V. Erdman. Garden City, N.Y.: Doubleday & Co., 1970.

Duncan, David James. "Man of Two Minds." *Sierra* (September–October 2000): 52–57, 75–76.

"Environmental Activist David Brower Dies at Age 88." *Associated Press,* San Francisco, 7 November 2000. Rpt. in the *Great Falls (Montana) Tribune,* 7 November 2000, 7A.

London, Jack. "The Call of the Wild" and "White Fang." In *Great Short Works of Jack London*. New York: Harper & Row, 1970.

Muir, John. *Stikeen*. Boston: Houghton Mifflin, 1909.

Slovic, Scott. "Politics in American Nature Writing." In *Green Culture: Environmental Rhetoric in Contemporary America,* ed. Carl G. Herndl and Stuart C. Brown, 82–110. Madison: University of Wisconsin Press, 1996.

Wordsworth, William. "Lines Composed a few miles above Tintern Abbey." In *The Prelude: Selected Poems and Songs,* ed. Carlos Baker. New York: Holt, Rinehart and Winston, 1948, 1954.

Contributors

KARLA ARMBRUSTER is assistant professor at Webster University in St. Louis, where she teaches American literature, professional writing, and interdisciplinary studies. She has published book chapters on Terry Tempest Williams, Dian Fossey, Ursula Le Guin, Josephine Johnson, and television nature documentaries. She is co-editor (with Kathleen R. Wallace) of *Beyond Nature Writing: Expanding the Boundaries of Ecocriticism* (2001).

DIANA L. ASHE coordinates the professional writing program and teaches at the University of North Carolina at Wilmington. Her research examines the discourse strategies used by government and grassroots groups in fighting local environmental battles. She is currently studying one such battle between the United States Navy and activists on Vieques Island, Puerto Rico.

THOMAS BAILEY is associate provost at Western Michigan University in Kalamazoo, where he has worked and taught English for thirty-one years. He has written and reviewed widely on such writers as John McPhee, Amy Clampitt, Alison Deming, Pattiann Rogers, and Linda Hasselstrom, and is working on a study of Robert Frost's nature poetry and a monograph on the contemporary georgic.

MICHAEL P. BRANCH is associate professor of literature and environment at the University of Nevada, Reno. He is a co-founder and past president of the Association for the Study of Literature and Environment (ASLE) and the book review editor of the journal *ISLE: Interdisciplinary Studies in Literature and Environment*. He is co-editor of *The Height of Our Mountains: Nature Writing from Virginia's Blue Ridge Mountains and Shenandoah Valley* (1998) and *Reading the Earth: New Directions in the Study of Literature and Environment* (1998) and textual editor of *John Muir's Last Journey: South to the Amazon and East to Africa* (2001).

TERRELL F. DIXON teaches literature and environment courses at the University of Houston, University Park, where he has served as director of the Interdisciplinary Scholars' Community as well as graduate director and chair of the English Department. He is editor of *City Wilds: Stories and Essays about Urban Nature* (2002) and co-editor (with Scott Slovic) of *Being in the World: An Environmental Reader for Writers* (1993).

JIM DWYER has been head of Bibliographic Services at California State University, Chico, since 1986. He also provides reference service, bibliographic instruction, and collection development in the humanities. He is the author of *Earth Works: Recommended Fiction and Nonfiction about Nature and the Environment* (1996).

TERRY GIFFORD is reader in Literature and Environment at the University of Leeds, United Kingdom, and director of the annual International Festival of Mountaineering Literature, now in its fifteenth year. He is the author of *Green Voices: Understanding Contemporary Nature Poetry* (1995), *Pastoral* (1999), and *Whale Watching with a Boy and a Goat* (1998), his fifth collection of poetry. He edited the complete works of John Muir in two omnibus editions: *John Muir: The Eight Wilderness-Discovery Books* (1992) and *John Muir: The Life and Letters and Other Writings* (1996).

HENRY HARRINGTON is professor emeritus of environmental studies and English at the University of Montana. He is the author of numerous articles on the literature of natural history and other subjects and co-editor (with John Tallmadge) of *Reading under the Sign of Nature: New Essays in Ecocriticism* (2000).

RICHARD HUNT teaches at Mesabi Range College in Virginia, Minnesota. His research interests include the connections and interactions between science and faith as expressed through American nature writing.

Jonathan Johnson teaches in the Master of Fine Arts creative writing program at Eastern Washington University. His poems have appeared in various national magazines, including *Best American Poetry 1996*. His first book of poetry, *Mastodon, 80% Complete,* is forthcoming from Carnegie Mellon University Press, and he has recently completed *Hannah and the Mountain,* a work of nonfiction.

Richard Kerridge is senior lecturer in English, course director in the Master of Fine Arts creative writing program, and subject leader in creative studies at Bath Spa University, United Kingdom. He is co-author of *Nearly Too Much: The Poetry of J. H. Prynne* (1995) and co-editor of *Writing the Environment* (1998). He received the BBC Wildlife Award for Nature Writing in 1990 and 1991.

Thomas J. Lyon taught at Utah State University for thirty-three years, edited *Western American Literature* from 1974 to 1997, and served as senior editor for *A Literary History of the American West* (1987) and *Updating the Literary West* (1997). A revised edition of his book *This Incomperable Lande: A Book of American Nature Writing* is forthcoming.

Gregory L. Morris is professor of American literature at Penn State Erie, the Behrend College. He is the author of *Talking Up a Storm: Voices of the New West* (1994), a collection of interviews with contemporary Western fiction writers, and of the chapbooks, *Frank Bergon* and *Gretel Erlich* (2001), for the Western Writers Series.

Scott Slovic teaches environmental literature at the University of Nevada, Reno. He served as the founding president of the Association for the Study of Literature and Environment (ASLE) and has written, edited, or co-edited eight books, including *Seeking Awareness in American Nature Writing* (1992), *Literature and the Environment: A Reader on Nature and Culture* (1998), and *Getting Over the Color Green: Contemporary Environmental Literature of the Southwest* (2001).

O. Alan Weltzien is professor of English at the University of Montana–Western and author of the chapbook *Rick Bass* (1998) for the Western Writers Series. He is also co-editor of *John McPhee and the Art of Literary Nonfiction* (2002) and author of *At Home on Camano: Summers in a Puget Sound Life* (forthcoming).

Index